MERRY AND MCCALL SMITH'S ERRORS, MEDICINE AND THE LAW

SECOND EDITION

ALAN MERRY

The University of Auckland

WARREN BROOKBANKS

Auckland University of Technology

CAMBRIDGE
UNIVERSITY PRESS

CAMBRIDGE
UNIVERSITY PRESS

University Printing House, Cambridge CB2 8BS, United Kingdom

One Liberty Plaza, 20th Floor, New York, NY 10006, USA

477 Williamstown Road, Port Melbourne, VIC 3207, Australia

4843/24, 2nd Floor, Ansari Road, Daryaganj, Delhi – 110002, India

79 Anson Road, #06–04/06, Singapore 079906

Cambridge University Press is part of the University of Cambridge.

It furthers the University's mission by disseminating knowledge in the pursuit of education, learning, and research at the highest international levels of excellence.

www.cambridge.org
Information on this title: www.cambridge.org/9781107180499
DOI: 10.1017/9781316848050

© Alan Forbes Merry and Alexander McCall Smith 2001
© Alan Forbes Merry and Warren Brookbanks 2017

First published 2001
Third printing 2004
Second edition 2017

Printed in the United Kingdom by Clays, St Ives plc

A catalogue record for this publication is available from the British Library.

Library of Congress Cataloging-in-Publication Data
Names: Merry, Alan F., author. | Brookbanks, Warren J., author.
Title: Merry and Mccall Smith's errors, medicine and the law / Alan Merry, Warren Brookbanks.
Other titles: Errors, medicine, and the law | Errors, medicine, and the law | Cambridge bioethics and law.
Description: Second edition. | Cambridge ; New York, NY : Cambridge University Press, 2017. | Series: Cambridge bioethics and law | Preceded by: Errors, medicine, and the law / Alan Merry and Alexander McCall Smith. 2001 | Includes bibliographical references and index.
Identifiers: LCCN 2016047827| ISBN 9781107180499 (Hardback) | ISBN 9781316632253 (Paperback)
Subjects: | MESH: Medical Errors – legislation & jurisprudence | Medical Errors – prevention & control | Malpractice – legislation & jurisprudence | Liability, Legal | Quality of Health Care – standards
Classification: LCC R729.8 | NLM WB 33.1 | DDC 610.28/9–dc23
LC record available at https://lccn.loc.gov/2016047827

ISBN 978-1-107-18049-9 Hardback
ISBN 978-1-316-63225-3 Paperback

MERRY AND MCCALL SMITH'S
ERRORS, MEDICINE AND THE LAW

SECOND EDITION

There is an understandable tendency or desire to attribute blame when patients are harmed by their own healthcare. However, many cases of iatrogenic harm involve little or no moral culpability. Even when blame is justified, an undue focus on one individual often deflects attention from other important factors within the inherent complexity of modern healthcare. This revised second edition advocates a rethinking of accountability in healthcare based on science, the principles of a just culture and novel therapeutic legal processes. Updated to include many recent relevant events, including the Keystone Project in the USA and the Mid Staffordshire scandal in the UK, this book considers how the concepts of a just culture have been successfully implemented so far and makes recommendations for best practice. This book will be of interest to anyone concerned with patient safety, medical law and the regulation of healthcare.

ALAN MERRY practices in anaesthesia and chronic pain management at Auckland City Hospital. He is Head of the School of Medicine at the University of Auckland, Chair of the Board of the NZ Health Quality and Safety Commission and a board member of the World Federation of Societies of Anaesthesiologists and Lifebox. His research and publications reflect interests in medical law, human factors, patient safety and global health. He is an Officer of the New Zealand Order of Merit and a Fellow of the Royal Society of New Zealand.

WARREN BROOKBANKS is a legal academic, and former practising lawyer and probation officer, now Professor of Law and Director for the Centre for Non-Adversarial Justice at AUT Law School in Auckland. He has written extensively in areas of criminal law, psychiatry and the law and therapeutic jurisprudence, and was previously President of the Australian and New Zealand Association of Psychiatry, Psychology and Law (ANZAPPL). His textbooks on criminal law and mental health law have been past winners of the JF Northey Memorial Book Prize.

CAMBRIDGE BIOETHICS AND LAW

This series of books was founded by Cambridge University Press with Alexander McCall Smith as its first editor in 2003. It focuses on the law's complex and troubled relationship with medicine across both the developed and the developing world. Since the early 1990s, we have seen in many countries increasing resort to the courts by dissatisfied patients and a growing use of the courts to attempt to resolve intractable ethical dilemmas. At the same time, legislatures across the world have struggled to address the questions posed by both the successes and the failures of modern medicine, while international organisations such as the WHO and UNESCO now regularly address issues of medical law.

It follows that we would expect ethical and policy questions to be integral to the analysis of the legal issues discussed in this series. The series responds to the high profile of medical law in universities, in legal and medical practice, as well as in public and political affairs. We seek to reflect the evidence that many major health-related policy debates in the UK, Europe and the international community involve a strong medical law dimension. With that in mind, we seek to address how legal analysis might have a trans-jurisdictional and international relevance. Organ retention, embryonic stem cell research, physician assisted suicide and the allocation of resources to fund health care are but a few examples among many. The emphasis of this series is thus on matters of public concern and/or practical significance. We look for books that could make a difference to the development of medical law and enhance the role of medico-legal debate in policy circles. That is not to say that we lack interest in the important theoretical dimensions of the subject, but we aim to ensure that theoretical debate is grounded in the realities of how the law does and should interact with medicine and healthcare.

Series Editors

Professor Graeme Laurie, *University of Edinburgh*

Professor Richard Ashcroft, *Queen Mary, University of London*

CONTENTS

CONTENTS

FOREWORD

Who amongst us has not made a mistake? Human error is ubiquitous and completely unavoidable; it is, quite simply, part of being human. Our response to error, though, does not always take this into account and this may result in our blaming people for things for which they do not deserve to be blamed. And with blame comes punishment. Yet, as a general rule, any punishment that carries moral opprobrium should only be imposed when there has been culpable wrongdoing – anything else is harsh and unjustifiable.

These fundamental notions lie at the heart of any sophisticated legal system, and yet there are occasions when a legal system might lose sight of them. This happens when society becomes unduly eager to blame people for adverse events – perhaps because it is felt that because something has gone wrong then somebody must be seen to account for it. That view ignores the fact that some mishaps are simply inevitable – given human limitations – and that accidents will happen.

Alan Merry and I became concerned about this issue some years ago when we were involved in a campaign to reform a particular provision of New Zealand criminal law relating to negligent manslaughter. What had happened in New Zealand was that some doctors involved in medical mishaps were being prosecuted for a serious criminal offence in circumstances where, in spite of doing their best for their patient, an error on their part had had disastrous results. The injustice of this situation was there for all to see, and it struck us as indefensible that morally innocent people could be convicted of manslaughter when they had made a mistake that did not in any way reflect recklessness or malign intention on their part.

The more we investigated the issue, the more it seemed to us that courts and legislators needed to clarify their approach to error. In particular, thought needed to be given to the question of which errors are culpable – and deserving of punishment – and which are simple accidents involving no reprehensible conduct on the part of the actor.

It also became apparent to us that the law needed to be more attentive to the causation issue and to recognise that mishaps often involve a complex chain of causative factors in which more than one person will be involved. An adverse event, then, may not be the work of just one person – the person who *appears* to be responsible – but may flow from the input of many others.

This new edition, based on our original work, is again the result of co-operation between medicine and the law. The medical side of the work remains in the hands of Alan Merry, while Warren Brookbanks, one of New Zealand's most distinguished legal academics, has brought his wide experience and understanding of criminal law to bear on the issue. Both of the authors have been long-standing friends of mine and it is with the greatest pleasure that I have seen the fruits of their collaboration. The issue is still a live one, and I hope that this book will help preserve awareness of just how vigilant we must be to ensure that punishment is reserved for those who really deserve it and not imposed on those who have not demonstrated any morally culpable state of mind. That the innocent should not be punished is something recognised a very long time ago by Greek philosophy; the truth of that proposition is as strong today as it was then.

Alexander McCall Smith

ACKNOWLEDGEMENTS

Acknowledgements for the First Edition

We wish to acknowledge the help which we have received in the planning and writing of this book. In particular, we wish to record our gratitude to Bruce Corkill, Dr Denys Court, Margaret Deith, Diana Emmens, Gaeline Phipps, Bill Runciman, Craig Webster and to an anonymous, but immensely helpful, reviewer in the United States. We were enabled to spend several periods working together in Canada thanks to the hospitality of Barbara Parker and Iona and John Copping of Vancouver, and of Douglas and Nadia Parker of Toronto, during which, and other times, Dr Sally Merry and Dr Elizabeth McCall Smith provided unstinting support for the project. Finally, no praise would be too great for the editorial support of Finola O'Sullivan of Cambridge University Press.

Acknowledgements for the Second Edition

We wish to thank Mike Merry, Dr Jacqueline Hannam and Professor Jan M Davies for carefully reviewing the text and providing insightful commentary on our ideas. We are very grateful for the support for this project of Sally Merry (once again) and Glenys Brookbanks.

Introduction

Early one morning in 2015, a young mother left home for work, taking her baby son with her to be dropped off at his crèche. She had worked beyond midnight the previous day. She secured her son safely in an approved child restraint seat, in the back of the car. As she later said, she was 'on autopilot', with her mind on her work. Without noticing, she missed the turning to the crèche, proceeded directly to her workplace, parked, hurried inside and resumed her duties from where she had left off the previous evening. She forgot altogether that her son was still in the car.

Several hours later she noticed a text message from the crèche. It asked whether her son was sick. She replied twice (with texts) that he had been fine in the morning. She also asked if something was wrong with him now. A staff member from the crèche then phoned her, and the realisation struck that she had not dropped her son off, after all. She ran to the car, but it was too late. The little boy had succumbed to heatstroke and dehydration, and could not be resuscitated.

The line that separates each of us from disaster can be very fine indeed. If only this mother's mind had not been on her work that morning, if only the crèche staff member had called earlier, if only a passer-by had noticed the child in the car and intervened, if only the weather been milder ... there were so many simple ways in which this disaster could have been averted.

Surprisingly, it turns out that events like this occur often enough to have a name – the 'forgotten baby syndrome'. Busy or distracted parents do simply forget their baby from time to time, in circumstances that matter. Chance then plays a major role in determining whether or not the child comes to harm, through factors such as the duration of the episode, the ambient temperature, the actions of passers-by and the age and resilience of the baby. Unfortunately, chance was not on the side of this particular mother.

Strictly speaking, the term 'syndrome' is not justified, because no mental or physical pathology characterises these cases. These parents are normal parents. There is also no suggestion of intentional neglect or abuse of the children who have died in this way, and seldom any evidence of substance abuse either. On the contrary, these events are simply classic failures of normal human cognition.

This young mother pleaded guilty to a charge of manslaughter, but the judge granted an application for a discharge without conviction. In doing so, Simon France J said that 'a conviction here would undoubtedly do more harm than good'.[1] His judgement shows deep insight and illustrates a central point of this book: when serious accidents[2] follow unintentional errors on the part of well-motivated people trying to do the right thing, the law, as a minimum, should not add to the harm that has already been done. A second central point illustrated by this story is that the principles discussed in this book apply generally, not just to doctors. As it happens, this mother did work in healthcare, but her tragic story could have involved anyone. We have taken medicine as the central focus of this book not because there is anything special about doctors and other health professionals, but because the problem of unintended harm to patients is both substantial and topical.

Modern medicine is highly effective. It is also available to greater numbers of people than ever before, but preventable injury has been identified as a strikingly common occurrence in all aspects of modern healthcare. The term 'epidemic of error' has been coined. In the United

[1] The *Queen* v. *X* [2015] NZHC 1244. The cited source of framing the test of whether conviction would do more harm than good was Lord Hoffman in *Sepet* v. *Secretary of State for the Home Department* [2003] UKHL 15 at [34]. The judge also provided name suppression and limited his written judgement in length and detail to reduce the chance of identifying the mother, her husband or her baby. We would like to thank Professor David Diamond of the Departments of Psychology and Molecular Pharmacology and Physiology at the University of South Florida (http://psychology.usf.edu/faculty/diamond), and also Associate Professor Susan Hatters Friedman, a forensic psychiatrist at the University of Auckland, for information on these events. Professor Diamond has acted as an expert witness and been interviewed by the media in several cases of this type: see for example L. Hilton, '"Good parents" denial puts kids at risk for heat stroke', Contemporary Pediatrics (2014) http://contemporarypediatrics.modernmedicine.com/contemporary-pediatrics/content/tags/icymi/good-parents-denial-puts-kids-risk-heat-stroke accessed 27 December 2016; 'Forgotten baby syndrome explained by neuroscientist' (2015), www.dailymail.co.uk/video/news/video-1107664/Forgotten-baby-syndrome-explained-neuroscientist.html, accessed 27 December 2016.
[2] The term 'accident' is controversial: see for example: R.M. Davis and B. Pless, 'BMJ bans "accidents"' (2001) 322 *British Medical Journal* 1320–1. We do not dispute that the word is often used inappropriately, but we think it does have value. In Chapter 1 we will discuss an operational definition of 'accident' which serves the purposes of this book.

States, the Institute of Medicine, acting under the National Academy of Sciences, has identified errors in healthcare as a leading cause of death and injury, comparable with that of road accidents. The precise extent of this problem is open to question, but it is beyond argument that an unacceptable number of people suffer serious harm or die as a result of 'avoidable adverse events'. Sometimes these events are attributable to negligence. However, it is often simple human error, operating in an intrinsically hazardous system, that results in an unnecessary death or serious injury. For the person concerned, and for the person's family and friends, the consequences of a deceptively simple mistake may be a tragedy of the first order. In addition, there may also be grave implications for a doctor or nurse at whose door the blame for the accident is laid, with consequences for his or her family as well.

This book is a study of how mishaps occur and how people are blamed for them. In many areas of human activity there is a strong tendency to attribute blame for events that, on further investigation, may be shown not to involve any culpable conduct. This is a particular issue in healthcare, where an error or a violation may contribute to serious consequences. The desire to blame leads to official inquiries, and in many cases to legal proceedings. In many parts of the world this has gone hand in hand with a marked increase in medical litigation, reflecting heightened public concern over the level of iatrogenic harm. The Institute of Medicine, the Institute of Healthcare Improvement and many other organisations have set targets for the reduction of errors in healthcare. Much investment has been made in many countries into improving the safety and quality of healthcare. However, as one commentator, writing in the *New England Journal of Medicine*, has pointed out, 'Any effort to prevent injury due to medical care is complicated by the dead weight of a litigation system that induces secrecy and silence.'[3]

In this book we present an argument that many of these events do not involve moral culpability. This argument is supported by the extensive research that has been carried out into the principles underlying the generation of human errors and into failures in complex systems. We examine the moral and legal basis for the attribution of blame and conclude that in many cases where there is a finding of blameworthy conduct, this in fact may not be justified in respect of the individual, but may often reflect institutional failures or unavoidable human error.

---

[3] T. A. Brennan, 'The institute of medicine report on medical errors – could it do harm' (2000) 342 *New England Journal of Medicine* 1123–5.

Paradoxically, by focusing on an individual, such inquiries or proceedings often fail to identify systemic deficiencies that predispose to error, or fail to protect the patient against the consequences of inevitable error. Blaming the person 'holding the smoking gun' may simply leave the scene set for a recurrence of the same tragedy.

An often misunderstood point is that human error, being by definition unintentional, is not easily deterred. Furthermore, to be effective, deterrence must be directed at those who are able to effect change within the system. For example, convicting two junior doctors of manslaughter after the incorrect injection of the drug vincristine into the spinal cord failed completely to prevent the same tragedy from happening again, with two more junior doctors some years later – a mistake which has now been made many times in British hospitals. Violations are a different matter from errors. Violations involve choice. Not all violations are reprehensible, and some may be forced upon individuals by the system, but in principle violations can be deterred. The cognitive mechanisms that underlie violations are quite different from those leading to error. It is important to distinguish these different types of human behaviour if we are to make our healthcare systems safer for patients and our legal systems fairer for those whose well-intended care sometimes goes astray. Attempts to modify human behaviour by regulation or legal processes are entirely appropriate, but need to be well informed. The current standard by which negligence is assessed in the law is that of reasonableness in respect of knowledge, skill and care. However, a great deal depends on the way in which this is tested. If the line of questioning focuses on the action, many statistically inevitable errors appear unreasonable. An expert can hardly be expected to say that it is reasonable to give the wrong drug, for example. However, if the questioning focuses on the person, who is a human being, and asks, 'Was this the sort of mistake a reasonable practitioner might make?' the answer will often be different. As we shall see, there is overwhelming evidence that, in fact, all practitioners make errors at some time, including errors in drug administration. It follows that errors can be made by the reasonable doctor. There are other actions, such as leaving an anaesthetised patient unattended, which no reasonable practitioner would do. In the latter case a punitive response may well be called for.

When a patient is unintentionally injured during healthcare, the response may typically involve disciplinary procedures, civil legal action or the criminal law. In some cases these responses will be appropriate; in others, they may actually be counter-productive. This book is as much about understanding those situations in which blame *is* appropriate as about knowing when it is not. The book has at its centre concern for the patients who are injured, but alongside that it makes the point that some practitioners, by unwittingly contributing to such injury, become victims themselves – often quite innocently. The impact on the practitioner is at times underestimated, and acknowledgement of its true extent should not be seen as diminishing the importance of the primary victim, the patient. Regrettably, current legal responses to inadvertent adverse events often help neither the harmed patients nor those responsible for their care. There is certainly room for improvement in the safety of healthcare, but it is equally true that there is room for improvement in the legal and regulatory responses to failures in care. When a patient is injured during conscientiously administered treatments by well-motivated clinicians, an ideal response would mitigate the consequences to the patient, provide compensation when appropriate, preserve trusting relationships with his or her doctors and other healthcare providers and improve systemic safety in the longer term. Inspiration can be found in the field of law related to mental health, in the emerging concept of therapeutic jurisprudence.

Ultimately, the best response for both patients and those responsible for the provision of healthcare is to make healthcare safer. Unfortunately, error will never be completely eliminated, and there will always be some practitioners whose behaviour is frankly culpable. There are no simple answers, but a better understanding of the factors which underlie the different types of human failing associated with iatrogenic harm is fundamental to improving the way in which we regulate medicine, hold practitioners and healthcare organisations accountable and compensate those who are harmed in the course of receiving treatment.

The problem of unintended harm in healthcare affects all societies. The issues discussed in this book apply generally, although some of the examples relate to specific countries. The legal principles involved are mostly discussed in the context of common-law systems. While they may differ in detail, these systems share the same basic approach. Reference is therefore made to the decisions of courts in England and Wales, Scotland, the United States, New Zealand, Australia and Canada. Because errors and violations raise issues of both civil and criminal liability, and may also fall within the scope of professional discipline, we have taken all these jurisdictions into account.

In Chapter 1, we introduce the concept that the pervasive nature of blame in contemporary society is distorting reactions to adverse events in medicine and other activities. To illustrate this we give some actual examples of severe consequences that have followed relatively minor errors committed during normal medical practice. The cases are used to exemplify the concepts discussed in subsequent chapters. The language used to describe these events can be important. The term 'accident', for example, is exculpatory, and may have value in distinguishing between situations of culpability and those not warranting blame.

In Chapter 2, we discuss how human beings function not in isolation, but in the context of today's complex technological organisations. Successful human endeavour in medicine and other fields has been the result of man's ability to communicate, cooperate, develop technology and function within a mechanised and skill-demanding world. Medicine is no longer the cottage industry it once was, centred on individual general practitioners working in isolation to treat, to the extent possible, whatever problems their patients presented with. Healthcare is much more effective today, in no small part because of the combined efforts of clinicians from multiple disciplines working together, supported by laboratories and technology that themselves are run by specialists. This has made teamwork and coordination fundamental to the success and safety of modern healthcare. The cognitive processes that have produced these successes are the same processes as those that predispose to certain forms of error. These should therefore be viewed as strengths rather than weaknesses, in comparison with the less error-prone but also less flexible attributes of machines.

A proper understanding of the human actions that lead to adverse events in medicine requires a knowledge of the nature of error. In Chapter 3, a precise definition of error is followed by a detailed discussion of its underlying cognitive processes and an outline of its taxonomy. The thesis is that errors should not necessarily be viewed as random acts or manifestations of carelessness, but rather that even inexplicable and bizarre actions or mistakes can often be understood, and even predicted, from particular circumstances. Deterrence will not prevent errors – their reduction depends on understanding the processes involved. However, not all unsafe acts are errors. In Chapter 4, we discuss violations, beginning with their definition. An understanding of violations facilitates the discussion of the difference between culpable and non-culpable failures in human activity.

The discussion now shifts to culpability. In Chapter 5, we explore the concepts of negligence, recklessness and blame, referring to the insights derived from our discussion of errors and violations. Negligence does not

necessarily imply blameworthiness, but may carry considerable overtones of moral opprobrium. Drawing on the theory developed in the
previous three chapters, we suggest a classification of blame into five
levels, ranging from pure causal responsibility to intentional harming.
The implication of this for our response to adverse events is explored.
Negligence in the law is based on the standard of care expected of the
reasonable person. In Chapter 6, we scrutinise how the standard of care is
set by the law. To assist in the recognition of failures to meet this
standard, courts have relied on evidence of professional custom. In this
chapter we explore how the test of the standard of care has tended to
move from what can reasonably be expected to what ought ideally to have
been done. There are risks of injustice in simplistic applications of either
test, and we argue that evaluations of culpability should be informed by
greater cognisance of the insights of psychology and accident theory
discussed in the preceding chapters. The role of the expert witness in
setting the standard of care is considered in Chapter 7. Evidence provided
by clinical experts tends to reflect ideal practices rather than a customary
standard of care. This has contributed to the development of the unrealistic standard discussed in Chapter 6, and expert evidence on human
cognition and performance within complex systems is also important for
a proper understanding of failures in care.

In Chapter 8, we consider various possible reforms to shift the focus
from blame with a view to improving the response of the law to the
injured patient, to the need to promote safety in healthcare and to the
reduction of inappropriate findings of culpability in doctors. We address
at some length the concept of no-fault compensation and consider
various possibilities for improving the tort system.

In Chapter 9, we turn to the role of the criminal law in healthcare.
In 2001, when the first edition of this book was published, it seemed
unlikely that the criminal law would often be evoked in common-law
countries in the context of failures in the care of patients unless there
was clear evidence of recklessness or intent to harm. New Zealand had
been an exception, with nine health professionals facing charges of
manslaughter in the 1980s and 1990s after patients died as
a consequence of errors in their clinical care. For a country of under
4 million people (at that time), this was a disproportionately high
number of such prosecutions. New Zealand's codified law at the time
had defined criminal negligence in terms normally considered more
appropriate to the purposes of civil law. However, advocacy had
resulted in a change to relevant legislation, and the threshold for

criminal prosecution of negligence had been aligned to that of comparable jurisdictions. It seemed that the matter was settled and of little interest to those living in other countries. Unexpectedly, after the turn of the millennium, criminal prosecutions of health professionals increased dramatically in England and Wales. Perhaps the public outrage associated with events such as the deliberate murder of more than 200 patients by the English general practitioner Harold Shipman and the scandal at the Stafford Hospital contributed to this development. In Chapter 9, we consider the limitations and implications of criminal prosecution in the context of healthcare. Our reservations over the appropriateness of civil law suits in cases of simple human error are considerably increased in relation to the criminal law. These reservations have nothing to do with the profession of the accused. Of course doctors like Shipman, who set out to harm their patients, are criminals, and jail is the right place for them. However, we believe there are very few practitioners of this type. For the vast majority of cases in which harm reflects failures in well-intentioned, but inherently dangerous activities (of which healthcare is but one example), we argue that the criminal law is an expensive, blunt and inappropriate instrument. We show that it is ineffective in promoting safety, frequently fails to provide either true justice or a desired outcome for those who loved the deceased patient and typically makes bad situations much worse than they already were.

We conclude, in the final chapter, that a failure to understand the role of blame, along with considerable contemporary enthusiasm for finding scapegoats, has led to what might be termed an inflation of blame. The consequences of this are particularly serious – and costly – in the area of medical mishaps. We extend the ideas developed in Chapter 8, drawing from successful models of healthcare improvement, to bring together the strands developed in the book and argue for coherent, rational and well-informed analysis of blame to underpin a more therapeutic framework for regulating healthcare in the interests of patients and doctors, and all others for whom safety in medicine is a priority.

1

Accidents

We begin with a chapter on accidents. The accident *par excellence* of the twentieth century was the loss of the RMS *Titanic*, which on the night of 12 April 1912 collided with an iceberg in the North Atlantic. Who, or what, was to blame for this incident, which was to become so enduring and potent a cultural symbol? There are numerous potential explanations: the iceberg might have been sighted in time, but was not. A warning message was sent, but not passed on. The metal used for the construction of the ship's rivets contained impurities, with the result that they gave under strain. The ship's architects had miscalculated the ability of sealed-off compartments to maintain buoyancy. A wireless operator on a nearby ship, which could have arrived on the scene to rescue the passengers, had turned off his set, only twenty minutes earlier, with the result that Mayday messages were not received. If the crew had been equipped with binoculars, the watch might have been alarmed in time. All of these played some role in the final disaster.[1]

The equivalent in our own times of the loss of the *Titanic* – in the sense that it demonstrated the same essential vulnerability of grandiose human ambitions – was the explosion of the space shuttle *Challenger* in 1986, 73 seconds after launch.[2] It is clear that ring seals failed, causing the explosion of escaping fuel, but this failure would not have occurred had the seals not been exposed to low temperatures on the ground. The problem was not a new one: engineers had expressed concern over the issue but this concern had not been translated into action within the labyrinths of

---

[1] The literature on the *Titanic* disaster is extensive. See Parliament of Great Britain, *Report on the Loss of the SS Titanic* (New York, St. Martin's Press, 1998 – original report 1912); T. Kuntz (ed.), *The Titanic Disaster Hearings. The Official Transcripts of the 1912 Senate Investigation* (New York, Pocket Books, 1998).

[2] United States Government, *Report of the Presidential Commission on the Space Shuttle Challenger Accident* (Washington, D.C., US Government Printing Office, 1986); L. C. Bruno, 'Challenger explosion (1986)', in N. Schlager (ed.), *When Technology Fails: Significant Technological Disasters, Accidents, and Failures of the Twentieth Century* (Detroit, Gale Research, 1994), 609–16.

the space programme. The launch was approved, but this decision might not have been taken had a number of those responsible not been grossly sleep deprived at the time of the crucial meeting, and under pressure to meet deadlines. The impact of sleep deprivation on intellectual processes is well understood, and decision makers had been deprived of normal sleep for many days. This, of course, was not necessarily a situation of their own making. They were under immense pressure to ensure that the launch proceeded according to schedule – a pressure that reflected the operational culture of NASA, and which led to managers overruling advice from engineers concerning the risk of ring-seal failure. And this, in due course, stemmed from budgetary pressure applied by politicians.[3] The range of potential causes was therefore wide, and the points of possible responsibility for the accident somewhat scattered. Can any one person, or even group of persons, be said to be to blame for this loss of life and material? What is the liability of organisations involved in this project?

These are well known, extensively documented incidents, the background of which has been closely scrutinised. Most accidents are considerably more mundane, occurring on the roads, in the home, or, as W. H. Auden observed in his poem on the fall of Icarus, against a backdrop of people simply going about their normal business.[4] Many medical accidents fall into this category. They occur in the context of routine treatment and are frequently not the subject of inquiry or proceedings. The Harvard Medical Practice Study, for example, which investigated the incidence of such accidents in the state of New York, revealed a remarkably high rate of such incidents, but only a small proportion of them resulted in formal legal action.[5] The question of

---

[3] For an account of the human factors involved in the *Challenger* disaster, see R. Boisjoly, E. F. Curtis and E. Mellican, 'The Challenger disaster: organizational demands and personal ethics', in M. D. Ermann and R. J. Lundman (eds.), *Corporate and Governmental Deviance: Problems of Organizational Behavior in Contemporary Society* (New York, Oxford University Press, 1996), 207–31.

[4] W. H. Auden, 'Musée des Beaux Arts', in *Collected Shorter Poems* (London, Faber and Faber, 1966).

[5] D. M. Studdert, M. M. Mello and T. A. Brennan, 'Medical malpractice' (2004) 350 *New England Journal of Medicine* 283–92; T. A. Brennan, L. L. Leape, N. M. Laird, L. Hebert, A. R. Localio, A. G. Lawthers, . . . H. H. Hiatt, 'Incidence of adverse events and negligence in hospitalized patients – results of the Harvard Medical Practice Study I' (1991) 324 *New England Journal of Medicine* 370–6; L. L. Leape, T. A. Brennan, N. Laird, A. G. Lawthers, A. R. Localio, B. A. Barnes, . . . H. Hiatt, 'The nature of adverse events in hospitalized patients. Results of the Harvard Medical Practice Study II' (1991) 324 *New England Journal of Medicine* 377–84; A. R. Localio, A. G. Lawthers, T. A. Brennan, N. M. Laird, L. E. Hebert,

responsibility for these incidents may be as complicated as the question of responsibility for major, highly publicised accidents, and it is for this reason that medical mishaps can make a very useful case study for the general question of responsibility for untoward events.

In all events of this nature, whether they are spectacular disasters (*Titanic, Challenger, Chernobyl*), or whether they involve the injury or death of a single person, the same questions of causal complexity will be involved. Causal investigations are familiar territory now to the public, which has become accustomed to publicity given to the proceedings of committees of inquiry, coroners and criminal courts, and in general we are rather more sophisticated in our appreciation of the multi-factorial features of many of these incidents. Yet this ability to appreciate that adverse events may be caused by more than one factor has not necessarily been accompanied by a change in blaming behaviour. Locating causal responsibility for an event may precede blaming, but is not in itself sufficient for an attribution of blame. There is a marked tendency to look for a human actor to blame for an untoward event – a tendency that is closely linked with the desire to punish. *Things have gone wrong, and therefore somebody must be found to answer for it.* The crudity of this statement is apparent on the face of it, and yet, to an extraordinary extent, it represents a widely held view. It is this attitude which fuels media and political campaigns for the identification and punishment of those responsible for whatever tragedy or social problem has seized the attention of the public. It is the psychology of the moral panic and it threatens certain fundamental values of a liberal, humane society: namely, that censure and punishment should be reserved – as far as is possible – for those whose actions reveal morally relevant wrongdoing.[6] Such analysis is often conspicuously lacking from both moral and legal

---

L. M. Peterson, . . . H. H. Hiatt, 'Relation between malpractice claims and adverse events due to negligence' (1991) 325 *New England Journal of Medicine* 245–51. The Harvard study is discussed in greater detail on p. 55. See also P. M. Danzon, *Medical Malpractice: Theory, Evidence, and Public Policy* (Cambridge, MA, Harvard University Press, 1985); P. C. Weiler, *Medical Malpractice on Trial* (Cambridge, MA, Harvard University Press, 1991).

[6] There will be some circumstances in which strict liability will be acceptable. In these cases punishment may be justified by the community's interest in the protection of a value or interest which cannot otherwise be protected; road traffic offences provide an example of this. Offences which involve real moral opprobrium require correspondingly real moral guilt, a distinction formally recognised in all common-law jurisdictions. For general discussion, see K. W. Simons, 'When is strict liability just?' (1997) 87 *Journal of Criminal Law and Criminology* 1075–137.

judgements – a situation prompting the moral philosopher Jean Hampton to remark: 'Accusing, condemning, and avenging are part of our daily life. However, a review of many years of literature attempting to analyze our blaming practices suggests that we do not understand very well what we are doing when we judge people culpable for wrong they have committed.'[7] Morally relevant wrongdoing can only properly be identified if the actions of those whose responsibility is in question are subjected to analysis designed to identify states of mind that are truly culpable. A refined system of criminal justice, with its elaborate notions of *mens rea* (guilty mind doctrine) and its carefully defined defences, is capable of achieving this degree of discrimination between the blameworthy and the blameless. However, many processes of calling to account – including many legal proceedings of both a civil and a criminal nature – fall far short of this goal.[8]

The central argument put forward in what follows is that the process of blaming, as it is practised in contemporary society, is in danger of losing sight of these moral values. It is a matter for remark that this should happen at a time when our understanding of human action, and therefore our ability to appreciate the full complexity of faulty human behaviour, has made substantial progress. The insights of psychology and accident theory are available to the law and to other institutions of blame; yet they are widely ignored. There are a variety of reasons why this should be so. To an extent, it is because of an understandable – and necessary – belief in individual accountability. But there are less acceptable reasons behind the phenomenon as well. These are the reasons that find their root in an atavistic human response of scapegoating. It is easier to blame others for mishaps than to accept the inevitability of human loss, and it is for this reason that crude solutions to the problem of human accidents strike a strongly responsive chord.[9]

---

[7] J. Hampton, 'Men s rea', in E. F. Paul, F. D. Miller and J. Paul (eds.), *Crime, Culpability and Remedy* (Oxford, Basil Blackwell, 1990), 1–28, quote at p.1.

[8] In one view, this goal is practically unattainable and, in any event, is not defensible. In criminal law theory there is a continuing tension between subjectivism and objectivism in the attribution of liability. In practice, most criminal justice systems place objectively determined limits on the extent to which certain conditions are capable of excusing those who cause actual harm to others. For discussion of the issue see A. Ripstein, *Equality, Responsibility, and the Law* (New York, Cambridge University Press, 1999); R. H. S. Tur, 'Subjectivism and objectivism: towards synthesis', in S. Shute, J. Gardner and J. Horder (eds.), *Action and Value in Criminal Law* (Oxford, Clarendon Press, 1993), 213–37.

[9] For discussion of blaming behaviour, see H. Tennen and G. Affleck, 'Blaming others for threatening events' (1990) 108 *Psychological Bulletin* 209–32.

Our investigation of the phenomenon of blame and negligence focuses predominantly on medical accidents. This is not only because of the frequency of such mishaps, but because such incidents occupy a central role in the contemporary drama of blame. Health professionals are frequently blamed for bad outcomes of medical treatment. Of these, doctors probably feature most often in lawsuits, disciplinary processes and criminal actions arising from allegedly negligent healthcare. However, nurses,[10] pharmacists and other practitioners may also be the subject of these proceedings and the net is being cast increasingly widely, occasionally catching even those with administrative or political responsibility for the delivery of healthcare.[11] In some of these cases, blame is justified; in others it is clearly not. Our aim is to examine the whole issue of blame in this context, in an attempt to show that the background to a mishap is frequently far more complex than may generally be assumed, and also to demonstrate that actual blame for the outcome must be attributed with great caution. It is our belief that society has become too ready to attribute blame without the discriminating, in-depth analysis that this process requires. This not only represents a moral affront, but also threatens the very safety goals we profess to embrace.

Blame

When a patient unexpectedly dies or is harmed in the course of a medical procedure, a common reaction is to attribute responsibility for the death to one of the practitioners involved. Not only may this be done by the family, but often the hospital itself will tend to lay the blame on the individual practitioner. There may be occasions when this will be entirely

---

[10] For an example see P. D. G. Skegg, 'Criminal prosecutions of negligent health professionals: the New Zealand experience' (1998) 6 Medical Law Review 220–46.

[11] Examples in which doctors with administrative responsibility have been held to account for harm to patients include the events at Bristol discussed later in this chapter, and the scandal involving France's blood transfusion services. In the latter example three government ministers (including the Prime Minister) were also prosecuted for manslaughter; the minister of health was convicted but discharged without penalty. See D. L. Breo, 'Blood, money, and hemophiliacs – the fatal story of France's "AIDSgate"' (1991) 266 Journal of the American Medical Association 3477–82; A. Dorozynski, 'Former French ministers on trial over blood' (1999) 318 British Medical Journal 419; M. Simons, 'France convicts 3 in case of HIV-tainted blood' (1992) New York Times 1, 5; 'Blood scandal ministers walk free' (1999) http://news.bbc.co.uk/2/hi/europe/293367.stm, accessed 29 November 2015.

appropriate, and where the problem clearly does lie with an individual practitioner. Very often, however, the situation is much more complicated. The delivery of healthcare today is typically dependent on the combined efforts of many people, working to a greater or lesser extent as a team, within a complex social and technological system.[12] The inadequacies of this system (particularly in relation to failures in communication), the specific circumstances of the case, the nature of human psychology itself and sheer chance may have combined to produce a result in which any individual practitioner's contribution is either relatively or completely blameless, or in which any blame should, in justice, be shared with others.[13]

Blame is rarely a simple matter. It is our view that the complexity of medical treatment and the human and technological systems involved are such that many of the allegations of medical fault are misplaced or misdirected. Conversely, current processes may fail to identify and address the important lessons to be learned from a tragedy simply because they focus on blame, and typically on blaming a single individual. For example, a particular practitioner's behaviour may not constitute a legally actionable wrong or sustain a criminal or disciplinary charge, but may nevertheless warrant constructive intervention, which may need to extend to others within the organisation as well.

What is required is an enhanced understanding of the underlying causes of iatrogenic harm. This necessitates a more sophisticated appreciation of how things go wrong. It is also important to distinguish between notions of best practice and the reality of how healthcare is actually delivered, usually by teams of people and often in the face of pressing need, constrained timeframes and limited resources. Finally, the ways in which the standard of care is assessed are themselves subject to a number of limitations: for example, expert evidence is frequently important, but often turns out to be a poor indicator of what should reasonably be expected in a particular case.

The case for reassessing our current approaches to harm of this nature is prompted not merely by concern that legal and disciplinary procedures should be properly founded on firm moral and scientific grounds; it is

---

[12] We discuss the influence of teamwork on patient outcomes in more detail in Chapter 2, and the implications of this for liability when things go wrong in healthcare in Chapter 10.

[13] We will expand on the idea of collective responsibility in later chapters of this book, but note that we do not interpret the notion that several people may be responsible when avoidable harm occurs to a patient as implying that no one should (or can) therefore be held accountable.

also motivated by the conviction that patients will be better served if the real causes of harm are properly identified and appropriately acted upon. We have chosen various cases, drawn from healthcare and other activities,[14] to illustrate some of the issues at stake. These cases provide a starting point for an analysis of the nature of negligence and the difficulties of determining culpability when injury or death occurs as a consequence of medical intervention.

Illustrative Cases

One theme of this book is that quite minor errors may have consequences completely out of proportion to their moral culpability. This applies not only in healthcare, but in all walks of life. Indeed, we opened the Introduction to this book with our first illustrative case, the story of the forgotten baby, which could have happened to any mother, and which provides a compelling illustration of this point. It is appropriate, therefore, that most of the cases dealt with involve tragedies in which patients or other people lost their lives. Some have been the subject of criminal prosecution, but could equally have resulted in a civil action (and indeed, the former does not rule out the latter). A disproportionate number of the cases are from New Zealand, where the issue of medical negligence was the subject of particular scrutiny during the 1990s and where there has been an extended political debate about medical accidents and culpability. Many occurred at a time when the New Zealand law provided (under certain circumstances, including but not restricted to medical practice) that there could be criminal liability where death resulted from a relatively low level of negligence – a level no higher than that required for civil purposes. This law has subsequently been amended to allow for such prosecution only where there has been a 'major departure' from the required standard of care. This in effect means that gross negligence is now required and brings New Zealand law into line with the vast majority of common-law jurisdictions (including those of the United States and the UK).[15] We shall return in Chapter 9 to the place of criminal prosecution for

---

[14] Many of the principles discussed in this book apply beyond the boundaries of healthcare.

[15] See Skegg, 'Criminal prosecutions of negligent health professionals'. It is interesting, however, that the use of the criminal law in the context of allegedly negligent harm in healthcare, a key element of that debate in New Zealand, has subsequently increased in England (and perhaps in some states of Australia as well): see R. E. Ferner and S. E. McDowell, 'Doctors charged with manslaughter in the course of medical practice, 1795–2005: a literature review' (2006) 99 *Journal of the Royal Society of Medicine* 309–14.

negligent injury; what concerns us at this stage is the variety and complexity of the influences that contribute to the causation of unintended harm, particularly in the context of healthcare, but also in other potentially hazardous activities. Many of these influences have not been adequately recognised by the law, with the result that there is frequently a gap between legal discussions of negligence and reality (i.e. reality as understood from the perspective of theoretical and empirical science, notably the science of human cognition and behaviour within complex systems).

An Anaesthetic Drug Error[16]

Dr Yogasakaran was an anaesthetist who had recently immigrated to New Zealand and had been given provisional registration with the expectation that he would work in a hospital post under some degree of supervision for a year. He obtained a position in the small provincial town of Te Kuiti, where it seems he was probably the best trained anaesthetist in the hospital. While there, he undertook the anaesthetic of a 'high-risk' patient for gall bladder surgery. At the end of the operation an emergency developed. During emergence from general anaesthesia the patient began to bite on her endotracheal tube (by which oxygen is administered to the lungs), became unable to breathe and developed cyanosis. It seems that the help immediately available to Dr Yogasakaran might not have been optimal at this moment, the surgeon and scrub nurse having already left theatre, and the nurse who regularly assisted the anaesthetist having been relieved by someone less experienced in this role. Dr Yogasakaran decided to inject the drug doxapram (*dopram*), an analeptic agent with the property of stimulating arousal of the central nervous system. Unfortunately, someone (who was never identified) had placed an ampoule of *dopamine* in the section of the drug drawer labelled 'dopram'. This is an inotrope (a drug used to stimulate the heart), and quite different from doxapram. As presented, it would normally require dilution and administration as an infusion over time, not as a bolus injection. There was a similarity in presentation of the two agents, however, and in his haste to treat the developing crisis Dr Yogasakaran injected the entire contents of the dopamine ampoule in error. It has always been accepted that this dose of dopamine produced

---

[16] R v. *Yogasakaran* [1990] 1 N.Z.L.R. 399; D. B. Collins, *Medical Law in New Zealand* (Wellington, Brooker and Friend, 1992).

cardiac arrest and was responsible for the subsequent demise of the patient. Dr Yogasakaran succeeded in resuscitating her, and transferred her to the regional centre of Waikato, in Hamilton, where she was admitted to the intensive care unit for ventilation and further management. Unfortunately, it became clear over the next day or two that she had suffered irreversible brain damage, and she eventually died.

Dr Yogasakaran returned to Te Kuiti, went back to the operating room, and only then discovered (himself) the empty ampoule of dopamine. He realised what had happened and immediately informed the doctors at Waikato Hospital, and reported the matter to the authorities in his own hospital. It was his honesty in bringing to light the drug error that led to the laying of charges by the police and to his ultimate conviction for manslaughter.

At his trial the expert witness for the defence was asked whether he would ever administer a drug without checking it. He said that he would not, and that one should always check every drug before administration. He then sought to qualify this position by a description of certain well-known features of human psychology, including the concept of 'mindset' and the fact that people often see what they expect to see in any given situation, not what is actually there – especially when there is a similarity between the two. This further evidence was objected to on the grounds that the witness was an anaesthetist, not a psychologist, and was ruled inadmissible (personal communication, Dr H. Spencer). Dr Yogasakaran was convicted, and then discharged without sentence. It was acknowledged that the conviction alone was a serious punishment for a doctor in these circumstances. His conviction was upheld at the Court of Appeal; the Privy Council in London (at that time the ultimate court of appeal from New Zealand) declined to interfere with what was seen as a policy decision of the New Zealand courts. On the face of it, this was a straightforward example of negligence. Dr Yogasakaran failed to check the drug, a requirement acknowledged even by the expert called by the defence. On closer inspection, a number of other factors emerge as relevant to the standard of care in this incident. In the first place, a small provincial hospital was hardly a suitable place for a doctor deemed to require supervision, even if the level of supervision needed was fairly minimal. A system that sets such a requirement should also ensure that the arrangements actually made are appropriate. This was a systems failure at a fairly general or high level. Similarly, the case selection in a small hospital with limited expertise and resources is questionable. It is quite possible that this death would have been averted had this patient been transferred to a major centre for her operation, if only because more immediate support would have been on hand at the time of the primary event – the initial development of cyanosis. There may well have been better ways to deal with the problem of increased tone of the muscles of the jaw during emergence from anaesthesia, and more expert assistance might also have made a difference to the success of the subsequent resuscitation. At any rate, placing a relatively junior doctor in a situation in which he had no choice but to deal with these challenges on his own was not ideal – although quite typical of the time at which it occurred.[17]

We have already intimated that many incidents involve a contribution from more than one person, and this case is an example. It illustrates the tendency to blame the last identifiable element in the chain of causation – the person holding the 'smoking gun'. A more comprehensive approach would identify the relative contributions of the other failures in the system, including failures in the conduct of other individuals – in this case the unidentified person who placed the wrong ampoule in the relevant compartment of the drug drawer, for example.[18]

On closer analysis, it seems compelling that Dr Yogasakaran's error was a slip or lapse of the type well recognised as an inevitable part of human behaviour. As we shall discuss in Chapters 2 and 3, there are ample data to show that all human beings make mistakes of this general type and that anaesthetists giving drugs are no exception. Stated simply, people frequently see what they expect to see rather than what is there. While the resolution of this problem is in fact very difficult, it seems reasonable to expect that the legal process would take greater account of current knowledge of normal human cognitive processes. The conclusion that Dr Yogasakaran's act was culpable must therefore be open to question, particularly since his handling of the crisis, once it developed, appears to have been both responsible and competent, if not exemplary.

---

[17] One interesting limitation of criminal prosecution in contexts such as this is the lack of evaluation of the overall management of the case; administering doxapram was accepted as a reasonable response to this situation, albeit that the use of this drug was more common in the UK than in New Zealand at the time, and would probably have been viewed as somewhat dated by most anaesthetists in the latter country. The criminal case hinged on a single mistake – so the possibility of better responses was never explored and no recommendations for improved management in future similar circumstances emerged, or could have emerged.

[18] It is not clear how things might have played out if this person had actually been identified, but the conviction of Dr Yogasakaran for his error suggests that relatively little importance was placed on this antecedent event.

When attributing blame, we often concentrate on a single, discrete act without paying adequate attention to the overall performance of the individual in the context of the entire event. This is the way in which the law frequently operates. It does not necessarily concern itself with what happened before and after an isolated act of alleged negligence: it focuses upon a single act and draws conclusions as to culpability purely on the basis of this act. It would therefore be quite misleading to describe Dr Yogasakaran as a 'negligent doctor' on the basis of one incident, just as it would be misleading to describe a driver as a negligent driver on the basis of one momentary lapse in attention. Indeed, in his summing up in the Yogasakaran case,[19] the judge alluded to this difficulty by saying:

> It is certainly not suggested by the Crown that Dr Yogasakaran is a poor doctor. The Crown says he is a highly trained, experienced, responsible man, whom the Crown says made a mistake, through carelessness, on this one occasion.

There are obviously times when it is appropriate to judge people on the basis of single acts. In the context of medical practice, though, it is particularly important that the cause of a problem is identified as soon as possible, and the way in which the problem is then handled becomes highly relevant. It is often said in medical training that mistakes are inevitable, but that the important thing is to know that one has made them and to deal with them appropriately. Viewed from this perspective, Dr Yogasakaran appears to have met all the requirements that could reasonably be expected of an anaesthetist in the circumstances. His only failing appears to have been a normal human error of the type that all anaesthetists will inevitably make from time to time, particularly in an emergency.[20]

The value of punishment in a case like that of Yogasakaran is far from clear. The need for compensation, of course, is a different matter, and there may well be justification for this. Punishing the last person in the chain, however, usually fails to address the underlying problems that predispose to harmful events. More importantly, however, it might amount to a lost opportunity to improve the overall safety of healthcare for the future, at least locally, and possibly more widely as

---

[19] Summing up of Justice Anderson, High Court, Hamilton, CR.56/88 p. 19.
[20] See, for example, A. F. Merry and D. J. Peck, 'Anaesthetists, errors in drug administration and the law' (1995) 108 *New Zealand Medical Journal* 185–7; B. A. Orser, R. J. B. Chen and D. A. Yee, 'Medication errors in anesthetic practice: a survey of 687 practitioners' (2001) 48 *Canadian Journal of Anesthesia* 139–46.

well if the issues are of a general nature. It is doubtful whether deterrence is effective in preventing slips and lapses of this type. Even removing the individual without correcting the system simply creates a situation where his or her replacement will be vulnerable to a recurrence of the same problem.

A Matter of 'Momentary Carelessness'[21]

Dr Morrison, a radiologist, was handed the wrong contrast medium by his assistant, an experienced radiographer, and injected it into a patient's spinal canal without first checking it. Death resulted two days later. Dr Morrison accepted that he had been negligent in injecting fluid without an adequate check, and pleaded guilty to manslaughter. He was convicted and discharged, the judge noting that the omission had been 'contributed to, indeed initiated, by the act of another person also qualified and experienced and with whom the accused was accustomed to work'. He also accepted that the omission 'was a matter of momentary carelessness in circumstances where he had no reason to be on guard'.

At a subsequent hearing the Medical Council placed certain require-ments for supervision on Dr Morrison for a defined period, and also asked that guidelines be developed for such injections. These were published in the Medical Council newsletter,[22] and, although headed as coming from the College of Radiology, the implication was that they were applicable to all injections of drugs. The key feature was a requirement for two people to check every injection by means of a 'chant' in which the key information was read out by one to the other. This approach has long been used by nurses, but has not always prevented errors.[23] It is not clear that it would always be practical in other situations, such as during anaesthesia, where the frequency of injections and potential to disturb other activities is high, or in general practice, where doctors may give injections in the home without the availability of a suitable second person. Furthermore, a subsequent survey (involving anaesthetists) revealed that only a minority of practising clinicians were aware that the guideline existed.[24]

[21] R v. Morrison, High Court, Dunedin, CR. 7/91, 23 April 1991.
[22] Medical Council of New Zealand, Safe administration of drugs, vol. 5 (Wellington, 1992), 4.
[23] Merry and Peck, 'Anaesthetists, errors in drug administration and the law', 185–7.
[24] A. F. Merry and D. J. Peck, Unpublished survey data.

At first glance, the negligence in this case seems clearer than that in the Yogasakaran case. Unlike the latter, there was no urgency here. However, there was once again an important contribution by a second person, and once again at least part of the problem, not just on the part of Dr Morrison and his assistant, but also on the part of the wider radiological community, lay in the system and its lack of established formal procedures for checking during the administration of drugs into the spinal canal. This was acknowledged by the Medical Council, and at least some attempt was made to address this safety issue through the development of guidelines. While this may have gone some distance towards improving the situation in radiology, it does seem that a greater effort to deal with wider problems of injectable drugs across all specialities might have been warranted.[25] Also, guidelines are of little use if not adequately promulgated.

An important difference between this case and the previous one is the particular vulnerability of the spinal cord. Injections into the spinal canal require meticulous care. The central point of the whole procedure was the administration of a single drug into a hazardous site. Although the error in this case is entirely understandable – in the sense that it is easy to see how it came about – this is a situation in which an enhanced level of care is warranted. It is, therefore, disconcerting to find that inadvertent injections of the wrong drug into the spinal canal occur over and over again (not only in New Zealand).[26] This example demonstrates that culpability has to be judged in the light of all aspects of the particular case, including the level of risk and the degree of urgency, but empirical data on similar occurrences are also relevant: if many well-intentioned people have made the same mistake the underlying problem is likely to be

---

[25] In fact, much has been done since that time. See, for example: J. Eichhorn, 'APSF hosts medication safety conference: consensus group defines challenges and opportunities for improved practice' (2010) 25 *APSF Newsletter* 1–7; A. F. Merry, C. S. Webster, J. Hannam, S. J. Mitchell, R. Henderson, P. Reid, ... T. G. Short, 'Multimodal system designed to reduce errors in recording and administration of drugs in anaesthesia: prospective randomised clinical evaluation' (2011) 343 *British Medical Journal* d5543.

[26] D. M. Berwick, 'Not again!' (2001) 322 *British Medical Journal* 247–8; P. Gilbar, 'Inadvertent intrathecal administration of vincristine: has anything changed?' (2012) 18 *Journal of Oncology Pharmacy Practice* 155–7; Anonymous, 'Miss-'n-mix and mimics. Tetraplegia following erroneous epidural injection' (2001) 52 *Acta Anaesthesiologica Belgica* 205–6; Clinical Safety Quality and Governance Branch, Safety Notice 010/10. Correct identification of medication and solutions for epidural anaesthesia and analgesia (2010), www.health.nsw .gov.au/sabs/Documents/2010-sn-010.pdf, accessed 29 November 2015.

systemic rather than the result of culpable behaviour. We do not believe that an incident of this sort, subsequently handled appropriately and with complete honesty, should merit the severity of a criminal prosecution, and we shall return to this point in Chapter 9.

Both these cases also bring to the fore the crucial importance of result in the criminal law. Criminal justice focuses on the effects produced by the conduct in question.[27] These effects may sometimes be out of all proportion to the seriousness of the wrongdoing, and indeed may be a matter of chance or what in philosophical discussion is referred to as *moral luck*. A momentary lapse of attention while driving would often go unnoticed and unpunished, or if it were to be detected and punished, the punishment would be very slight. However, if moral luck dictates that a pedestrian is killed, the punishment is likely to be considerably more serious, *even though the wrongdoing is identical in each case*.

Similarly, we know that many, if not most, practitioners whose work requires regular administration of drugs have administered the wrong drug to a patient at some time.[28] In most cases this is done without serious consequence and attracts little comment. However, if a patient dies or is otherwise seriously harmed as a result, two factors may come into play. One is that the likelihood of legal or disciplinary proceedings becomes very high; the other is that the phenomenon known as 'outcome bias'[29] will tend to induce a much harsher appraisal of the degree of negligence involved. This point is further explored in Chapter 7.

---

[27] It is a very basic point, but worth recalling, that views on what constitutes 'wrongful' conduct differ between communities and within any one community over time; changes in the legal position on homosexuality in many countries is but one example of this.

[28] The literature on medication errors is large. See, for example, D. W. Bates, 'Medication errors. How common are they and what can be done to prevent them' (1996) 15 *Drug Safety* 303–10; D. W. Bates, L. L. Leape and S. Petrycki, 'Incidence and preventability of adverse drug events in hospitalized patients' (1993) 8 *Journal of General Internal Medicine* 289–94; K. C. Nanji, A. Patel, S. Shaikh, D. L. Seger and D. W. Bates, 'Evaluation of Perioperative Medication Errors and Adverse Drug Events' (2015) *Anesthesiology* 124: 25–34; K. Taxis and N. Barber, 'Causes of intravenous medication errors: an ethnographic study' (2003) 12 *Quality and Safety in Health Care* 343–7; C. S. Webster, A. F. Merry, L. Larsson, K. A. McGrath and J. Weller, 'The frequency and nature of drug administration error during anaesthesia' (2001) 29 *Anaesthesia and Intensive Care* 494–500.

[29] R. A. Caplan, K. L. Posner and F. W. Cheney, 'Effect of outcome on physician judgments of appropriateness of care' (1991) 265 *Journal of the American Medical Association* 1957–60.

Perverting the course of justice[30]

A contrast can be drawn between the manner in which Drs Yogasakaran and Morrison responded to and dealt with the results of their errors and that followed by a British general practitioner who inadvertently prescribed a beta-adrenergic blocking agent (beta-blocker) to a patient with asthma. Asthma was considered to be a known contra-indication to the use of the selected drug. Fatal bronchospasm followed. In the resulting criminal trial for manslaughter, the court took a lenient view of the doctor's medical error, but sentenced him to six months' imprisonment for falsifying the relevant records with the intent of perverting the course of justice.

This illustrates neatly the distinction in terms of culpability between an understandable mistake (prescribing the beta-blocker) and a deliberate and unacceptable violation (altering the evidence). The attribution of blame seems entirely appropriate in respect of the doctor's deliberate choice to commit the offence of falsifying evidence.

Unsupervised Junior Doctors [31]

Malcolm Savage, a sixteen-year-old boy, who had had leukaemia since the age of four (and was found at post-mortem examination to be in remission), was admitted to Peterborough District Hospital in 1990 for his monthly treatment with cytotoxic drugs. Under the supervision of Dr Barry Sullman (a house officer), Dr Michael Prentice (a pre-registration house officer) injected vincristine (which should have been given intravenously) into the patient's cerebrospinal fluid instead of methotrexate. It appears that Dr Sullman misunderstood his role, and believed himself to be supervising only the lumbar puncture while Dr Prentice believed his colleague to be supervising the overall procedure of administering the cytotoxic medication. The boy died two weeks later. In summing up, the judge said, 'It seems to me you could have been helped more than you were helped.' He also said, 'You are far from being bad men; you are good men who contrary to your normal behaviour on this one occasion were guilty of momentary recklessness.' Both doctors

---

[30] D. Brahams, 'Medical manslaughter' (1994) 344 *Lancet* 256.

[31] G. Korgaonkar and D. Tribe, 'Doctors' liability for manslaughter' (1992) 47 *British Journal of Hospital Medicine* 147; *R* v. *Prentice* [1993] 3 WLR 927; *R* v. *Prentice, R* v. *Sullman, R* v. *Adomako, R* v. *Holloway* [1994] QB 302; D. Brahams, 'Manslaughter and reckless medical treatment' (1991) 338 *Lancet* 1198–9.

were convicted of manslaughter and given nine-month suspended prison sentences, but this conviction was overturned by the Court of Appeal.

In a very similar case, also involving junior doctors, vincristine was given intrathecally instead of intravenously once again, this time into a twelve-year-old child, Richie William. Charges against Dr John Lee, a specialist registrar in paediatric anaesthesia, and Dr Dermot Murphy, a registrar in haematology, were withdrawn on the grounds that failures in the system operated by Great Ormond Street Hospital for Children had played a significant part in the events. For example, the patient was admitted to a general ward instead of the ward that specialised in the treatment of malignancies. The injection was then deferred because he had eaten a biscuit. The result of this was that the senior registrar who should have administered the chemotherapy was off duty by the time the injection could be given. Vincristine was incorrectly sent to the operating theatre by a nurse against a rule that prohibited this. It was injected by Dr Lee, who had never previously administered chemotherapy into the spine, after Dr Murphy advised him, over the telephone, to administer the drugs.

The case of Prentice and Sullman was of importance in the development of the English position on the criminal prosecution of negligence, and the decision of the Court of Appeal confirmed the requirement of gross negligence for this purpose. A striking feature of this case, and that of Dr Lee, is the lack of any senior doctor or hospital authority amongst the defendants. A second feature is the fact that the very high-profile prosecution of Drs Prentice and Sullman appears to have had little if any benefit in avoiding recurrences of the same mistake or of errors in drug administration in general.[32] Finally, in both cases, it can be seen how factors in the system may contribute to the generation of an error.

A Highly Complicated Emergency [33]

Dr Hugel, a specialist anaesthetist, was charged with manslaughter after a thirteen-year-old boy, Benjamin Thorne, died following a minor procedure on an infected knee. The child was fit and active, and the tragedy of this case was particularly poignant. His mother had expressed anxiety about the risks of anaesthesia, but had been told that the

---

[32] See footnote 28.
[33] The details of this case are known to one of the authors (Merry), who acted as an expert witness. See also Skegg, 'Criminal prosecutions of negligent health professionals'.

operation could not be done under local anaesthetic and that under the circumstances there was little to fear.

After some pre-trial proceedings, the charge was confined to an allegation that Dr Hugel's failure to identify and remove a blocked filter had been negligent. Expert evidence called by both the prosecution and the defence concurred that the preliminary problems in this case were nothing to do with the filter, but rather the result of aspiration of stomach contents into the larynx. This, it was thought, produced laryngospasm, which led on to the well-recognised syndrome of negative pressure pulmonary oedema and probably bronchospasm as well.[34] Dr Hugel immediately called for the help of an anaesthetic colleague, but this was nearly thirty minutes coming and the contribution of various junior doctors who did arrive was relatively ineffectual. It was accepted by both sides that a filter used to protect the anaesthetic circuit from possible contamination by patient secretions was indeed blocked by the time the second anaesthetist arrived, and that its removal at that point did result in a rapid improvement of the boy's oxygenation and general condition. Unfortunately, he had suffered irreversible brain damage by this stage, and life support was discontinued the following day. The defence led evidence to the effect that it was unlikely that this blockage occurred until relatively late in the proceedings. None of the experts was able to relate the time that irreversible brain damage occurred to the time at which the filter blocked. All four experts said that the general conduct of the resuscitation was adequate, and none was prepared to criticise without reservation Dr Hugel's failure to identify the problem with the filter. It was agreed that she had not followed a protocol known as 'COVER ABCD'[35] in that she had not expressly eliminated the patient circuit and replaced it with a rebreathing bag. However, in the circumstances of the case, none of the experts was able to say confidently that this would have made any difference. Furthermore, one of the witnesses, the author of the protocol, pointed out that the protocol had failed to anticipate this particular problem and, if followed to the letter, would probably have been interpreted as requiring the filter to be retained because it was the means by which the carbon dioxide sampling line gained access to the circuit gases and the protocol expressly advised

[34] S. A. Lang, P. G. Duncan, D. A. Shephard and H. C. Ha, 'Pulmonary oedema associated with airway obstruction' (1990) 37 *Canadian Journal of Anaesthesia* 210–18.

[35] W. B. Runciman, R. K. Webb, I. D. Klepper, R. Lee, J. A. Williamson and L. Barker, 'Crisis management – validation of an algorithm by analysis of 2000 incident reports' (1993) 21 *Anaesthesia and Intensive Care* 579–92.

the retention of this line. He said the protocol had now been modified to make the need to eliminate a filter explicit. In the result, the jury returned a verdict of not guilty.

One of the most important features of this case is its 'smoking gun' aspect. A very obvious problem – the blocked filter – suggested itself as the cause of the death. A superficial inquiry might have gone no further, but on more mature reflection and more detailed examination of the facts it became obvious that this was but one of several difficult and dangerous problems that faced the anaesthetist. It was, furthermore, one that seems to have developed late in the proceedings. A second feature underlined by this case is the fact that certain medical procedures (notably the administration of anaesthetics) are inherently hazardous, and may allow very limited time for response to problems when they do develop. Dr Hugel had no more than a few minutes to evaluate and resolve a complex and rapidly evolving emergency. We are once again confronted with the human being as the limiting factor in the complex system.[36] No matter how competent a person may be, there will always be challenges that exceed his or her ability to react adequately and in time.

The strikingly emotive nature of this case, involving, as it did, the totally unexpected death of a healthy thirteen-year-old undergoing a minor procedure, makes some form of blame attribution almost irresistible. Yet it is important that the desire to blame does not prevent a proper and objective evaluation of what went wrong.

Another feature illustrated by this case is the uncertain nature of medical knowledge. The algorithm COVER ABCD was developed on the basis of an analysis of the first 2,000 incidents reported to the Australian Incident Monitoring Study (AIMS). It was (and is) an excellent approach to facilitating the management of a crisis in anaesthesia. It was understandable for the prosecution to assume that this protocol represented a statement of the standard of care for managing the sort of situation faced by Dr Hugel. On closer analysis, however, it emerged that the protocol was flawed in the very respect applicable to the case in question. This was a reflection of the fact that no similar incident had been reported to the AIMS database. A further point is that the protocol was not in fact universally accepted. Not all practising anaesthetists in New Zealand were aware of its existence, and it is uncertain how many anaesthetists outside Australasia would have been familiar with it.

---

[36] G. H. Sigurdsson and E. McAteer, 'Morbidity and mortality associated with anaesthesia' (1996) 40 *Acta Anaesthesiologica Scandinavica* 1057–63.

A Sleeping Anaesthesiologist[37]

Joseph Verbrugge, a Denver anaesthesiologist, was convicted of negligence after an eight-year-old patient, Richard Leonard, died following ear surgery in 1993. Dr Verbrugge was accused of having fallen asleep during the anaesthetic; he denied this, but admitted colleagues had confronted him about allegedly falling asleep during previous anaesthetics. There were a number of other features of this case which may have influenced the jury, who concluded that Dr Verbrugge's conduct amounted to 'an extreme deviation from generally accepted standards of medical practice', but were unable to agree unanimously that this constituted criminally negligent homicide or reckless manslaughter.

The most important point in this case is the fact that Dr Verbrugge's falling asleep during previous anaesthetics had been raised with him. Whether or not he was in fact asleep on the occasion of Richard Leonard's death, it does seem that something more should have been done to reduce the risk created by this problem. It might be thought that an anaesthetist has a responsibility to respond to manifestations of an inability to stay awake at work. It could also be argued that those who identified this problem had a responsibility to take action. The public is rightly concerned about the repeated failure of the available mechanisms to identify medical practitioners who are a risk to their patients, or to take adequate measures to safeguard patients when such doctors are identified.

A 'Systems Double-bind'[38]

At about 6 p.m. one evening, a mature woman was admitted to a district hospital in New Zealand following a road traffic accident. She had multiple orthopaedic injuries, but none of them were life-threatening. Both the orthopaedic surgeon and the anaesthetist who were on call had completed a long day's work. The anaesthetist assessed the patient soon

---

[37] Anonymous, 'Anesthesiologist is convicted in death of patient' (1996) *The New York Times* A22. The conviction was appealed: *People* v. *Verbrugge* 998 P 2d 43 (1999). Note that the term 'anesthesiologist' is used in the United States (and some other countries) to describe medically qualified anaesthetists, but is generally spelled 'anaesthesiologist' in the UK and several other countries, as for example in 'The World Federation of Societies of Anaesthesiologists'.

[38] Inquest into the death of Patricia Margaret Ross, Coroner's Court, Rotorua, 17 October 1997; D. Diaz, 'Doctor's slip led to death, inquest told', *New Zealand Herald* (16 October 1997), A4.

after admission and then attended to two other urgent cases. At about 10 p.m., he was free to take the patient who had had the accident to the operating theatre. The proceedings became quite protracted and the blood loss significant. To manage this better, the anaesthetist elected to insert a central venous catheter (CVC). This procedure was made more difficult by the fact that it was undertaken during the operation rather than before it, and unfortunately, unbeknown to the anaesthetist, in the process of insertion of the CVC, damage was done to the carotid artery. Blood loss became an increasingly difficult problem. What in fact was happening was that blood from the carotid artery was tracking into the thorax. The anaesthetist did consider this possibility, and made some attempts to investigate it. By this time, however, it was after 3 a.m. and these attempts may have been less determined than normal.

The surgery was completed at about 7 a.m. By this time, the doctors concerned had been working for almost 24 hours without rest. The patient was handed over to intensive care staff and the doctors departed. Shortly afterwards, cardiac arrest occurred and the patient died. The post-mortem examination confirmed that the cause of death was bleeding into the thorax from the damaged carotid artery.

At the coroner's hearing (presided over by a district court judge), the expert witness gave evidence that the actual insertion of the CVC had been entirely competent, and that the problem that had occurred was a recognised complication of CVC insertion. She did express criticism, though, of the failure to diagnose and treat the problem adequately. The judge commented on the possible contribution made by fatigue to this failure. He took note of evidence testifying to the adverse effect of fatigue on performance. On the basis of other evidence presented, he eventually acknowledged that the hours worked by the doctors in this case were accepted as inevitable in both anaesthesia and orthopaedic surgery. It was pointed out that it would be difficult to staff hospitals of this type without exposing doctors to the occasional requirement to work all night after a full day. On these grounds the judge declined to criticise the individual doctors, but recommended that the relevant colleges re-evaluate their guidelines with regard to hours of work.

There is now increasingly convincing evidence of the negative impact of fatigue on performance in many fields, including medicine.[39] It is now

---

[39] A. F. Merry and G. R. Warman, 'Fatigue and the anaesthetist' (2006) 34 *Anaesthesia and Intensive Care* 577–8.

widely accepted that working continuously for a period such as that involved in this case should be seen as a violation of safe practice.[40] The hours worked, the nature of the work and the time of day may all have contributed to a decrease in performance. This incident is a prime example of a violation made unavoidable by the system. Reason has called this a 'system double-bind'[41] – the doctors may understand and wish to avoid the unsafe behaviour, but they are unable to do so because of the constraints of their working arrangements.

Once again, this example reinforces the need to evaluate events in their wider context. Concentrating on human error alone may produce a misleading picture of the true cause of the problem. As we have observed previously, simply to punish, or even to remove the individual without addressing the deficiencies in the system, is to invite a repetition of the event, albeit with different players. It is significant that the judge was prepared to identify fatigue as a possible contributory factor in this patient's death. Such an awareness has often been absent in the law, and it is only recently that the courts are beginning to be aware of the full impact of fatigue on human activity. The challenge is to translate this awareness into effective measures to promote more sensible practices. We shall return in later chapters to the question of holding organisations accountable for the performance of their employees.

A Culpable Violation[42]

Dr Channagiri Manjanatha, a Saskatchewan anaesthetist, was the first Canadian doctor to be gaoled as the result of criminal negligence causing bodily harm. He had left the operating room to make a personal telephone call during the anaesthetic of his seventeen-year-old patient, Ryan Braumberger, who was undergoing surgery to repair a broken leg, without arranging for a suitable person to monitor the situation. The patient became disconnected from the ventilator, and was left in a vegetative state. Two of the ventilator's alarms had been switched off. Dr Manjanatha was also found by the judge to have falsified, to some degree, his report of the incident.

---

[40] Violations and errors are distinct: see Chapters 3 and 4.
[41] J. Reason, *Human Error* (New York, Cambridge University Press, 1990).
[42] L. S. Williams, 'Anesthetist receives jail sentence after patient left in vegetative state' (1995) 153 *Canadian Medical Association Journal* 619–20; *R* v. *Manjanatha* (1995) 131 *Saskatchewan Reports* 316.

For an anaesthetist to leave a patient unattended is quite different from any of the medical errors outlined above. This is a matter of deliberate choice – a clear violation of the rules of safe anaesthesia. A central theme of this book is that human error is inevitable; equally central, however, is the point that violations are a different matter. Thus it is unreasonable to require that, in an entire career, an anaesthetist should never make a slip/lapse error of the type made by Dr Yogasakaran, but it is quite reasonable to require, in the absence of compelling cause, that no patient should be left unattended in the manner of this case.

The Bristol Cardiac Surgeons[43]

This well-known case involved the performance over an extended period of time of two cardiac surgeons at Bristol Royal Infirmary, in relation to difficult operations on paediatric patients with congenital heart abnormalities. Of fifty-three operations involving arterial switches and atrioventricular septal defects, twenty-nine resulted in the death of the patient. In addition, four of the surviving patients suffered brain damage. These results were considerably worse than those obtained in other centres. The central issue related to the persistence of these surgeons in continuing these procedures in the face of poor results. Attempts to raise the matter by others were discounted by the surgeons and by a hospital administrator. Indeed, it seems that the anaesthetist who expressed

[43] P. M. Dunn, 'The Wisheart affair: paediatric cardiological services in Bristol, 1990–5' (1998) 317 *British Medical Journal* 1144–5; C. Dyer, 'Bristol doctors found guilty of serious professional misconduct' (1998) 316 *British Medical Journal* 1924; Editorial, 'First lessons from the Bristol case' (1998) 351 *Lancet* 1669; I. Murray and A. Lee, 'Baby death surgeons ignored warnings' (1998) *The Times*; R. Smith, 'All changed, changed utterly. British medicine will be transformed by the Bristol case' (1998) 316 *British Medical Journal* 1917–18; J. Warden, 'High powered inquiry into Bristol deaths' (1998) 316 *British Medical Journal* 1925; C. W. Dyer, 'Whistleblower in Bristol case says funding was put before patients' (1999) 319 *British Medical Journal* 1387; I. Kennedy, *The Report of the Public Inquiry into Children's Heart Surgery at the Bristol Royal Infirmary 1984–1995: learning from Bristol* (London, T. S. Office, 2001); Secretary of State for Health, 'Learning from Bristol: The Department of Health's Response to the Report of the Public into children's heart surgery at the Bristol Royal Infirmary 1984–1995', TSO (2002): www.gov.uk/government/uploads/system/uploads/attachment_data/file/273320/5363.pdf, accessed 29 November 2015; B. Keogh, 'The legacy of Bristol: public disclosure of individual surgeons' results' (2004) 329 *British Medical Journal* 450–4; C. Dyer, 'NHS has still not learnt the lessons of Bristol' (2006) 333 *British Medical Journal* 220; C. R. V. Tomson and D. M. Berwick, 'What can the UK learn from the USA about improving the quality and safety of healthcare?' (2006) 6 *Clinical Medicine* 551–8.

concern over the high mortality rate had little choice but to leave Bristol and to find employment outside Britain. The parents of the patients were quoted standard risks rather than being told the actual results of the unit in question.

This complicated story raises a number of issues. It illustrates the problem of individual technical competence of doctors, who undertake difficult procedures when they simply are not sufficiently skilled, or perhaps not sufficiently well supported by their unit, to achieve an acceptable success rate. It also raises issues of audit, of how such doctors are to be identified and of the difficulties faced by whistle-blowers. The culpability in this case is rather different from that in the preceding examples, because of the drawn-out nature of the course of conduct, and also because of the complexity of the issues at stake. For example, the point has been made that the results of a unit such as this depend not only on the surgeons but also on a number of other members of the team. Indeed, evidence supporting the importance of teamwork in surgery has continued to accumulate since the time of these events.[44] Furthermore, it is no simple matter to demonstrate that results in a relatively small series of high-risk cases are indeed beyond the limits of acceptable variation.[45] Nevertheless, the decision to take a risk and persist with the operations in the face of mounting evidence of unacceptable outcomes was unfortunate. Furthermore, being deliberate, in this case once again the actions of the doctors have the appearance of a violation rather than an error. Disciplinary proceedings by the General Medical Council resulted in the deregistration of both surgeons, and of the medically qualified hospital administrator whose response to expressions of disquiet was considered inadequate.

The Failure at the NHS Mid Staffordshire Trust

It is difficult to know the full extent of the events at Stafford Hospital (in Stafford, England) between 2005 and 2008. An excess in hospital

[44] See discussion of teamwork in Chapter 2.
[45] For discussion of the general issues, see: K. Walker, J. Neuburger, O. Groene, D. A. Cromwell and J. van der Meulen, 'Public reporting of surgeon outcomes: low numbers of procedures lead to false complacency' (2013) 382 *The Lancet* 1674–7; R. Hamblin, C. Shuker, I. Stolarek, J. Wilson and A. F. Merry, 'Public reporting of health care performance data: what we know and what we should do' (2016) 129 *New Zealand Medical Journal* 7–17. In respect of the Bristol affair, see also D. J. Spiegelhalter, 'Mortality and volume of cases in paediatric cardiac surgery: retrospective study based on routinely collected data' (2002) 324 *British Medical Journal* 261–3.

mortality rate was one of the factors that alerted authorities to the extent of the problems in this hospital.[46] Amongst many widely publicised examples, toilets were dirty, some patients were left by nurses to lie in their own excreta and others had to resort to drinking water from the flower pots on their bedside tables.

Perhaps the most concerning aspect of this scandal is the length of time and number of inquiries required to identify that this organisation was seriously dysfunctional. The extent of the disconnect between assessment of hospitals in the NHS at that time and the reality of what was actually happening on the wards and in the operating theatres is shown by the remarkable fact that the Mid Staffordshire hospital trust succeeded in gaining the coveted status of a foundation trust during the very same period. The inquiry by Robert Francis QC[47] was the fifth inquiry into this hospital. The persistent efforts of a group of consumers called 'CURE the NHS', led by Julie Bailey, the daughter of Isabella Bailey, an elderly patient who had died in Stafford Hospital, was pivotal in bringing about this inquiry. Julie Bailey was subject to widespread harassment and criticism in relation to this work. It has been said that senior (or indeed any) medical and nursing staff failed to raise concerns and insist on some sort of response. It seems clear that considerable anxiety prevailed about the consequences of speaking up. However, Jones and Kelley have argued that many efforts were made in this regard, but ignored. They refer to a 'Deaf Effect' on the part of organisations, and also to the substantial barriers to whistle-blowing in any organisation (indeed, we have already mentioned the consequences that followed for the anaesthetist who did this in Bristol).[48]

The report by Robert Francis QC is more than 1700 pages long.[49] The executive summary contains a table of 290 recommendations. A National Advisory Group on the Safety of Patients in England, led by Don Berwick, provides a more practical set of ten

---

[46] S. Goodacre, M. Campbell and A. Carter, 'What do hospital mortality rates tell us about quality of care?' (2015) 32 Emergency Medicine Journal 244–7.

[47] R. Francis, 'The Mid Staffordshire NHS Foundation Trust. Public Inquiry Chaired by Robert Francis QC. Report of the Mid Staffordshire NHS Foundation Trust Public Inquiry. 3 vols', Stationery Office (2013) www.midstaffspublicinquiry.com, accessed 2 July 2016.

[48] A. Jones and D. Kelly, 'Deafening silence? Time to reconsider whether organisations are silent or deaf when things go wrong' (2014) 23 BMJ Quality & Safety 709–13.

[49] Francis, 'The Mid Staffordshire NHS Foundation Trust'.

recommendations.[50] Both reports have received considerable attention internationally, and a great deal has been written about the implications of this subject.[51] Many people with responsibilities in healthcare in the UK and other countries have pondered the question 'could something like the events at Mid Staffordshire be happening in my institution – and how would I know if it was?'

An Airline Disaster[52]

It is often said that civil aviation is a shining example of the successful adoption of a systems-based approach to safety and that healthcare need look no further than the airline industry for guidance on how to solve its own problems. There is much truth in these points, but it is salutary to remember that airline pilots are as susceptible to human error as any other professionals, and that even well-intentioned and well-designed engineering and organisational initiatives to ensure safety may not always prove adequate.

On 1 June 2009, Air France Flight 447 (an Airbus A330) departed from Rio de Janeiro for Paris. Because the flight was expected to take thirteen hours, three pilots were on board to allow rests to be taken in turns (the A330 is actually designed to need only two pilots, so this was an active step to promote safety). As it happened, the captain took his turn to rest early, soon after cruising altitude had been reached. At least some sources indicate that he may have had less sleep than he would have liked on the previous night. In any event, he was not on deck when the airbus reached an (anticipated) area of bad weather. The co-pilots on deck decided to climb above the worst of the turbulence.

---

[50] D. Berwick, 'A promise to learn – a commitment to act: improving the safety of patients in England', Department of Health (2013) www.gov.uk/government/publications/berwick-review-into-patient-safety, accessed July 2016.

[51] See, for example, G. P. Martin and M. Dixon-Woods, 'After Mid Staffordshire: from acknowledgement, through learning, to improvement' (2014) 23 *BMJ Quality & Safety* 706–8, and the references within this paper.

[52] A great deal has been written about this event, including the official reports; see in particular: Bureau d'Enquêtes et d'Analyses pour la Sécurité de l'Aviation Civile, *Final report on the accident on 1st June 2009 to the Airbus A330–203 registered F-GZCP operated by Air France Flight AF 447 Rio de Janeiro – Paris* (2012). In this very brief account we have tried to capture some key points that relate to the nature of error, rather than to enter into a detailed analysis of precisely what went wrong and why. Wikipedia provides an overview supported by a long list of references. See Wikipedia contributors, Air France Flight 447, *Wikipedia, The Free Encyclopedia*, https://en.wikipedia.org/wiki/Air_France_Flight_447, accessed 30 June 2016.

The A330 makes considerable use of computers to increase safety by reducing dependency on error-prone humans: in effect, pilots usually spend only a small proportion of time actively flying the A330, mainly during take-off and landing (apparently, the behaviour of aeroplanes is different at high altitude).

The A330 used a set of small 'pitot' tubes in the measurement of airspeed. These tubes were rendered dysfunctional by ice crystals in the bad weather. In consequence, indications of airspeed became intermittent and inaccurate, and the autopilot system switched to manual. Thus, the pilots found themselves having to fly the aeroplane themselves, in very unfamiliar circumstances – high altitude with at least some dysfunctional monitoring equipment. A feature of manual mode (so-called 'alternate law') is that the computerised functionality that would normally have made it impossible for them to stall the aircraft was disabled – a distinction they may not have fully appreciated in the heat of the moment.

Notwithstanding extensive investigation, the exact details of the subsequent events are not perfectly clear, but there does seem to have been some important failures of coordination and communication between the two co-pilots and a failure on the part of all three pilots to understand the situation as it developed.

Unlike a Boeing, which has traditional joysticks, the A330 is 'fly-by-wire' in design,[53] and has side-stick controls very much like those used for many computer games today. These side-sticks move independently of each other with very little tactile feedback to either pilot, and their position is not particularly obvious from even a slight distance (the other seat in the cockpit, for example). Amongst other things, it appears that a situation arose in which turbulence, a series of confusing alarms, and a general sense of things going wrong led to a misunderstanding in which each of the two pilots on the deck failed to appreciate what the other was doing. It has been suggested that, at one point, they were trying to fly the aircraft at the same time, one trying to lift the nose and the other trying to lower it, with the net effect that their respective inputs cancelled each other out. At the very least, misinterpreting the information intermittently presented by the instruments, one of the co-pilots repeatedly attempted to lift the nose of a plane that was already flying far too slowly (lowering it

---

[53] In other words, the links to the aircraft's ailerons, flaps, rudder and so on are electronic rather than mechanical.

would have been more appropriate), without the other realising that this was happening.

Late in the sequence of events, the captain returned to the cockpit. He took one of the second row seats to oversee the situation, unaware that time was not on his side. A substantially functional commercial aircraft had stalled and was falling from the sky, with 228 people on board. Extraordinary as it may seem, this was not obvious to the crew, in part because there would have been no sensation of falling. The last recorded words spoken by the captain were, 'Damn it, we're going to crash . . . This can't be happening!'

A key feature of this story is the failure of teamwork. There were obvious failures in communication between the three people responsible for flying the aeroplane, but reference has also been made to alleged deficiencies in their training (notably in cockpit resource management) and to alleged shortcomings in the safety culture of Air France at that time. Design features of this aeroplane also contributed to the difficulties that arose. The 'team' in many challenging endeavours extends beyond those who function at the 'sharp end'. We will return to these concepts in Chapter 2, but it is worth commenting here that one of the biggest changes in our understanding of the genesis of avoidable harm in healthcare since the publication of the first edition of this book lies in our increased appreciation of the importance of teamwork and communication. In fact, we alluded to these issues in many parts of the first edition, but since then a great deal more evidence has accumulated about these aspects of human performance in healthcare. It was clear then, but it is even clearer today, that singling out individuals for punishment seldom makes sense when things go wrong in a complex system that depends on many people working in concert at multiple organisational levels. This is not to say that no one is responsible, but rather that it is unusual for failures at the point of patient care to reflect an isolated error by a single individual in an otherwise highly functional system. This point goes beyond ideas (discussed in the next three chapters) of latent factors in equipment (such as the vulnerability of the pitot tubes to ice) or capability of individuals (such as lack of experience in flying this type of aeroplane at altitude in manual mode) to encompass the ways in which people interact with each other effectively, particularly under constraints of time. A central point of this book is that any sophisticated analysis of blame should at least consider the wider context in which accidents occur, and the point here is that teamwork is an important part of that context.

Perhaps the most striking difference between this story and the others outlined in this chapter is that the professionals involved in the accident all died. It is sometimes said that a major reason for the safety of air travel is that the pilots are themselves at risk – this is sometimes framed in terms of the position of the pilots 'in the front of the plane' or of the weak joke that they 'tend to be the first people to reach the scene of the accident'.[54] These are ideas that we will discuss in greater detail, but airlines have not always been safe. Until the mid-1950s, accidents in aviation were very common. The thing that changed for airlines was not the position of the pilots (they have always taken their full share of the risk of crashing). It was the adoption of a system-based approach to organisational safety underpinned by a just culture in which the reporting of close calls was encouraged and made safe, but compliance with safety procedures was made non-negotiable. The people at the centre of the other accidents discussed in this chapter did not lose their lives, but one can be sure that they did suffer substantial and prolonged emotional distress, as well as harm to their careers and to people close to them. The term 'second victim'[55] has been used to make this point. Many a mother would see the loss of a baby as rivalling the loss of her own life, yet in the Introduction to this book we outlined the story of a mother who, through distraction, made an error that cost her baby's life. This example from aviation, which is not isolated, makes it clear that the fear of consequences is not sufficient on its own to prevent error. We will discuss this fundamental aspect of human error in greater detail in Chapter 3.

Naming and Blaming

Our examples illustrate how failures – at times quite minor failures – in medical care can at times have tragic consequences for patients. How we react to events of this sort is, in one sense at least, dependent on how the event is described. Event descriptions carry a great deal of moral weight,

---

[54] The apparent safety of air travel is probably overstated, anyway. Travel in a scheduled commercial aircraft is safer than other forms of transport if measured by distance covered, but if measured by hours of exposure or number of trips, buses turn out to be safer. Travel in modern motor cars is, deceptively, very safe – at least in high-income countries. The design and construction of cars and roads has improved enormously in the last few decades, and has been supported by increasingly effective approaches to the regulation of traffic. The reason that travel by motor car appears to be particularly dangerous is because the exposure of most people to this form of travel is so high – two or three trips a day, typically, in contrast to a flight every year or so perhaps.

[55] A. W. Wu, 'Medical error: the second victim' (2000) 320 *British Medical Journal* 726–7.

and our choice of description may well be decisive in determining the outcome of any legal or moral inquiry into the event. For example, to describe an event as an accident is often taken to mean that it was a 'matter of chance' and carries strong implications of blamelessness. At the other end of the spectrum, to describe it as deliberate or intentional implies a high level of culpability.[56] Yet between these two extremes of complete chance and intentional harm, there may be varying degrees by which behaviour knowingly contributes to the risk of harm. For example, the drunk driver may not intend harm, but must be held responsible for the consequences of deliberate risk-taking. Such a driver may protest that the knocking down of a pedestrian was unintentional and was therefore an accident. This would not be accepted, and it could be pointed out that the event was not accidental in that it could have been avoided by modifying a decision within his or her control – the decision to drive while under the influence of alcohol.[57] By contrast, if an apparently well-maintained tyre blows out, perhaps because it has run over a jagged stone in the road, that would seem to be beyond the control of the driver and would be truly accidental. It might be viewed as reflecting inadequate maintenance of the road, and in that context be seen as a systems-based problem. However, the design of systems is itself subject to limits, including those on resources, and in this example there is a sense that, given the current state of tyre technology and the impossibility of keeping roads free of all debris, it would have been beyond the ability of anybody to prevent this. This event was simply not preventable – it was an accident in the purest sense.

If it is the case that the term 'accident' carries with it an exculpatory, or even mitigating, meaning, it is important to identify exactly what this word means. One definition describes an accident as something which is 'largely, if not completely, unintentional, unforeseeable – and harmful'.[58]

Does this definition serve our purposes adequately? Probably not. To begin with, the inclusion of the concept of harm must be taken as a matter of arbitrary definition and is unnecessary; it is possible to

---

[56] R. A. Duff, *Intention, Agency and Criminal Liability: Philosophy of Action and the Criminal Law* (Oxford, Basil Blackwell, 1990). See also M.S. Moore, 'Intention as a marker of moral culpability and legal punishability' in R.A Duff and S.P. Green (eds.), *Philosophical Foundations of Criminal Law* (Oxford, Oxford University Press, 2013) 179–205.

[57] J. Rumgay, *Crime, Punishment and the Drinking Offender* (London, Macmillan, 1998).

[58] J. Dowie, 'Would decision analysis eliminate medical accidents?', in C. Vincent, M. Ennis and R. J. Audley (eds.), *Medical Accidents* (New York, Oxford University Press, 1993).

imagine an event which all would agree is accidental but which causes no harm. Indeed, there is even the concept of the happy accident, which describes an occurrence which may be fortuitous but which is regarded as positive. Missing a flight that subsequently crashes comes to mind as an example.

Intentionality is certainly relevant. It is obvious that no harm was intended in any of the cases dealt with in this chapter. Were these, then, all accidents? If they were, does this imply that there should be no blame attached to any of them?

A particular feature of medical practice, well illustrated in the cases presented, is that, so far from any intention to harm, there is actually a duty of care to help, and almost always a genuine intention to do so. This is in contrast to the situation where a driver knocks over a pedestrian. In the latter case there may be no intention to harm the pedestrian, but in fact, apart from the technical duty of care on the part of the driver not to cause harm to the pedestrian, there is no intent either way in relation to the particular individual. When a doctor accepts responsibility for a patient, there is an explicit responsibility to try to help that patient, or at the very least not to harm him or her. Sadly, however, unintentionality alone does not provide a sufficiently narrow filter to preclude all cases in which blame may reasonably be attributed. There are many examples of consequences which may be neither intended nor desired by the actor, but which nevertheless may be the subject of blame and may therefore need to be excluded from the category of accidents. In the example of an armed robber who points a weapon at a shopkeeper with the intention only of frightening him, the law nevertheless quite rightly holds the robber responsible for the consequences if the gun goes off and the shopkeeper is killed or injured. It would certainly be unacceptable to describe this as an accident, even if the robber genuinely had no intention of shooting. What makes the situation non-accidental is the element of foreseeability. Even if the robber did not foresee the possibility of the weapon going off, any reasonable person would have seen the risk of this happening. The term 'accident' has a strongly normative element to it; it is not merely descriptive and cannot be understood outside the framework of the normative evaluation of the behaviour in question. Clearly, then, in evaluating the sort of case described above, intentionality, although an important component of our definition of an accident, must be taken as given and is of little use on its own.

A more significant element would seem to be foreseeability. As with intentionality, this concept is one of the important elements in determining whether an occurrence is accidental but, of itself, it too is insufficient. By convention, foreseeability in this context means reasonable foreseeability. If an event is foreseeable, then there is a duty to take precautions to prevent its occurrence. A failure to do so is culpable and justifies the conclusion that what happened was not an accident. There is, though, a further requirement. It is only reasonable to hold a person responsible for a foreseeable event if it was realistically within his or her power to prevent it. Thus it is foreseeable that an anaesthetist's failing to stay awake is, in the end, likely to result in a tragedy – and something can be done about this by the practitioner concerned.[59] As with the drunken driver, if a patient died because of a practitioner's known tendency to fall asleep while working we would not call this an accident. Similarly, it is foreseeable that failing to adequately supervise junior doctors will over time increase the number of errors in a hospital. Again, it should be possible to deal with problems of this type, given adequate resources, but in this case the onus would seem to lie substantially with the supervisors, and only partly with the junior doctors. We need to find effective ways to shift the focus of accountability from individuals to teams. The limitations of human behaviour must also be taken into account. In the following chapters we shall build on the argument that it is foreseeable that every practitioner will eventually make certain types of error, and some of these will contribute to harming patients. As with the junior doctors, we shall emphasise the importance of designing the system to reduce the likelihood of such harm occurring. However, if it is accepted that errors are an inevitable accompaniment of the human condition, it then follows that it is not realistically within the power of human practitioners to eliminate them. Given a reasonably well-designed and resourced system, an error (as defined in Chapter 3) must be accepted as unintended and unavoidable – and therefore as an accident.

---

[59] This is true, despite the surprising finding from a study in a simulated clinical environment that sleep-deprived participants experienced increased sleepiness while providing anaesthesia but this did not affect clinical performance; it seems that the link to brief periods of inattention is less immediate than when driving a car, for example. See S. K. Howard, D. M. Gaba, B. E. Smith, M. B. Weinger, C. Herndon, S. Keshavacharya and M. R. Rosekind, 'Simulation study of rested versus sleep-deprived anesthesiologists' (2003) 98 *Anesthesiology* 1345–55. Nevertheless, patients are at risk when anaesthetists fall asleep, and perhaps the most fundamental point here is that colleagues who become aware of this type of impairment (perhaps in an older practitioner who may also be losing insight) are also responsible and must act.

We would suggest, then, that an event can be defined as an accident if and only if the following conditions are met: (i) that it was unintended; and *either* (ii) it was reasonably unforeseeable *or* (iii) it was foreseeable (in a general or statistical sense at least) but could not realistically have been prevented in the particular instance in question. The second and third of these criteria should be applied in the context of practice, knowledge and context at the time of the event: defining an event as an accident does not imply that nothing should be done to prevent the same thing happening again, or that events of the same type would necessarily qualify as accidents in the future. The moral and ethical onus here should be on learning from mistakes.

This definition might be tested further against others of the cases mentioned above. We have already noted that the first condition is met in all the cases: none of the people in question intended to cause harm. As far as the second and third requirements are concerned, judgements on foreseeability and preventability in these cases depend to some degree on the weight given to the contemporary understanding of the nature of human error. Thus, in Dr Yogasakaran's case one might say that failing to read an ampoule's label is preventable, and that one could foresee the risks entailed in such a failure. A view more compatible with our knowledge of human psychology is that this was an example of a slip/lapse error. The fatal failure by a mother to remember that her baby was in her car was also a lapse, albeit a more prolonged one. We shall expand on the nature and classification of human error in Chapter 3, but all the evidence suggests that lapses are inevitable concomitants of the human ability to deal with complex situations. They cannot be prevented by exhortation, punishment or any other direct attempt to modify human behaviour. They are particularly understandable in the context of an unplanned and unexpected emergency, but lapses are equally likely during routine activities. The difference between the routine and the urgent lies more in the opportunity for systematic checking. For example, in the planned injection of a single drug into a hazardous location by Dr Morrison, it does seem that more could have been done to ensure that a proper check was carried out. While no amount of care can guarantee that all such errors will be prevented, the introduction of precautions along the lines subsequently recommended by the College of Radiologists recognised a failure of process, which, if addressed, could make this type of error substantially preventable – at least in the future. In effect, more could reasonably have been done. Furthermore, it could reasonably have been predicted that the failure to follow such precautions might eventually result in a disaster. There are grounds for suggesting, therefore, that the case of Dr Yogasakaran was an accident, while that of Dr Morrison was not.

In spite of this, it seems harsh to place the entire responsibility for the event on Dr Morrison, partly because of the contribution of a second person (the radiologist), but more importantly because the evidence points to the lack of a properly defined procedure for radiologists administering such an injection at the time. Had a proper protocol been in general use when the injection was undertaken, there would be little doubt about Dr Morrison's culpability in choosing not to follow it. In fact, it was only after the event, and at the instigation of the Medical Council, that the College of Radiologists produced a suitable protocol. Dr Morrison chose to plead guilty to the charge against him; it might have been possible for him to defend himself on the grounds that his overall approach was consistent with the norms applicable at the time. If one accepts this proposition, his only error was, like Dr Yogasakaran's, a momentary lapse – something very difficult to prevent. At that time and in that context, it was an accident. It would be more difficult to construe an otherwise identical event as an accident if it occurred *after* the recommendations of the College of the Radiologist had been promulgated and they had then been flaunted.

Similarly, there was a clearly preventable component in the case involving fatigue, one which might foreseeably compromise performance. It is far from ideal for doctors to work for excessive periods without a break, and it ought to be possible to avoid this. For this reason, in one view, this case should not be called an accident. Yet in an alternative view, even if it was not an accident and was therefore attributable to a deliberate violation of a general principle in relation to fatigue, responsibility for the incident did not rest primarily with the doctors. In Chapter 4 we shall consider the contribution of system double-binds to the generation of violations. It may be neither possible nor desirable to single out individuals responsible for the system failure in a situation of this type, although sometimes this can and should be done. For the doctors concerned, in the circumstances, working while fatigued was not preventable. Once again, under this construction, the patient's death might be thought accidental.

In the case of Dr Hugel, it is understandable that the completely unexpected death of an essentially healthy child, taken together with the discovery of a blocked filter, might be construed as a simple matter constituting negligence – and therefore not an accident. On closer enquiry, the case (as we have described) involved multiple factors in a complex and rapidly evolving emergency. It is hard to see how a sequence of events such as this could have been predicted, and at her trial for manslaughter no measures were identified which, without the benefit of hindsight, could reasonably have been expected from a competent practitioner and which would clearly have prevented the loss of the patient.[60] Once again, therefore, we can conclude that this incident was an accident.

An important feature in understanding this case is its progressive nature. The overall incident may be viewed as having been made up of a series of developments which were dependent upon one another. The management of the case cannot be evaluated by looking at a single decision or act within the series. One must take into account the overall picture and how the reaction to each stage may have been affected by what had preceded it. How the boundaries of an event are defined may be crucial to its evaluation. In this case the prosecution laid great store by the doctor's failure to identify a blocked filter. The defence view, though, was that the blockage of the filter was a late and largely irrelevant development. Furthermore, while one might have expected an anaesthetist to identify a blocked filter as an isolated problem at the beginning of a case, diagnosing a late blockage in the context of numerous other problems is a different matter. The subjective reaction of the anaesthetist to a relentlessly developing crisis in which a child is dying is likely to be severe and, indeed, to become overwhelming as bad event succeeds bad event. The point to be made here is that human behaviour has

---

[60] It is worth noting that tragic deaths attributable to unanticipated problems in managing patients airways during anaesthesia, in intensive care units and in emergency departments, do occur on a regular basis; these are true crises in which little time is available to rescue a rapidly deteriorating situation, and much effort is being put into finding improved ways of responding when they occur. Thus, as with drug errors, empirical data support the view that terrible things can happen to the patients of competent and conscientious practitioners. See T. M. Cook, N. Woodall and C. Frerk, 'Major complications of airway management in the UK: Results of the Fourth National Audit Project of the Royal College of Anaesthetists and the Difficult Airway Society. Part 1: Anaesthesia' (2011) 106 *British Journal of Anaesthesia* 617–31; T. M. Cook, N. Woodall, J. Harper and J. Benger, 'Major complications of airway management in the UK: Results of the Fourth National Audit Project of the Royal College of Anaesthetists and the Difficult Airway Society. Part 2: Intensive care and emergency departments' (2011) 106 *British Journal of Anaesthesia* 632–42; C. Frerk, V. S. Mitchell, A. F. McNarry, C. Mendonca, R. Bhagrath, A. Patel, ... Difficult Airway Society intubation guidelines working group, 'Difficult Airway Society 2015 guidelines for management of unanticipated difficult intubation in adults' (2015) *British Journal of Anaesthesia* 1–22.

a chronological dimension and performance must be judged in temporal context. What might be considered preventable at the beginning of a sequence may be made inevitable by the limitations of human beings confronted with the informational and emotional overload which develops as a crisis unfolds.[61]

It is possible to analyse the remaining cases in somewhat similar terms. The point of this exercise is not to endorse or reject the decisions of the courts, but rather to emphasise the need for some sophistication in analyses of this type. It is essential to look beyond the 'smoking gun' (the filter in Dr Hugel's case, for example) and identify the full sequence of events, the nature of any antecedent factors, the cognitive processes involved in the incident and the contribution of other players and of the system in general. The story of the Mid Staffordshire NHS Trust makes it clear that the focus of any investigation, or any initiative to improve care, must extend beyond any one individual and encompass the entire 'teams' (which may imply the entire institutions) that deliver healthcare today.

There is no doubt that many people use the term 'accident' rather loosely, and would include within it at least some untoward incidents in which there is an element of fault or blame. Indeed, it is in this sense that we used the word in the opening sentence of this chapter. This usage, though, deprives the term of a useful evaluative role. In a technical context we talk, for example, *of non-accidental injury* in children, and this is a convenient term, which signals the presence of some element of culpability. The concept of accident and the accidental, as we have defined it, is a useful aid to differentiate blameworthy from blameless behaviour, and is in accordance with one form of everyday use. It is obvious from the above discussion that the dividing line between accidental and non-accidental events may be hazy and subject to differences of interpretation. In Chapter 5 we shall extend this distinction, and identify five levels of blameworthiness. Clarifying the boundaries between them depends on a proper understanding of the insights that the science of psychology has brought in relation to the ways in which the limitations of human behaviour contribute to adverse events.

---

[61] For a discussion on the effect of cognitive overload on performance, see J. W. Rudolph and N. P. Repenning, 'Disaster dynamics: understanding the role of quantity in organizational collapse' (2002) 47 *Administrative Science Quarterly* 1–30.

Accidents, Errors and Violations

A useful starting point in deciding whether an event should be judged as accidental or non-accidental is a proper classification of the cognitive processes underlying the human behaviour that have contributed to its occurrence. Errors need to be distinguished from violations. Errors are characteristically never deliberate. Violations, on the other hand, must be defined in the context of accepted rules, norms or principles, and constitute a deliberate deviation from them. They are not inevitably reprehensible, and indeed may be motivated by the best of intentions. Yet they do involve choice – there is in a violation a clear volitional component. Violations are therefore generally avoidable, although factors within the system or organisation may at times make it very difficult in practice to avoid them. Errors, by contrast, are unintentional and cannot be avoided simply through the exercise of choice.

Errors may involve an action or a plan. Skill-based errors are either slips or lapses, and can also be thought of as unintended actions. Errors involving unintended actions can be differentiated from *mistakes*, in which the action is intended but there is some flaw in the plan. Mistakes may be further subdivided according to the type of cognitive processing involved in the generation of the event. Much is known about each type of error and about different forms of violation. Indeed, it is often possible to predict what type of error is most likely to occur in a particular set of circumstances. This systematic approach should greatly facilitate assigning accidental or non-accidental status, or, in a more general sense, blameworthiness. In Chapters 3 and 4, we shall enlarge upon each of these error types and on violations, and relate each to medical practice. A further theme of this book is that the proper understanding of errors and violations goes beyond the knowledge and experience of the lay person, and is not a matter which the court should determine for itself without the help of an expert. On the contrary, analysis of these events requires familiarity with a substantial body of knowledge based on empirical research. Indeed, certain attributes of error are counter-intuitive. For example, we shall see that, surprisingly, although experts are less likely than novices to make errors overall, they may be more prone than novices to slips and lapses – a factor of obvious importance in the evaluation of an event.

Explaining and Blaming

The Quest for Truth

Misfortune invites explanation. When things go wrong in human affairs, the almost inevitable response is to seek an explanation for what happened. This can be explained in various ways. At the most general level, human curiosity about the world compels us to try to understand the events that touch upon our lives. This curiosity prompts us to try to understand the past, in order to make sense of our relationship with it. Every human institution, every human life has a history, and the urge to see coherence in the events of our lives and to resolve the unresolved is very powerful. Even if the knowledge that we acquire as to what has happened were to have no practical value – in the sense that it would not alter how we conduct our affairs or even how we deal with them legally – it may still be important to us for its own sake. The truth is always important to people, whatever other motivations may also contribute to the search for the facts.

The Pursuit of Safety

Curiosity apart, there are good pragmatic reasons for seeking an accurate account of events that have caused harm. Foremost amongst these is the desire to prevent the recurrence of such harm. What distinguishes this motivation from others is the fact that it is forward-looking and is therefore arguably of greatest use. In the scientific and technological realms in general, and in medicine in particular, the need for comprehensive and scientifically based evaluation of incidents is well understood, and significant resources are committed to this sort of inquiry.

The emphasis is on identifying the truth rather than on attributing blame. This is shown by the way in which inquiries of this sort will seek to encourage maximum disclosure by focusing on the information itself rather than by seeking to establish authorship and responsibility. This also recognises that the individual operator is only one component of the complex system, and often the least important one. The use of confidential reporting, notably in aviation and medicine, is widely accepted as being of great value. Typically, in a hospital using this system, a report will be submitted by the practitioners concerned with the incident. This may be anonymous, although in practice it may be difficult to conceal the relevant identities. The vital requirement is for those concerned not only to explain the facts, but also to offer their opinions about what went wrong. In this situation, the right to silence is being set aside. There is also a significant chance that these opinions may take too little account of all the circumstances and may even be unnecessarily self-critical. With this in mind, arrangements have been made in many countries for such opinion to be privileged to a greater or lesser degree. This privilege results in no loss for police or other investigative agencies; all the normal sources of information remain open to them, including patient notes and the testimony of witnesses, for example. The process to which privilege applies is additional to the existing avenues of enquiry. It is regrettable that, in a number of countries, legislators struggle to accept the value of such provisions. In aviation, the value has long been recognised of a process of learning from confidential reports, compiled by any member of aircrew or ground staff. These reports are analysed centrally by bodies concerned with air safety. One medical example of a similar, centralised process of anonymous incident reporting is that which was established under the auspices of the Australian Patient Safety Foundation.[62] Incident reporting systems that extend across specialties and disciplines have been adopted in many hospitals around the world, but with various disparate arrangements in relation to anonymity and privilege.

The overriding goal of all these activities is the pursuit of greater safety. The aim is to circumvent the barriers created by the legal process – whether civil or criminal – to the comprehensive and open elucidation of adverse events. It should, of course, be possible to obtain an understanding of an event through the use of legal or disciplinary proceedings, but in practice such proceedings may be unreasonably protracted, and even then may often fail to get to the truth, in part because some of those involved are likely to have powerful reasons to conceal or even distort

---

[62] W. B. Runciman, A. Sellen, R. K. Webb, J. A. Williamson, M. Currie, C. Morgan and W. J. Russell, 'The Australian Incident Monitoring Study. Errors, incidents and accidents in anaesthetic practice' (1993) 21 *Anaesthesia and Intensive Care* 506–19; R. K. Webb, J. H. van der Walt, W. B. Runciman, J. A. Williamson, J. Cockings, W. J. Russell and S. Helps, 'The Australian Incident Monitoring Study. Which monitor? An analysis of 2000 incident reports' (1993) 21 *Anaesthesia & Intensive Care* 529–42. More recent examples of this type of incident reporting in anaesthesia include the web-based Anaesthetic Incident Reporting System ('WebAIRS') developed by the Australian and New Zealand Tripartite Anaesthesia Data Committee (ANZTADC), the Swiss Critical Incidents Reporting System, and the Anesthesia Incident Reporting System (AIRS) established by the Anesthesia Quality Institute in the United States.

information. Indeed, the advice of lawyers to those involved is often to refrain from comment, and certainly to avoid self-incrimination.[63] In the legal context, the adversarial process does not always lead to the disclosure of the entire picture; amongst the reasons for this are the rules of evidence and the limitations of expert witnesses. We shall consider the role of the expert in Chapter 7.

Blaming and Compensation

The need to compensate for injury was recognised in the earliest legal systems. Early law favoured a crude system whereby fixed measures of compensation closely linked with the nature of the injury suffered were provided for, purely on the grounds that the defendant had caused injury. Such systems did not concern themselves with blame, and it is only later, with the development of the Roman law concept of *culpa*, that notions of blame came to underpin the duty to compensate. The concept of *culpa* as an abstract legal notion was not developed to any great extent in Roman law itself, but came to the fore in the work of the canon lawyers, who introduced into Western European law strong moral notions of fault as the basis of the duty to provide compensation.[64] By the time of the great codifications of the nineteenth century, a concept of fault had developed which was heavily influenced by the notion of moral blame. A parallel development occurred in English law, where the notion of negligence required that there should be a failure on the part of the defendant to meet an expected standard of behaviour. This failure was inevitably expressed in the language of shortcoming or wrongdoing. As a result, except in those areas where the law allowed for compensation based on strict liability, the law of torts proceeded on the assumption that the duty to compensate was based on a moral duty to provide reparation for the consequences of faulty conduct.

---

[63] Over the last decade, in parallel with increased emphasis on the importance of open disclosure, some legal advisors in some countries (notably, but not only, New Zealand) have begun to advocate a more constructive approach. We will enlarge later on the theme that everyone benefits from openness, but until we reach a point where the vast majority of practitioners and their legal advisors are unequivocally convinced of this, a parallel process that provides a way for practitioners to go further in disclosure than might otherwise feel safe has merit.

[64] J. Gordley, 'Tort law in the Aristotelian tradition', in D. G. Owen (ed.), *Philosophical Foundations of Tort Law* (Oxford, Clarendon Press, 1995), 131–58; R. Zimmermann, *The Law of Obligations: Roman Foundations of the Civilian Tradition* (Cape Town, Juta, 1990), 1033.

It is significant that, although the law referred to negligence liability being based on fault, the standard by which conduct was judged was an objective rather than a subjective one. Conduct then could be described as 'faulty' or 'wrongful' even if the individual had no intention of behaving wrongfully, and even if he or she was making his best efforts to avoid harming others. In other words, the external judgement of fault had nothing to do with the internal, subjective mental state of the defendant. In the definition of an accident that we have proposed, it is the elements of foreseeability and preventability, rather than that of intentionality, that would create liability for compensation. Because it would not be foreseeable, or if foreseeable it would not reasonably be preventable, an accident, as defined above, would not merit compensation.

The objective nature of the concept of negligence, as applied in the law of torts, is absolutely central to our discussion of negligence. In the context of compensation, the law is seeking to establish whether the external features of the defendant's conduct 'fit the pattern' of negligent conduct as defined by the law. For this purpose, it does not matter whether the defendant is morally culpable; all that matters is that the conduct in question was deemed faulty, which is another way of saying that it was deemed to be substandard or inadequate in the circumstances. There is therefore no necessary connection in law between moral culpability and liability for negligence. Such a connection may exist in individual cases (as, for example, in the case of a person who deliberately omits safety precautions for unjustifiable reasons), but this is not essential to liability. The use of 'fault' in this context is therefore potentially misleading, if one reads into 'fault' any moral significance.

How can this be justified? If a person may be obliged to make reparation for an act that shows no subjective moral fault, then it would appear that the obligation to pay compensation has nothing to do with blameworthiness. This is in fact true (at least in theory – in Chapter 5 we shall discuss the extent to which it is or is not true in practice). The objective of the law of torts is to provide compensation to those whose interests have suffered as a result of the act of another. In selecting those acts that will warrant the award of compensation, it identifies acts that unjustifiably intrude upon the interests of others. Such acts cause unjustified harm, and our sense of what is fair or just dictates that this disturbance be rectified and the people harmed be put back, as far as possible, into the position in which they were before the untoward interference with their interests. To give a simple example, if A throws an object out of the window without checking whether anybody is in the street below, he is liable for the damage he causes to a passer-by who is injured by it. It may be that *A* believed that there was nobody in the street and that he would not have wished to cause injury. This, however, is not the point. The possibility of injuring a passer-by was foreseeable and preventable, so the law prefers the interests of the passer-by, who has a right to be compensated.

An accompaniment to liability for compensation is the effect it has on the conduct of members of society in general. The risk of being made to pay compensation is thought to serve as a deterrent for negligent behaviour as well as positively encouraging initiatives to reduce risk and enhance safety. Inevitably, but usually not by intention, civil liability also carries an element of punishment. In rare cases, the level of compensation may be fixed at a punitive level to reflect the court's belief that the defendant's conduct merits some form of financial punishment.

The requirement for some element of fault is related to the fact that the right to compensation is exercised against the person who actually causes the damage. There is evidence that this system is quite inefficient. Civil litigation often fails to compensate those who most deserve it and gives money in circumstances that are less appropriate.[65] It is also slow and expensive. An alternative is to impose the duty to compensate on the state and extend the right for compensation to all personal injuries arising from 'accidents', whether fault is involved or not. This approach has been tried in a number of countries, most notably in New Zealand. Under this approach, there is not the same need for explanation of how an incident occurred; the important matter is that the incident is confirmed as a non-natural occurrence. An effect of this general approach, of course, is that those who are injured may achieve compensation but may not get a full explanation of what happened. This aspect has also been criticised as resulting in reduced accountability, and in New Zealand provisions have been made to take account of this objection.[66] In Chapter 8 we shall

---

[65] Localio et al., 'Relation between malpractice claims and adverse events due to negligence'; P. Fenn, 'Compensation for medical injury: a review of policy options', in C. Vincent, M. Ennis and R. J. Audley (eds.), *Medical Accidents* (New York, Oxford University Press, 1993).

[66] M. Bismark and R. Paterson, 'No-fault compensation in New Zealand: harmonizing injury compensation, provider accountability, and patient safety' (2006) 25 *Health Affairs* 278–83.

return to the difficult question of how injured patients should in fact be compensated, and consider these issues in more detail.

Blaming and Sanctioning

The search for explanation is linked to the universal human desire to punish wrongdoing. Wrongdoing gives rise to reactive attitudes; we resent the wrongdoer and feel that a response to the wrongful act is both justified and necessary.[67] This response commonly takes the form of a call for retribution, inspired by a belief that the moral balance, which is upset by the wrong, will somehow be restored through punishment. Retribution has been the subject of immense debate in the philosophy of punishment and, in spite of the objections that it represents a crude, revenge-based approach, it still plays a major role in penology. Moreover, retribution cannot be ignored, however uncomfortable we may feel about it. Its popularity, and the degree to which it accords with the moral feelings of the community, secure for it a central place in our social practices.

There are other theories used to justify the practice of punishment. The declaratory theory, for example, believes that punishment underlines and vindicates the interest that has been wronged by crime.[68] In punishing, then, the courts are seen to be announcing their support for the victim and denouncing the conduct of the defendant. Deterrent theories similarly see the good of punishment in the notion that it prevents crime. In this view, the wrongdoer may be expected to make the calculation that committing an offence is simply not worth the risk of detection and punishment.

The declaratory and deterrent views of punishment do not necessarily support the notion that only the deserving should be punished (although they tend to assume that). By contrast, theories of retribution are under-pinned by the notion of desert. Retribution is limited to those who deserve to be punished on account of their culpable conduct. Desert requires more than mere authorship of the wrong; it stipulates that the defendant should have acted in a morally culpable state of mind. This close connection between desert and punishment means that blame

---

[67] P. Strawson, 'Freedom and resentment', in G. Watson (ed.), *Free Will* (New York, Oxford University Press, 1982), 59–80.

[68] J. Feinberg, 'The expressive function of punishment', in *Doing and Deserving: Essays in the Theory of Responsibility* (Princeton, Princeton University Press, 1970), 95–118.

should only be placed on those who are morally culpable.[69] Strict liability is quite different: it merely requires that the defendant should have acted in a particular way and pays no attention to his or her state of mind at the time of acting. In any developed system of morality or jurisprudence, the impulse to blame will always be subject to the recognition that some persons who cause harm simply are not blameworthy. This is because they either fail some test of responsibility (they are too young, for example, or they are mentally disordered) or because the state of their mind is clearly not blameworthy. The question of which states of mind are blameworthy is contested. We probably all agree on some cases at either end of the spectrum. Between these extremes, however, considerable debate may arise as to the blameworthiness of the individual under the circumstances.

Whether an individual merits punishment is often a complex issue, requiring cautious and well-informed judgement. The desire to blame and punish for misfortune is at times very strong, and concerns have been voiced that blaming behaviour in recent decades has been unduly encouraged by the public media and certain consumer-oriented pressure groups. The idea that life's misfortunes are usually attributable to failure on the part of others to prevent them is a seductive one. Every death in an institution, or every loss of a child at the hands of an abusive parent, raises demands for an inquiry into where fault lies. This culture of blaming has led to a high level of civil litigation in many countries, notably the United States.

In medicine, this attitude has contributed to a marked increase in various types of action against doctors and other practitioners, including civil claims, disciplinary proceedings and criminal prosecutions. The growing frequency with which civil claims are now brought against doctors in many countries points to a much greater willingness of patients to attribute blame for medical misfortune. Many of these claims are, of course, legally justifiable; their significance, however, lies in the fact that they signal the growth of a blaming mentality.

A real danger in this area is an excessive readiness to blame others for events which in fact they might not have been able to prevent. There is

---

[69] Blame is to be distinguished from guilt. We may feel guilty for things we have done, even if we are not to blame: H. Morris, 'Responsibility, Character and the Emotions', in F. Schoeman (ed.), *New Essays in Moral Psychology* (Cambridge, Cambridge University Press, 1987), 220. Elsewhere, Morris has drawn attention to the uncoupling of liability and moral culpability: H. Morris, 'The decline of guilt' (1988) 99 *Ethics* 62–76.

a risk that this will give rise to an undiscriminating attitude towards the process of dealing with harmful events, and at times with inevitable misfortune. A number of undesirable consequences may ensue. These include increased costs, victimisation and a breakdown in trusting relationships. Blame not only requires culpability; it needs cool analysis. A rush to blame, particularly when fuelled by a natural tendency to focus on those aspects of an incident that are dramatic and obvious rather than systemic and underlying, is likely to be counter-productive and obscure opportunities to improve safety. It also creates a serious risk of injustice.

2

The Human Factor

Our knowledge of the workings of the human brain has progressed enormously over recent decades, not only in respect of the receptors, transmitters and pathways that form the physical matrix of the brain, but also in our understanding of human cognition, and of how people communicate and interact with each other to complete tasks together that could not be undertaken successfully alone. It is our human cognitive ability that has given us our highly organised and technologically sophisticated societies, with all their advantages and disadvantages. Yet it is precisely these cognitive processes that also make human beings prone to error. To this risk must be added the fact that the technology and complexity which characterise modern life, and which have resulted from our ability to think, have created an environment in which the opportunities for error are numerous and in which errors may readily contribute to serious harm. Error, then, should be viewed not as an unfortunate frailty on the part of human beings, but rather as an inevitable concomitant of the powerful cognitive processes that have permitted us, collectively, to extend the limits of human achievement.

There have been good observational data concerning human error since the work of Freud first suggested that errors were not necessarily random events attributable to carelessness, but could be meaningful in terms of a person's psychology. Today, cognitive science can provide considerable insight into the workings of the human mind. This knowledge is of more than theoretical significance: a wider understanding of the processes that underlie our decisions and our actions is essential if we are to make progress in improving safety in complex systems that involve humans (such as medical practice). This knowledge is, in fact, relied upon by those concerned with designing systems that will lead to the optimising of the human performance of technical tasks. It has proved to be less accessible to those concerned with the judging and regulation of human behaviour – in particular, it is not always considered relevant in a legal context. This is unfortunate: legal inquiries are about justice and social utility, and these goals would be greatly assisted if the law were to pay adequate attention to what this information can tell us about how people behave and, most importantly, how they can realistically be expected to behave.

Error and Progress

The remarkable material and scientific progress humankind has made does not reflect a progressive increase in what we might call our raw intelligence. It is not the computing power of our brains that has improved. Instead, it is a function of the growth in our language and knowledge, of our ability to communicate sophisticated ideas and cooperate with one another and of our talent for working together to create and utilise the increasingly powerful technology which today supports and facilitates our cognitive processes.

Obvious advantages have accrued from our astonishing progress in almost every field of human endeavour. Our ability to organise ourselves into large but coherent functional groups, added to the sophistication and power of our continuously accumulating knowledge and technology, has allowed us to perform numerous complex and useful tasks. Unfortunately, there have also been some less desirable consequences of our increasing reliance on activities based upon ever more complicated technology and dependent upon co-operation within and between complex organisations. Amongst these has been a marked increase in the number of ways in which we can make errors, and in the degree of devastation now possible when accidents occur. Even those human activities that are peaceful and well intended have a tendency to go badly wrong, sometimes with consequences so serious that it might have been better never to have embarked on them in the first place.

Many of our daily activities are highly complicated and depend on the skills, expertise and judgement of many people – either at the time of the activity or before it, by way of design, organisation or other contributory processes. The surprising thing is not that something will go wrong eventually; rather, it is astonishing that we can successfully undertake some of our modern-day functions at all. People's actions must be viewed against a backdrop of this fertile ground for error: it is a fundamental mistake to describe, study or judge people out of context, without considering the social structures, groups, rules (written or simply understood), methods of communication and technologies that form their world. We shall return in Chapter 5 to the tendency of the law to make just this mistake.

Iatrogenic Harm – A Statistical Inevitability

Our particular concern is errors and violations in medicine. Medical practice is a good example of the kind of high-level achievement that groups of people are capable of, and that has been made possible by language, technology, research, training and co-operation. It is also highly prone to things going wrong. A series of studies, from several countries, based on the screening of random samples of medical records by trained reviewers[1] have made it increasingly clear that *preventable* adverse events *resulting from medical therapy* are much more common than had previously been supposed.[2] The Harvard Medical Practice Study is perhaps the best known of these. This study involved structured reviews of 30,121 randomly selected case records from 51 randomly selected acute care non-psychiatric hospitals in the state of New York in 1984. Adverse events occurred in 3.7 per cent of admissions ('hospitalizations'), and 27.6 per cent

[1] D. H. Mills, *Report on the Medical Insurance Feasibility Study* (San Francisco, Sutter Publications, 1977).

[2] T. A. Brennan, L. L. Leape, N. M. Laird, L. Hebert, A. R. Localio, A. G. Lawthers, J. P. Newhouse, P. C. Weiler and H. H. Hiatt, 'Incidence of adverse events and negligence in hospitalized patients – results of the Harvard Medical Practice Study I' (1991) 324 *New England Journal of Medicine* 370–6; L. L. Leape, T. A. Brennan, N. Laird, A. G. Lawthers, A. R. Localio, B. A. Barnes, L. Hebert, J. P. Newhouse, P. C. Weiler and H. Hiatt, 'The nature of adverse events in hospitalized patients. Results of the Harvard Medical Practice Study II' (1991) 324 *New England Journal of Medicine* 377–84; R. M. Wilson, W. B. Runciman, R. W. Gibberd, B. T. Harrison, L. Newby and J. Hamilton, 'The quality in Australian health care study' (1995) 163 *Medical Journal of Australia* 458–71; E. J. Thomas, D. M. Studdert, J. P. Newhouse, B. I. Zbar, K. M. Howard, E. J. Williams and T. A. Brennan, 'Costs of medical injuries in Utah and Colorado' (1999) 36 *Inquiry* 255–64; C. Vincent, G. Neale and M. Woloshynowych, 'Adverse events in British hospitals: preliminary retrospective record review' (2001) 322 *British Medical Journal* 517–19; T. Schioler, H. Lipczak, B. L. Pedersen, T. S. Mogensen, K. B. Bech, A. Stockmarr, A. R. Svenning, A. Frolich and S. Danish Adverse Event, 'Incidence of adverse events in hospitals. A retrospective study of medical records' (2001) 163 *Ugeskrift for Laeger* 5370–8; G. R. Baker, P. G. Norton, V. Flintoft, R. Blais, A. Brown, J. Cox, E. Etchells, W. A. Ghali, P. Hebert, S. R. Majumdar, M. O'Beirne, L. Palacios-Derflingher, R. J. Reid, S. Sheps and R. Tamblyn, 'The Canadian Adverse Events Study: the incidence of adverse events among hospital patients in Canada' (2004) 170 *Canadian Medical Association Journal* 1678–86; P. Davis, R. Lay-Yee, R. Briant, W. Ali, A. Scott and S. Schug, 'Adverse events in New Zealand public hospitals I: occurrence and impact' (2002) 115 *New Zealand Medical Journal* U271.

of these were attributed to negligence. Of the adverse events, 2.6 per cent caused permanently disabling injuries and 13.6 per cent led to death. These results were extrapolated to suggest that 27,179 injuries, associated at least in part with 13,451 deaths and 2,550 cases of permanent total disability, resulted from medical care in New York State in 1984. The 'Quality in Australian Health Care Study' was very similar in design. Investigators reviewed 14,179 records from 28 hospitals in New South Wales and South Australia in 1992. The main outcome variable was an 'adverse event', defined as 'an unintended injury or complication which results in disability, death or prolonged hospital stay and is caused by health care management'. Adverse events occurred in 16.6 per cent of admissions, 51 per cent of which were judged to be 'highly preventable' – a phrase used to circumvent the debate over what constitutes negligence and to avoid the negative connotations of that term. Death occurred in 4.9 per cent of the patients suffering an adverse event, and permanent disability in 13.7 per cent.

Amongst the dramatic claims which have been made on the basis of these data have been suggestions that more people die on an annual basis from medical negligence than on the roads, and that the number of deaths in the United States equates to three jumbo jets full of passengers crashing every two days.[3] Makary and Daniel have recently suggested that medical error is the third biggest cause of death in the United States.[4] Comments of this type serve to emphasise the magnitude of the problem, but in doing so they tend to reflect only the debit side of the account. They fail to remind us that, in the absence of figures describing positive outcomes to provide balance, the data from these studies do not reflect the *net effect* of medical practice. Also, these analogies may not adequately reflect the fact that many of the patients identified in these studies as having been harmed are not in a comparable state of health to those in road traffic or airline accidents; many are elderly and/or very sick: in one study few would have been alive, well and at home three months later.[5] This is not to say that inadvertent harm to such patients does not matter. Rather, it is to ask

[3] L. L. Leape, 'Error in medicine' (1994) 272 *Journal of the American Medical Association* 1851–7; D. Blumenthal, 'Making medical errors into "medical treasures" [editorial]' (1994) 272 *Journal of the American Medical Association* 1867–8.

[4] M. A. Makary and M. Daniel, 'Medical error-the third leading cause of death in the US' (2016) 353 *British Medical Journal* i2139.

[5] R. A. Hayward, 'Counting deaths due to medical errors' (2002) 288 *Journal of the American Medical Association* 2404–5.

whether the balance between harm and good is being taken into account. One of the challenges for healthcare is the imperative to treat the very sick. One way to avoid harming patients directly by healthcare would be simply not to treat them. The question that has not properly been addressed is that of the net effect of healthcare – the balance between the harm done and the good. It would also be wrong to assume that these data mean that the problem of iatrogenic harm is new, or even that it is necessarily getting worse. In the first edition of this book we noted that the exponential rise in the number of aeroplanes in the sky means that, in the absence of improvements in aviation safety, a stage would be reached when one major crash was occurring per fortnight. The fact that this has not yet happened, perhaps because safety in aviation is improving alongside the increasing number of flights, does not detract from the underlying point. The public would probably find it difficult to accept disasters occurring at this frequency, even if the level of safety had improved from that pertaining today.[6] In a similar way, it may be the *perception* rather than the *reality* which has changed in relation to safety in medicine. Indeed, it is very probable that the increase in data concerning iatrogenic harm reflects a renewed emphasis on safety and a growing commitment to identifying and dealing with problems in the health system. Notwithstanding these caveats, it is obvious from the above studies that iatrogenic harm in general is a significant problem in hospitals, and that it is often the consequence of imperfect practice. Furthermore, despite authoritative calls for improvement[7] and considerable investment in initiatives to that end,[8] there is little evidence of a substantial reduction in the rate of unintended harm in healthcare,[9] except in a few outstanding examples of success.[10] As the stories in Chapter 1

---

[6] D. E. Maurino, J. Reason, N. Johnston and R. B. Lee, *Beyond Aviation: Human Factors: Safety in High Technology Systems* (Aldershot, Ashgate Publishing Limited, 1995).

[7] For example, in 1999 the Institute of Medicine in the United States called for a 50% reduction in iatrogenic harm in five years: see L. T. Kohn, J. M. Corrigan and M. S. Donaldson (eds.), *To Err Is Human: Building a Safer Health System* (Washington, D.C., National Academy Press, 1999).

[8] The establishment of the Institute of Healthcare Improvement in the United States, and the Health Quality and Safety Commission in New Zealand are just two examples of this investment.

[9] L. L. Leape and D. M. Berwick, 'Five years after To Err Is Human: what have we learned?' (2005) 293 *Journal of the American Medical Association* 2384–90; C. P. Landrigan, G. J. Parry, C. B. Bones, A. D. Hackbarth, D. A. Goldmann and P. J. Sharek, 'Temporal trends in rates of patient harm resulting from medical care' (2010) 363 *New England Journal of Medicine* 2124–34.

[10] P. Pronovost, D. Needham, S. Berenholtz, D. Sinopoli, H. Chu, S. Cosgrove, B. Sexton, R. Hyzy, R. Welsh, G. Roth, J. Bander, J. Kepros and C. Goeschel, 'An intervention to

illustrate, many people die, or are seriously injured, who expected healing rather than harm, so an expectation for a response from legal or regulatory authorities is entirely understandable. The data provide compelling evidence of the imperative to respond to the problem of inadvertent harm in healthcare without any need for hyperbole. When we are seeking to attribute blame, however, it is important to keep in mind that this iatrogenic harm occurs in the context of a great deal of essential, effective and successful medical treatment. For an individual patient during one admission, the chances of suffering a serious adverse event are actually quite low (although not as low as they should be); on the other hand, for an individual practitioner, working with thousands of patients over a career of thirty or forty years, the chances of accidentally causing such an adverse event are high. The consequences to each are different, of course, since it is the patient, not the practitioner, who is injured. Nevertheless, the consequences to clinicians may also be considerable, psychologically and in relation to their reputations and careers. The idea, mentioned in Chapter 1, that staff involved in accidents in healthcare may also be 'victims' of these accidents has gained increasing recognition in recent years.[11] Emotional distress is to be expected from any caring person who injures another, particularly when a duty of care pertains, there are times when other adverse consequences to a clinician, including punishment, may also be appropriate, but the disciplinary or legal processes that may flow from such events should distinguish genuinely culpable practices from the human errors that are inevitable in any clinician's career.

Drug Administration Errors as an Example

In the Harvard Medical Practice Study, 19.4 per cent of adverse events involved drug errors. These errors constituted the largest single category, and 14.1 per cent of them led to serious disability.[12] In the first 2,000 anaesthetic incidents reviewed by the Australian Incident Monitoring Study (AIMS), 144 (about 7 per cent) involved the wrong drug.[13]

decrease catheter-related bloodstream infections in the ICU' (2006) 355 *New England Journal of Medicine* 2725–32.

[11] For example, see chapter 8 in: B. Runciman, A. Merry and M. Walton, *Safety and Ethics in Healthcare: A Guide to Getting It Right* (Aldershot, Ashgate, 2007).

[12] Leape, 'Error in medicine'.

[13] M. Currie, P. Mackay, C. Morgan, W. B. Runciman, W. J. Russell, A. Sellen, R. K. Webb and J. A. Williamson, 'The "wrong drug" problem in anaesthesia: an analysis of 2000 incident reports' (1993) 21 *Anaesthesia and Intensive Care* 596–601.

In 4 American hospitals, voluntary 'critical incident' reporting showed that 6 per cent of critical incidents in anaesthetic practice were wrong-drug errors.[14] In a British hospital, 9.2 per cent of nurses admitted having given the wrong drug to a patient, and 62 per cent admitted errors of omission, while 30 per cent of interviewed anaesthetists had administered the wrong drug at some time.[15] Chopra's group reported 16 drug errors (including 2 which involved giving the wrong blood) out of 148 incidents from 113,074 anaesthetics over 10 years in one hospital in the Netherlands.[16] In an Australian intensive care unit, drug errors were the second most frequent category of incident (after problems with equipment), constituting 122 of 390 reported incidents for 2,153 admissions over 24 months.[17] In a series of more recent studies, facilitated incident reporting has been used, in which information is collected on every anaesthetic rather than just those in which an error occurs. When this approach has been used, much higher rates of error have been observed.[18] The use of direct observation, in simulated anaesthetics or in clinical practice, has shown that the true rates of drug administration error are even higher, and that errors in the recording of administered drugs are also common.[19] It is therefore not surprising

[14] J. B. Cooper, R. S. Newbower and R. J. Kitz, 'An analysis of major errors and equipment failures in anesthesia management: considerations for prevention and detection' (1984) 60 *Anesthesiology* 34–42.

[15] G. D. Smellie, N. W. Lees and E. M. Smith, 'Drug recognition by nurses and anaesthetists' (1982) 37 *Anaesthesia* 206–8.

[16] V. Chopra, J. G. Bovill and J. Spierdijk, 'Accidents, near accidents and complications during anaesthesia' (1990) 45(1) *Anesthesia* 3–6.

[17] G. K. Hart, I. Baldwin, G. Gutteridge and J. Ford, 'Adverse incident reporting in intensive care' (1994) 22 *Anaesthesia and Intensive Care* 556–61.

[18] C. S. Webster, A. F. Merry, L. Larsson, K. A. McGrath and J. Weller, 'The frequency and nature of drug administration error during anaesthesia' (2001) 29 *Anaesthesia and Intensive Care* 494–500; R. L. Llewellyn, P. C. Gordon, D. Lines, A. Reed, A. D. Butt, A. C. Lundgren and M. F. M. James, 'Drug administration errors: A prospective survey from three South African teaching hospitals' (2009) 37 *Anesthesia and Intensive Care* 93–8; Y. Zhang, Y. J. Dong, C. S. Webster, X. D. Ding, X. Y. Liu, W. M. Chen, L. X. Meng, X. Y. Wu and D. N. Wang, 'The frequency and nature of drug administration error during anaesthesia in a Chinese hospital' (2013) 57 *Acta Anaesthesiologica Scandinavica* 158–64.

[19] A. F. Merry, C. S. Webster, J. Hannam, S. J. Mitchell, R. Henderson, P. Reid, K. E. Edwards, A. Jardim, N. Pak, J. Cooper, L. Hopley, C. Frampton and T. G. Short, 'Multimodal system designed to reduce errors in recording and administration of drugs in anaesthesia: prospective randomised clinical evaluation' (2011) 343 *British Medical Journal* d5543; K. C. Nanji, A. Patel, S. Shaikh, D. L. Seger and D. W. Bates, 'Evaluation of perioperative medication errors and adverse drug events' (2016)124(1) *Anesthesiology* 25–34.

that 89 per cent of the respondents to a survey of New Zealand anaesthetists reported having made drug administration errors at some stage
in their careers, most more than once, and 12.5 per cent reported having
actually harmed patients in this way. To place this finding in context, it
should be appreciated that most anaesthetists administer drugs at least
250,000 times during their working lives, and for many the number of
administrations would exceed 500,000.[20]

To the lay public, a drug administration error is hard to comprehend.
It does not seem a difficult matter to give the right drug in the right dose
to the right patient at the right time by the right route and to record this
correctly.[21] Yet we can see that the facts belie this understandable
assumption. The truth is that errors of drug administration occur in all
medical and nursing disciplines in all countries. It is precisely because
they are common but not immediately understandable that they are
a good example of the type of error that pervades healthcare. In part,
the issue is a lack of awareness of the complexity of some of the activities
in question. Most people understand that a major surgical operation is
a difficult undertaking, but it is perhaps less widely appreciated that an
anaesthetic may often involve the administration of ten, and in some
cases more than thirty, intravenous boluses of drug.[22] As with many tasks
in medicine, this has to be achieved under pressure of time and while the
anaesthetist is also attending to a number of other duties (as in the case of
Dr Yogasakaran). The difficulty lies not in giving the right drug once, but
rather in giving the right drug on every occasion, hundreds of thousands
of times in a working life, often under circumstances which are far
from ideal. A more significant issue illustrated by these drug errors,
however, is a widespread failure to understand the nature of human
error and the way in which errors may occur even during tasks that are
straightforward.

Most drug errors are harmless, and as such pass unpunished and
almost without comment. Again, this is typical of many forms of error
in healthcare, and goes some way to explaining why, in a system that is

---

[20] A. F. Merry and D. J. Peck, 'Anaesthetists, errors in drug administration and the law'
(1995) 108 *New Zealand Medical Journal* 185–7.
[21] A. F. Merry and B. J. Anderson, 'Medication errors – new approaches to prevention'
(2011) 21 *Paediatric Anaesthesia* 743–53.
[22] C. S. Webster, L. Larsson, C. M. Frampton, J. Weller, A. McKenzie, D. Cumin and
A. F. Merry, 'Clinical assessment of a new anaesthetic drug administration system:
a prospective, controlled, longitudinal incident monitoring study' (2010) 65 *Anaesthesia*
490–9.

often stretched to the limit of its resources and in which many other matters constantly demand attention, they are tolerated. However, harm does occur occasionally. When it does, the severity of the consequences may be quite out of proportion to the magnitude of the errors. In fact, the outcome of a failure in patient care is often related to chance more than to the degree of negligence involved. It is therefore worrying, not so much that a tougher approach seems to have been taken by the courts in some countries in recent years when harm does follow a simple error of this general type,[23] but more that this tougher approach has tended to focus on the individual practitioner rather than the system. Four of the examples given in Chapter 1 are cases in point (those of Drs Yogasakaran and Morrison, of the general practitioner who prescribed a beta-blocker to an asthmatic patient, and of the vincristine administered intrathecally by junior doctors). The prosecution of a junior doctor in Northern Ireland, following her accidental administration of a drug into the wrong tube while she was fatigued, is also an example of this.[24] As we emphasise throughout this book, it is not our position that errors like these should be accepted – indeed, much greater effort is warranted to reduce their occurrence. However, given the frequency of drug errors overall, the conclusion does seem inescapable that the factor which plays the greatest role in the allocation of blame for these errors is their outcome. It is the result that is being judged, not the action. In other words, *outcome bias* is compounding the effect of *moral luck* – phenomena to which we shall return in Chapters 6 and 7.

Complexity

A process or system can be simple, complicated or complex.[25] Changing the wheel of a car is relatively simple. Making the car is complicated, but the process, once understood can be repeated reliably.

[23] S. E. McDowell and R. E. Ferner, 'Medical manslaughter' (2013) 347 *British Medical Journal* f5609; R. E. Ferner and S. E. McDowell, 'Doctors charged with manslaughter in the course of medical practice, 1795–2005: a literature review' (2006) 99 *Journal of the Royal Society of Medicine* 309–14. See also: P. D. G. Skegg, 'Criminal prosecutions of negligent health professionals: the New Zealand experience' (1998) 6 *Medical Law Review* 220–46.

[24] C. Dyer, 'Doctors cleared of manslaughter' (1999) 318 *British Medical Journal* 148.

[25] S. Glouberman and B. Zimmerman, *Complicated and Complex Systems: What Would Successful Reform of Medicare Look Like?* (Commission on the Future of Health Care in Canada, Saskatoon, 2002); A. Gawande, *The Checklist Manifesto* (New York, Metropolitan Books, 2009).

Bringing up a child is the classic example of a complex process. Some general principles apply, but the fact that one has had previous success in this endeavour does not guarantee future success. Similar considerations apply to systems. The weather is the classic example of a complex system. The key feature of a complex system is that its future state can be predicted, but only over a fairly short time frame, after which it is necessary to start again with renewed baseline data and repeat the process of prediction. Healthcare systems are, in general, complex. Any system in which humans play a crucial role will be complex, at least to some extent, because human cognition and performance are themselves complex.

Driving in traffic provides a useful illustration of the interdependence of people and technology, and of many aspects of human cognition and error. This example is especially useful because it is familiar to most people – so familiar, in fact, that we tend to take many quite astonishing aspects of this modern phenomenon for granted. Consider for a moment some of the steps involved in driving a motor car from one place to another in heavy traffic. The car and all its component parts had to be conceptualised, designed and manufactured, its fuel obtained and supplied, the roads surveyed and built, and a set of rules created and implemented to deal with the ebb and flow of traffic. At the end of all this research and development, the driver had to learn to operate the car, follow the roads and keep to the rules, while at the same time avoiding running into other drivers, all of whom are engaged in similar endeavours. In most aspects, the process of driving a car tends to be complicated rather than complex, but the interdependence of many human beings that characterises traffic is complex and the unpredictable is always possible. It is quite remarkable how well most people master the challenge of driving in traffic, to the extent that they may often drive almost automatically, often chatting to a passenger, listening to a radio or talking on a cell phone (perhaps illegally) at the same time as controlling the car. And yet most drivers will almost always see – and respond to – an unexpected event such as a child running into the road ahead. Almost always, but not quite always. Occasionally we fail to respond in time, and a crash results. As human beings we are capable of the most extraordinary feats of individual and collective accomplishment, but, because we are not machines, we are also capable of lapses and failures in performance.

'Normal Accidents' and the Utilitarian View of Punishment

The individual who, after many years of driving safely, eventually makes a serious mistake may not only be punished as criminally negligent but is often portrayed as deficient, incapable and worthy of censure or disparagement. This may occur even when the mistake is entirely under-standable. The attention paid to the contribution of other people involved in the activity, either at the time or in some antecedent way, is seldom in proportion to its importance. Typically, failure is judged as if the last person in the line were the primary cause of a problem that, on closer inspection, often turns out to reflect some antecedent failure. The presence of the wrong ampoule in the compartment of the drug drawer in Dr Yogasakaran's case is one example of a *resident pathogen* resulting from a *latent factor*,[26] and the fact that the members of the team were chronically short of sleep in the *Challenger* disaster is another. The reality is that accidents in complex systems are not all primarily manifestations of avoidable human misdemeanours. Instead, they are often the result of unpredictable interactions between errors and one or more of the innumerable components and activities that are involved in any sophisticated endeavour within large organisations of people and machines. The idea that such events are inevitable in complex organisa-tions has been developed by Charles Perrow and encapsulated in the title of his study, *Normal Accidents*.[27] Perrow classifies activities on two axes. On one axis, complexity is represented, on the other coupling. An activity is highly coupled to its outcome if the consequences of an action are relatively certain, and loosely coupled if not. Perrow argues that it is not possible to have the benefits of human progress without a certain inci-dence of failure, particularly in complex systems in which actions or events are tightly coupled to potentially serious consequences. In the past this seems to have been quite well appreciated, and people have been willing to accept that things do go wrong occasionally. As our technolo-gical sophistication has increased, the risks involved in certain activities have tended to shift. To some degree, it may simply be that one must accept new risks as the price of greater achievement. In addition, how-ever, developments in technology have a tendency to produce hazards which are unexpected, and which in some cases would have been very

---

[26] J. Reason, *Human Error* (New York, Cambridge University Press, 1990); J. Reason, *Managing the Risks of Organizational Accidents* (Aldershot, Ashgate, 1997).

[27] C. Perrow, *Normal Accidents: Living with High Risk Technologies*, 2nd edition (Princeton, Princeton University Press, 1999).

difficult to predict. Thus, aeroplanes are safer today than ever before – but because more people fly further and faster than in the past, the total number of deaths associated with aviation has increased. Medicine, too, is certainly more effective now than ever before, and in general safety has also increased; for instance, anaesthesia has become progressively safer, at least in high-income countries: the risk of dying directly from anaesthesia has changed from 1 in 2,000 cases in the nineteenth century to about 3 per 10,000 anaesthetics in the middle of the twentieth century, to about 1 per 50,000 anaesthetics today.[28] Indeed, there has been a change in the way deaths associated with anaesthesia are perceived: the notion that anaesthesia itself caused death in some mysterious way was first challenged in the years following the Second World War, notably by Robert McIntosh,[29] who pointed to common failures in the standard of care that provided perfectly plausible explanations for many of these deaths. This type of honesty in analysis contributed enormously to improving the safety of anaesthesia over subsequent years, but also opened opportunities for legal or regulatory responses: it is more difficult to blame clinicians for poorly understood influences of a powerful and essential treatment than for openly admitted mistakes. Furthermore, as this objective analysis has led to progressively improved standards of anaesthesia, the complexity and risk associated with many of the treatments now being undertaken in greater numbers of progressively sicker patients has created new opportunities for iatrogenic harm to occur. Again, one may find an example in anaesthesia – the filter that became blocked in the Hugel case (see Chapter 1) would not have been part of routine anaesthesia ten years earlier. Filters of this type were introduced to reduce a small risk of infecting patients with microorganisms from circuits potentially contaminated by previous patients. In solving one

---

[28] A. P. Adams, 'Standards and postgraduate training', in J.S. Walker (ed.), *Quality and Safety in Anaesthesia* (London, British Medical Journal Publishing, 1994) 27–47; R. F. Armstrong, 'Monitoring in anaesthesia', in Walker (ed.), Quality and Safety in Anaesthesia, 173–89; N. Gibbs (ed.), *Safety of Anaesthesia in Australia. A review of anaesthesia related mortality 2006 to 2008* (Melbourne, Australian and New Zealand College of Anaesthetists, 2012). In some parts of the world the risk of dying from an anaesthetic may be 1,000 times higher than in countries like Australia and the UK – see I. A. Walker and I. H. Wilson, 'Anaesthesia in developing countries – a risk for patients' (2008) 371 *Lancet* 968–9.

[29] R. R. Macintosh, 'Deaths under anaesthetics' (1949) 21 *British Journal of Anaesthesia* 107–36. See also: A. S. Keats, 'What do we know about anesthetic mortality?' (1979) 50 *Anesthesiology* 387–92; W. K. Hamilton, 'Unexpected deaths during anesthesia: wherein lies the cause?' (1979) 50 *Anesthesiology* 381–3.

problem (with a sophisticated filter), technology has created a different (rare, but potentially lethal) alternative problem. In part, this is because the overall increase in the complexity of anaesthetic equipment makes the identification of unusual problems such as this more difficult, particularly in the constrained time limits of a crisis. Unpredicted hazards of improved technology have been referred to as 'revenge effects'.[30] Ironically, the advances in aeronautical, medical and other activities seem to have created expectations that are fundamentally unattainable. The tendency today when there is an accidental death is to call for accountability and compensation with scant regard for the fact that some accidents are inevitable. People seem less willing than before to accept that the occurrence of an accident does not necessarily mean that someone must be to blame. On the contrary, a widely held view in modern society seems to be that safety will only be achieved if we can identify and punish or eliminate all wrongdoers. This idea lies at the heart of utilitarian justifications for punishment, based on the notion of deterrence. However, this concept requires that the deterrent be effective in producing the desired result.

In fact, there is not much evidence to support the view that either tort law or criminal law as deterrents are effective in producing the desired safer behaviour in medicine. For example, Shuman has reviewed the psychological basis for the belief that tort law will achieve deterrence, considering each school of psychology in turn. He finds little, if any, theoretical basis for believing that the civil law is likely to be effective in this regard.[31] An interesting finding of the Harvard study was that litigation following an adverse event was not closely linked to the presence of negligence. Few of the cases in which negligence was identified by the authors resulted in litigation, and in many of the cases in which litigation occurred the authors could find no evidence of negligence. They concluded that 'medical-malpractice litigation infrequently compensates patients injured by medical negligence and rarely identifies, and holds providers accountable for, substandard care'.[32] As to the role of the criminal law, there is little evidence to suggest that the highly

---

[30] E. W. Tenner, *Why Things Bite Back – Technology and the Revenge of Unintended Consequences* (New York, Vintage Books, 1997).

[31] D. Shuman, 'The psychology of compensation in tort law' (1994) 43 *Kansas Law Review* 39–77.

[32] A. R. Localio, A. G. Lawthers, T. A. Brennan, N. M. Laird, L. E. Hebert, L. M. Peterson, J. P. Newhouse, P. C. Weiler and H. H. Hiatt, 'Relation between malpractice claims and adverse events due to negligence' (1991) 325 *New England Journal of Medicine* 245–51.

publicised prosecutions (reviewed in Chapter 1) of Drs Yogasakaran and Morrison for their drug administration errors have led to widespread improvements in approaches to drug administration. The studies referred to above indicate that drug administration errors have continued to occur frequently. Furthermore, a system developed by one of the authors of this book in an attempt to reduce errors in drug administration has been adopted more for its subsidiary purpose of producing an electronic anaesthesia record than for enhancing safety: compliance with its safety principles was found to be poor in an observational study of its use,[33] notwithstanding the fact that double checking (one of these principles) was expressly recommended by the New Zealand Medical Council following Dr Morrison's case. Similarly, the case involving Drs Murphy and Lee indicates that the lessons of the very similar earlier experience of Drs Prentice and Sullman were not learned, notwithstanding the considerable publicity associated with their prosecution and initial conviction. Indeed, it was reported that the same error (administering vincristine intrathecally instead of intravenously, which is made more likely because it is given with intrathecal methotrexate) has now occurred at least fifteen times in Britain and many more times in other countries as well.[34] In Chapter 3 we shall return to the point that even the prospect of injury or death is not effective in deterring errors.

The fact that deterrence is relatively ineffective in this regard does not imply that nothing can be done about the problem of error. Perrow argues that the most effective approach to minimising the occurrence and consequences of human error lies in considering all the components of the system in question. He lists these under the acronym DEPOSE, as design, equipment, procedures, operator, supplies and environment.[35] Not only is it too limited to focus on the operator, but in reality the

---

[33] Merry et al., 'Multimodal system designed to reduce errors in recording and administration of drugs in anaesthesia: prospective randomised clinical evaluation'.This randomised controlled study provided evidence that use of a system designed to reduce errors in the administration and recording of drugs during anaesthesia was effective despite variable and generally poor compliance with its safety principles; also, better compliance was associated with a lower rate of errors.

[34] D. M. Berwick, 'Not again! Preventing Errors lies in Redesign not in Exhortation' (2001) *British Medical Journal* 322(7281) 247–8; Joint Commission Sentinel Alert on Vincristine Administration Errors. 2005, available from: www.ons.org/practice-resources/clinical-prac tice/joint-commission-issues-sentinel-alert-vincristine, accessed 11 November 2015; P. Gilbar, 'Inadvertent intrathecal administration of vincristine: has anything changed?' (2012) 18 *Journal of Oncology Pharmacy Practice* 155–7.

[35] Perrow, *Normal Accidents: Living with High Risk Technologies*.

operator is the part of the system most difficult to make error-free, because, of course, operators are human. Unit-dosing systems have been developed to help nursing staff reduce drug errors on wards, and several systems-oriented approaches to improving the way drugs are given in anaesthesia have been developed over the last two decades.[36] The success of these initiatives has varied, but some have been highly effective. For example, addition of devices to prevent the fitting of incorrect cylinders and pipelines to anaesthetic machines[37] and the widespread adoption of pulse oximetry[38] have been much more effective in reducing accidents in relation to the administration of adequate concentrations of oxygen to anaesthetised patients than has the conviction for manslaughter of an anaesthetist who failed to give oxygen to a child in New Zealand during an anaesthetic in 1982.[39]

Criminal and civil liability can result in pressure on organisations (such as hospitals) to change their systems. However, the facts belie the notion that the elimination of a small number of so-called 'incompetents' or 'error-prone individuals' is likely to improve the performance and safety of an organisation as a whole. This applies most particularly if the individuals concerned are not really 'incompetents' at all, but instead are competent and conscientious practitioners who have simply been unfortunate enough to have made errors that contributed to harm, perhaps under circumstances which may have been far from ideal.[40] In the airline industry the point has been made that a pilot whose errors or violations has resulted in a crash is less likely than most to make those particular errors or to commit those violations again – even assuming he or she survives. In a sense, by virtue of the costs associated with a crash, the airline has invested heavily in this pilot's training. Assuming that

[36] R. L. Cooper and A. Merry, 'Medication Management', in J. Stonemetz and K. Ruskin (eds.), *Anesthesia Informatics* (London, Springer, 2008). J. Eichhorn, 'APSF hosts medication safety conference: consensus group defines challenges and opportunities for improved practice' (2010) 25 *APSF Newsletter* 1–7.

[37] W. B. Runciman and A. F. Merry, 'A brief history of the patient safety movement in anaesthesia', in E. Eger II, L. Saidman, and R. Westhorpe (eds.), *The Wondrous Story of Anesthesia* (New York, Springer 2014) 541–56.

[38] I. A. Walker, A. F. Merry, I. H. Wilson, G. A. McHugh, E. O'Sullivan, G. M. Thoms, F. Nuevo and D. K. Whitaker, 'Global oximetry: An international anaesthesia quality improvement project' (2009) 64 *Anaesthesia* 1051–60.

[39] Skegg, 'Criminal prosecutions of negligent health professionals'.

[40] D. M. Berwick, 'Continuous improvement as an ideal in health care' (1989) 320 *New England Journal of Medicine* 53–6; G. Laffel and D. Blumenthal, 'The case for using industrial quality management science in health care organizations' (1989) 262 *Journal of the American Medical Association* 2869–73.

the accident was isolated, and in the absence of evidence to show that the individual's performance has been systematically below standard over a period of time, the dismissal of this person from the airline would seem to be misguided.

The unfounded belief that complex human activities can be conducted on an ongoing basis without ever having a significant failure has other important implications. It is very important to realise that human error is, in the end, inevitable. With this in mind, Perrow argues that it is necessary to consider the possible consequences of the accidents that will eventually happen in every branch of human endeavour and weigh these against the social utility of the activity in question. In the case of the nuclear industry, he concludes that the potential consequences of an accident are so serious that its continuation cannot be justified. On the other hand, he suggests that the occasional loss of life, or even the quite serious disasters that occur from time to time in aviation, medicine, shipping and mining, for example, are justified in relation to their magnitude and to the overall benefits to society of these activities.[41] This does not mean that nothing should be done about accidents in these fields of endeavour. Although it has to be accepted that accidents will never be eliminated completely, the focus should always be on improving the system to ensure the greatest possible level of safety. This requires an understanding of how humans co-exist with the machines that provide the advantages which a technological age takes for granted.

Human Beings and Machines

So much do we interrelate with and depend upon our technology that society needs to be seen not just as a grouping of people but as a highly complex human–machine conglomeration in a world subject to many unpredictable and variable influences, including the effects of chance. The closeness of this relationship between us and our machines (in the widest sense of the word 'machine') is such that it seems to have influenced our expectations both of ourselves and of our machines. To a degree we are starting to expect machines to behave like human beings. We expect increased sophistication, flexibility and the ability to be interactive. The idea that machines may one day be able to think has gained weight with the development of chess-playing devices that

[41] Perrow, *Normal Accidents: Living with High Risk Technologies*.

outperform the masters (something which was a long time coming), computers which use 'neural nets' and are capable of 'learning from experience' and real progress towards the development of artificial intelligence. In reality, these are very much the exceptions, and any similarities with human beings are still but pale imitations of the real thing and fall within highly circumscribed limits. In fact, the difference between machines and humans underpins a test for artificial intelligence described by Alan Turing. In this test, an intelligent questioner interrogates an unseen human and an unseen machine with a view to telling which is which; if the answers do not permit the one to be distinguished from the other, the machine is deemed intelligent. Although there has been debate about the validity of this test, it provides an intuitive insight into the different nature of the two; to date, it would not be too difficult to distinguish even the most powerful of computers from a person.[42] If neural-net technology were to produce a machine so human-like that it was able to respond with both the strengths and weaknesses of a human, then for the purposes of our discussion it would have become a human, and, like us, it would be subject to human error. In the end, an entity not subject to error could not truly resemble a human.

Their lack of humanness is not a reason to denigrate machines. After all, they are not human. Machines can do many things that humans cannot. The strength and the precision of which they are capable far exceed that of human beings – they can cater for the fine and delicate or the large and brutish with equal facility. They can make possible activities that would otherwise be beyond our capability – prodigious feats of calculation, flight, communication and all the other things that would have been deemed evidence of magic as recently as a hundred years ago.

Machines are typically very single-minded. Tasks which are boring or repetitive are ideally suited to machines, which, having once been set up properly, will go on doing the same thing over and over again for as long as power and lubrication are provided, with a reliability that we take for granted. Within quite wide limits, it matters not that the clock has passed five, that the tea break has been missed, that the day is hotter than usual, that a distracting story is being recounted by another occupant of the room – the machine will stick to the task in hand, uncomplaining and focused, getting it right.

[42] Interestingly, impressive progress continues to be made in the development of artificial intelligence. For example, see D. Geere. Uh-oh, a robot just passed the self-awareness test, 16 July 2015; available from: www.techradar.com/news/world-of-tech/uh-oh-this-robot-just-passed-the-self-awareness-test-1299362, accessed 15 January 2016.

Regrettably, we have come to expect the same thing of humans, and to see it as a weakness when people prove to be distractible and fail to meet the exacting standards set by their machines in the particular attributes of behaviour that suit machines but not human beings. In fact, some people have learned to do machine-like activities astonishingly well. Traditional production line activities are highly repetitive and tedious. So is sewing, whether by a seamstress or a surgeon closing the skin after an operation. Monitoring a patient during a long anaesthetic in which each successive reading is much the same as the one before is also a task more suitable for a machine – and the same applies to monitoring the instruments in a nuclear plant or on an aeroplane. Human beings are able to do these things very adequately most of the time, but these are not tasks that play to their strengths.

In the same way that we should not denigrate machines for failing to be people, people have no need to apologise for their failure to achieve machine-like standards in those activities for which machines are best suited. They are good at other things – original thought, for one; empathy and compassion, for another. It should not be forgotten that one of our strengths is our ability to create the very machines with which we are, increasingly, at risk of being unfavourably compared. It is true that people are distractible – but in fact this provides a major survival advantage for them. A machine (unless expressly designed to detect such an event) will continue with its repetitive task while the house burns down around it, whereas most humans will notice that something unexpected is going on and will change their activity to make an appropriate response. When they are used to monitor routine signals in medicine or industry, machines far exceed humans in their reliability in detecting anticipated possibilities – a fall in blood pressure, for example. Humans come into their own in having the flexibility to detect things that were never anticipated, and in their ability to respond in a variety of resourceful and imaginative ways when things do go wrong. Humans can also often tell, in the absence of anything specific enough to trigger an alarm, that things simply don't 'feel' right, that something is going wrong and that further enquiry is needed to diagnose an incipient problem. This form of 'intuition' involves the ability of humans to store vast numbers of mental pictures or patterns derived from previous experience, and to retrieve them when they are needed, not by the relatively rigid and sequential algorithms of traditional machines but by multiple processes operating in parallel, creatively, instinctively, as needed and, concomitantly, a little unreliably. Human performance can be spectacularly inspiring or terribly disappointing. In the former case the humanness of the achievement is often accepted with complacency – people have done so many astonishing things that one more goes almost without note. In the latter case, however, there is a tendency towards harsh criticism; in many cases people who have made an error are judged as if they were machines.

In his book *Things That Make Us Smart*,[43] Norman has developed these ideas much more fully, concluding that many of today's problems actually arise from a failure to allocate machine-oriented tasks to machines and human-oriented tasks to people. There is often a failure to appreciate that humans have difficulty in adapting to poorly designed machines, whereas it is often possible for machines to be designed to take account of human characteristics and requirements. He uses the term 'soft technology' to describe machines which are designed to facilitate human endeavour by working for and with people, relieving them of the tasks for which they are poorly suited, adding strength to their abilities and protecting them from their human tendency to make certain types of error. He argues, however, that the reverse often happens, and he uses the term 'hard technology' to describe situations in which machines are allocated tasks because they *can* do them rather than because they *should* do them. A prime example of this is the use of recorded messages on answer-phones and automatic switchboards. There may be some financial savings in the use of these devices, but their effect is to increase the difficulties and frustrations of those on the other end of the line who are trying to reach a human being. Taken to absurdity (but not beyond the bounds of possibility), the application of this technology to emergency support services or help lines for people contemplating suicide provides an excellent example of something which a machine *can* do, but which is better left to people. Where the machine might be more usefully employed is in tracking and recording the source of the call – an application we shall return to the section on skill-based errors in Chapter 3.

An understanding of the distinction between machines and human beings, and of the fact that society is in reality an integrated network of many people with many machines, permits us to design systems which are more effective, more satisfying to work in, and much safer. It is also very important in helping to place human behaviour in its appropriate

[43] D. Norman, *Things That Make Us Smart – Defending Human Attributes in the Age of the Machine* (Reading, Perseus, 1993). See also: D. A. Norman, *The Psychology of Everyday Things* (New York, Basic Books, 1998).

context when the allocation of blame for things which go wrong is being evaluated. It is irrational to judge human actions in isolation or by the standards that we would apply to the functioning of a machine. An individual's actions should be judged in relation to the other people and technologies involved. Such judgements should also take account of the ways in which the human mind actually works.

Human Cognition and Performance

Reason,[44] reviewing the development over the last century of the science of human cognition, makes the point that, until the early 1970s, research into human judgement and inference had a markedly rationalist basis. According to the 'Subjective Expected Utility Theory', it was assumed that human beings make decisions in accordance with logical principles, and form judgements by processes analogous to the use of Bayesian statistics. In the same way, much of American economic theory assumed that people actually know what they want and that they typically choose the optimal route to getting what they want. This was a very machine-like model of the human brain. It is interesting to speculate on the degree to which this general view of the mind pervaded the development of legal concepts of responsibility and accountability during the first three-quarters of the twentieth century.

Freud challenged the assumption that humans are rational beings, and psychological research has gone on to make it abundantly clear that human cognitive processes are often far from rational. It is now appreciated that human rationality is usually *bounded*; in other words, human decision-making may be severely hindered by restricted or 'keyhole' views of the information in relation to any particular problem. Our rationality is also frequently *imperfect* (that is, not Bayesian at all) and *reluctant* (that is, people prefer to apply a rule, even an imperfect rule, than to think out a problem from first principles). The true motivation behind our actions may at times be subconscious. Prejudice is often influential, and often subconscious. It may relate to gender, race, age, height, accents, dress and many other factors. Subtle clues may bias our decisions – for example, the positioning of products on supermarket shelves, the order in which information is presented, the way in which facts are framed, the things others own or the decisions they make (particularly decisions made by people perceived as authoritative) or

---

[44] Reason, Human Error.

fear of embarrassment (which may exceed fear of death).[45] There are occasions when human behaviour can only be described as irrational, particularly under the influence of group dynamics. It is hard to ascribe some of the activities associated with war to any plausible rationality, for example. From these insights a much more human-like model of the way in which human decisions are made and implemented has emerged, and, with it, a much more sophisticated appreciation of the nature of human error has been developed.

In any analysis of the ways in which human cognitive processes can go astray, the question of context is very important. Exactly the same external events may represent the endpoints of completely different cognitive processes, and actions cannot be evaluated adequately in isolation. As human beings have extended the boundaries of possibility by means of increasingly sophisticated and complex systems involving both humans and machines, hitherto unattainable standards of quality and safety have been achieved in many industries, including healthcare. Unfortunately, as we have already noted, one result of this has been to create expectations amongst the population of near-infallibility. Infrequently, but inevitably, these systems fail. They do so because their design and operation depend on human beings. When such failures are being judged, whether to reduce the likelihood of their recurrence or in the interests of justice, it is very important that we see beyond machine-like models of human cognition and retain a human-oriented perspective based on a proper understanding of the basic premises of modern cognitive psychology.

How We Think

It is obvious that our general understanding of the fundamental anatomy, physiology and chemistry involved in the functioning of the brain has expanded rapidly over the last century, but perhaps less obvious that much of our modern knowledge of the processes of human cognition derives from several strikingly different fields of scientific and medical research. For example, much has been learned about memory from

---

[45] R. Thaler and C. Sunstein, *Nudge: Improving Decisions About Health, Wealth and Happiness* (New Haven, Yale University Press, 2008); D. Kahneman, *Thinking, Fast and Slow* (London, Penguin Books, 2011); A. de Botton, *Status Anxiety* (London, Penguin Books, 2005). See also P. Lyons, 'Judicial Decisions: Sanism v Self-Reflexivity: A Case for Circuits of Psychic Reflexivity without end' in W. Brookbanks (ed.), *Therapeutic Jurisprudence: New Zealand Perspectives* (Wellington, Thomson Reuters, 2015).

patients who have undergone surgical procedures or suffered injuries to various areas of their brain, such as Henry Molaison, who underwent bilateral medial temporal lobe resections for intractable epilepsy in 1953. From this work it first became clear that different aspects of memory depend substantially on different structures. Some functions important in the formation and recall of information depend substantially on the medial temporal lobes, notably the hippocampus, while others are more widely distributed, notably through the neocortex.[46] More recently, functional magnetic resonance imaging, positron emission tomography and other sophisticated techniques have made it possible to observe changes in different areas of the brain associated with different kinds of mental activity. For example, observations before and after practice show differences in the neural circuitry supporting performance of tasks in the naïve and practised states.[47] Experimental work in various animals has added to concepts of the anatomy and physiology of memory and thinking, and continues to do so.[48] In parallel, empirical evidence from experimental work with normal human subjects in laboratories and from observational work in the field[49] has informed a substantial body of theoretical knowledge about the way in which we think.

It is sometimes difficult to find the precise links between the language and findings that have emerged from these substantially different approaches to cognitive science, and our understanding of this whole field of science is continually being refined and expanded. The detail of the functioning of the human mind is enormously complicated, and indeed much information is continuing to emerge from these various fields of research. However, there are some fairly clear and well-established themes that go a long way towards explaining the various ways in which human error occurs. In the pages that follow we have tried to synthesise a selection of the relevant concepts.

If a single theme has emerged in this regard, it is that more than one cognitive system or process is involved in the related activities of assimilating, storing and recalling information, carrying out highly skilled

---

[46] D. A. Wolk and A. E. Budson, 'Memory systems' (2010) 16 *CONTINUUM: Lifelong Learning in Neurology* 15–28.

[47] M. E. Raichle, 'The neural correlates of consciousness: an analysis of cognitive skill learning' (1998) 353 *Philosophical Transactions of the Royal Society of London, Series B* 1889–901.

[48] N. M. White, M. G. Packard and R. J. McDonald, 'Dissociation of memory systems: The story unfolds' (2013) 127 *Behavioral Neuroscience* 813–34.

[49] Reason, *Human Error*; G. Klein, *Sources of Power: How People Make Decisions* (Cambridge, MA, The MIT Press, 1999).

physical tasks and making decisions. More than one cognitive process typically operates at any given time. These processes usually interact effectively and thus increase the success of human endeavour. Occasionally they compete, so that one process may undermine another, and thereby give rise to failures in human performance. Alternatively, some failures may arise out of just one process. Either way, similar failures in cognitive process may produce outcomes that vary from trivial to catastrophic.

Although some oversimplification will inevitably follow, it is helpful (and, we believe, substantially accurate) to think of human decisions and actions as subserved by two basic types of cognition, which occupy two parts of a continuum of thought process within which characteristic subtypes can be discerned.

At one end of this continuum is the automatic, effortless, rapidly responsive processing by which an action is performed or a decision made virtually instantaneously. At the other end is the slow, active, effortful thinking by which we solve problems which are new to us, or to which we do not already know the answer. Various terms have been used to describe these processes. Norman refers to *reflective* and *experiential* thinking.[50] Reason, following Rasmussen, refers to the first, effortful type of reasoning as *knowledge-based*, and divides the effortless processing into *rule-based*, in the case of decision-making, and *skill-based*, in the case of actions.[51] Kahneman refers to *slow* and *fast* thinking,[52] but also advocates the use of the terms introduced by Stanovich and West: System I and System II.[53] System I thinking is fast, effortless, associative, unconscious, rule-based and feed forward in nature. System II thinking is slow, effortful, deductive, conscious or self-aware, logical and feed back in nature.

There is general agreement that the more automatic processes of System I thinking tend to be used by default. Klein and others have taken research in decision-making out of the laboratory and into the field, and studied high-stakes situations in which time is critical. From this, the concept of recognition-primed naturalistic decision-making has emerged – essentially System I thinking.[54] These ideas have been

---

[50] Norman, Things That *Make Us Smart.*   [51] Reason, *Human Error* (1990).

[52] Kahneman, Thinking, Fast and Slow.

[53] K. E. Stanovich and R. F. West, 'Individual differences in reasoning: implications for the rationality debate?' (2000) 23 *Behavioral & Brain Sciences* 645–65; commentary 665–726; Kahneman, Thinking, Fast and Slow.

[54] Klein, *Sources of Power.*

expressed by Rouse's statement that 'humans, if given the choice, would prefer to act as context-specific pattern recognisers rather than attempting to calculate or optimize'.[55] In fact, as Kahneman explains, these concepts are representational rather than real, in the sense that there aren't actually two physically discrete systems within the brain. Furthermore, few decisions are made or actions taken in isolation. More typically, complex activities involve multiple actions taken in a sort of rapid-fire sequence with decisions being made in response to a changing and developing situation. There is a spectrum rather than a dichotomy, and cognitive processes shift rapidly back and forward along this spectrum. Some degree of System II oversight of System I processes is usually involved, as a form of supervisory metacognition. Even deep thought (involving System II thinking) is often accompanied by some simultaneous activity under largely subconscious (System I) control, such as walking or making notes.

The Mind's Eye – Mental Models of the Real World

When we make decisions, our functional relationship with the 'real world' is indirect. We depend on a conceptual 'map' of our surroundings – often called the *mental model* of the situation.[56] The correspondence between our internal and external (or 'real') environments is usually close enough for all functional purposes, but the internal map is always different from the real world in at least some aspects. If one closes one's eyes and tries to enumerate as much detail as possible about one's immediate surroundings, it is very unlikely that even all the main features will be accurately recalled. This is particularly so in situations that are transient and novel – at a restaurant or in an airport lounge, for example. In a reasonably crowded room it is very unlikely that one would be able to say, after closing one's eyes, how many people were present; one person's best guess is likely to differ from another's, even though they may be sitting next to each other and conducting the experiment at the same time. Similarly, details such as the clothes other people are wearing, the colour of their hair, the pictures on the wall and so on are likely to be recalled inaccurately and to different degrees by different individuals. This phenomenon is well known and very important in relation to the

---

[55] W. B. Rouse, quoted in Reason, *Human Error*, p. 44.
[56] R. Lipshitz and O. Ben Shaul, 'Schemata and mental models in recognition-primed decision making', in *Naturalistic decision making* (Mahwah, Lawrence Earlbaum Associates, 1997) 293–303.

testimony of witnesses at the scene of an accident or crime – at times the accounts of what happened are so different that it seems the individual witnesses must be describing different scenes. The success with which we can perform this type of recall, whether in an experiment or in the context of providing an account of some important event, will vary from person to person, and for the same person at different times depending on the degree to which his or her attention has been focused on other things. Nevertheless, we seldom, if ever, know more than the broad outline of our surroundings at any given time, and this is actually a good thing. It is only by filtering, ordering and interpreting the barrage of incoming information that we are able to function efficiently. Failures in these processes may contribute to certain forms of mental disorder.[57] The mind operates from a set of facts that may have been assimilated in the order of their salience but are only understandable after they have become organised in a way that takes account of their pertinence, their significance and their interrelationships.

One reason why we do not have to have every detail of our surroundings clear in order to function adequately is that much of the information is accessible – 'in the world', as Norman says – if we need it. This idea – that we operate on the basis of *information in the world* and *information in the mind* – is very important when it comes to design. If a thing is well designed we should not need much instruction in its purposes and uses, because they will be obvious from its *affordances* – the applications to which it lends itself, in other words. For example, a chair (even a chair that we have never seen before) is easily identified as a chair, and it is possible for us to sit on it quite easily, but rather difficult to use it to cut up a piece of steak. Many other things are also easy enough to sit on, but for some of these this affordance is misleading, and the object may turn out to be poorly constructed to support the weight of a person. In the same way, a steak knife in a restaurant may look a little different from one's familiar cutlery at home, but few people would struggle to identify its intended purpose (and fewer still would try to sit on it) even in the absence of any instruction in its use. Many things have more than one affordance – knives and forks lend themselves to being poked into things, for example. This can be very useful but also very dangerous in unedu-cated hands, such as those of a child, particularly in the presence of

[57] D. J. Siegel, 'Perception and cognition', in H. I. Kaplan and B. J. Sadock (eds.), *Comprehensive Textbook of Psychiatry*, 6th edn (Baltimore, Williams and Wilkins, 1995) No. 1 277–90.

another device whose own affordances create the possibility of an inadvisable application of the former implement. Electric toasters, for example, lend themselves to being poked, particularly if the toast becomes stuck. The consequences of this particular juxtaposition of the unintended affordances of two commonplace things whose primary uses are entirely benign is potentially lethal. In *The Psychology of Everyday Things*,[58] Norman discusses in detail how the good and bad design of things used in daily life can influence the ease and safety of human experience. Our primary interest at present, however, is in the fact that we routinely function on the basis of schematic mental representations of the world, and that this is made possible because we are able to check, modify and refine our internal representation of our surroundings by reference to the information that resides in the world about us. In addition, we may refer to knowledge stored in our brains. These two sources of information together form our *knowledge base*. Thus, for example, if we really needed to know how many people were in the room, we could count them, provided the numbers were not too large. If it was a very large number, and the reason for knowing was important, then, as humans, we would find a way of estimating the number to a reasonable degree of accuracy. We might do this by reference to a previously learned rule stored in our brain, or we might derive a novel approach working from first principles. One of our strengths is that we can find new and imaginative ways to solve problems.

Unfortunately, this mechanism of regularly reviewing our internal map by reference to our surroundings and our interpretation of this information in relation to the knowledge stored in our memories is subject to failure. Numerous examples have now been published of cases where a mismatch develops between the external or 'real world' situation and its internal or mental representation. The starting point of such a dichotomy is often one erroneous piece of information which is either presented incorrectly (a wrong name on a map, for example) or which is incorrectly perceived (a correct name, misread).

Perrow reports in detail a truly illuminating example of this, in which the initiating event involved a mistake by the captain of the coastguard training vessel *Cuyahuga* in 1978, in Chesapeake Bay. He saw only two of the lights being carried one night by another ship, when in fact there were three. This led him to believe that the ship was sailing away from him,

---

[58] Norman, *The Psychology of Everyday Things*.

when in fact it was approaching. Once a firm, but incorrect, interpretation has been made in any set of circumstances, the stage is set for the gap between perception and reality to widen. This undesirable dichotomy is contributed to by a phenomenon called *confirmation bias*. The effect of this is that, having once formulated an idea of events or of their surroundings, people have a strong tendency to interpret other information in such a way as to confirm or strengthen their initial interpretation of circumstances. In Perrow's example, two more bits of information were available to the captain: the image on the radar which appeared to be that of a small object, and the fact (presumably also derived from the radar) that the two ships were closing rapidly. Instead of interpreting this last point correctly as a *countersign*, the captain took from it the inference that the other ship was very small and very slow, and that his own ship was therefore overhauling it rapidly, thus adding to the conviction with which he held his incorrect internal view of the world. His first officer – who understood the real situation – could see that the captain was attending to the available information but, in the absence of explicit communication, he had no way of knowing that the captain's picture of the world differed from his own, and therefore saw no need to comment. As a result of this, the captain, just at the moment when (by virtue of his internal scheme of things) he believed that his vessel was about to overtake the 'smaller' boat, 'realised' that in doing so he would cut it off from the entrance to the Potomac river. He therefore ordered a sudden change in direction to allow the 'fishing boat' better access to an entrance to the harbour. This was an entirely well-intentioned manoeuvre, based on a now fairly detailed but seriously flawed idea of what was happening. The result was a last-minute swerve by the captain's ship under the bows of a large vessel sailing in the opposite direction and a disaster ensued in which eleven people died. On superficial inspection, the captain's actions were bizarre and inexplicable. They were certainly unexpected. Interestingly, Perrow makes the point that this example is not exceptional but in fact typifies the way in which ships tend to collide (which, apparently, they do disconcertingly often).[59]

Perrow's example is particularly graphic, but the underlying principles illustrated by it are very common in medicine. In the case of Dr Hugel, for example, which we outlined in Chapter 1, it is clear that a contributory equipment-related problem from a blocked filter did develop at some time during the crisis. Dr Hugel, however, had been presented with

---

[59] Perrow, *Normal accidents*, 215–24.

a clear, patient-related problem at the outset of the incident: difficulty in breathing. This was followed by pulmonary oedema, which continued to froth from the lungs very dramatically, continuing to suggest that something was seriously wrong with the patient. The fact that the patient's lungs became progressively more difficult to ventilate was therefore attributed by Dr Hugel to an ongoing problem within the patient himself, and taken as confirmation of the presence of serious spasm within the lungs. At some stage in the proceedings this perception changed from being an accurate description of what was happening to being an outmoded and seriously wrong one. Whether or not the filter took over as an important cause of the obstruction to ventilation at a point early enough to have made it a leading cause of the patient's ultimate death is pure conjecture, but by the time useful help (in the form of a second anaesthetist) arrived, the filter was completely blocked. Dr Hugel (now beside herself with desperation) was still convinced that she was dealing with a patient-related problem, and was continuing to interpret all the signs of obstruction to ventilation as pointing to a problem within the patient's lungs. The fact that a second anaesthetist was able to identify the blocked filter almost as soon as he arrived made Dr Hugel's failure seem very incompetent. In reality, several factors contributed to the speed with which the problem was discovered when help arrived. Simply having two people instead of one was very valuable – Dr Hugel actually handed the rebreathing bag to the new anaesthetist for him to hold while she disconnected the anaesthetic circuit to suction out the endotracheal tube; holding the bag with the circuit disconnected made it obvious that there was a problem with the equipment – the answer was literally handed to the newcomer. However, it is very likely that his perspicacity was also attributable to the fact that he was bringing a fresh mind to the situation, without the confounding influence of having partaken in an unfolding sequence of events in which the signs were highly misleading. For Dr Hugel, all the information could be explained in a way that supported her original interpretation of the situation. For example, the event had occurred at the end of an anaesthetic during which the filter had given no trouble. Also, she had checked the anaesthetic circuit (including the filter) at the outset and had found it to be in working order. More than one person had noted that air entry into the chest was diminished but present – and this too could be fitted into her concept of a patient-related problem. Each fact would have been added to the previous ones to build a convincing but incorrectly evolving mental picture of events.

This kind of incorrect mental model of the environment can underlie or initiate any of the error types we shall discuss in Chapter 3.

A more mundane example of how information can be misinterpreted or variously interpreted is found in many books of psychology. A very well-known picture can be seen as either a beautiful young girl or an ugly old woman. Even those who have seen it before often find it quite difficult to switch between the two, and tend to favour one or other interpretation quite strongly. There are many other puzzle-pictures of this kind.[60] The printing of the same word twice (as in this sentence) often goes unnoticed, particularly if the repetition is split by the end of a line. Anyone who has undertaken the proofreading of a manuscript will know how difficult it can be to detect certain errors, and it is often harder to see one's own mistakes than those of someone else. The reason for this is quite simple – one tends to see what one expects to see, rather than what is before one's eyes. Thus, if a writer used a word similar but not identical to another (intended) word, it is quite likely that he or she would subsequently also read it as the intended word. A second person, having no preconceptions, would be more likely to detect the error.

These trivial examples become very important when applied to reading drug labels or prescriptions. Dr Yogasakaran may or may not have looked at the label on the ampoule of dopamine. It was said in court that he did not, but it is far more likely that he did at least glance at it (his memory for an event of that sort would be unreliable, and very probably overwhelmed by the subsequent tragic events). If he did glance at it, it is not at all surprising that he would have read the word 'dopamine' as 'dopram' – the drug he expected to be in the ampoule. This type of misreading has been reported on a number of occasions[61] and probably represents a major factor in the causation of drug administration errors. The particular example of giving the wrong drug, if undetected, may be compounded by subsequent errors of interpretation based on the unexpected response or lack of response that ensues from the given rather than the intended drug. For example, some years ago a junior anaesthetist failed to realise that the device for administering the anaesthetic vapour was not properly attached to

[60] E. G. Boring, 'A new ambiguous figure' (1930) 42 *American Journal of Psychology* 444–5.
[61] M. R. Cohen, 'Drug product characteristics that foster drug-use system errors' (1995) 52 *American Journal of Health-System Pharmacy* 395–9; B. A. Orser and D. C. Oxorn, 'An anaesthetic drug error: minimizing the risk' (1994) 41 *Canadian Journal of Anaesthesia* 120–4.

the anaesthetic machine, with the result that a patient who had received a muscle relaxant, and who was therefore unable to move, was awake during a surgical operation. The anaesthetist attributed the failure of increasing doses of the agent to control a rapidly rising blood pressure to the elderly patient's age and pre-existing hypertension – another example of confirmation bias reinforcing an incorrect mental image of events. Only on the arrival of a supervisor (one of the authors) was her *mindset* broken and the real problem identified, regrettably too late. The correct diagnosis was more obvious to the newcomer not only because of his greater experience but (as in the case of Dr Hugel) also because of his fresh perspective on events. He was not nearly so strongly influenced as the first anaesthetist by the way in which events had unfolded. A variation of this problem is that doctors faced with a particular set of signs and symptoms have a strong tendency to make a diagnosis that falls within their own field. Thus, consulting a series of specialists from different fields about the same symptom may at times result in being given a different diagnosis by each of them. In each case the diagnosis would be of a disease process commonly seen in the particular doctor's own speciality. This illustrates once more the way in which people tend to see what they expect to see: they interpret information to fit the 'diagnosis' with which they are familiar. Any new information is also interpreted in this way, if at all possible, so that the practitioner's conviction becomes progressively stronger under circumstances in which, to a fresh and more objective observer, the correct diagnosis might appear increasingly obvious. Behaviour that is completely bizarre and inexplicable from the perspective of the real world – particularly when interpreted with hindsight – may become understandable if seen in the context of the individual's internal representation of events. The potential gap between the world and one's mental model of it is a very dangerous force in the generation of errors.

Cognition: Chunking, Processing and Responding to Information

We have seen that the human brain is capable of dealing with a large amount of information at one time. This ability can be enhanced by training and experience. As we have already observed, driving a motor car in traffic provides a good example of an ordinary activity that is, on reflection, an impressive accomplishment. This is true in the broader sense of the way in which society works as a whole, but also in the individual sense of the highly efficient way in which our minds are capable of functioning, particularly with the benefit of practice. A novice placed at the wheel of a car and launched into the rush-hour traffic of a large city would be overwhelmed by the range and subtlety of physical actions required to guide the vehicle successfully to its destination. He or she would struggle with the gear changes, the need to use the clutch properly, the nuances of acceleration and braking, and even with the relatively straightforward matter of steering the car. These activities are essentially a matter of skill, and this requires time and practice to build up. For an expert, on the other hand, many of these processes have become highly integrated and are mostly automatic. Accelerating, changing gear and steering are done by experienced motorists largely subconsciously, not as individually planned actions but as unified sequences, conceptualised at a subconscious level as quite large *cognitive chunks*.[62] In effect, as tasks become more routine they are incorporated into reflex-like action sequences which can be executed as integrated conceptual units, rather like subroutines in a computer program. This is Rasmussen's *skill-based* level of human performance, at the extreme end of System I thinking. Although it is necessary for an experienced person to disassemble these cognitive units or chunks into their individual components only when something slightly unusual causes an interruption in the automatic sequence, it may then sometimes be quite difficult to resume from exactly the place in the sequence where one left off, such is the fixedness of the chain of actions in which the individual task is embedded.

For the novice driver, lack of skill would be only part of the problem. It is obvious that the need to interact with other traffic, respond to road signals, deal with lane changes, avoid running over pedestrians and at the same time stay within the limits of the law would present an overwhelming task to the beginner. He or she would need to process far too much information at one time. Decisions which, for the novice, would necessitate detailed and careful thought would have to be made rapidly. Even the preliminary matter of assembling the important facts in the forefront of the mind, while at the same time setting aside the other myriad of

[62] G. A. Miller, 'The magical number seven, plus or minus two: some limits on our capacity for processing information' (1956) 63 *Psychological Review* 81–97; A. M. Graybiel, 'The basal ganglia and chunking of action repertoires' (1998) 70 *Neurobiology of Learning and Memory* 119–36; M. Davis. Psycholinguistic evidence on scrambled letters in reading. Undated; Available from: www.mrc-cbu.cam.ac.uk/people/matt.davis/cmabridge/, accessed 16 January 2016.

(possibly conspicuous) unimportant bits of incoming information, would be very difficult, particularly if this had to be done at the same time as actually driving the car. The novice has no choice but to think through the implications of each successive situation and work out effortfully and logically (using System II thinking) what to do in every circumstance. As indicated above, in the Reason/Rasmussen classification, this is called *knowledge-based* decision-making.[63]

The expert driver in the same situation would function quite differently from the novice. The mass of irrelevant detail would automatically be filtered out by the mind. The name of the streets he is driving along, the name of the last intersecting street, the corresponding features on the map and the details of the intended route, the position of other cars, the rules of the road and the presence of various signs and signals are all examples of facts relevant to the driver trying to find her way in traffic. These facts would need to be selected from the barrage of other information competing for attention at the same time – the colour of the buildings, the details of pedestrians' clothes, the type of clouds in the sky, the music on the radio and so on. Again, the expert will have an advantage over the novice. This is because the vitally important process of rejecting information likely to be unhelpful in the resolution of a given problem while at the same time focusing on the key facts that actually matter is more instinctive to an experienced person than to a beginner. The expert is able to synthesise the complex mass of incoming information into a small number of distinct patterns, or *schemata*, recognisable on the basis of previous experience. These schemata might themselves be synthesised into a larger and essentially unified picture, or *mental model*, of the situation. In much the same way as our minute by minute appreciation of our surroundings tends to be an approximate rationalisation of what is really there, these schemata are not thought to be exact representations of previously encountered individual situations but are considered more likely to be conceptualisations of the essential features of idealised versions of various similar situations. Thus, a room may be conceptualised as having four walls, a ceiling, doors, windows and so forth. This view is supported by evidence that memories of briefly seen

---

[63] Although errors that arise in this process often reflect deficiencies in the knowledge base, this name is not particularly descriptive of the distinguishing features of System II thinking, which are that it is effortful, self-aware and feed back (or trial and error) in nature. Furthermore, it can be seen from this discussion that rule-based decisions are also made on the basis of mental models (or schema) formed from the decision-maker's knowledge base at the time.

objects tend to be recalled in an idealised rather than an accurate fashion. Thus, for example, a clock on the wall of a room to which a subject in an experiment has been briefly exposed will often be recalled as having hands even if the hands have in fact been removed from it. At the subconscious level this reworking, or ordering and simplifying of the information stored in our memory is a very powerful mechanism for rapidly making sense of complicated situations. Schemata may be refined, so that increasingly more specific versions of a general situation may be stored in a sort of hierarchy, to cope with the variety of situations that characterise our existence. Even these lower-level patterns or templates will tend to be conceptualisations of the important (possibly the exceptional) features of a given place or event rather than photo-graphically accurate representations of them.

To return to our expert driver: a schema would usually be available which would correspond, at least approximately, to situations seen before. The driver would therefore know what to do on the basis of a previously learned 'rule', or response, which he or she knows has worked well before in similar circumstances. It would not be necessary to analyse the problem in detail. The process would be: if situation x do action y. In the Reason/Rasmussen classification, this is known as *rule-based* performance. This is System I thinking, and requires far less effortful processing of information than System II thinking.[64] The given situation would be identified as approximately equivalent to a particular conceptual representation already stored in the mind. The expert has a large store of such patterns and a similarly large store of rules that are known from experience to produce a satisfactory result if applied in the presence of the corresponding schema. All that is required is to recognise the pattern and respond by applying the most appropriate rule – a rule known to have worked previously on similar occasions. Only when an unfamiliar situation arises must the expert resort to more effortful delib-eration using System II. Expert chess players are able to reconstruct complex positions from real games with ease, but interestingly they are no better than novices at recalling the positions of pieces placed at random about the board.[65] Again, this reflects the way in which mean-ingful information can be brought together and retained within one's store of knowledge as unified blocks, while meaningless patterns are less

[64] Kahneman, *Thinking, Fast and Slow*.
[65] F. Gobet and H. A. Simon, 'Expert chess memory: revisiting the Chunking Hypothesis' (1998) 6 *Memory* 225–55.

readily remembered. The expert has moved from predominantly System II thinking (working out each move from first principles) to a much greater ability to resolve problems with System I (recognition of patterns, and matching these to stored schemata that encapsulate the key elements of appropriate responses).[66] Similarly, in finding his or her way, a driver will follow a familiar route with ease, and with little need for conscious thought, but, once hitherto unexplored territory is entered, it becomes necessary to rely once more on the slow and deliberate process of identifying relevant facts and then working out from first principles how they should be interpreted.

In practice, people switch from fast to slow thinking and back again as the evolving circumstances demand, and some degree of conscious oversight (through slow, System II, thinking) is usually maintained over the fast and unconscious processes (System I) by which most decisions are made in the context of daily activities. Even decisions made through System II thinking may be implemented by sequences of actions that are largely automatic – the application of a rule or the use of a skill-based response to a familiar situation. Often it is necessary to continue to deal with one task unconsciously with fast, automatic skill-based and rule-based responses to keep the activity on track, while at the same time processing information more slowly and consciously to specify the next major task. In this way it is possible to do several different things simultaneously – so-called *multi-tasking*. It is much more difficult to carry out two tasks simultaneously if both involve System II.

As already indicated, earlier theories of human behaviour presumed that human cognition was essentially rational, and underpinned by Bayesian logic. In fact, as we have observed, humans seem to have a very strong preference for responding to situations by using a pre-formulated rule than by thinking things out from first principles – a phenomenon known as *reluctant rationality*. It may be thought that the application of pre-formed rules to situations identified as corresponding to appropriate schemata is rational enough, but in fact the process of retrieving a schema or selecting a rule to apply in a given situation is not necessarily either logical or rational. For one thing, as already discussed, there are many factors that operate subconsciously to influence the way

---

[66] This is somewhat counter-intuitive, given that chess has the reputation of being fundamentally a game that requires active and effortful problem solving – and of course, both System I and System II are involved even with an expert – it is just that a greater proportion of the cognitive load is being handled by System I.

people respond to situations – whether they be bus drivers, surgeons or even judges.[67] The relatively subconscious choice of a particular rule is also strongly influenced by factors such as how recently the rule was last used successfully, the frequency with which it has worked before successfully and the strength of the emotional experience associated with its previous use. Even with careful deliberation, decisions seldom follow rational lines in the Bayesian or statistical sense. One major reason for this is that the set of facts available for making decisions – the *problem space* – is often incomplete or inadequate. This applies both to the information in the world and to the information available from memory. In a medical example, there may be a very large number of facts relevant to a patient's condition, available as information in the world (which includes information in other people's minds and information stored in books, or in patient notes), but some of these might not be provided or readily available to a practitioner when needed. For example, a patient may forget to mention the history of a previous illness or allergy, which might subsequently prove relevant. Alternatively, a patient may provide this information to one practitioner (perhaps a nurse, or a junior doctor) and assume (reasonably, but perhaps incorrectly) that the information will be passed on to all who need it. In order to manage each patient's problem properly, clinicians must rely on a great deal of information stored in their memories, some of which may be missing, inaccurate or difficult to retrieve at the time required. There is much in medicine that is rare, arcane and easily forgotten – an unusual interaction between two classes of drug, for example. The solution to a problem may be logically sound even with incomplete information – such a solution is sometimes referred to as *satisficing*.

The naturalistic decision-making framework grew out of empirical study of how experts make decisions in the field, under stress – while fighting fires, for example. In this framework satisficing[68] is seen as finding a workable solution quickly through what is sometimes called the *recognition-primed decision* model rather than comparing all alternatives in pursuit of an optimal solution. This is entirely consistent with the idea of learned responses to stored patterns. More than one possible response may be considered, and an effort made to select the best of these, but there is a trade-off between time and reliability. In a sense, an

---

[67] See footnote 43.

[68] H. A. Simon, 'Rational choice and the structure of the environment' (1956) 63 *Psychological Review* 129–38.

attempt is made to find the best balance between intuition (doing the first thing that comes to mind, which often but not always turns out to be right) and analysis (for which there usually isn't enough time in high-risk activities). There is no substitute for experience in this context, but it is possible to improve the performance of experts through appropriate training.[69]

Clearly, however, the lack of a complete set of pertinent facts and the incorrect nature of some of the information which is available militate against the reliability of a decision made in this way: sometimes it will be wrong. Furthermore, there is a problem in assembling the necessary information in the front of the mind – our ability to think of all the various aspects of a complex problem at once is quite limited. If the problem space is thought of as a blackboard full of facts, then for human beings it is a blackboard illuminated by a narrow beam of light whose movements from one place to another are largely random and only partly responsive to voluntary control. This feature of the human condition is known as *bounded rationality*.

Expertise

There is, of course, a gradation between the complete novice and the inveterate master, and people cope with different activities (including driving) by using different levels of skill and experience. Each individual's store of retained patterns and rules will also differ, both in its size and in the precise nature of the conceptualisations and corresponding pre-formulated responses. A major objective of training a person to be competent at a particular activity is to create greater conformity of the schemata and rules in the individual's store to those known by the teacher to be relatively reliable. Rules need to be matched to their appropriate schemata, and they need to be sound, robust and (so far as possible) capable of working in all the circumstances to which they are appropriately applied. Expertise goes beyond factual knowledge, and includes the ability to apply that knowledge effectively in a variety of complex and dynamic situations. The expert who has benefited from a well-designed and administered training programme is more likely to have sound conceptual patterns and robust rules for doing this than the self-taught person, and also a better understanding of the principles that explain and underpin these rules. The expert will spend less time in the System II part

[69] Klein, *Sources of Power*.

of the thinking continuum than the novice, and more in System I. When System II thinking is required, it will be facilitated by a larger store of schemata representing previously experienced situations and responses that worked or failed before. Thus, the grand master of chess may think out a position using first principles with as much effort and conscious thought as a club player, but will typically do so more effectively, by using much larger chunks of pre-stored information.

It follows that expertise is highly desirable. The ability of human beings to undertake complex activities is only possible because of the inherent properties of the human mind which facilitate the filtering and processing of information, and allow rapid and skilled responses to difficult and dynamically changing challenges. Equally, many contemporary human activities are only possible on account of the social fabric of human society, which permits co-operation between individuals and allows knowledge and skill to be passed from one person to the next. These factors are manifest to a very high degree in an activity such as the practice of medicine. It would be quite impossible for doctors to function in their various and often concurrent roles as diagnosticians, advisers, technicians and counsellors if it were not for the way in which the human mind works, the way in which people interact and the technology with which they can enhance their abilities. Modern healthcare is a team activity, with different members contributing different but essential skills to the endeavour in a coordinated manner. Furthermore, the skills of each participant must be exercised substantially in real time. If a doctor, for example, had to start afresh from first principles every time a procedure was undertaken or a patient examined, little would get done. Some technical specialists (some neurosurgeons, for example) have honed their psychomotor and analytical skills to very high levels in order to undertake extremely difficult operations or other procedures on, for example, tiny babies or infirm elderly patients. In doing this, they are in no small way like professional sportsmen whose natural ability has been developed by training and practice to produce a very high level of skill, although the range of activities and the theoretical knowledge involved in medical practice exceeds that in most sporting activities.[70] Even top batsmen (for example) do get bowled out from time to time, and in the same way surgeons, through technical failures, occasionally fail to

---

[70] On the other hand, doctors in more generalist fields (general practitioners, but also general physicians, for example) may be confronted with a wide variety of novel situations, which create a very different kind of challenge.

achieve the outcome they intended for a patient, sometimes to the extent that injury or death is the result, instead of healing. But this analogy is limited, and depicts only part of the complex process necessary for the achievement of excellent results in surgery today. Success depends also on many other people, including nurses and junior doctors involved in the care of each patient on the wards before and after surgery, anaesthetists with skills in maintaining life while rendering patients oblivious to pain during the procedure and at the same time managing the substantial physiological responses to the assault of surgery, highly skilled specialist nurses who assist in the operation and subsequently during the immediate postoperative period of recovery from anaesthesia, doctors and nurses who specialise in intensive care, and a small army of supporting medical, nursing, technical and administrative staff who provide laboratory, radiological, and other essential services. Not only must each of these people undertake his or her role with considerable knowledge, skill and care, but the efforts of each need to be coordinated with those of all the others. Failure at any step along the path from admission into hospital to discharge home can undo even the most technically brilliant surgical procedure. For example, a lapse in hand hygiene three days later can result in the infection of an otherwise perfectly inserted hip joint replacement, and a postoperative pulmonary embolism that could have been prevented had the correct medication been administered on time can prove lethal. Modern medicine, as we have said, is a team game. Perhaps the analogy works better if the comparison is made with the bowler, rather than the batsman, because the bowler's success depends to a large extent on ten fielders, not just to gain the batsman's wicket but also to limit harm (in the form of runs) when balls are bowled less than perfectly. None of this discussion is intended to distract from the importance of the considerable technical skills required by surgeons, anaesthetists, and other proceduralists in healthcare. We shall discuss technical failures in Chapter 3, under the heading 'technical errors', but, as in sport, perhaps the most surprising thing in medicine is that some of the more difficult procedures are possible at all.

Memory

We have seen that expertise is a concept that captures a wide range of abilities, but one thing it depends upon is memory. Memory has been described as declarative or non-declarative. Declarative memory is divided into episodic and semantic categories. Declarative memories can be accessed consciously and expressed in words. Examples of episodic memory might include remembering receiving a present on one's tenth birthday, or recalling an occasion in which the administration of a drug produced a profound drop in blood pressure. Semantic memory is more conceptual – recalling that one tends to get presents on one's birthday, for example, or that the drug that caused the drop in blood pressure has this particular pharmacological characteristic in general, and so is likely to produce this effect again, if administered in the future. Working memory is an important subset of declarative memory: whereas other forms of memory may be stored for years, working memory is generally held in the conscious mind for a matter of seconds or a minute or two at most. Most people can hold a number of six or seven digits in working memory for a short time by actively rehearsing it (a telephone number, for example) but unless working memory is somehow converted to long-term memory, this information will be lost as soon as one's mind is diverted to something else.

Non-declarative memory involves procedural activities. Learning to ride a bicycle or water-start a windsurfer are classic examples. Before being learned, the procedure is too difficult, and the cyclist will almost certainly fall off the bicycle and the novice windsurfer will swallow large quantities of sea or lake water without succeeding in using the wind to mount the board. Once learned, the procedural skill is retained indefinitely – even after many years without use. Yet it is not easy to articulate the elements of the skill in such a way that a novice could apply the information without the benefit of learning through repeated attempts. It is true that coaches can articulate aspects of procedures that may help or hinder acquisition of the skill, and this demonstrates the usual point that the boundaries between categories of cognitive process are seldom sharp, but practice is still required to attain a procedural skill. Interestingly, language and mental arithmetic depend heavily on similarly subconscious memory processes (although declarative processes are also involved) and skill in these activities depends heavily upon practice. Similarly, surgery and anaesthesia (and the various other fields of healthcare as well) call on mixes of strictly practical procedural skills with more abstract elements of recognition and recall, as well as semantic declarative memory. Non-declarative memory is, of course, relevant to an understanding of skill-based errors, because these errors manifest through skills that are practised unconsciously.

As we have already said, much of our understanding of memory has been acquired through the study of patients with memory deficits.

The human errors in which we are primarily interested mostly involve normal people rather than patients with pathology, but it is too simplistic to assume that all the processes that support memory function equally well in all healthy people, or even in any one person at all times. For example, there is a difference between familiarity and recall – one may recognise a person as familiar, but have difficulty recalling her name. Furthermore, recall of a name may appear to be blocked either spontaneously or by the distracting influence of an unwanted thought that has emerged – of a slightly different name, for example. Yet this does not mean that the memory has been lost – some time later it may emerge easily and perfectly, but too late to be of great use. This phenomenon of 'blocking' does seem to increase with age, and does not necessarily indicate any other form of mental difficulty or pathology. The point of real interest is one we have made earlier: we rely on our memories for some of the information that forms the knowledge base used in making decisions, but we may not be able to access all the relevant facts, even if some of them are demonstrably available within our memory before and after the event: some facts are simply not accessed at the time they are needed, whether the person concerned is aware of knowing them and attempts to access them or not. Also, some facts that one might expect to be stored in memory simply are not; they never move from working memory, and in some cases may not even pass through working memory.

In the case of the forgotten baby, described in the Introduction, one might hypothesise an explanation for the events as follows. The young mother's thoughts were, presumably, completely focused on her work. The process of putting her child into the car seat would have been automatic, using procedural (non-declarative) memory. She had presumably done this many times before, and it would have been second nature to her; someone, such as a grandparent, doing the same thing on an occasional basis would have needed to use System II thinking, supported by declarative memory (semantic, and possibly episodic as well), and some trial and error. This would have involved engagement of the conscious mind in a way that was not necessary for a mother expert in the use of baby seats, and would have made forgetting the presence of the baby much less likely. The normal course of events, through which the child would have been dropped off at the crèche, would also have involved a sequence of almost automatic activities, using substantially non-declarative memory, the elements of which would have to be chunked into a subconscious cognitive whole. The fact that a key part of the journey to work was omitted would never even have entered the mother's working memory – had she realised for one moment that she had missed the turning to the crèche she would certainly have turned back, and dealt with the omission. So this information never became part of even her short-term memory, let alone her long-term memory.

This raises the question of why, on receiving the first text from the crèche, she did not immediately remember her mistake. The processes involved in the storage and consolidation of memory are very complex. The primary distinction seems to be between working memory and longer-term memory. The simple view is that facts held only in working memory are not stored at all, but this is not entirely clear. There is evidence that some information may be stored unconsciously as well as through the conscious process of repeated rehearsal in working memory.[71] As we have already discussed, information accessed from the external world seems typically to be rationalised and simplified into schema and then filed in the brain, as it were. However this doesn't only happen once. The process of consolidation of memory seems often to involve iterative cycles of retrieval, reframing and restoring. Over time, people tend to recall memories and retell the stories of the events to themselves, perhaps modifying details in subtle and unconscious ways to make sense of the inexplicable aspects of the memory, or to reduce discomfort arising from the implications of the memory. The restored version becomes the memory – or perhaps it becomes a version of the memory. Depending on the exact methods used to retrieve the memory, some evidence suggests that the original version may be retained, but this point seems still to be controversial. What is clear is that false memories are easily created by various factors, of which suggestion is particularly powerful. In a classic experiment, subjects are exposed to a yield sign. It is subsequently suggested that there was a stop sign in the scene. Many will then recall the sign, incorrectly, as a stop sign. Alternatively, some memories that are painful, perhaps because they are associated with highly traumatic events, are suppressed. Given that the ways in which people view and assimilate information in the first place are limited, it is clear that episodic memory is unreliable and becomes more so with the

---

[71] It has even been suggested that memory may be formed while under anaesthesia: see R. A. Veselis, 'Memory formation during anaesthesia: plausibility of a neurophysiological basis' (2015) 115 Suppl 1 British Journal of Anaesthesia i13–i19. K. Leslie, P. S. Myles, A. Forbes, M. T. V. Chan, S. K. Swallow and T. G. Short, 'Dreaming during anaesthesia in patients at high risk of awareness' (2005) 60 Anaesthesia 239–44.

passage of time and the influence of new information. Work by Elizabeth Loftus and Jim Coan using the 'lost in the mall' technique showed that it is possible, through suggestion, to implant a memory of being lost in a shopping mall as a child in, perhaps, a third of adults who have never experienced such an event – in other words, memories can be created de novo. Certain people, including the very young and the very old, seem to be more susceptible to this phenomenon. It is even possible to create (and demonstrate) false memories in certain non-human animals. Furthermore, the degree of certainty with which a memory is recalled may have very little relationship with the likelihood of its being correct. Thus, several witnesses to an accident may provide very different accounts of what actually happened, but, in fact, none may be entirely accurate, particularly if the events occurred a long time in the past.[72]

False memories have created considerable controversy in the courts. The advent of DNA testing led to the exoneration of many people previously convicted on the strength of evidence from eyewitnesses. In the past, many cases of alleged child abuse hinged on testimony recounting allegedly suppressed memories retrieved using techniques that are now believed likely to promote the creation of false memories. Perhaps the most disturbing point that arises from these unfortunate mistakes lies in a view that was sometimes taken over expert witnesses and memory: it was argued that experts on memory were not required, because the veracity of a memory was something for juries to determine. The reality, of course, is that survey data show clearly that potential jurors frequently hold beliefs about memory that are contradicted by science. A very similar view has sometimes been taken in the past about expert evidence in relation to human error, and we will return to the importance of appropriate expert testimony later in the book. Fortunately, it does seem that these issues are becoming better understood today than in the past.[73]

It is a useful exercise to think back over a period during which one has been concentrating intensely. One will often find that striking events have

---

[72] E. F. Loftus, 'Remembering what never happened', in E. Tulving (ed.), *Memory, Consciousness, and the Brain: The Tallinn Conference* (Philadelphia, Psychology Press, 2000) 106–18. E. F. Loftus, 'Memory distortion and false memory creation' (1996) 24 *Bulletin of the American Academy of Psychiatry & the Law* 281–95. E. F. Loftus, 'Planting misinformation in the human mind: a 30-year investigation of the malleability of memory' (2005) 12 *Learning & Memory* 361–6.

[73] E. F. Loftus, '25 Years of Eyewitness Science . . . Finally Pays Off' (2013) 8 *Perspectives on Psychological Science: A Journal of the Association for Psychological Science* 556–7.

occurred of which one has no recall at all – sometimes even conversations with familiar people (notably spouses or children to whom one has responded subconsciously – what one might call the 'Yes dear' phenomenon). Returning to the young mother and her recall of events, it seems clear enough that a sense of having dropped her child off could quite plausibly have developed from a firm conviction that this was what she always did and the absence of any memory to the contrary.

Teamwork

During these first two chapters we have repeatedly alluded to the importance of teamwork in modern healthcare. This theme will be developed further in our deliberations over the most effective and just approach to the regulation of healthcare and the legal response to inadvertently caused harm. Therefore, it is important to understand what we mean by the term 'team'.

Teams and 'Tribes' in Healthcare

A team is something more than just any group of individuals who happen to find themselves interacting together in some way at some point in time. One of the most strikingly effective teams in recent years has been the All Blacks, New Zealand's national rugby union team. From a sporting team of this sort one can form a mental image of what a team might ideally look like: a group of individuals, with different but related skills, led by a charismatic captain, who know each other well, train together regularly and collectively possess the skills needed for achieving a shared common goal, supported by coaches and bonded by a strong sense of shared identity.

In fact, teams in healthcare seldom fit this image. For a start, somewhat surprisingly, individuals seldom identify as belonging primarily to the same team focused on a particular group of patients with common problems.[74] Instead, they typically identify more strongly with their

---

[74] The cardiothoracic surgical unit ('CTSU'), led for many years by Sir Brian Barratt-Boyes, at Green Lane Hospital in Auckland was actually an exception to this: its multidisciplinary members did see their affiliation to the CTSU as at least equal to their affiliation to their professional disciplines. This culture was subsequently weakened by a process of relocation and restructuring that occurred at about the turn of the millennium. For more discussion of this particular example of teamwork, see A. F. Merry, J. Weller and S. J. Mitchell, 'Teamwork, communication, formula-one racing and the outcomes of cardiac surgery' (2014) 46 *Journal of Extra-Corporeal Technology* 7–14.

professional disciplines, as nurses, surgeons, anaesthetists, cardiologists, perfusionists, pharmacists and so forth. The term 'tribalism' has been coined to capture this observation. This phenomenon can be seen in the meetings held within hospitals to discuss patient care, review events in which harm has occurred, develop policy and so forth. There are exceptions, and some hospitals have done much to address these problems, but in general far more of these meetings seem to be held within each of these discrete 'tribes' than with all 'tribes' brought together. Also, it is typical to have separate heads of nursing, surgery, anaesthesia, pharmacy and so forth, with relatively little emphasis on the integration of these services. Even when a chief medical officer is appointed to a hospital, this appointment is often matched by a chief nursing officer. With the increasing advent of chief executive officers who are not clinically qualified, the separation of the 'tribe' of administrators from the multiple 'tribes' of clinicians is typically even more notable. This last problem is made more acute by the fact that administrators often function through meetings scheduled during the very hours that the clinicians are fully occupied with patient care.

Another key difference between healthcare and sporting teams lies in the stability of the teams that actually provide care to patients at any particular moment. In healthcare, these teams (or perhaps sub-teams) are often dynamic, and formed as needed, by individuals who have the required skills but may or may not know each other and may or may not have perfectly aligned understandings of the situation and the common goal. Imagine a cardiac arrest call in the middle of the night: the people who typically respond will be those who happen to be in the hospital and close at hand on the time. They coalesce at the patients' bedside and somehow quickly establish who should do what, and initiate cardio-pulmonary resuscitation promptly but with variable collective effectiveness, sometimes only to discover some minutes later that the patient who has arrested has an advanced care plan recorded in the notes that specifies a desire to be allowed to die in peace. It may seem astonishing, but it is quite common for none of the people responding to a cardiac arrest call to actually know the patient, or in the heat of the moment to have the time to read the relevant information in the notes before initiating inappropriate emergency treatment. It is true that many hospitals have formalised emergency response teams of one sort or another, but even these teams will be formed on a daily basis according to rosters, rotational training schemes and so forth, and would be unlikely to know any particular patient in a large hospital. Many hospitals also have protocols to record whether patients should or should not be resuscitated. Despite these efforts, on the one hand resuscitative efforts often fail, and on the other inappropriate resuscitative attempts are carried out all too often (although clearly with good intentions).[75] In particular, it is still quite unusual for a team that forms to respond to an emergency of this sort to have practised together and honed their ability to coordinate their considerable individual skills to a common end.

Even in the context of routine work, on hospital wards or during routine surgical lists for example, the teams that form on any particular day will often contain different individuals from those who worked together the week before, or the week before that. This problem has become more marked in many countries in recent years, with shortened work hours for junior doctors resulting in increased frequency of transfer of care from one to another, and also with shortages of nurses and increased usage of agency staff. This problem is also more characteristic of large hospitals than small ones: some smaller hospitals and some units within large hospitals do have considerable staffing stability, but unfortunately this is often not the case. The question arises, then, as to when one can say that the groups of doctors, nurses and others who actually care for patients really do constitute teams in the true sense, and when they are instead just random groups of poorly coordinated people with moderately aligned responsibilities and goals.

A team has been defined as a 'distinguishable set of two or more people who interact dynamically, interdependently, and adaptively toward a common and valued goal, who have each been assigned specific roles or functions to perform, and who have a limited life-span membership'.[76] Salas et al. have drawn from a broad body of empirical evidence to formulate a theoretical model incorporating five dimensions for effective teamwork: team orientation, team leadership, mutual performance monitoring, backup behaviour and adaptability. These dimensions are underpinned by three coordinating mechanisms: mutual trust, closed

---

[75] An example supporting this contention can be found in proposals recently submitted to the New Zealand Health Quality and Safety Commission calling for initiatives to ensure earlier detection of deterioration in patients' condition and greater emphasis on the appropriateness or otherwise of intervention in the face of such deterioration: the proposal reflected concern over the need for greater success in resuscitation when appropriate and better recognition of patients' desires when not.

[76] E. Salas, T. L. Dickinson, S. Converse and S. I. Tannenbaum, 'Toward an understanding of team performance and training', in R. W. Swezey and E. Salas (eds.), *Teams: Their Training and Performance* (Norwood, Ablex, 1992), p. 4.

loop communication and shared mental models within the team.[77] To rephrase the ideas in this definition and this list of elements, the most important prerequisites for effective team work would seem to be that members of the team all agree that they do belong to the team, that they trust one and other, that there is some clarity over leadership and that there is effective communication between them. There also needs to be at least some alignment or sharing of relevant elements of the individual members' mental models, certainly in relation to objectives and the broad plan for achieving them.

Given this view of teamwork, one can conclude that it is certainly possible for a group of professionals who do not know each other personally to gather together when needed, assign or acknowledge a leader, adopt various specific roles and function together as described towards a common goal. In fact, notwithstanding the challenges to teamwork that we have just outlined, this is what happens every day in hospitals, and, incidentally, also in the cockpits of commercial airlines where it is the norm for the pilots to be unacquainted. It is clear, then, that modern healthcare is nearly always provided by teams. What is less clear is the degree to which the teamwork in healthcare is effective in promoting a successful outcome for patients. To answer this it is useful to consider the empirical data.

Teamwork and Outcomes in Healthcare

Reports of serious adverse events to agencies such as the New Zealand Health Quality and Safety Commission regularly include examples of failures in communication that lead to patient harm. Similarly, many studies have now provided evidence linking teamwork and communication to the genesis of adverse events in surgery, in postoperative care and in healthcare more generally.[78] In one example, Lingard identified failures in more than 25 per cent of observed communications in operating theatres, many of which resulted (amongst other things) in inefficiency, waste of resources and delays or errors with procedures.[79] Work in

---

[77] E. Salas, D. Sims and C. Burke, ' Is there a "Big Five" in teamwork?' (2005) 36 *Small Group Research* 555–99.

[78] See A. F. Merry and J. M. Weller, 'Teamwork and minimizing error', in P. Alston, P. Myles and M. Ranucci (eds.), *Oxford Textbook of Cardiothoracic Anaesthesia* (2015) 461–7.

[79] L. Lingard, S. Espin, S. Whyte, G. Regehr, G. R. Baker, R. Reznick, J. Bohnen, B. Orser, D. Doran and E. Grober, 'Communication failures in the operating room: an observational classification of recurrent types and effects' (2004) 13 *Quality & Safety in Health Care* 330–4.

paediatric cardiac surgery by Marc de Leval, James Reason, Charles Vincent and others has added considerably to the evidence that teamwork in general and communication more particularly are related to patient outcomes. Minor events during this type of surgery may be without consequence individually, but collectively they are clearly linked to outcome. They need to be declared and addressed, which again depends on communication and teamwork.[80] The Flawless Operative Cardiovascular Unified Systems project was established to promote harm-free cardiac surgery in the United States. This project started with a substantial systematic review of the relevant literature: one of the key recommendations that emerged was the promotion of good teamwork and communication. A subsequent observational study again explicitly concluded that improving communication and teamwork was essential for improving the outcomes of cardiac surgery.[81] Finally, the story of the Mid Staffordshire NHS Trust (outlined in Chapter 1), is a graphic illustration of the importance of culture and integration across an entire organisation: this was a failure in teamwork of the first order.

It is also relevant that there is evidence that teamwork and communication in healthcare can be improved through training and the introduction of relevant tools and processes.[82] Substantial improvements in patient outcomes have followed interventions that include the WHO Surgical Safety Checklist (the Checklist), briefings and other initiatives designed to improve teamwork and communication. The Checklist includes an explicit requirement for everyone in the operating theatre

---

[80] M. R. de Leval, J. Carthey, D. J. Wright, V. T. Farewell and J. T. Reason, 'Human factors and cardiac surgery: a multicenter study' (2000) 119 *Journal of Thoracic and Cardiovascular Surgery* 661–72; I. L. Solis-Trapala, J. Carthey, V. T. Farewell and M. R. de Leval, 'Dynamic modelling in a study of surgical error management' (2007) 26 *Statistics in Medicine* 5189–202. K. R. Catchpole, A. E. B. Giddings, M. Wilkinson, G. Hirst, T. Dale and M. R. de Leval, 'Improving patient safety by identifying latent failures in successful operations' (2007) 142 *Surgery* 102–10.

[81] E. A. Martinez, D. A. Thompson, N. A. Errett, G. R. Kim, L. Bauer, L. H. Lubomski, A. P. Gurses, J. A. Marsteller, A. Mohit, C. A. Goeschel and P. J. Pronovost, 'High stakes and high risk: a focused qualitative review of hazards during cardiac surgery' (2011) 112 *Anesthesia & Analgesia* 1061–74; A. P. Gurses, G. Kim, E. A. Martinez, J. Marsteller, L. Bauer, L. H. Lubomski, P. J. Pronovost and D. Thompson, 'Identifying and categorising patient safety hazards in cardiovascular operating rooms using an interdisciplinary approach: a multisite study' (2012) 21 *BMJ Quality & Safety* 810–18.

[82] E. Salas, D. DiazGranados, C. Klein, C. S. Burke, K. C. Stagl, G. F. Goodwin and S. M. Halpin, 'Does team training improve team performance? A meta-analysis' (2008) 50 *Human Factors* 903–33.

to be introduced, and for information to be shared about important issues or anticipated problems. The introduction of the Checklist in eight institutions around the world resulted in improved compliance with basic safety processes and a substantial reduction in mortality and other pre-specified surgical complications.[83] Two further major studies in the United States and Europe demonstrated similar improvements in outcomes through initiatives which included checklists, briefings and relevant training.[84] Simulation-based training of entire operating teams together (surgeons, anaesthetists and nurses) has been undertaken in New Zealand, with promising improvements in perceived communication practices persisting for at least some months after the training.[85]

The Collective Nature of Human Performance in Healthcare

In the majority of this chapter we have discussed the extent to which human performance depends on the representation of external facts by conceptualised mental models, the recognition of patterns within these models and the selection or appropriate responses to situations from previously stored schemata laid down through experience over time. We have also pointed out that the fast and efficient System I cognition of this type is monitored by the slower, more deliberative processes of System II, and discussed various influences on cognition overall, notably biases of various types. In this penultimate section of the chapter we introduced the rather striking concept that healthcare is almost always delivered by teams, and that many of the failures in healthcare actually

---

[83] A. B. Haynes, T. G. Weiser, W. R. Berry, S. R. Lipsitz, A. H. S. Breizat, E. P. Dellinger, T. Herbosa, S. Joseph, P. L. Kibatala, M. C. M. Lapitan, A. F. Merry, K. Moorthy, R. K. Reznick, B. Taylor and A. A. Gawande, 'A surgical safety checklist to reduce morbidity and mortality in a global population' (2009) 360 *New England Journal of Medicine* 491-9.

[84] J. Neily, P. D. Mills, Y. Young-Xu, B. T. Carney, P. West, D. H. Berger, L. M. Mazzia, D. E. Paull and J. P. Bagian, 'Association between implementation of a medical team training program and surgical mortality' (2010) 304 *Journal of the American Medical Association* 1693-700; E. N. de Vries, H. A. Prins, R. M. P. H. Crolla, A. J. den Outer, G. van Andel, S. H. van Helden, W. S. Schlack, M. A. van Putten, D. J. Gouma, M. G. W. Dijkgraaf, S. M. Smorenburg, M. A. Boermeester and S. C. Group, 'Effect of a comprehensive surgical safety system on patient outcomes' (2010) 363 *New England Journal of Medicine* 1928-37.

[85] J. Weller, D. Cumin, J. Torrie, M. Boyd, I. Civil, D. Madell, A. MacCormick, N. Gurisinghe, A. Garden, M. Crossan, W. L. Ng, S. Johnson, A. Corter, T. Lee, L. Selander, M. Cokorilo and A. F. Merry, 'Multidisciplinary operating room simulation-based team training to reduce treatment errors: a feasibility study in New Zealand hospitals' (2015) 128 *New Zealand Medical Journal* 40-51.

arise through failures in communication between individuals and in the ways in which groups of healthcare professionals work together in teams. We have indicated that the effectiveness of teamwork in healthcare typically leaves much room for improvement, and also that the composition of the teams may be quite substantial. In particular, patient outcomes may depend as much on administrators or support services (such as radiology, pharmacy and laboratory services) as on the doctors and nurses who interact with patients directly.

Different institutions obtain different outcomes, and at least one study has linked superior outcomes in the management of acute myocardial infarction to a culture of excellence throughout every layer of the organisation.[86] A substantial recent review of the relevant literature has added further weight to the contention that outcomes depend more on the way units and institutions function collectively than on the excellence of any particular surgeon, or other clinician, within the institution.[87] It follows that we need to think of human performance more collectively, and think beyond the mental models of individuals to the sharing of those models within groups. We also need to extend our analysis beyond the skills and behaviours of individuals to the overall capability and culture of the institution as a whole. These observations are profoundly important for any initiatives to improve patient outcomes and reduce unintended harm from healthcare. They are also relevant to considerations of justice and effectiveness in the regulation of healthcare and the response to things that go wrong. We will return to these themes throughout the remainder of this book, and deal with them in some depth in Chapter 10.

The Price of Success

This chapter has stressed human abilities and achievements. The way in which our minds work has permitted us to develop a highly technological society, and to function within it. Many of the cognitive processes that have allowed humans to function successfully in the world are so

---

[86] L. A. Curry, E. Spatz, E. Cherlin, J. W. Thompson, D. Berg, H. H. Ting, C. Decker, H. M. Krumholz and E. H. Bradley, 'What distinguishes top-performing hospitals in acute myocardial infarction mortality rates? A qualitative study' (2011) 154 *Annals of Internal Medicine* 384–90.

[87] R. Hamblin, C. Shuker, I. Stolarek, J. Wilson and A. F. Merry, 'Public reporting of health care performance data: what we know and what we should do' (2016) 129 *New Zealand Medical Journal* 7–17.

successful precisely because of our flexible, distractible and interpretative nature. These attributes are the ones that also underlie the predisposition of human beings to error. The technology and complexity that we have created in our modern society, and our ability to work together in a coordinated fashion, have increased the demands on our abilities to reason accurately, share thoughts, respond promptly with the correct rule for any given situation and carry out actions requiring considerable skill. They have also produced scenarios in which the consequences of error may be very serious indeed; we have reviewed data confirming that accidental harm is a major problem in modern healthcare.

The informed response to harm from errors does not lie in a denial of the existence or nature of human error, and it is therefore worrying that medical practitioners and the courts often take a view of error that sits more readily with a model of people as machines and as individuals operating in isolation than with the insights of contemporary psychology and of the collective nature of healthcare delivery. Justice and safety would both be better served by a more sophisticated appreciation of the relationship between the highly desirable achievements of today's society and its inherent vulnerability to accidents. In particular, the inevitability of human error should be seen not so much as evidence of a primary human weakness, but rather as an inevitable concomitant of our impressive cognitive ability and evolutionary success.

3

Errors

We all know that everyone makes errors – but are everyday errors (misplacing a household item or misdialling a telephone number) really equivalent to inadvertently administering the wrong drug to a patient? There is an understandable view that professionals are trained and paid precisely to ensure that they do in fact do the right thing. The problem of iatrogenic harm in healthcare described in Chapter 2 demands a response. The first reaction to accidents in medicine is often punitive, and based on a denial of the nature of human error. The culture of clinical practice is in general one of relentless dedication to high achievement, and the medical profession is the foremost culprit in perpetuating the myth of professional infallibility. It is not surprising that the courts and disciplinary authorities have often taken their lead from doctors themselves and have at times seemed to treat any kind of failure in medical practice as unacceptable.

In Chapter 2 we discussed some of the processes involved in human cognition and described the ways in which the mind may mislead an actor and create a situation in which bizarre and apparently inexplicable actions become perfectly understandable. We now explore the nature of error in more detail. We distinguish between different types of error and investigate the degree to which it is possible to predict when certain types of error are most likely to occur. We discuss reasons for believing that errors are both understandable and inevitable, even for a highly trained and regulated professional. However, not all unsafe acts are errors. If we are to gain any useful insights into the issue of blame from our consideration of the ways in which human cognitive processes can fail, it is essential to distinguish unintentional *errors* from deliberately unsafe acts, or *violations*. Violations will be the subject of Chapter 4, and then, in the rest of the book, the distinction between errors and violations will be important to our discussion of blame and of the relationship between the law and safety in healthcare.

Definition of Error

In his book *Human Error*, Reason defines 'error' as a generic term encompassing 'all those occasions in which a planned sequence of mental or physical activities fails to achieve its intended outcome, and when these failures cannot be attributed to the intervention of some chance agency'.[1] Reason's book provides one of the most authoritative and comprehensive accounts of human error available, but it is explicitly not concerned with blame, and consequently this definition does not fully delineate the characteristics of error that are important for our purposes.

First, a violation may also meet the criterion of being 'a planned sequence of mental activities ... that ... fails to achieve its intended outcome'. And second, we do not think outcome is helpful in judging whether or not an error or a violation has occurred.

Drug administration illustrates these points. As explained in Chapter 2, the process of drug administration often goes wrong. Most of these occasions are the result of errors, but some events that might seem to be errors reflect failures that are violations of acceptable practice – choosing not to label syringes, for example. Most of these events are without any noticeable consequence at all – quite often no one even knows they have been made. Occasionally, as in the cases of Dr Yogasakaran and Dr Morrison for example, the consequences are disastrous. This difference in outcome relates primarily to chance. In most cases, outcome provides no clue as to whether or not something has gone wrong with drug administration, and where it is known that something of this sort has happened, it provides even less of a guide to the nature of the failure – to whether it reflected an error or a violation.

It seems to us that definitions of error and violation should reflect the cognitive processes and states of mind involved in their generation. It is these processes, we suggest, that should underpin an understanding of the culpability of actions that cause unintended harm.[2]

We recognise that there is a semantic sense in which it could be argued that the desired outcome of the decisions and actions in the context of drug administration is to give the correct drug. We would suggest,

---

[1] J. Reason, *Human Error* (New York, Cambridge University Press, 1990), 9. See also J. Reason and K. Mycielska: *Absent Minded? The Psychology of Mental Lapses and Everyday Errors* (Englewood Cliffs, New Jersey, Prentice-Hall, 1982).

[2] It will be obvious that this view resonates with the idea that *mens rea* is important in the criminal law.

instead, that giving the right drug is only part of the process by which the intended outcome of a therapeutic effect is to be achieved, and simply administering the drug successfully is not in itself that outcome. After all, the outcomes that tend to attract the attention of the law are typically those of direct importance to patients – things such as dying or sustaining serious permanent injury, for example.

It may be worth exploring this point in a little more depth. Many very difficult procedures are undertaken in healthcare in which quite high mortality rates are normal. Emergency surgery for Type A dissection of the ascending aorta is an example. This is a terrifying condition that often strikes relatively young people – often in their fifties or sixties. The aorta (the vessel carrying all the blood from the heart to be distributed through the arterial tree to the body) develops a crack into which blood (under pressure) slowly forces itself, opening a gap between its concentric layers. In the absence of treatment, the aorta eventually bursts, and death is virtually certain. Emergency surgery in good units carries an early mortality rate of about 11 per cent.[3] What can outcome tell us about the care provided to an *individual patient* with this condition? If such a patient dies does it mean an error has occurred? If such a patient lives, and returns to good health, does it mean care was perfect?

The surgery of acute dissection of the aorta is a very challenging and complex undertaking, which often takes place at night and lasts for many hours. The care that follows surgery is as critical to outcome as the surgery itself. Very high levels of skill and attention are required from surgeons, anaesthetists, nurses, intensive care specialists and many others. These people have to perform really well in their individual capacities, but they also have to coordinate their efforts, communicate with each other and work well together, as a team. Errors in minor aspects of this formidable undertaking are, in effect, inevitable. On its own, any one of these errors may or may not have a material influence on outcome, but most do not.

Rates of mortality over time do provide a normative indication of how well a particular unit or team is performing. For example, in the case of Bristol (discussed in Chapter 1), it was an unacceptable mortality rate that showed that something was wrong. However, in a series of patients in which the overall mortality rate is high (11 per cent, for example) the

---

[3] K. Suehiro, P. Pritzwald-Stegmann, T. West, A. R. Kerr and D. A. Haydock, 'Surgery for acute Type A aortic dissection a 37-year experience in Green Lane Hospital' (2006) 15 *Heart, Lung and Circulation* 105–12.

death or survival of an individual patient does not in itself provide any indication at all about the presence or absence of errors in that patient. It is common (and appropriate) to review the care of any patient who dies after surgery to see whether anything could have been done better. However, even that might provide misleading information – reviewing patients who survive will often identify very similar imperfections in care, because few complex cases are managed so well that no areas for possible improvement can be found.

It is very important to appreciate that we are not discounting the importance of the errors that occur in healthcare, including those that occur when managing complex and difficult cases. We are not, for example, saying that nothing should or can be done about errors that might make healthcare safer. Errors whose consequences are major are obviously a problem but, as we indicated in Chapter 2, even those with little obvious potential to cause harm do matter, taken collectively: there is good evidence that reducing the number of errors made in complex surgical procedures, or responding effectively to them when they occur, can improve overall outcomes.[4] Also, the importance of timely 'rescue' of patients whose condition is deteriorating has emerged in recent years as a key element in achieving good outcomes from surgery.[5] Our points are simply that that the expectation for absolute perfection in healthcare is often unrealistic, and that clinical outcomes reflect a wide range of factors, some of which are beyond the control of clinicians. It follows that the outcome of any individual case, in itself, may not be a good marker of failures in the process of care.[6]

---

[4] K. R. Catchpole, A. E. B. Giddings, M. Wilkinson, G. Hirst, T. Dale and M. R. de Leval, 'Improving patient safety by identifying latent failures in successful operations' (2007) 142 *Surgery* 102–10.

[5] There is a substantial variation in hospital mortality after surgery that is explained not by the rate of complications in the first place, but rather by the rate of failure to rescue after complications occur. See J. H. Silber, S. V. Williams, H. Krakauer and J. S. Schwartz, 'Hospital and patient characteristics associated with death after surgery. A study of adverse occurrence and failure to rescue' (1992) 30 *Medical Care* 615–29; A. A. Ghaferi, J. D. Birkmeyer and J. B. Dimick, 'Complications, failure to rescue, and mortality with major inpatient surgery in Medicare patients' (2009) 250 *Annals of Surgery* 1029–34; A. A. Ghaferi and J. B. Dimick, 'Variation in mortality after high-risk cancer surgery: failure to rescue' (2012) 21 *Surgical Oncology Clinics of North America* 389–95, vii; M. Johnston, S. Arora, D. King, L. Stroman and A. Darzi, 'Escalation of care and failure to rescue: a multicenter, multiprofessional qualitative study' (2014) 155 *Surgery* 989–94.

[6] The outcomes of large series of cases can provide insights into systemic or recurrent shortcomings in care, but isolated serious mistakes tend to be difficult to identify other than through the honest testimony of the clinicians involved.

This point applies more generally, beyond the boundaries of health-care. Errors were made during Flight 447 (see Chapter 1). Arguably, however, the factor that contributed most to the tragic outcome was the failure to rescue the situation. Had the captain returned to the cockpit a little earlier, he might have had enough time to evaluate what was happening and intervene effectively, and a completely different outcome might have been achieved. This would not have changed the fact that errors were made – for example, in the interpretation of the situation and in the un-coordinated use of the side-sticks by the co-pilots.

We do agree that error can only be understood in relation to an intention to achieve a particular result or outcome – acts that originate spontaneously, in the absence of any intention, should be excluded. From a legal perspective, acts of this type are sometimes called 'automatic' – but it is important to understand that we are referring here to things like muscle spasms that occur because of disease processes, for example, rather than the subconscious decision-making that characterises much of System I thinking. Nevertheless, an error may be made after which the intended overall *goal* is still successfully achieved, while the failure to achieve the overall goal of a complex endeavour is not a reliable indicator that errors have been made. It is fundamental to the arguments in this book that the appropriateness of an act or decision cannot be reliably assessed on the basis of its outcome or result. In general, errors (and violations) do tend to reduce the chances of achieving a given outcome or to reduce the margin of safety associated with a particular activity. We would probably have little interest in errors that had no potential to contribute to either of these results, but these are not the critical aspects of the definition of an error.

In error, the failure lies in the faultiness of some aspect of a particular *act* or *plan* that is part of the process of achieving a goal. To qualify as an error, this failure in planning or acting must be *unintentional*. As discussed in Chapter 4, we would classify an act or decision that knowingly falls short of a reasonably expected standard as a *violation*, even though there may be no intent to cause harm or to jeopardise a particular goal. Knowingly exceeding the speed limit is a violation even if a driver believes this will get him to his destination sooner, with no material loss of safety. Giving the wrong drug to a patient is usually an error because the practitioner intends to give the right drug, with a view to achieving a therapeutic goal. The caveat is that, for an act to qualify as an error (rather than as a foreseeable consequence of a violation), every effort should have been made to follow accepted process.[7] There can be no suggestion in the case of an error that a faulty action or decision was undertaken in the knowledge that it was faulty, but in the belief that this faultiness did not matter. Indeed, the actor is often completely unaware at the time that the error has occurred – a salt-for-sugar substitution is often only identified on tasting the tea, for example, and many drug errors go completely undetected by the person concerned, to be identified later by their consequences, or perhaps by a second practitioner (such as a supervisor) who notices the empty ampoules. When we are evaluating events for the purpose of attributing blame, these are important points, because our focus needs to be on the actions and thought processes themselves, not on their results. In fact, this discussion reflects agreement with Reason that 'the intervention of a chance agency' does not constitute grounds for judging a decision or action as erroneous. It is central to our argument that the outcome of a complex process is often influenced by many other factors that are not reasonably knowable at the time and events that are not reasonably foreseeable (including those apparently attributable to chance). Therefore, before defining error and (later) violation, we need to start by stating that:

> Decisions and their consequent actions should be judged only on the basis of information and events that were reasonably accessible or foreseeable at that time.

Thus, no error should be imputed if an unforeseeable[8] event occurs (such as a bird flying across the path of a ball heading directly towards the hole after a perfectly executed golf shot, for example) that thwarts the intended outcome of the correct execution of a sound plan.

With this clear, we can then say, in colloquial terms, that an error is *when one tries to do the right thing but actually does the wrong thing.*

---

[7] We have already mentioned the example of choosing not to label syringes; again, we would take the view that administering a drug correctly involves a sequence of steps, including selecting an ampoule, transferring its contents to a syringe, labelling the syringe, checking the identity of the patient and so forth. See A. F. Merry, D. H. Shipp and J. S. Lowinger, 'The contribution of labelling to safe medication administration in anaesthetic practice' (2011) 25 *Best Practice and Research Clinical Anaesthesiology* 145–59; Australian and New Zealand College of Anaesthetists, *Guidelines for the Safe Administration of Injectable Drugs in Anaesthesia (Policy Document PS 51)* (Melbourne, The College, 2009). It makes little sense to argue that the administration itself was an error if the practitioner had chosen to omit from the overall process steps that are widely accepted as important.

[8] It is a somewhat esoteric point, but worth emphasis, that many an unforeseeable event, despite appearances, is not truly due to 'a chance agency'. It is an inherent property of complexity that events that are not random may nevertheless be too difficult to predict.

More formally, we propose the following definition:

> An error is unintentional; it involves the use of a flawed decision or plan to achieve an aim, or the failure to carry out a planned action as intended.[9]

This definition retains the principle that errors are not associated with automatic actions, and that there must be some intended aspect of the act or plan which 'goes wrong', although the error itself is unintentional; it explicitly shifts the focus from the outcome of an act or plan to a failure in the act or plan itself.

Taxonomy of Error[10]

There are various ways in which errors may be classified, but for evaluating events with a view to the possible attribution of blame, there is great value in an approach that draws on the principles of cognitive psychology, which we have discussed in Chapter 2. In this approach errors are classified on the basis of the type of cognitive processing involved at the time they were made. Reason, in describing a 'Generic Error Modelling System', refers to *skill-based, rule-based* and *knowledge-based errors.* Skill-based errors involve actions and are often the result of *distraction.* Rule-based and knowledge-based errors are problem-solving failures, or planning failures, and may be grouped together under the heading of *mistakes.*

This classification is well known and has been very helpful in understanding the nature of human error. However, every action that is not involuntary must be preceded by a decision, albeit that the decision may be made entirely subconsciously and almost instantaneously. Also, as explained in Chapter 2, *every* decision involves interpreting the knowledge base available at the time. This is a key concept. The interpretation and framing of situations within a conceptualised *mental model* renders them understandable. It is our mental models rather than the objective facts of any situation that inform our decisions and often explain our errors – of whichever category.

The knowledge base of an individual consists of knowledge in his or her own mind and knowledge in the rest of the world. Examples of

[9] This definition has the same sense as the definitions proposed in the first edition of this book and subsequently in W. B. Runciman, A. F. Merry and F. Tito, 'Error, Blame, and the Law in Health Care – An Antipodean Perspective' (2003) 138 *Annals of Internal Medicine* 974–9. However, there are slight differences in wording.

[10] J. Reason, *Human Error*, 9–13.

knowledge in the rest of the world, relevant to our discussion, include knowledge in the minds of other people (colleagues, students, patients, patients' family members and so on), and information in notes, in textbooks, on the web and in physical form that can be inspected directly or indirectly. For example, a doctor can see that a jaundiced patient is yellow, or hear that a patient with asthma is wheezing audibly and can obtain additional information from blood tests or radiographs.

In healthcare, and notably in medicine, much emphasis is placed on learned knowledge – the information in a doctor or nurse's memory. *Expertise* is an excellent term to encapsulate this part of the knowledge base used in making decisions. As discussed in Chapter 2, expertise goes beyond information and includes the ability to apply that information effectively and in a variety of complex and dynamic situations. Much of healthcare does not lend itself to System II thinking, supported by undue reliance on external sources of information – there is simply not time to look everything up, and anyway it would often be difficult to know where to start in the absence of expertise.[11] For these reasons, a huge amount of effort is invested in training practitioners. Many errors in healthcare do reflect deficiencies in expertise and the solution to these may well be more (or better) training. Alternatively, they may reflect transient failures in *memory* rather than actual gaps in knowledge, and, if so, other solutions (such as the use of cognitive aids) may be more appropriate.

It seems to us that the distinction between skill-based and some rule-based errors may be quite slight. The primary distinction seems to lie in the concept that the former always involve actions that seem to be automatic, whereas in the latter the emphasis is on decisions. Nevertheless, skill-based errors do involve decisions, albeit that these are completely subconscious. Thus, the actions associated with these errors are not automatic in the sense that would be understood in the law – a reflex jerk of an arm, for example. Also, a lapse often manifests as the lack of an action – no action is involved in forgetting to put salt into the rice because of a distraction (for example). Conversely, rule-based errors often lead promptly to actions and the degree of consciousness involved in a decision may be very slight – many rule-based decisions are made completely subconsciously.

---

[11] In fact, part of medical and nursing expertise is the ability to access enough relevant information from all available sources to make good decisions, using history-taking, clinical examination, the notes, the laboratory and x-ray results and so forth.

As explained in Chapter 2, these various forms of cognition and consequent action typically take place in the context of complex activities, in a sort of quick-fire sequence of decisions and actions.[12] A mixture of cognitive processes is usually at play, often involving predominantly automatic (System I) thinking supplemented by a degree of supervisory or monitoring oversight that is conscious and slower in nature (System II).

Taking all of this into account, we think, nevertheless, that there is considerable utility in retaining the idea that slips and lapses form a distinct category of error, which we see as reflecting failures in System I thinking but at the extreme end of the spectrum, with no conscious element at all. These terms capture the characteristics of these errors very well, and slips and lapses can have consequences totally out of proportion to the magnitude of cognitive failure involved in their generation – a momentary failure that would usually be trivial can be lethal in the wrong circumstances. Errors in System I thinking can thus be seen as encompassing both slips and lapses and rule-based errors. On the other hand, we wonder whether the term *knowledge-based errors* really captures the *distinguishing* features of these mistakes. We suggest that it would be clearer to simply refer to these failures as errors in System II thinking.[13] For both systems, it is then worth considering the extent to which an error is attributable to deficiencies in the knowledge base, the subsequent processing of that information, or both. The truth is that all decisions (conscious or subconscious) and their consequent actions reflect the mental model of the actor at the time, and this depends substantially on the knowledge base upon which it has been constructed. Thus, the mental model of the actor is the best place to start from in the analysis of any error, wherever it lies along the spectrum of cognitive processes from slips and lapses at one end to the formal application of Bayesian logic at the other. Failures in the knowledge base are very common, and an understanding of an actor's mental model (or frame) can go a long way towards understanding otherwise inexplicable perceptions, decisions and actions. Having clarified the mental model, other important factors to consider include distraction, failures in logic and the invidious influence of subconscious bias or prejudice.

There is one more nuance to this characterisation of unintentional failures in thinking and acting – the question of how to determine that

---

[12] This is well illustrated in the example of Flight 447.

[13] D. Kahneman, *Thinking, Fast and Slow* (London, Penguin Books, 2011).

there has actually been a failure in the first place? How do we distinguish an error from an acceptable decision or action? To some extent, the determination is normative. We say a decision or action is an error because most people, usually including the person making the error, agree that it is. Often there is no dispute – in the case of an inadvertent syringe swap, for example, an anaesthetist who intends to give the sedative drug midazolam to a patient but actually gives a paralysing drug is unlikely to dispute that this was an error. However, there are contexts in which the normative element comes into play more strongly, and we shall discuss two of these later in this chapter: *technical errors* and *errors of judgement.*

Errors Associated with System I Cognition

These are the errors in which actions follow almost automatically from decisions made with little if any conscious awareness, but there is a spectrum from apparently automatic actions, subject to slips and lapses, to decisions in which System I cognition begins to merge into System II and a blend of logic and rules is applied with at least some degree of awareness.

Slips and Lapses

Slips or *lapses*[14] typically occur as a result of *attentional capture* or distraction – which may be momentary. Thus, a lapse involves a failure of attention that results in the omission of some intended action, whereas in a slip something is done which was not intended, also because of a failure in attention. Both are typical of learned or familiar sequences of actions, which are usually carried out more or less automatically. Forgetting to switch off the house alarm on returning home is an example of a lapse. Typically this might happen if some minor but unexpected distraction diverted one's attention during the critical period between opening the front door and going to the alarm keyboard. Driving through a stop sign would be an example of a lapse with more serious potential consequences, and again, this would usually be attributable to a moment of distraction in which one's attention was captured by something else. Failing to give a drug that one had intended to administer is an example

---

[14] It is useful to refer to these, collectively, as *slip/lapse or skill-based errors*, to stress that they are of the same general type.

ERRORS   113

of a lapse, and giving an unintended drug, perhaps in substitution for the correct one, is an example of a slip. In the case of Dr Yogasakaran,[15] for example, the error may have been a lapse – one explanation for his having given the wrong drug is that he unintentionally omitted to check because his attention was distracted by the developing emergency.[16] The forgotten baby story also involved a lapse, and we will expand on this example later in the chapter.

Inadvertently adding milk to one's tea a day or two after deciding to give up this practice provides a trivial example of a slip. The tendency to revert from an exceptional or new way of doing things to a well-established routine is a very powerful force in the generation of slips and lapses. Human beings are very inclined to run on automatic pilot whenever possible, operating by the exercise of learned sequences of skilled actions in response to context-specific patterns in their surroundings. Driving home from work after moving from a long-established residence makes this clear – there is a good chance of finding oneself back at the old house without much idea of how one actually got there. Typically, the new route will begin along the same route as the old and well-established way home, but at a particular point it may turn away and proceed along new, unfamiliar roads. A point such as this, in which an active decision needs to be taken, may be thought of as a *decision node*. Driving a car along a well-known route really depends on a combination of declarative and non-declarative memory; most of the time the skills of driving within the constraints of the law, the traffic and the conditions at the time are applied automatically, using non-declarative memory and responding subconsciously to situations recognised as corresponding to pre-stored schemata, but when a decision node is reached, declarative memory is needed and conscious attention is required. Distraction at a decision node will often lead to missing the moment and therefore to an error – typically a lapse.

The distraction, or *attentional capture*, which is a characteristic feature in the genesis of these errors, can involve over-attention as well as inattention. Checking is a process that can break into a sequence of events and cause an operator to lose his or her precise place, with the result that a particular step, which may well have been undertaken correctly if the routine had simply been allowed to run as usual, is either missed or

---

[15] See Chapter 1.
[16] An alternative explanation, discussed in Chapter 2, is that in reading the label he saw the name he expected to see rather than the one that was actually there.

repeated. This can occur with drug administration errors, particularly in certain branches of anaesthesia where, at times, over thirty drug administrations need to be given in one anaesthetic. It is quite possible for one drug to be missed or given twice because the doctor, in pausing to check, loses track of his or her place in a well-established sequence of administrations. Interestingly, Daniel Wegner has demonstrated that simply trying harder to avoid a particular action or thought can, ironically, make that action or thought more likely.[17]

One way or another, it follows that slips and lapses are not necessarily manifestations of carelessness.[18] A resolve always to pay close attention to the many routine but dangerous tasks that form part of one's regular duties is an appropriate response to the obvious need to take care, but such a resolve (on its own) is doomed to failure over any prolonged period of time. We noted in Chapter 2 that the distractibility of human beings is a survival advantage rather than a weakness. Distractibility is a requirement if we are to notice when the house is on fire or when some unexpected event occurs during a surgical operation, and so, at some stage in any prolonged or often-repeated activity, distraction is inevitable – and may occasionally result in an error.

A Hang-gliding Lapse

Several features of slips and lapses are graphically illustrated by an event reported in a daily newspaper.[19] As a Christmas present from his partner, a man had been given an introductory hang-gliding lesson. While the instructor was getting ready, he was momentarily distracted by a puff of wind and failed to secure his harness properly. Putting on his harness would have been, for the expert instructor, an automatic sequence of events, and the effect of a momentary distraction in producing a break in this sequence and precipitating a subsequent failure to complete it properly is typical of

---

[17] D. M. Wegner, *White Bears and Other Unwanted Thoughts: Suppression, Obsession and the Psychology of Mental Control* (New York, The Guilford Press, 1989); D. M. Wegner, 'Ironic processes of mental control' (1994) 101 *Psychological Review* 34–52; D. M. Wegner, M. Ansfiled and D. Pilloff, 'The putt and the pendulum: ironic effects of the mental control of action' (1998) 9 *Psychological Science* 196–9.

[18] For certain important and likely slips or lapses, cognitive aids can be useful. In some circumstances it could be argued that a decision to avoid using a potentially available cognitive aid represents a degree of carelessness. See J. M. Weller and A. F. Merry, 'I. Best practice and patient safety in anaesthesia' (2013) 110 *British Journal of Anaesthesia* 671–3.

[19] A. Horwood, 'Hang this gliding lark says novice after solo flight' (1996) *New Zealand Herald* 1.

a lapse. On launching, the instructor fell some distance, injuring himself – and leaving his pupil to soar out into the sky, alone, on his first ever flight. Fortunately, he too survived, with relatively minor injuries.

This example illustrates several points. The first is the role of distraction in the generation of lapses – the puff of wind, in this case. The second point is that these errors do not necessarily represent *carelessness*. It is inconceivable (short of suicidal intention) that the instructor would not have cared about securing his harness. Similarly, it is reasonable to presume that airline pilots care about avoiding crashes in which they will be leading participants. If care were all that were needed, airline pilots would never make errors (of any type) – but they certainly do: the story of Flight 447 makes this abundantly clear. Obviously carefulness and attention are distinguishable from care in the sense of concern about consequences, but the important conclusion from this example is that deterrence cannot eliminate slips and lapses, or indeed any type of error. Another example illustrating this point is to be found in the case of the observer on a police traffic-spotting plane who walked into a spinning propeller during a fuel stop.[20] There is no suggestion other than that this action on the part of an experienced professional was a lapse. The idea of walking into a propeller on a light aircraft is particularly unpleasant and the hazardous nature of a propeller is very obvious. It is not possible to avoid slips and lapses by choice, by good intention, by strict regulation combined with draconian punishment or by the risk of harm inherent in a dangerous situation; the remedy has to be sought elsewhere, notably in the way systems are designed.

The third point is that slips and lapses are characteristic of experts – in the hang-gliding case it was the instructor, not the pupil, who was subject to the lapse. Indeed, experts make all kinds of errors – the members of the crew on Flight 447 were all expert – but being an expert tends to predispose to slips and lapses and does not necessarily prevent loss of situational awareness or the development of flawed mental models. This point is counter-intuitive, and it often leads to much misunderstanding, especially in the legal and disciplinary proceedings that may follow such errors. It is often said that the person responsible for a slip or a lapse was trained in the field and therefore could have been expected not to make an error, particularly of the very basic sort typical of slips and lapses. Giving a wrong drug is a good example – on the face of it, it seems easy enough to give the right drug, and it is difficult to see why a competent and careful

---

[20] 'Propeller kills traffic observer' (17 February 1996) *New Zealand Herald* 1.

professional would fail in this elementary aspect of the job. It is sometimes even suggested that the money paid to professionals justifies the expectation that errors of this type should not be made, and this view is understandable. It is based, however, on a misconception: namely, that expertise or incentives or threats create a situation in which an individual can suddenly stop being human and, on the basis of choice alone, avoid unintended actions (such as slips or lapses) that occur independently of choice. Experts may reasonably be expected to remain sober and to be attentive, but it is not reasonable to suggest that they should somehow become superhuman and thereby never make an error. Thus, in Chapter 1 we were able to make a distinction between the deliberate neglect by one expert anaesthetist (Dr Manjanatha) of his responsibility to attend to his patient and the accidental administration of the wrong drug (almost certainly a slip/lapse error) by another (Dr Yogasakaran).

It is expertise that makes a difficult and dangerous task possible at all – the instructor was capable of flying a hang-glider, the novice was not. The expert's knowledge is deeper, and more robust, than the novice's, and expertise reduces the likelihood of error overall; there are many reasons for this, but a particularly relevant one is that an expert would have a large number of well-practised rules at his or her disposal and so would be less reliant on error-prone deliberation than a novice; he or she would also have a better understanding of the fundamentals of the subject if System II thinking actually was required. In addition, one component of the development of expertise involves the learning of techniques to counter the risk of particular skill-based errors – the use of a double-checking protocol as advocated after the case of Dr Morrison, for example. In fact, for many competent experts the overall likelihood of making a mistake that results in harm is so low that expectations have become unrealistically high, which contributes to the likelihood of a potentially inappropriate legal response when things do go wrong. However, the fact remains that errors, including skill-based errors, are impossible to eliminate completely; it is unrealistic to assume that, simply on the basis of good intentions, anyone can successfully avoid ever making a slip/lapse error again. These errors are inextricably linked with the way in which the multi-tasking and distractible human mind works. It is the nature of expert activity to rely heavily on automatic skills for the undertaking of several activities simultaneously, while counting on human distractibility to identify and respond to unexpected or new developments. It follows that expert or highly skilled activity actually *predisposes* to slips or lapses at the same time as it reduces (but does not eliminate) the chances of other types of error.

Finally, the hang-gliding example clearly illustrates the very powerful influence of outcome on the judgement of an action. Because nobody was seriously injured, the matter was treated as worthy of little more than an amusing newspaper article. Had the pupil died, it is very likely that the instructor's lapse would have been subject to much stronger criticism.[21] There may be a pragmatic justification for reserving the resources needed to undertake a detailed investigation of an event for those situations in which serious harm has occurred – but, as discussed above, there is no rational justification for judging the culpability of an act by the severity of its unintended consequences. On the contrary, the argument that dangerous activities warrant a high level of care – which we fully accept – is in fact a reason to investigate those close calls in which the outcome is fortunate just as closely as events in which it is disastrous.[22]

Calls for Help

Slips and lapses are not only the province of the professional – they are a feature of everyday life. This is made clear in another example from the daily papers. It was reported that the fire brigade was receiving a surprisingly high number of calls to burning houses in which the wrong addresses were being given. It transpired that the callers were people who had recently moved home and that the wrong addresses were in fact those of their former residences. This is very similar to the example of driving home to a previously occupied house and not knowing how one has got there. As with the hang-gliding story, however, it does make clear the fact that this type of error does not represent carelessness. These people must have cared – that was why they were telephoning for help. It is even harder to construe their failure in terms of carelessness than in the case of the hang-gliding instructor. These were people whose whole attention was focused on communicating their need for help – and yet they were getting the information wrong. The deterrence of losing their house by failing to give the correct address did nothing to prevent their

---

[21] Tragically, similar events have subsequently occurred with fatal results and consequent prosecution and conviction for manslaughter: 'Kiwi hang-glider pilot jailed over fatal flight', New Zealand Herald (12 February 2014) www.nzherald.co.nz/news/print.cfm?objectid=11200684, accessed 1 December 2015.

[22] In practice, it is not affordable to investigate every near miss in detail. In healthcare today, it is common for incident reports to be assessed on the basis of their potential consequences as well as their actual consequences. Those with potential (or actual) consequences that are sufficiently serious and sufficiently likely to recur are then investigated more thoroughly.

error and, from the opposite perspective, the possible reward of saving their home was equally ineffective in modifying their behaviour. Again, a systems-oriented approach would be more likely to produce an effective solution than simply trying to modify people's behaviour. For example, advances in technology have made it possible for emergency services of this type to obtain and record automatically the locations from which callers are telephoning. This is an effective response to the problem, using technology to compensate for the failings inherent in human cognition.[23]

Forgotten Babies

We began this book with the tragic story of a young mother who left her baby in the back of her car while she went into work, completely unaware of what she was doing. This rather extended series of events involved a lapse with the unusual feature that it appears to have been a prolonged lapse. In fact, there was probably only one momentary error – the mother's failure to take the turn off to the crèche. This is a classic lapse, exactly equivalent to absentmindedly driving to one's old home after moving house. At the decision node (the turn off), it seems that the mother was distracted by her thoughts of the coming day's work. The moment came and went without being noticed. It made no impact on her conscious mind. Had this lapse involved failing to put sugar in her tea, for example, she would have identified it moments later, at the first sip. In this case, hours passed before she received any feedback from her error. During this time she retained as her working mental model the normal sequence of events on any other day – on arriving at work she would not normally look in the back of the car, because there would be no need – her baby would have been dropped off at the crèche, not sitting in the car seat. She would normally just get out of the car and go into the building, so that is what she did. She would not normally carry out any other checks about the baby, because the baby would be safely at the crèche, and she could rely on the staff to call her if need be. This day (and it seems probable that it was a busy day) must have felt to her like any other day at work, and there would be nothing about it that would make her even think about her child, or if she did (perhaps recalling a pleasant moment from earlier in the week or anticipating a plan for the weekend) there would be no reason for the thoughts to be about whether her child

---

[23] The advent of widespread use of mobile phones (a further advance in technology) has, ironically, made it more difficult to track the location of a caller.

might need her. There was nothing to trigger an alarm bell in her mind until she received the first text from the crèche. So, although the story has a feel of a prolonged and persistent failure, it almost certainly hinges on a single, momentary lapse, from which everything else followed without the need for additional errors (or violations). As to the mother's first response to the text, it seems that this message must have been ambiguous. We have outlined the importance of failures in communication in healthcare in Chapter 2, and this story illustrates how easily these can occur. It can be seen that the mother might draw a very different interpretation from a message like 'we wonder why you have not dropped your baby off today' than from one that said something like 'is your baby OK?'[24] Her response (she texted back to ask if her baby was unwell) strongly suggests that she interpreted the text to imply that her baby was at the crèche, but possibly unwell.

Once again we can see that carelessness was not a factor here, in the sense of caring about something – it is hard to imagine something that a mother would care about more than the welfare of her child. Even if the word 'careless' is interpreted as 'taking care' in the context of the specific instance, there was evidence of taking care as well – in the careful placing of the child in an approved rear facing car seat. It is also relevant that chance (or, at the least, events that were unforeseeable) played an important role in the tragic outcome of this momentary lapse (we enlarged on this point in Chapter 1).

A final point brought out by this story is the striking similarity that can be seen in the characteristic features of errors generated by the same underlying cognitive processes, even if at first appearance they seem very different. In the hang-gliding story, the phone calls for help, driving home to a new house, the drug error of Dr Morrison and the story of the forgotten baby we see (to varying degrees) an element of self-interest[25] to motivate carefulness, expertise, routine activity, decision nodes and distraction – all culminating in lapses. In the case of

---

[24] The content of the actual text message is not in the public domain, so these are speculative examples to illustrate a point. It is, incidentally, also interesting to reflect on the increased reliance placed on text messages by many people today, and on the difference a brief telephone conversation might have made.

[25] To avoid doubt, notwithstanding the fact that patients are the primary victims of medical error, there is good reason to believe that considerable self-interest motivates the avoidance of error by doctors: the potential professional and legal consequences of error are considerable. See, for example, W. Cunningham and S. Dovey, 'The effect on medical practice of disciplinary complaints: potentially negative for patient care' (2000) 113 *New Zealand Medical Journal* 464–7.

Dr Yogasakaran, these elements are once again all present, but with the additional components of time pressure, look-alike ampoules and the stress of an emergency as well.

Technical Errors

Runciman and his colleagues have delineated a particular variation of error, common in medicine, which they have called 'technical errors'.[26] These errors do involve actions and skill, but they are quite different in nature from slips and lapses. These authors give the example of failing to place an epidural catheter correctly, in such a way that the needle is inserted too far, causing the complication of a dural tap,[27] or in such a way that the correct space is not entered and no block results. The plan and choice of technique are appropriate, no slip or lapse occurs and there is also no suggestion of a violation – but there is a failure to carry out the intended action successfully.

Two factors contribute to these errors. The first is patient variability. Runciman's group refers to this problem as 'under-specification of the task', by which they mean that any abnormality in the anatomy of a patient may be unknown and unknowable. If every practitioner produced the same result in the same circumstances, then one would have to conclude that the adverse event was due to circumstances beyond any practitioner's control.

This is not the case, however, because of the second factor, which is the variability of the skill and knowledge of individual practitioners. Skill in this context is learned, and reflects the non-declarative procedural memory built up by an individual through practice, as well as innate ability. Skill varies, both from one practitioner to another, and also in the same practitioner on different days, or perhaps at different times of day and night and in the presence of different levels of fatigue. Thus, the incidence of dural taps differs between anaesthetists. In general, the frequency of this complication diminishes with increasing training, experience and skill of the operator. It is never possible to eliminate the problem

---

[26] W. B. Runciman, A. Sellen, R. K. Webb, J. A. Williamson, M. Currie, C. Morgan and W. J. Russell, 'The Australian Incident Monitoring Study. Errors, incidents and accidents in anaesthetic practice' (1993) 21 *Anaesthesia & Intensive Care* 506–19.

[27] In a dural tap, the needle penetrates too deeply and pierces the *dura mater* – the membrane surrounding the spinal cord and encapsulating the cerebrospinal fluid. A leak of cerebrospinal fluid ensues, with various potential consequential complications.

altogether, and some practitioners seem to perform better in this regard than others, even when they are all fully trained and equally experienced.

Another example from sport may help us to understand the issues involved with technical errors. A weekend golfer will set out to drive the ball straight down the fairway, but will often fail to achieve this goal. The failure will generally occur despite an appropriate decision, and in the absence of a slip or a lapse. The task is just too difficult. Note that it is not too difficult for even an average golfer to hit a good drive occasionally. The difficulty lies in doing it over and over again. This point was well illustrated in a recent series of tests undertaken for an article in a golfing magazine. A professional golfer, a player with a handicap of seven (a strong amateur player) and one with a handicap of fourteen (an average golfer, who was said to play twice a week) were asked to perform the same tasks. In the driving test, the first drive of the fourteen-handicapper was accurate (landing on the fairway) and very nearly as long as the professional's. However, the professional hit only one out of ten drives into the rough, against four out of ten on the part of each of the amateurs.[28]

We referred earlier in this chapter to Wegner's work on the ironic control of the mind.[29] Trying to avoid a particular action may often make that action more rather than less likely. Any golfer who has hit a ball into water while concentrating intensely on avoiding this particular outcome will understand this aspect of the way our minds work – in the context of golf, water, trees, course boundaries and other prominent hazards appear to emanate a mysterious attraction for the ball. Concentrating on avoiding them often seems to produce exactly the opposite effect. In a similar way, focusing very hard on avoiding a dural tap may, ironically, make the dural tap more likely. It seems that an increase in expertise may mitigate this aspect of the way the mind works, perhaps through focusing on the attainment of success rather than on the avoidance of failure.[30] Once again we see that the factors that influence the outcome of any given human endeavour may not all be obvious.

In this analogy, one might hope that health practitioners would be more like *professional* golfers than amateurs. This may often be true in the context of specialist practice, but much medical practice is generalist,

[28] P. Masters, 'How much better are the pros?' (2000) 41 *Golf World* 112–21.
[29] See footnote 17.
[30] This idea is integral to the notion of 'Safety-II'. See J. Braithwaite, R. L. Wears and E. Hollnagel, 'Resilient health care: turning patient safety on its head' (2015) 27 *International Journal of Quality in Health Care* 418–20; E. Hollnagel, *Safety-I and Safety-II: The Past and Future of Safety Management* (Aldershot, Ashgate, 2014).

and even in specialist practice the problems faced by practitioners are highly diverse and often quite rare, and therefore often unfamiliar. Rates of success do tend to reflect deliberate practice[31] in doing the same thing over and over again, so it is not surprising the success rate of professional golfers is very good, but even professionals fail to hit the fairway on occasion – as demonstrated in the above test. There is also a difference between professionals. A few stand out as more consistently successful than the majority, even though the majority perform very well indeed. Many factors contribute to these differences.[32] In the same way, returning to the subject of epidurals, some anaesthetists experience more dural taps than others. Can these extra taps be characterised as errors? An alternative view might be to treat them as evidence of technical incompetence. In either case it is generally agreed that, if an individual practitioner's rate of any complication is 'too high', some intervention is called for, such as additional training or redeployment into a less technically demanding field. Thus, the categorisation of these events as errors or as reflecting inadequate technical competence is essentially normative, and tends to depend on their rate over time rather than on the features of any single occasion. The difficulty lies in knowing where to draw the line – an issue we shall consider further in Chapter 7.

Apply these thoughts to surgery. Many cardiac surgical units experience a certain mortality rate for first-time coronary artery surgery – possibly about 1 per cent. In some the rate is higher; in some it is a little lower. Part of this variation relates to differences in the characteristics of the different patient populations, but at least some of it relates to other factors. Clearly, a major contribution to the incidence of the complication of death in these patients comes from the skills of the surgeon, the anaesthetist, the intensive-care specialists, and from the overall standards of the unit in which these specialists work.[33]

In the highly publicised Medical Council proceedings involving cardiac surgery in Bristol, the performance of the surgeons concerned seems

[31] R. H. Hastings and T. C. Rickard, 'Deliberate practice for achieving and maintaining expertise in anesthesiology' (2015) 120 *Anesthesia & Analgesia* 449–59.

[32] D. Z. Hambrick, E. M. Altmann, F. L. Oswald, E. J. Meinz and F. Gobet, 'Facing facts about deliberate practice' (2014) 5 *Frontiers in Psychology* 751.

[33] G. T. O'Connor, S. K. Plume, E. M. Olmstead, L. H. Coffin, J. R. Morton, C. T. Maloney, ... J. E. Wennberg, 'A regional prospective study of in-hospital mortality associated with coronary artery bypass grafting' (1991) 266 *Journal of the American Medical Association* 803–9; A. F. Merry, M. C. Ramage, R. M. L. Whitlock, G. J. A. Laycock, W. Smith, D. Stenhouse and C. J. Wild, 'First-time coronary artery bypass grafting: the anaesthetist as a risk factor' (1992) 68 *British Journal of Anaesthesia* 6–12.

to have fallen below an acceptable standard, although questions have been asked about the possible contribution to the Bristol unit's results of other members of the team.[34] It is only fair to the surgeons to note that the technical skill associated with the successful conduct of paediatric cardiac surgery is very high indeed. It seems probable that poor results in this type of situation would be attributable, at least in part, to inadequacies of surgical technique. However, these inadequacies can be judged only in relation to the performance of other institutions undertaking the same work. If the results of all units in paediatric cardiac surgery had been similar to Bristol's, the same level of performance would have to be accepted as the best that could be done at the time. Similar comments apply to other disciplines. For example, one of the challenges of specialist anaesthetic, intensive care and emergency medicine practice lies in the potential for the development of unmanageable problems with patients' airways, leading to hypoxemia. These feared events are very rare, so individual practitioners are unlikely to encounter them more than once or twice in a career. Nevertheless, a recent major audit showed, amongst other things, that brain damage and death from this cause still occurs disconcertingly often in a country the size of the UK, typically in patients who would otherwise be expected to do well, and with variation in rate that suggests a considerable difference in capability between these three specialist groups in the anticipation and management of these dangerous and challenging problems.[35] There is, of course, also variation in the abilities of individuals within each of these disciplines, and in the difficulty presented by different patients. The line between notions of insurmountable challenge, error in the context of competence and frank incompetence may be quite difficult to draw.

It can be seen, then, that technical errors are an important category of error in medical practice. Given that specialists are being called upon to undertake increasingly difficult and hazardous procedures, often in association with excessive workloads and limited resources, technical challenges are likely to be even more prominent in the future. It is likely to be

---

[34] See Chapter 1. The importance of teamwork for the outcomes of surgery is discussed in Chapter 2.

[35] T. M. Cook, N. Woodall and C. Frerk, 'Major complications of airway management in the UK: Results of the Fourth National Audit Project of the Royal College of Anaesthetists and the Difficult Airway Society. Part 1: Anaesthesia' (2011) 106 *British Journal of Anaesthesia* 617–31; T. M. Cook, N. Woodall, J. Harper and J. Benger, 'Major complications of airway management in the UK: Results of the Fourth National Audit Project of the Royal College of Anaesthetists and the Difficult Airway Society. Part 2: intensive care and emergency departments' (2011) 106 *British Journal of Anaesthesia* 632–42.

very difficult to evaluate the degree of blame due when a generally competent individual who tries conscientiously to undertake a technically challenging procedure fails to succeed in an individual case. This situation may be highly analogous to that of a golf shot that an otherwise very successful professional golfer just happens on one occasion to hit out of bounds. On the other hand, this analogy may not adequately reflect the point that some of the potentially lethal and technically difficult challenges faced in healthcare are seen quite infrequently by any individual practitioner. Either way, while the golfer is judged on his total score for the competition, and indeed on his overall performance over many years, a surgeon or anaesthetist faced with a dead or injured patient may (understandably) have a hard time explaining what went wrong. In particular, any prosecution for negligence would focus on the isolated failure and discount the doctor's many previous successes.[36]

Rule-based Errors

Rule-based errors involve some failure in the process by which a set of circumstances is recognised and an appropriate rule applied. This failure might occur because the pattern of events is incorrectly recognised and interpreted.[37] The overall mental model may be flawed, or it may be sound but the pattern may be matched to an inappropriate schema stored in memory, or an appropriate schema may trigger the application of a wrong or inadequate rule.

Many decisions in medicine are made by *frequency gambling*. Frequency gambling, like skill-based activity, is typical of experts, often

---

[36] An example can be found in an event, known to one of us (AM), in which a highly competent cardiac surgeon inadvertently and uncharacteristically left a clamp in place for too long during a difficult operation in a child with a complex cardiac abnormality. The baby died, leaving its mother understandably devastated. The police initiated criminal proceedings and at least one court hearing took place before all charges were withdrawn. See footnote 34 in P. P.D. G. Skegg, 'Criminal prosecutions of negligent health professionals: the New Zealand experience' (1998) 6 *Medical Law Review* 220–46.

[37] Note again that deficiencies in the knowledge base may explain some rule-based errors. The interpretation of any situation involves the formation of a schema that in effect synthesises its key elements into a manageable representation that is also *framed* from a certain perspective: for example, the same set of facts may be interpreted differently if (amongst other sources of information) it includes comments from a trusted friend on the one hand or a despised enemy on the other. Many a statement has been made in haste and regretted at leisure because of a rule-based response to a situation in which framing contributed to emotion.

in the context of heavy workloads. The essential idea expressed by this term is that people tend to choose a rule known to have worked on many previous occasions in more or less the current circumstances, without necessarily establishing beyond doubt that the circumstances really are equivalent to those in which the rule was previously applied. Doctors are taught to work in this way and the concept has been encapsulated in the adage 'When you see hoof prints, think of horses, not zebras'. The difficulty is to know precisely when to look more closely in case the animal actually *is* a zebra! Thus, a general practitioner faced with a pyrexial and unwell patient might diagnose influenza on the basis that he or she had seen ten cases of this illness in the previous two days, in all of whom many of the same features were present. In doing this, the doctor runs the risk of missing distinguishing but less obvious features – neck stiffness or a purpuric rash, for example – which might warn of the possibility of the more serious but less common condition of meningo-coccal infection. An excessive amount of work may create pressure to resort to frequency gambling; thus a usually conscientious practitioner, exhausted by the demands of an influenza epidemic, might be tempted to provide advice over the telephone, late at night, in the belief that he or she is dealing with yet another case of 'flu', instead of insisting on seeing the patient in order to undertake a full physical examination. Frequency gambling usually works, and may allow a practitioner to cope with a heavier load than would otherwise be possible. Indeed, to some degree most medical diagnosis involves frequency gambling – the main variable being the depth of enquiry which precedes any decision. In this example, a careful practitioner would formally eliminate neck stiffness to rule out meningitis, and might perhaps also look for specific signs of various other conditions. Blood tests and a chest radiograph might be considered, as well as a lumbar puncture. At some stage, however, a halt must be called, and a diagnosis made on the basis that any alternatives not yet fully eliminated are too unlikely to warrant the expense and additional risk to the patient entailed in the further investigations that would be required to rule them out completely. The precise point at which this halt is called will depend on the circumstances, but also on the training and experience of the individual practitioner. Typically, it is the more experienced doctor who does the fewer tests, but it is also the more experienced doctor who (usually) knows precisely when the extra test is indicated. For most doctors the response to a given clinical situation will involve the use of a rule or set of rules, but the complexity and robustness of the rules, and the degree to which their use is reinforced by System II deliberation, may vary substantially.[38]

The types of error possible in rule-based processing are relatively limited in variety and reasonably predictable from identifiable inadequacies in the rules themselves and in the ways in which rules are selected. We have already discussed the fact that the strength with which a rule is likely to present itself for selection depends on a number of factors, some of which do not necessarily promote rational decisions. Rules which have been used frequently and recently will be more attractive than those which have lain dormant for a long time. A rule which has produced an unusual but highly adverse result may be eschewed, quite irrationally, on an emotional basis; thus, doctors often change their practice because of one bad experience with a certain treatment, even though the logic of the situation might suggest that this experience was a rare event unlikely to be repeated.

As indicated in Chapter 2, prejudice is a powerful factor in the making of decisions, notably – but by no means only – in rule-based decisions.[39] To the extent that System II thinking is conscious, and people can monitor themselves for evidence of bias, it might be thought that prejudice is most important when System I thinking is at play. However, subconscious prejudice can often influence System II thinking as well. Few people truly appreciate all of the factors that influence their decisions.[40] In healthcare, ethnicity is a powerful determinant of outcome.[41] There are many reasons for this, but prejudice is

---

[38] A tragic illustration of these points is to be found in the death of a fourth year medical student in 2009 in Auckland; the student was admitted to the emergency department of Auckland City Hospital during an influenza epidemic; there were delays in his full assessment and the initiation of treatment, and he subsequently died of meningococcal septicaemia. Frequency gambling is deeply embedded in medical practice, for the reasons outlined, but it is potentially very dangerous. See 'DHB pays out family over meningitis death', New Zealand Herald (27 June 2013) www.radionz.co.nz/news/national/138702/dhb-pays-out-family-over-meningitis-death, accessed 2 December 2015.

[39] M. Gladwell, *Blink. The Power of Thinking Without Thinking* (New York, Little, Brown and Company, 2005); R. Thaler and C. Sunstein, *Nudge: Improving Decisions About Health, Wealth and Happiness* (New Haven, Connecticut, Yale University Press, 2008); Kahneman, Thinking, Fast and Slow; R. H. Thouless, *Straight and Crooked Thinking* (London, Pan Books, 1953).

[40] It can be very illuminating to take a few Implicit Association Tests. See https://implicit.harvard.edu/implicit/takeatest.html.

[41] K. Pickett and R. Wilkinson, *The Spirit Level* (New York, Bloomsbury Press, 2009). J. M. McWilliams, E. Meara, A. M. Zaslavsky and J. Z. Ayanian, 'Differences in control of cardiovascular disease and diabetes by race, ethnicity, and education: US trends from 1999 to 2006 and effects of medicare coverage. [Summary for patients in Ann Intern Med.

unquestionably one of them. Importantly, these same factors influence those who implement society's legal and regulatory processes, from police officers to the judiciary (we return to this issue in Chapter 9).[42] Patients' access to means of redress for harm experienced in healthcare may also vary by ethnicity and by indicators of deprivation, even in countries (like New Zealand) where complaints processes are freely available, without any need to retain the services of lawyers.[43]

The control of rule-based activity is referred to as *feed-forward*; this implies that rules are applied with objectives in mind, on the basis of previous experiences in similar circumstances. Thus, situations may arise in which it is believed that a particular objective (the patient's safety, for example) will be achieved by the use of a particular rule – but in which the conviction with which that rule is selected is quite misplaced; this phenomenon is referred to as the application of a 'strong but wrong' rule.

Experts are not immune from making rule-based errors, but rule-based errors become less likely with increasing expertise, because experts develop better and more comprehensive sets of rules with a wider range of stored patterns (based on experience) to use in selecting the appropriate rule. This process of acquiring a larger repertoire of more robust rules also increases the possible range of activities. In the end, the only way many activities can be carried out at all is by the use of rule-based performance. One aspect of expertise lies in reducing the need to resort to deliberative cognitive processing by having rules for almost all circumstances – it is this that permits doctors (and other experts, whether in healthcare or many other fields) to cope with heavy workloads in reasonable time.

As noted above, rule-based cognitive processing seldom takes place in a pure way, isolated from subconscious exercise of skills that depend on

2009 Apr 21;150(8):I-26; PMID: 19380848]' (2009) 150 *Annals of Internal Medicine* 505–15; A. J. Kerr, A. McLachlan, S. Furness, J. Broad, T. Riddell, R. Jackson and S. Wells, 'The burden of modifiable cardiovascular risk factors in the coronary care unit by age, ethnicity, and socioeconomic status–PREDICT CVD-9' (2008) 121 *New Zealand Medical Journal* 20–33.

42 C. T. Ross, 'A Multi-Level Bayesian Analysis of Racial Bias in Police Shootings at the County-Level in the United States, 2011–2014' (2015) 10 *PLoS ONE [Electronic Resource]* e0141854; O. Quick, 'Medical Manslaughter and expert evidence: the roles of context and character', in D. Griffiths and A. Sanders (eds.), *Bioethics, Medicine and the Criminal Law*, vol. 11 (Cambridge, Cambridge University Press, 2013).

43 M. M. Bismark, T. A. Brennan, R. J. Paterson, P. B. Davis and D. M. Studdert, 'Relationship between complaints and quality of care in New Zealand: a descriptive analysis of complainants and non-complainants following adverse events' (2006) 15 *Quality and Safety in Health Care* 17–22.

non-declarative memory and more self-aware processes that involve System II cognition. Rules are usually developed by the passive mechanisms associated with experience, but they may be improved, added to and even generated by slow and conscious System II thinking. Thus, at one end of the scale, reasoning from first principles may be used to develop rules and to select, check and support the application of the best rule, and at the other, rules may be applied 'on the fly' to direct and control automatic, skilled technical activities.

In our example of a general practitioner evaluating a pyrexial patient, it is important to understand that pattern recognition is fundamental to diagnosis, but that the full spectrum of cognitive processing is typically involved. In fact, reaching a point of comfort that the relevant pattern has been recognised may often seem to be a slow process rather than a fast one. Much time is taken in identifying the necessary elements of the knowledge base to build up the relevant schemata, within an overarching mental model, to test against stored patterns representing different medical conditions. Interestingly, first impressions are very powerful and often (but not always) correct.[44] System II thinking serves to monitor the process and test and refine one's confidence in the correctness of the recognised pattern. However, this System II thinking may go wrong for many reasons, as discussed in the next section. Also, selected rules may turn out to be flawed (because of inadequate training, or inexperience, or because of unsuccessful frequency gambling), or a lapse might result in the failure to apply a rule at the right time. A moment's distraction, for example, might lead the normally careful practitioner to omit one step of her usual examination without realising it, and as a result she might miss information that she would normally elicit (the sign of neck stiffness in relation to meningitis, for example). And, of course, timeliness may be critical, and this factor may be obvious, or deceptive – as in the tragic example of the medical student admitted with meningitis alongside many other patients with influenza.[45]

Errors Associated with System II Cognition[46]

System II thinking is slow, works logically from first principles and uses induction or deduction rather than pattern recognition. In System II

---

[44] Gladwell, Blink.   [45] See footnote 40.

[46] These are Reason's 'knowledge based errors'; in the first edition of this book we called these 'errors of deliberation'.

thinking, progress is often tentative and controlled by feedback from the results of each action, iteratively, on the basis of trial and error. This is in contrast to rule-based reasoning, in which (as we have seen) control is feed-forward and goals can be achieved fairly assuredly on the basis of applying a rule known from past experience to be correct.

Many rules used in everyday life concern exceptions that simply don't make sense from a logical perspective. Much of the physical world is relatively resistant to logic, or to the process of arguing from apparent facts and principles to a conclusion that ought to be right. To a large extent this reflects limitations on the information that is available to any individual at any particular time. This is the concept of bounded rationality, discussed in Chapter 2. Typically, the information available for solving a problem is incomplete, the facts to hand may not be the most useful and some may not even be correct. The deficiencies may lie in the knowledge stored in memory or in the knowledge available from the events and circumstances of a situation. The analogy of a blackboard full of facts but only partly illuminated was used in Chapter 2 to illustrate this idea. It is because of the importance of deficiencies in knowledge in the generation of errors during active reasoning that the term 'knowledge-based errors' has been applied to them, but, as we have said, problems with the 'knowledge base' are just as likely to contribute to rule-based errors. A person whose perception of a situation is inadequately informed is equally likely to apply a rule (which will probably be the wrong rule) as to resort to deliberative reasoning to reach a solution (which is also likely to be the wrong solution in the circumstances). Also, as explained, it is common for both cognitive systems to be employed in parallel. Whichever system is in play, the consequences of a faulty knowledge base may be compounded by a developing – and increasingly faulty – appreciation of a particular situation built progressively on a sequence of incorrect conclusions.[47] The distinguishing feature of errors of System II thinking is the slow, deliberative, feedback nature of the processing involved. This type of reasoning is a powerful process by which even extremely difficult problems can be solved, but only if there is adequate time, and only if a trial-and-error approach can be tolerated. The process involves formulating an idea, testing it, finding it to be imperfect (or in error), modifying the idea, retesting it and so on. Because it is an *error-driven* process, it follows that System II thinking will inevitably be prone to error, especially at an early stage in the iterative

[47] See the discussion of confirmation bias in Chapter 2.

process of working towards a satisfactory solution to a problem, and particularly in unfamiliar circumstances. The implications of this for the management of a crisis are very important, and will be considered below.

Scientists have recognised the difficulties of finding correct answers to problems on the basis of theoretical reasoning alone. They have developed the process known as 'scientific method' to allow for the inconvenient intrusions of what *does* happen into what *ought to* happen. Scientific method is a highly developed and formalised example of System II reasoning, illustrating particularly well the feedback nature of this type of cognitive processing. This method involves stating a hypothesis derived from logical interpretation of the observed facts, which form the knowledge base at that point in time, and then testing this hypothesis by experimentation. The feedback from these experiments either supports the hypothesis or adds new information to the knowledge base that allows the hypothesis to be refined and then tested again. This process produces an iteratively updated and increasingly useful hypothesis, but few hypotheses explain all the observed data in all situations, and so, as new facts continue to emerge, the process of refinement continues to be needed. In this way science has developed from Newton's observation of a falling apple to modern theories of nuclear physics. In healthcare, the translation of knowledge from established biological principles to clinical practice through experiments in animals, healthy volunteers and finally sick patients is fraught with uncertainty. The randomised controlled trial is considered by many to be the 'gold standard' of establishing the value of a new therapy.[48] The net effect of iteratively collecting and interpreting data in this slow and effortful way has unquestionably proven very powerful in advancing knowledge in medicine.[49] In a similar way, but less formally, a decision or plan formulated in daily life by effortful reasoning from known facts and principles will be tested against the results of its implementation, and then refined and tested again. One of the results of such activity is an increase in an individual's store of rules. Iterative deliberation adds knowledge

---

[48] For an alternative view see A. F. Merry, J. M. Davies and J. R. Maltby, 'Editorial III. Qualitative research in health care' (2000) 84 *British Journal of Anaesthesia* 552–5.

[49] However, some of the conclusions from apparently sound randomised controlled trials subsequently turn out to be incorrect. See, for example, J. P. Ioannidis, 'Why most published research findings are false' (2005) 2 *PLoS Medicine/Public Library of Science* e124. Another difficulty relates to knowing how far it is valid to apply the results of studies of particular groups of patients to the management of individuals who may or may not have much in common with the sample studied. For these and other reasons, many decisions in healthcare have to be made on an uncertain knowledge base.

that we can formulate into schemata or heuristics, to which we can return in the future without the need to repeat the processes by which they were derived.

It has sometimes been suggested that the quality of decision-making in medicine could be improved by applying Bayesian principles in a formal way – in a sense, the ultimate application of System II thinking.[50] For example, applying decision theory might involve allocating ten points to one possible outcome of therapy and a hundred to another, and then multiplying each by the probability of its occurrence. Doing this for each of two different methods of treatment would provide an allegedly objective estimate of their relative utility. In this way an attempt could be made to be systematic in formulating all decisions. Computers could facilitate the calculations, and have been used to aid in diagnosis. However, there are many difficulties in this approach. Bayesian logic requires prior knowledge of the likelihood of the outcomes from different interventions, and in practice this is often missing. Also, the importance placed on various possible outcomes is highly subjective. How does one quantify the difference between losing a limb and losing one's life, for example? In the end the most powerful barrier to the use of formal decision theory in medicine is that humans very much prefer to work by rule-based pattern matching rather than by effortful deliberation – humans are simply not inherently Bayesian. We vastly prefer to use a combination of intuition and heuristics to formal logic. It seems that even many professional statisticians tend to resort to heuristics that are inherently unreliable rather than carry out the formal calculations that would be required to make objectively rational decisions.[51]

Errors of Judgement

When things go wrong in medicine it is quite common for a mistake to be called an error of judgement. In order to exercise judgement, at least some degree of conscious thought is required – for a decision that is entirely subconscious, no judgement is involved. Thus, alleged errors of judgement typically arise in the context of decisions made with slow thinking in relation to relatively complex situations.

---

[50] D. L. Sackett, W. S. Richardson, W. Rosenberg and R. B. Haynes, *Evidence Based Medicine* (New York, Churchill Livingstone, 1997), 99–104.
[51] This theme is discussed in detail in Kahneman, *Thinking, Fast and Slow*.

This term is often used when the decision in question might have produced its desired goal, but didn't. People are often credited with good judgement when things work out well, even if the odds were against a good outcome and chance just happens to have had an influence on events.[52] Either way, outcome is a poor guide to the quality of a decision. A perfectly rational decision on the basis of the facts known at the time may not produce the desired result. This can be seen in examples of betting. It would be perfectly rational to take a bet on the chance of winning $3 if tails comes up or losing $1 for heads on a single toss of a fair coin – but one might still lose. One might argue against betting at all, but many decisions that have to be made in medicine are essentially of this type, in that they contain an element of uncertainty and that their outcome is to some degree unknowable. The question, then, should not be 'Did this decision turn out well?' It should be 'Could a better decision have reasonably been made without the benefit of hindsight?' The term 'error of judgement' is often used normatively to suggest that an individual's judgement tends to reflect a level of willingness to take risks different from those thought appropriate by the commentator, or perhaps by a group of colleagues.

Given our definition of the term 'error', a decision should be called an error only if the process by which it was made in the light of the information reasonably available at the time can be shown to have been unsound, perhaps because of a fault in logic or because of a deficiency in the information actually used as the knowledge base from which to form the mental model. If the decision was objectively faulty, there would be no distinction between an error of judgement and any other type of mistake. However, the evaluation of these errors is typically subjective. Somewhat circularly, a decision tends to be called an error of judgement primarily because it is *judged* to be an error by those who believe something different should have been done.[53] The Bolam principle (to which we shall return in Chapter 6) allows for differences in opinion between doctors, but (as we shall see) more recent decisions by the courts in Australia and the United Kingdom have set limits to the principle that it is a sufficient defence to have the support of a body of medical opinion (regardless of the size of that body). The courts have asserted their right to determine, not what *would* have been done by a reasonable

---

[52] At any rate, it is unusual to be criticised if things work out well, in part because scrutiny is less likely.

[53] Many of the examples of faulty heuristics for risk assessment discussed by Kahneman (see footnote 30) are of this type: objectively faulty, and therefore (at least arguably) errors.

practitioner (or even the majority of reasonable practitioners), but what *should* have been done. In other words, decisions taken by medical practitioners have been judged to be wrong even though they have had the support of other doctors. Thus, in *Rogers* v. *Whittaker* (a case involving an ophthalmologist and informed consent), for example, in awarding damages against the doctor, the court could be said to have concluded that he had made an error of judgement in failing to inform the patient of a material risk.[54] Arguably, this conclusion was predicated on little more than the judgement (i.e. the opinion) of the judge; given that this verdict was a departure from precedent, it is difficult to argue that the doctor made an error on the basis of the information available to him at the time, including his understanding of the norms of practice and expectations of the courts up to that time (whatever one's view of informed consent today). This is not to suggest that a judge should refrain from the exercise of judgement, particularly in light of evolution in the values of society. The point here is simply that, when judgement is concerned, it may be very difficult to distinguish between a matter that is no more than a difference of opinion and one that can justifiably be called an error.

It is tempting to suggest that there is really no such thing as an error of judgement – either a decision is an error or it is not. However, the exercise of judgement plays an important role in medicine (as it does in the law). Soundness of judgement is one of the attributes by which peers are evaluated. In practice, it seems to us that judgement is essentially the formation of an opinion on a matter that is open to differences of opinion. Arguably, when the answer is clear, no judgement is required – all reasonable opinions should align. Nevertheless, some opinions do seem better able to stand the test of time than others. Also, although we stand by our position that outcome should not be a key factor in the definition of error, some people do seem to make successful judgements more consistently than others. We come back to the idea that any evaluation of the soundness of judgement is at best normative, and at worst simply, in itself, a matter of opinion – and it can sometimes be very difficult to know who is correct when conscientiously formed opinions differ.[55] Evaluations, based on the collective consensus of a group of experts, of an individual's overall exercise of judgement are often more defensible than any one individual's evaluation of another person's

---

[54] [1957] 2 All ER 118. This case and the *Bolam* principle are discussed in more detail in Chapter 6.

[55] Again, the numerous examples provided by Kahneman show that decisions are far from objectively rational; see footnote 13.

judgement in a single instance.[56] Furthermore, as we have said, if judgement is to be evaluated in relation to an individual event, it is essential that the decision is considered on the basis of the facts available at the time rather than its outcome – but in practice, as we shall see in Chapters 6 and 7, there is a high risk that any such evaluation will be influenced by outcome bias.

Variations, Gradations and Overlaps

We have described the different types of error in such a way as to emphasise the distinguishing features and the underlying cognitive processes involved. However, the external features of an event may reveal little about the underlying mechanisms of an error, and differentiation between classes of error may be made more difficult by the way in which humans switch from one type of cognitive process to another, conducting several activities concurrently.[57] Thus, the classification of an error may depend on the honesty and accuracy of the account of his or her mental processes given by the person concerned.

Consider Perrow's ship captain, whose disastrous collision with another ship is outlined in Chapter 2. What type of error was involved in this accident? It is tempting to suggest a lapse, but in fact the evidence suggests that he was not distracted and actually had his mind focused on the task in hand and was thinking about his actions quite carefully. The fundamental problem was a flawed mental representation of events. This was precipitated by a failure in the information on which he was basing his analysis of the situation (the incorrect perception that there were only two lights instead of three). The final decision was probably the result of a synthesis of System I and System II thinking (as is often the case). The captain recognised the significance of the lights (using rule-based, System I thinking) but with the wrong visual information (seeing two when there were actually three); he analysed the data on the radar screen with correct logic (effortful, System II thinking) but faulty information, the faultiness being reinforced by confirmation bias. Finally, he made a wrong decision and turned, probably on the basis of applying a rule on the fly (System I thinking again). This rule would have worked

---

[56] The corollary of this is that clinical decisions requiring judgement can be better defended if made in consultation with an appropriate colleague.
[57] See Chapter 2.

adequately had the real world corresponded with his 'internal map' of things, but, of course, his mental model was faulty and disaster ensued. Obviously any post hoc analysis of this type must contain some judgements and be to some degree a matter of opinion. As with any attempt to classify and name phenomena, distinctions are difficult at the margins. This does not matter. Perrow's example illustrates perfectly how behaviour that, on the face of things, is inexplicable and apparently seriously negligent may become more understandable given an appropriate framework for the analysis. For the purposes of assessing blame it is not the precise category of error that matters, and considerable overlap may occur. The important thing is an appreciation of the various mental processes involved and an understanding of the ways in which well-intentioned, competent and sober professionals can sometimes do astonishingly inadvisable things.

It can be seen, then, that the administration of a wrong drug could be the result of a deliberate and careless failure to look at the label – which would be a violation (see Chapter 4). More commonly, however, it would be due to an error – a slip or a lapse. However, the same event could alternatively represent a failure to understand the properties of the drug. In this case it would be a rule-based error if little active thought had gone into the decision and the mistake simply reflected the lack of the right rule in the doctor's armamentarium. On the other hand, it could be an error in System II thinking if the doctor had actively attempted to work out the best choice from a range of possibilities, taking account of the patient's medical condition and his knowledge of pharmacology, but had come to the wrong conclusion either because of flawed reasoning or because of inadequate or incorrect (including incorrectly perceived or remembered) information. Thus, superficially identical events may arise from quite different types of cognitive process. It is important not to attribute an event to the most culpable option available without a proper consideration of the alternatives.

Crises and the 'Catch-22' of Human Monitoring

We have contrasted System II thinking, which is slow, effortful, time-consuming, unpredictable in its results and error-driven by feedback of the information derived from the results of iterative decisions with System I thinking, which is fast, rule-based, relatively predictable and controlled (or driven) by feed-forward considerations – that is, by the objective in mind. The typical occasion on which a practitioner is required to abandon predominantly System I thinking and resort to predominantly System II thinking is in a crisis – when the store of applicable rules has run out; this is also the very situation in which System II thinking is least likely to be successful, primarily because of the constraints on time.

The problem of bounded rationality or keyhole vision of the problem space is also at its most serious in a crisis. In a routine situation, a great deal can often be done to improve the quality of decision-making by the allocation of adequate time to the task, by writing down the information in such a way that it can be reviewed, by reference to textbooks which contain the required information and so on. Co-operation in the form of consultation with a colleague may be helpful, particularly for inexperienced practitioners. However, in a crisis, time is limited and decisions must be made without the benefit of this type of support.

Every doctor will eventually meet a case with features not typical of his or her pre-stored patterns, and for which he or she has no previously learned rules. In these circumstances, taking a gamble that a rule will work that has been satisfactory in a more or less similar and relatively frequently occurring condition is very dangerous. In a crisis, however, the choices are often stark. For example, an anaesthetist facing a hypoxic patient with a difficult airway may have only two or three minutes to prevent irreversible brain damage. Very often the most attractive option (if not the only option) is to resort to frequency-gambling. In the case of an expert, this will often work, but problems arise when decisions, taken under intense pressure to act, lead to bad outcomes and are subjected to unsophisticated analysis with the benefit of hindsight.

In some areas of medicine, notably anaesthesia, and also in many areas of industry (including aviation and the nuclear industry), people may be required to monitor relatively stable situations in anticipation of the rare occasion in which a crisis might develop. Reason has referred to this as 'the catch-22 of human supervisory control'.[58] Machines are, in general, better than humans at monitoring routine data, such as blood pressures and pulse rates. Modern alarms are very reliable, but one valid function of the human is to back up the monitors in case they fail; thus, an anaesthetist may check a suspect pulse rate on an automatic monitor by feeling for the patient's radial or temporal pulse. The main reason for retaining a human in the system, however, is for his or her ability to do what machines cannot do: that is, to identify, analyse and cope with the unexpected – in other words, to manage a crisis should it occur.

[58] J. Reason, *Human Error*, 182–3.

The catch-22 lies in the fact that spending many hours monitoring normal vital signs provides little practice in handling an emergency. The safer the system, the more infrequent the crises, the less chance for experience in handling problems. In addition to this, the fear and emotional stress associated with a crisis often inhibit calm and rational thought. Add to that the fact that humans are not good at prolonged monitoring, suffer tedium poorly and have a tendency to see what they expect to see, and you have a situation tailor-made for eventual disaster. It is asking a great deal to expect a human being to stay alert for extended periods, notice the earliest signs of something going wrong, evaluate them correctly and then remain calm, skilled and effective while treating a life-threatening problem seldom, if ever, seen before, often without the benefit of help, and at times when he or she is significantly fatigued. Given the feedback, error-driven nature of deliberative cognitive processing, it is a testimony to the quality of human performance that professionals handle crises successfully as often as they do.

One important conclusion of this discussion relates to the evaluation of the moral culpability of apparent failures to do the right thing in an emergency (such as in the case involving Dr Hugel, described in Chapter 1): it is essential in such an evaluation to take into account the available alternatives (or lack of alternatives), the time frame in which decisions had to be made, and the limitations of the cognitive processes involved.

A second important conclusion relates to improving the safety of practice. In recent years there have been many examples in which an understanding of human factors has been incorporated with technical expertise to develop more effective approaches to both the monitoring of routine situations and the management of crises. Cognitive aids, such as checklists and algorithms, have been developed to facilitate logical decision-making under pressure of time. In anaesthesia, as in aviation, simulation has gained considerable traction as an educational tool. Highly realistic simulation of human patients is now possible, and courses have been developed to teach the effective management of crises without having to await the advent of rare events and then put patients at risk. These approaches are increasingly being extended to entire teams of clinicians.[59]

[59] J. Weller, D. Cumin, J. Torrie, M. Boyd, I. Civil, D. Madell, . . . A. F. Merry, 'Multidisciplinary operating room simulation-based team training to reduce treatment errors: a feasibility study in New Zealand hospitals' (2015) 128 *New Zealand Medical Journal* 40–51; A. F. Arriaga, A. M. Bader, J. M. Wong, S. R. Lipsitz, W. R. Berry, J. E. Ziewacz, . . . A. A. Gawande,

The 'Egregious Error'

Should errors ever be considered morally culpable? Given that our strict definition precludes any deliberate element to an error, it might seem that the answer should be 'no'. Consider, however, the practitioner who has been lazy throughout his or her training and has thereby failed to acquire the knowledge and skill that could reasonably be required of a medical practitioner. Such a practitioner might make an error (by our definition) that quite clearly ought to be avoidable. Thus, failing to check for neck stiffness in a case of possible meningitis through a lack of awareness that this examination is mandatory in the presence of certain signs and symptoms would be unacceptable, even if it was technically an error – although the same failure by a generally competent practitioner on account of a lapse might, under some circumstances, have quite different connotations. We shall see in the next chapter that the antecedent failure in application to training would be a recognisable violation, and it seems straightforward that at least some culpability should apply in such circumstances. It is slightly less straightforward to know where that culpability should lie. Should it lie entirely with the practitioner, or should it extend to include those responsible for training the practitioner, and those responsible for ensuring standards of care within his or her institution? This is a question that will be considered further in Chapter 10.

What if the underlying problem was not laziness, but simple inability on the part of the individual concerned? Perhaps the doctor in question is congenitally incapable of the cognitive or motor skills required of his or her particular speciality. This might well apply in a case involving technically difficult surgery. Alternatively, age or illness might lead to impairment in performance, perhaps without any appreciation on the part of the doctor that this has occurred. The test, as we shall see in Chapters 6 and 7, is an objective one. If such a person falls below the standard of the reasonable practitioner, then liability may apply, appropriately, even if the failure is an error. Again, however, it is at least arguable that much of the responsibility lies not only with individual practitioners but also with those responsible for poor training, or for a failure of the systems that should be in place to ensure the competence of practitioners and detect deterioration in that competence before they reach a position to cause harm.

'Simulation-based trial of surgical-crisis checklists' (2013) 368 *New England Journal of Medicine* 246–53.

The key to assessing these various situations lies in the application of the test of what is reasonable, and in Chapter 7 we shall discuss the importance of recognising that the reasonable person is human. There is a difference between a single slip or lapse in an otherwise competent practice and a repeated failure to achieve a required standard. Similarly, there is a difference between a mistake generated by a misunderstanding or by a failure to appreciate subtle nuances of a situation, and one generated by a lack of knowledge so basic that the vast majority of doctors would view the information as fundamental. Thus, errors may reflect antecedent negligence, and if the departure from the expected standard is major, this antecedent negligence may be substantial and justify a finding of gross negligence. Analysis along the lines proposed in this and the next chapter is not in any way aimed at exonerating all human failures; it is simply intended to bring a greater sophistication to the process of ensuring that blame *is* attributed where it is deserved, but *only* where it is deserved. Accountability is a slightly different issue: all concerned should be held accountable for taking all reasonable steps to understand why harm from error has occurred and seeking ways to make such harm less likely in the future.

Error, Safety and Blame

Modern authorities on the psychology of human behaviour are virtually unanimous in saying that certain types of error are inevitable in any human endeavour and in the technological systems devised by people. As we have been at pains to stress, this is not the same thing as saying that error should be tolerated. Every effort should be made to reduce the occurrence of error to the lowest level possible. Until recently, the prevailing failure in medicine (and other activities) to appreciate the need to engineer systems (in the widest sense) and introduce techniques and training designed to facilitate human function and compensate for its weaknesses has no doubt been one reason for the number of preventable adverse events which occur every day. In part this has been the result of an attitude of denial of the limitations of human cognitive performance and of a culture that has too readily asserted that the solution lies in employing the right type of individuals and getting rid of the others. Attitudes of this sort have been characteristic not only of healthcare, but of many other activities as well. Over the last two decades there has been a sea change in thinking and there is now a much greater awareness of the importance of human factors in the delivery of care to patients that is safe, and of a high quality in other ways as well. Unfortunately, there are still many people with responsibilities for the delivery of healthcare, from government ministers and senior administrators to those who actually deliver care to patients, who still hold the view that the most important thing to do when things go wrong is to identify the individual to blame – presumably because they still believe that someone always must be blameworthy. Also, the problem of unintended harm in healthcare has turned out to be more difficult to deal with through systematic approaches to improvement than perhaps anticipated – although there have been some notable recent successes in this regard.[60] In short, encouraging progress has been made, but there is still a long way to go on this journey towards greater safety in healthcare.

Further progress towards greater safety in medicine (and other activities) will be facilitated by a wider appreciation of the ways in which human cognitive processes can fail. The law has an important role to play in this. It is basically counter-productive to respond in a harsh and ill-informed way to the inevitable failures of well-motivated, well-trained and competent individuals who have been required to deal with situations of enormous difficulty in which there has been little time for response, or even to those failures that occur in less stressed situations, but clearly reflect the inevitable errors made by all people. Investigative approaches which delve beyond the 'smoking gun' into the antecedent and underlying causes of adverse events make better sense in the promotion of safer practice. Appropriate legal signals may provide pressures for organisational change and promote a culture of safety. We will expand upon these themes in Chapter 10.

When the outcome of an accident is harm or the loss of life, it is understandable that there will be blame. Individuals who have contributed to any such accident must expect to be called to account for their role in its generation. However, the degree to which such a person may be considered morally culpable will vary greatly depending on the circumstances involved. An appreciation of the processes which underlie human errors and contribute to many modern-day disasters is essential to any meaningful analysis of blame.

---

[60] Two examples both involve the introduction of checklists and related measures to improve process: see J. D. Birkmeyer, 'Strategies for improving surgical quality – checklists and beyond' (2010) 363 *New England Journal of Medicine* 1963–5; A. Gawande, *The Checklist Manifesto* (New York, Metropolitan Books, 2009); P. Pronovost, D. Needham, S. Berenholtz, D. Sinopoli, H. Chu, S. Cosgrove, ... C. Goeschel, 'An intervention to decrease catheter-related bloodstream infections in the ICU' (2006) 355 *New England Journal of Medicine* 2725–32.

4

Violations

It is not only error that contributes to the failure of human endeavour. People drink, drive and wreak havoc on the road. Substandard structures are erected, and collapse, with loss of lives. Clinicians in intensive care units fail in their hand hygiene practices between patients and contribute to the problem of hospital-acquired infection. There are many situations like these in which harm flows from actions, which, in contrast to errors, are quite deliberate in their conceptualisation and execution, even though no harm was intended. We have said that errors are entirely involuntary. The moral implications of an injury are quite different if some element of deliberate disregard for safety by the actor was involved in the decisions that led to its causation. Slips and lapses involve no conscious decision, but mistakes do. A mistake is defined as an *error* precisely because the actor believes that the decision in question is an appropriate way of achieving an objective safely. He or she is acting in good faith, trying to do the best possible thing, but failing. A decision or plan cannot be considered a mistake if the person concerned *knows* that an alternative is both reasonably available and more likely to achieve the given objective safely, and yet *deliberately chooses* the less satisfactory option. This element of consciously choosing to act in a way that falls short of some identifiable standard or creates an unnecessary and unjustifiable increase in risk defines an action as a violation rather than an error.[1] An important point about violations is that many violations tend to make errors more likely and more dangerous when they do occur.[2] This is often the reason that a rule has been created in the first place.

[1] The question of justifiable risk is discussed later in the chapter.
[2] This point is discussed more fully later in this chapter under the heading 'Violations as Antecedent Actions to Errors'.

Definition of a Violation

In his classic book, *Human Error*, Reason defined violations as 'deliberate – but not necessarily reprehensible – deviations from those practices deemed necessary (by designers, managers and regulatory agencies) to maintain the safe operation of a potentially hazardous system' and commented that 'violations can only be described with regard to a social context in which behaviour is governed by operating procedures, codes of practice, rules and the like'.[3] By the inclusion of the word 'deliberate' this definition distinguished violations from errors, but Reason made the point that '[t]he boundaries between errors and violations are by no means hard and fast, either conceptually or within a particular accident sequence'. Later, in *Managing the Risks of Organizational Accidents*, he defined violations more simply as 'deviations from safe operating procedures, standards or rules,' but explained that these deviations could be either deliberate or erroneous, and that some could be well intentioned (and therefore not reprehensible).[4] In both books he also distinguished violations, which involve no malevolence, from sabotage, which involves intent to harm.

The advantage of the later definition is that it is objective. Behaviours can be observed, and a broken rule is a broken rule. In contrast, it is difficult to know what people are thinking so it can often be difficult to establish the cognitive processes involved in an action, including the degree to which it was deliberate.[5] Nevertheless, on balance, we think the inclusion of the word 'deliberate' is helpful, and we also wonder whether either definition is quite broad enough to capture all the events that should be categorised as violations.

Human Error provided a straightforward and very helpful framework for the ways in which humans can fail: they can fail through error, violation, sabotage or chance. For our purposes – the evaluation of the blameworthiness of an act – the distinction between an error and violation is important, but we agree with Reason that the boundaries between

---

[3] J. Reason, *Human Error* (New York, Cambridge University Press, 1990), 195.
[4] J. Reason, *Managing the Risks of Organizational Accidents* (Aldershot, Ashgate, 1997), 72.
[5] The use of behaviourally anchored rating scales to evaluate actions in certain contexts illustrates this point: one can evaluate observable actions much more readily than subjective motivations: see D. A. Devcich, J. Weller, S. J. Mitchell, S. McLaughlin, L. Barker, J. W. Rudolph, ... A. F. Merry, 'A behaviourally anchored rating scale for evaluating the use of the WHO surgical safety checklist: development and initial evaluation of the WHOBARS' (2015) 25 *BMJ Quality & Safety* 778–86.

the two may be blurred. In particular, we think some intentional actions may knowingly create unjustifiable risk without breaking any formal rules. Two examples of this, which we discuss in detail later in this chapter, are the use of a cell phone while driving and the failure to wear a helmet while riding a motorcycle. These actions may not be malevolent and would not reflect the influence of chance, but because of the actor's insight into the deliberate taking of a risk they would not qualify as errors. How, then, should they be categorised? Should they be seen as acceptable simply because no relevant rule has been officially formulated? Or, instead, should a new category of human failure be described? Or should a new rule be created each time such an event is identified, in the hope that every organisation or society will eventually have enough rules to cover every contingency? None of these options seem to us to provide an adequate resolution to this issue.

From the point of view of the operation of organisations, the clarity provided by well-constructed rules is certainly very attractive. Many actions involve at least some risk. In the absence of a formal rule, the point at which an action becomes unacceptably risky may be difficult to determine, and may be open to debate. However, if interpreted narrowly, this view seems to place excessive responsibility for the moral behaviour of individuals on those whose role it is to create explicit rules, procedures, standards, laws or other forms of formal regulation – and thereby to diminish the role of personal responsibility, which we consider critically important to the safety and success of any organisation or society.

Rules have an important place in the safe running of organisations and society, but some rules may be inappropriate, at least under some circumstances. This does not create undue difficulty – the concept of an appropriate violation, discussed later in this chapter, covers situations in which rules may need to be broken. It also matters little that some rules are primarily to do with social expectations and norms – laws about alcohol during the period of prohibition in the United States, and today in some Islamic states, for example.[6] Traditionally, in the UK and many countries in the former British Commonwealth, doctors were judged by their professional bodies as much on the basis of their social behaviour as on patient care – hence the term 'conduct unbecoming'.[7] Breaking such

---

[6] There are many examples of laws that society has subsequently come to view as inappropriate, or that one society accepts and another society rejects.

[7] Fortunately, the emphasis today in the regulation of medical practice in most of these countries has become more strongly focused on the safety of patients.

rules would clearly constitute a violation in the context of the particular time and place, but the only immediate risk would probably arise from enforcement of the law.[8] In general, rules of this type can be judged on their merits. Our greater concern is with situations that have not been covered by any form of rule at all, and we are not convinced that the solution is simply to increase the number of rules. Too many rules may well create more problems than they solve, in part by reducing the scope for initiative.[9] The importance of some flexibility for individuals within an organisation to exercise initiative has been recognised in healthcare, in recent years, with a shift in emphasis from quality assurance (involving compliance with rules and regulations applied from above) to the engagement of each person in the organisation (particularly at the workface) in quality improvement. Both quality assurance and quality improvement are needed, but regulation is primarily limited to enforcing minimally acceptable standards or restricting harmful behaviour while quality improvement is more ambitious and seeks the continuous and ongoing improvement of the performance of an organisation. Interestingly, the latter approach does imply taking risks. Healthcare is too complex to have a rule for every situation. Every patient is unique, so clinicians often have to make decisions in situations that do not fall into well-recognised patterns with prescribed standards of management. The taking of risk is integral to clinical medicine. It is preferable to limit rules and regulations to those that are clearly useful and necessary and leave room for individual initiative, but this approach must obviously be predicated on the belief that people can be trusted to exercise responsibility in judging how much risk is reasonable, often on the basis of personal experience and common sense. The importance of trust in healthcare has been debated at length: clearly trust must be earned as well as given. It is true that there have been many examples in which practitioners, notably doctors, have failed to earn the trust of society, but there are also many examples in

---

[8] Obviously excessive consumption of alcohol carries risk in itself, but in many societies having one glass of wine with dinner would not be seen as a violation and is unlikely to carry material risk. See P. E. Ronksley, S. E. Brien, B. J. Turner, K. J. Mukamal and W. A. Ghali, 'Association of alcohol consumption with selected cardiovascular disease outcomes: a systematic review and meta-analysis' (2011) 342 *British Medical Journal* d671; S. E. Brien, P. E. Ronksley, B. J. Turner, K. J. Mukamal and W. A. Ghali, 'Effect of alcohol consumption on biological markers associated with risk of coronary heart disease: systematic review and meta-analysis of interventional studies' (2011) 342 *British Medical Journal* d636.

[9] The discussion of the question of excessive numbers of rules is continued later in this chapter under the heading 'Actions – Correct or Appropriate?'

which that trust has proven well placed, and we do not believe that rules are the key to trustworthiness. Similarly, we think that reasonable risk can usually be distinguished from unreasonable risk, whether relevant rules exist or not. If there is only one practical possibility, the situation is straightforward. If alternatives exist, the situation is more complicated but, in general, any increase in risk associated with a chosen alternative ought to be justifiable on other grounds, such as those of effectiveness or cost, for example. As always, there may be difficulty at the margins, but that probably does not matter: it is actions that clearly exceed the boundary of reasonable risk with which we are most concerned, and wish to capture in our definition of the term 'violation'.[10] Thus, we would argue that the suggestion that if no formal rule has been broken then no failure has occurred diminishes an important element of personal responsibility – the element that drives people do the right thing regardless of the rules.

Some of these points can be illustrated by considering the implications of conversing on a cell phone while driving a car, or of riding a motorcycle without a helmet.

Cell Phones and Driving[11]

In New Zealand, the use of cell phones while driving is common (as it is in many countries, a fact reflected by the increasing inclusion of support for cell phones into the design of new cars), and the perception of the risks associated with this varies considerably amongst members of the public. Legislation was introduced in 2004 that prohibited the use of hand-held, but not hands-free, cell phones while driving.[12] This legislation was supported by a campaign to discourage the use of hand-held cell phones while driving.

Taken collectively, the evidence relevant to this initiative leaves little doubt that having a conversation on a cell phone while driving does increase the risk of an accident (albeit that there have been many

---

[10] We will expand on this theme later in the chapter, when considering the various types of violation.

[11] C. Hallett, A. Lambert and M. A. Regan, 'Cell phone conversing while driving in New Zealand: prevalence, risk perception and legislation' (2011) 43 *Accident Analysis & Prevention* 862–9; C. Collet, A. Guillot and C. Petit, 'Phoning while driving I: a review of epidemiological, psychological, behavioural and physiological studies' (2010) 53 *Ergonomics* 589–601; C. Collet, A. Guillot and C. Petit, 'Phoning while driving II: a review of driving conditions influence' (2010) 53 *Ergonomics* 602–16.

[12] See Land Transport (Road User) Rule 2004, 7.3A(NZ).

different studies, with many equivocal or even contradictory findings). The primary mechanism by which risk is increased appears to be cognitive overload, with one task diverting attention from the other. Furthermore, a demanding conversation is much more likely to increase risk than a simple one, and this seems to be true whether the conversation is held by phone or with a passenger in the car. On the other hand, in a varying flow of traffic it is more difficult to pace a conversation with a physically remote person than with a passenger in the car, so there are reasonable grounds for banning the former while accepting the latter. It is relevant, though, that conversations are not the only source of distraction while driving – there are many other factors that determine the net risk at any particular moment. Context is important – for example, there are studies suggesting that conversations by means of headsets may reduce the risks of sleepiness for long distance truck drivers and thereby actually promote safety. Crawling along a straight motorway (substantially free from unexpected interactions with pedestrians or cyclists, or from side roads) in a traffic jam is very different from driving at higher speeds along secondary roads through built up residential areas. In the end, though, the one thing for which evidence seems to be particularly slight is the view that the use of a hand-held phone is significantly more dangerous than the use of a hands-free one. Apparently, it is the distracting effect of a conversation with a remote person that really matters. It could be argued, therefore, that the legislation does not go as far as it should. A needed rule is missing – a rule prohibiting the use of hands-free phones as well as hand-held ones.

As things stand, how should we analyse the decisions associated with an accident in which the use of a hands-free phone appears to have been a contributory factor? Do we call such use an error or a violation, or something else? Should we accept the use of a hands-free phone in all circumstances, simply because the law has not prohibited this?

We think that an actor's personal understanding of the risk of an action is at least as relevant to the evaluation of blameworthiness as the existence of a rule. If the driver did not know the relevant evidence it would be reasonable to categorise the use of a hands-free phone in inadvisable circumstances (in free flowing heavy traffic, for example) as an error – or, more precisely, a mistake. Indeed, one could not but have sympathy for a driver who considered such use of a hands-free phone to be acceptable – after all, the new legislation promotes this idea. On the other hand, if the driver was aware of the thrust of the scientific evidence and knowingly decided to take a risk anyway, we believe there would be justification for arguing that this was not an error. As usual, the situation may be nuanced. The driver may have known the evidence but incorrectly judged that the combination of traffic flow, road conditions and speed made this a safe occasion to use a cell phone. Alternatively, he or she might have appreciated that the situation was one that really did warrant the undivided attention of the driver but could not be bothered to pull over and stop to make the call, and instead decided simply to take a risk in the hope and expectation of getting away with it. This last scenario seems to have the hallmarks of a violation, albeit that no law was broken.

It is interesting to extend this analysis a little further. In this example the risk applied not only to the driver, but to other people as well, people who had not been asked if they were prepared to take such a risk. One view would be that this adds to the justification for classifying the action as a violation: on this particular occasion there would be no gain to offset the risk for these other people, so they would be unlikely to support the driver's decision. Alternatively, one could argue that the public had been represented through legislation, and that approval for use of a hands-free phone in this way could be assumed. This argument would suggest that the gain lies in the right of these other people to do the same thing in similar circumstances. It follows that legislation (and indeed any form of rule or regulation) is highly relevant to the analysis of an action such as this. Had the driver used a hand-held phone the situation would, arguably, be much graver (at least under New Zealand law). Not only would the law have been broken, but one could also say that a clear public warning had been issued and disregarded. The onus to understand and apply complicated scientific findings to one's actions in the absence of a clear rule is much lower than the onus to obey the law of the land.

Our position, then, is not that rules don't matter. Rather, our position is that there is an onus to apply one's knowledge and common sense in an effort to do the right thing even in the absence of rules (as well as, occasionally, in spite of rules). One test of whether this particular action was a violation would be to ask the driver whether he or she knew that a risk was involved that could not be adequately justified. If the answer was 'yes', then it was a violation. In practice, however, there is an obvious difficulty in the need to rely on honesty in making such a determination. In general, we advocate giving people the benefit of any reasonable doubt, but there are situations in which the risks are so obvious that protestations to the contrary become implausible. The wearing of motorcycle helmets provides a good example of such a situation.

Motorcycle Helmets[13]

In some countries, riding a motorcycle without a helmet will be a violation of a specific law requiring that such headgear be worn. In other countries there is no such legal rule. Nevertheless, it is widely understood that head injuries are a common consequence of riding motorcycles, and that helmets provide worthwhile protection against them. If, therefore, one wishes to avoid a head injury, one should not violate the obvious (on the basis of common sense) requirement to wear protective headgear. If, as a consequence of not wearing a helmet, a person suffers a serious head injury, it is only reasonable to attribute this to a violation, not an error, whatever the law. In effect, the person must take the blame for this decision. The main difference between this example and the previous one is that the evidence supporting this use of helmets is much clearer. Arguments discounting either the net potential value of wearing a helmet or the potential risk of riding a motorcycle without one simply do not stand up to scrutiny today.[14]

In this book we are concerned with the underlying cognitive processes that have led to particular actions. There is both theoretical and empirical evidence that errors and violations are mediated by different cognitive processes. Even the demographic profile of the individuals concerned may be different – violations decline with age, while errors do not, and

---

[13]   J. B. MacLeod, J. C. Digiacomo and G. Tinkoff, 'An evidence-based review: helmet efficacy to reduce head injury and mortality in motorcycle crashes: EAST practice management guidelines' (2010) 69 *Journal of Trauma-Injury Infection & Critical Care* 1101–11; C. Lam, M. R. Lin, S. F. Chu, S. H. Tsai, C. H. Bai and W. T. Chiu, 'The effect of various types of motorcycle helmets on cervical spine injury in head injury patients: a multicenter study in Taiwan' (2015) 2015 *BioMed Research International* 487985; K. G. Hooten and G. J. Murad, 'Helmet use and cervical spine injury: a review of motorcycle, moped, and bicycle accidents at a level 1 trauma center' (2014) 31 *Journal of Neurotrauma* 1329–33; A. J. Ogle and E. A. Tillotson, 'Should it be the law in Wisconsin that all motorcyclists are required to wear helmets?' (2008) 15 *Journal of Trauma Nursing* 43–6.

[14]   In effect, as with recklessness, some acts can thus be said to meet an objective standard of violation whether the actor understands the issues or not.

violations are more common in men than women at all ages.[15] There is more to the evaluation of the blameworthiness of an unsafe act than deciding whether the act was erroneous or a violation, but this is a useful place to start.

We suggest, therefore, that the definition of a violation should encompass any action that *deliberately* jeopardises the integrity of a system of rules, accepted principles of safety, the objectives of an undertaking, the ongoing function of a system or organisation, the accepted norms and expectations at a particular time of society or a group of people, or the reasonable considerations for safety that arise from each individual's own knowledge and common sense. The existence of a formal rule makes the violation clear. However, a rule formalised in writing or in any other way should not be seen as essential for an action to be categorised as a violation. It is enough that some identifiable principle, appreciated by the actor, has been knowingly breached. This principle may take the form of a broad legal proposition – for example, that one should not act in such a way as to cause foreseeable damage to others – or it may take the form of a rule that follows from scientific fact or from widely accepted standards of medical practice.

For our purposes, therefore, we suggest that deviations from formal rules, laws, procedures, standards and other regulations should be described objectively without use of the words 'error' or 'violation'. For example, the statement that a driver exceeded a particular speed limit at a certain time and place can be seen as an objective description of fact. The initial evaluation of the moral implications of this fact will then be facilitated by consideration of whether the act constituted an error, a violation or perhaps even an act of sabotage.

In simple terms one can then think of a violation as *when one deliberately does the wrong thing – but without malevolent intent.* For the reasons discussed above, we propose to adopt the following more formal definition, which is a slight expansion on the earlier of Reason's two aforementioned definitions:[16]

---

[15] Reason, *Human Error*, 197.

[16] The changes to Reason's definition are shown in normal text (rather than italics). Note that there is no fundamental conflict between this definition and the common usage definition given in *The Oxford English Dictionary*, although the latter is somewhat broader and outlines six senses in which the word may be used. The definition given here differs from that in the first edition of this book in that it places more weight on the presence of formal rules and also explicitly distinguishes violations from sabotage. Note that if an individual did not appreciate that a rule existed, breaking the rule would be unintentional and, therefore, an error. However, if the rule broken also constituted

A violation is an intentional – but *not necessarily malevolent and* not necessarily reprehensible – deviation from those practices deemed necessary (by designers, managers or regulatory agencies) *or appreciated by the individual as advisable* to maintain the safe operation of a potentially hazardous system.

The blameworthiness of violations varies. In effect there is a continuum from pure errors (which we consider to be blameless) to obviously blameworthy violations. Any decision should be judged on its merits at the time it was made rather than on its outcome.

Recklessness and Violations

The fact that a course of action constitutes a violation does not necessarily mean that it amounts to recklessness. Recklessness is a term that carries a considerable measure of moral opprobrium. To describe an action as reckless is usually (if not inevitably) to censure the actor. As already indicated, many acts will involve a risk to others, but this risk may be thought to be justifiable on the grounds of social benefit derived from the conduct in question. A surgical operation and the associated anaesthetic are good examples. Both carry risk – but if the risk is outweighed by the social value of the conduct, the action will not be reckless.

Recklessness implies knowing that an action or omission will involve an unnecessary and unjustifiable level of risk to someone or something, and deciding nevertheless to take that risk. Violations involve a decision to do something in the knowledge that the given action or decision will place at risk some aspect of safety or of the system. However, some violations constitute recklessness, while others do not. Few people would describe it as reckless to exceed the speed limit by 1 mile per hour, although it would be a violation to do this deliberately. Most would say that exceeding it by 50 miles per hour would be seriously reckless. Defining the point at which an action may be called reckless comes down to a matter of judgement as to the acceptability or otherwise of the level of risk involved, and needs to take account of all the circumstances of the particular instance.

a crime it would not excuse the actor, on the basis of the principle that ignorance of the (penal) law is no defence to a crime. An 'erroneous violation' seems to us to be an oxymoron, hence our suggestion that we distinguish the fact that a rule has been broken from the question of whether this constituted an error or a violation. The term 'deliberate' is critical in making this distinction.

Actions – Correct or Appropriate?

We discussed the concept of the 'happy accident' in Chapter 3, and saw that it is even possible for errors to be life-saving. In the same way, an action that is clearly a violation may have very satisfactory consequences. Reason discusses this issue, and introduces the idea of *correct violations*.[17] This approach categorises actions or decisions on the basis of their outcome and is intuitively attractive. If we bet on a horse and it wins, we have backed the right or correct horse. Similarly, if we buy a raffle ticket and win the prize, we have been fortunate enough to buy the correct ticket – and so on. If someone drives home at excessive speed while under the influence of alcohol, he or she may succeed in the objective of getting home sooner than a companion who chooses to take a taxi in the same circumstances. This person might well argue that the right (or correct) decision had been made. From the perspective of result on that occasion, the action was successful. However, as we have already emphasised, outcome often reflects the influence of chance and is not a sound basis for the moral evaluation of a decision or action.

The *appropriateness* of the action is a different matter. There may be circumstances in which all reasonable choices constitute violations and it becomes necessary to break a rule. For example, a double amputation carried out on a trapped man under part of a collapsed building during the Christchurch earthquake in February 2011[18] would have involved the breaking of many rules normally associated with surgery and anaesthesia, but saved a life. Violations of this type could be called 'appropriate violations'. In certain fields of medicine, notably anaesthesia and surgery, it is often necessary to act quickly and decisively, and a failure to do

---

[17] Reason, *Managing the Risks of Organizational Accidents*, 75.

[18] The following is cited verbatim from the June 2014 New Zealand newsletter ('Gasbag') of the Australian and New Zealand College of Anaesthetists: 'Dr Bryce Curran, a Christchurch anaesthetist, was awarded the New Zealand Bravery Decoration for the part he played in operating on and saving the life of a man trapped in the Pyne Gould Corporation building, which had collapsed in the February 22, 2011 earthquake in Christchurch. Australian urologist Dr Lydia Johns-Putra, who was in Christchurch at a conference, also received a New Zealand Bravery Decoration for her part in the same rescue. A firefighter and police officer made up the team of four who carried out a double amputation on Brian Coker who was trapped under concrete. They work[ed] in a confined, unstable, dark space with the constant threat of aftershocks and with minimal equipment (a Leatherman knife and hacksaw, with morphine and ketamine as anaesthetic) to free Brian Coker, who has since gone on to compete in the New York marathon on a hand cycle.'

anything may be the most certain route to disaster. Doctors face uncertainty every day, usually in situations more mundane than those of an earthquake. For example, psychiatrists frequently have to decide whether a patient may be a danger to him or herself, or to the public, and make a decision between restricting the patient's liberty and potentially placing the public at risk. The tendency in such circumstances is to praise a decision as showing 'good judgement' if it proves successful and to call it 'an error of judgement' if not.[19]

If an individual in such circumstances makes a decision in good faith that breaks a rule, but he or she can articulate a reasonable justification for it, *and* it is a decision that at least some other appropriately qualified individuals would have made in the circumstances, then the best way of classifying the action is to call it an *appropriate violation*. For the purposes of evaluating the quality of the decision, the concept of appropriateness is much more useful than the concept of correctness. Another way of looking at this is to ask whether a different person in the same circumstances, and with events unfolding in the same way, would have been likely to behave any differently, assuming that this hypothetical person came from the same general field of activity and had similar experience, abilities and qualifications. This is the basis of the Johnston 'substitution test'. If the answer is not in the affirmative, then, according to Johnston, there can be no justification for apportioning blame to the individual concerned, and indeed to do so simply creates a risk that any underlying contributory or systemic factors will be obscured.[20]

Obviously the individual may need to face the regulatory or legal consequences of any rules that have been broken; in law the defence of *necessity* may well be available. There are very strong arguments for other relevant authorities to take all circumstances into account in evaluating such situations, but of course there is no guarantee that they will exonerate an individual simply because he or she has acted in good faith. As we shall discuss in Chapters 5 and 6, the factor most likely to influence the result of any investigation or trial that ensues from an unfortunate accident is the outcome of the course of action pursued. Success tends to be seen as its own justification; failure needs a great deal of explanation.

[19] Outcome bias is discussed in more detail in Chapters 6 and 7.
[20] N. Johnston, 'Do blame and punishment have a role in organizational risk management?' (Spring 1995) *Flight Deck* 33–6. Quoted in Reason, *Managing the Risks of Organizational Accidents*, 208.

An appropriate violation (i.e. a well-intentioned decision to break a rule for reasons perceived as justifiable at the time) may turn out to be an error. If logical arguments or empirical evidence can subsequently be advanced to demonstrate that a better decision was possible at the time, without the benefit of hindsight, then the decision was simply a mistake. In this case the cause of the error would lie with the inadequacy of the knowledge-base or reasoning of the individual at the time of the action. If the criticism of the decision was based on opinion rather than objective criteria, then this would be called an error of judgement. If no logical, empirical or normative evidence can subsequently be advanced to demonstrate that a better decision was possible, then the judgement should be considered sound, not an error, and the violation considered appropriate whatever the outcome.

There are other situations in which an individual may elect in good faith to violate a rule, perhaps on the grounds that the rule was poorly conceived or has lost its rationale and become outmoded. On the other hand, some rules, such as those prohibiting sexual impropriety with patients, have a strong foundation, and it would be difficult to justify breaking them. One position is that the breaking of any rule is wrong because organisations and complex systems need rules and it cannot be left for an individual to pick and choose between those which need to be observed and those which can be ignored. In this view, such laxity would import a dangerous subjectivity and would compromise the efficiency – and indeed the safety – of the organisation. Such an argument is at its strongest when applied to the law of the land in a democratic society. In general, it is not possible to justify the selective observance of the law in this context. If a law is thought to be wrong, then procedures exist in most countries to seek its repeal or reform. An expectation of technical adherence to the letter of the law is, therefore, justified. In exceptional circumstances, such as those discussed above, the law recognises that an overriding principle may justify violating a legal rule. The defence of *necessity* is based on this premise. This defence may, in some limited circumstances, allow a person to break the law in the interests of protecting human life or limb from an otherwise unavoidable threat.

In the context of bureaucratic organisations the reality is often different. Again, this has been recognised by Reason. In such organisations there is often a tendency for the promulgation of excessive numbers of rules, and frequently these are simply added to existing ones rather than substituted for those that have become obsolete. This process may be well intentioned, but it may also be motivated by a perception that such rules provide protection for senior management or directors, who may be held liable in the event of an accident. Reason makes the point that continuously adding to the number of safety regulations tends to reduce the scope of action permissible for performing required tasks successfully. Thus, ironically, a situation may eventually be created by the very process of regulation in which violations become necessary, either routinely or in exceptional circumstances when operational conditions make this unavoidable.

The important thing is not just the existence of a rule; it is also necessary that the rule be generally accepted as well founded, and also that it should apply in the circumstances of the particular case. It is thus quite possible for a poor rule to be violated appropriately in the interests of safety, or in order to reduce the risk of an adverse outcome. Reason has gone so far as to say: 'The important issue in many hazardous technologies is not *whether* to violate, but *when* to violate – or perhaps, more importantly, when to comply.'[21]

Categories of Violation

As with error, it is possible to classify violations. In one approach, the primary division is between routine and exceptional violations.

Routine violations typically involve the cutting of corners in everyday tasks. They reflect the natural human tendency to take the path of least effort, and are made more likely by designs or procedural requirements that are perceived as unnecessarily cumbersome or restrictive. This is graphically illustrated by an example from landscape architecture. If a path takes a longer route around a lawn rather than simply going straight across it, perhaps for aesthetic rather than utilitarian reasons, there is a high probability that pedestrians will choose to take a short cut across the grass rather than follow the pathway around the perimeter. If a procedure is perceived as unreasonably arduous, there is a good chance that people will find ways to shorten it or to leave it out altogether. The literature is replete with evidence that health professionals routinely disregard the rules in respect to hand hygiene between patient contacts in situations where cross-infection is a known risk: indeed, major efforts have been made internationally to address this problem, with varying

---

[21] Reason, *Managing the Risks of Organizational Accidents*, 51.

degrees of success.[22] Another example of a violation of this general sort is to be found in anaesthesia. The anaesthetic machine should be checked before every anaesthetic to ensure that it is properly assembled and safe to use. Several protocols are available for this, notably one promulgated by the Australian and New Zealand College of Anaesthetists, which has been revised several times. This protocol was originally too long, and it took an anaesthetist several minutes to work through all the prescribed steps. Doing the full check before every case might add nearly an hour to the time needed to anaesthetise a list of seven or eight patients, so the process was often shortened by individual anaesthetists to a greater or lesser degree. Sometimes this was done in a well-thought-out way, which retained the most important steps; sometimes it was done inadequately; and on occasion the check was omitted altogether. The likelihood of a prescribed task of this sort being omitted is increased if the individual's workload is high, inadequate time is available for the completion of the task and the organisational culture values productivity and efficiency more than safety. Often the violation results in only a slight reduction in the margin of safety associated with a particular procedure or situation, and an adverse result is indeed quite unlikely. This is true in the case of the anaesthetic machine check, for example. In such circumstances, it is common for the individual concerned to believe that the rule is unreasonably restrictive and that the violation is actually a good thing, on grounds of economy or efficiency. The individual may believe that the organisation could not continue functioning if the proper procedures were followed, and it may be true that the organisation would at least face increased costs on account of conscientious and scrupulous

---

[22] D. Pittet, P. Mourouga, T. V. Perneger and Members of the Infection Control Program, 'Compliance with handwashing in a teaching hospital' (1999) 130 *Annals of Internal Medicine* 126–30; D. Pittet and L. Donaldson, 'Clean care is safer care: the first global challenge of the WHO World Alliance for Patient Safety' (2005) 33 *American Journal of Infection Control* 476–9; N. El Mikatti, P. Dillon and T. E. J. Healy, 'Hygienic practices of consultant anaesthetists: a survey in the North-West region of the UK' (1999) 54 *Anaesthesia* 13–18; B. Allegranzi, J. Storr, G. Dziekan, A. Leotsakos, L. Donaldson and D. Pittet, 'The First Global Patient Safety Challenge "Clean Care is Safer Care": from launch to current progress and achievements. On behalf of the World Health Organization (WHO) Global Patient Safety Challenge (Lead, Professor D Pittet), World Alliance for Patient Safety, WHO Headquarters, Geneva, Switzerland' (2007) 65 *Journal of Hospital Infection* 115–23. C. Kilpatrick and D. Pittet, 'WHO SAVE LIVES: Clean Your Hands global annual campaign. A call for action: 5 May 2011' (2011) 39 *Infection* 93–5. M. D. Koff, H. L. Corwin, M. L. Beach, S. D. Surgenor and R. W. Loftus, 'Reduction in ventilator associated pneumonia in a mixed intensive care unit after initiation of a novel hand hygiene program' (2011) 26 *Journal of Critical Care* 489–95.

compliance.[23] The latest version of the protocol is vastly improved, and is supported by an explanatory background paper. Successive versions have differentiated between three levels of checking, depending on whether the machine has just been commissioned or serviced (very detailed), is to be used for the first time at the beginning of a session (reasonably detailed) or is to be used for subsequent cases on the same list (brief, and focused on essential points). These changes have been accompanied by other initiatives[24] to improve compliance with the relevant essential checks at each level, with considerable success (at least within several hospitals in New Zealand, on the basis of the personal observation of one of the authors). Thus, it is important that rules are carefully constructed and reviewed in the light of experience. Also, since rules change, views on which practices should be construed as violations also change over time, and may differ between countries or organisations.[25]

A good non-medical example of a violation (or violations) that reflected a genuine effort to make a system function in the absence of adequate resources concerns the tragedy that occurred at Cave Creek in New Zealand in 1995. The construction of a viewing platform above a cliff was carried out with limited resources and almost entirely by volunteers. Little if any supervision was provided. The people who designed and approved the plans for the platform were not appropriately qualified and no building consent was obtained from the council (all obvious violations of good building practices). A procedural violation involved the use of nails instead of nuts and bolts in certain critical positions. After some years of apparently satisfactory function, the structure suddenly collapsed under the weight of a number of students on a field trip, with considerable loss of life. The actions that led to

---

[23] To a degree this is borne out by the notion of 'work to rule' as a means of industrial action.
[24] One of these initiatives, the use of a signed logbook, is discussed later in this chapter in the section on 'Promoting Compliance'.
[25] Australian and New Zealand College of Anaesthetists, *Guidelines on Checking Anaesthesia Delivery Systems PS31* (Melbourne, 2014). This document was originally promulgated in 1984, with revisions in 1990, 1996, 1997, 2003, 2012 and 2014. For similar, but not identical, guidelines, compare Association of Anaesthetists of Great Britain and Ireland, A. Hartle, E. Anderson, V. Bythell, L. Gemmell, H. Jones, . . . I. Walker, 'Checking anaesthetic equipment' (2012) 67 *Anaesthesia* 660–8. Guidelines for managing a difficult airway have also undergone many revisions over time, and even today those promulgated by different organisations differ in quite important ways (more so than those for checking anaesthetic delivery systems, in fact): for a recent example see C. Frerk, V. S. Mitchell, A. F. McNarry, C. Mendonca, R. Bhagrath, A. Patel, . . . Difficult Airway Society intubation guidelines working group, 'Difficult Airway Society 2015 guidelines for management of unanticipated difficult intubation in adults' (2015) *British Journal of Anaesthesia* 1–22.

the construction faults precipitating this disaster were entirely well motivated. It would have been believed, perhaps correctly, that only by means
of such voluntary work could platforms (and many other necessary
structures) be erected at all. Clearly, the most fundamental violation
was committed on behalf of the government department involved, in
permitting the unsupervised construction of a structure whose potential
dangerousness was foreseeable. Even this was probably well motivated.
It might have been thought fundamentally unhelpful to place excessive
restrictions on voluntary activities of this type. The Commission of
Enquiry noted that the Department of Conservation, responsible for
the project, was inadequately resourced and therefore did have
a culture of 'making do'.[26]

There are many examples of routine violations in medical practice.
These include: providing patients with less information than certain
regulatory bodies have prescribed for the purpose of obtaining informed
consent; failing to check results of clinical investigations (such as blood
tests) in a timely manner; eating and drinking within areas in which food
is prohibited, such as intensive care rooms and operating rooms; wearing
jewellery in the operating room; taking medical histories from patients in
open ward situations which fail to provide adequate privacy; filling in
labels incompletely; completing case notes inadequately. A specific
instance of the last example is provided by a study related to the accuracy
of anaesthesia records. The records of anaesthetists were compared with
those of an observer, present throughout the procedure, with the sole
purpose of documenting perioperative events. Eighty-six items of information were analysed for accuracy from 197 records. Information was
omitted from the record in respect of a mean of 35 per cent of the items,
and 3.4 per cent of recorded items were incorrect. Inaccuracies were
common for the majority of sites on the record, irrespective of whether or
not they reflected on the anaesthetist's performance. The authors concluded that the inadequacies in the anaesthetic records were not related
to any defensiveness on the part of the anaesthetists, but instead probably
reflected their attitudes to the value of the record and their response to
possible deficiencies in the record's design.[27] There has been much
interest in recent years in the development of electronic methods of

[26] Christchurch City Libraries, *Cave Creek* (Christchurch, undated); The Department of
Internal Affairs, *Commission of Inquiry into the Collapse of a Viewing Platform at Cave
Creek Near Punakaiki on the West Coast* (Wellington, 1995).
[27] L. Rowe, D. C. Galletly and R. S. Henderson, 'Accuracy of text entries within a manually
compiled anaesthetic record' (1992) 68 *British Journal of Anaesthesia* 381–7.

anaesthetic record keeping. This approach is not without its difficulties, but in the long term it is likely to provide an answer to what at present is an endemic problem, which even the obvious medico-legal risk associated with poor record keeping has done little to correct.[28]

An important characteristic of routine violations is that they often become a matter of habit and are repeated without much thought from occasion to occasion; the element of choice is often essentially historical – the choice was made at the time the violation was first committed. Nevertheless, these violations do involve an ongoing deliberate infringement of appropriate practices, and (in contrast to errors) there is no intrinsic reason why practitioners should not be able to avoid them, although a sudden change in the practice of one individual might create pressures that might be very difficult for that individual to handle.

The fact that routine violations are daily occurrences is one factor that helps to distinguish them from most errors. Errors are typically exceptional events, although it is possible to make an error of judgement about a common situation, obtain no negative feedback from the action and therefore adopt a faulty rule into one's repertoire of schemata without realising that it is faulty. In these circumstances an individual might repeat the same error many times. A variation on this theme is that one might learn the wrong way of doing something from a senior colleague for whom a particular method of carrying out some procedure is a violation which he or she has long since come to think of as acceptable. In this way a trainee anaesthetist might learn an inadequate method of checking an anaesthetic machine from a consultant, for example, and might not realise that the procedure he or she has been taught is in fact in violation of accepted protocol.

Exceptional violations are quite different from routine violations. They occur in situations that are themselves exceptional and which create conditions in which some rule that would normally be accepted as appropriate cannot easily be followed. The *appropriate violations* discussed above are typically exceptional rather than routine in nature,

---

[28] B. J. Anderson and A. F. Merry, 'Paperless anesthesia: uses and abuses of these data' (2015) 25 *Paediatric Anaesthesia* 1184–92; K. E. Edwards, S. M. Hagen, J. Hannam, C. Kruger, R. Yu and A. F. Merry, 'A randomized comparison between records made with an anesthesia information management system and by hand, and evaluation of the Hawthorne effect' (2013) *Canadian Journal of Anesthesia* 1–8; J. M. Van Schalkwyk, D. Lowes, C. Frampton and A. F. Merry, 'Does manual anaesthetic record capture remove clinically important data?' (2011) 107 *British Journal of Anaesthesia* 546–52.

but not all exceptional violations are appropriate. Usually, but not always, they are well intentioned. Exceptional violations are quite likely to occur in emergencies. For example, in an emergency an anaesthetist might elect not to expend resources on keeping an adequate anaesthetic record, a surgeon might omit to carry out a full hand-washing procedure or the process of obtaining informed consent from a patient may be reduced to take the least amount of time possible.

Having distinguished routine from exceptional violations, one can identify several subsets of violation that may fall into either of these two main categories.

Necessary violations are violations justified by unexpected and unpredicted situations (in the exceptional category) or by what Reason has referred to as *system double-binds*[29] (in the routine category). The examples given above, concerning the anaesthetic record and surgical hand-washing in an emergency, would qualify as necessary violations in the exceptional category if the patient's situation was so urgent and demanding of immediate attention that neither of the tasks mentioned was reasonably possible.

Another interesting example of a systems double-bind which produces routine violations involves the excessive hours regularly worked by many doctors. There is now considerable evidence to support the contention that fatigue contributes to errors and to diminished performance in general. The impact of fatigue on performance has been compared with that of alcohol.[30] However, many doctors find themselves in a situation where they are required to work for twenty-four, thirty-two, or sometimes even more hours at a time, often at high levels of intensity. An example of this is given in Chapter 1 (the case of the 'systems double-bind'), in which a coroner commented on how long a surgeon and anaesthetist had been working without a break at the time an accident occurred. He indicated that he considered the hours the doctors had worked at the time of the event to be unacceptable. At the same time, this coroner also recognised that these individual doctors were not primarily or solely responsible for the situation; the hours had not been worked by choice but had been forced on them by the system. He recommended that the hours doctors work in general should be re-examined. Much change has occurred in recent years in many countries in relation to the hours of

---

[29] Reason, *Human Error*, 196.
[30] D. Dawson and K. Reid, 'Fatigue, alcohol and performance impairment' (1997) 388 *Nature* 235.

work of junior doctors, but not usually to the same degree in relation to those of senior doctors. There is ongoing debate about whether the effects seen in experimental work are also seen in clinical practice, and on whether the advantages of reducing fatigue are offset by disadvantages such as the increased number times that the care of individual patients has to be handed over from one doctor to another.[31]

Optimising violations are violations for the thrill of it. Driving in excess of the speed limit would be an example if the motivation was the pursuit of excitement rather than the desire to get somewhere more quickly.

A characteristic of all the above forms of violation is that there is no actual intention to cause harm. In general, the perpetrator believes that the consequences of the violation will be neutral at worst, or even beneficial – in terms of greater efficiency, for example. Actions deliberately aimed at causing harm should be categorised as *sabotage*.

Violations as Antecedent Actions to Errors

Violations often create an increased risk of error and make the consequences more serious when an error does occur. Alternatively, like errors, they may make it more difficult to detect or deal with problems that subsequently arise. This is a very important aspect of violations, and a major reason why it is so important to take them seriously. Thus, speed itself may not cause motor accidents, but it reduces the time available for the driver to react to new situations and increases the chance of a mistake. If a mistake is made and an accident occurs, the energy associated with the crash increases in proportion to the square of the speed, so that the chance of serious injury or death is greatly increased.

A medical example of this principle is to be found once again in a case relating to an anaesthetic machine.[32] At the beginning of an operating session, a machine check by the anaesthetist identified a problem with part of the breathing circuit. The relevant piece of apparatus was dispatched to a technician for a small repair, while the surgeon proceeded

---

[31]   A. F. Merry and G. R. Warman, 'Fatigue and the anaesthetist' (2006) 34 *Anaesthesia and Intensive Care* 577–8; J. M. Rothschild, C. A. Keohane, S. Rogers, R. Gardner, S. R. Lipsitz, C. A. Salzberg, . . . C. P. Landrigan, 'Risks of complications by attending physicians after performing nighttime procedures' (2009) 302 *Journal of the American Medical Association* 1565–72; J. F. Cheeseman, C. S. Webster, M. D. M. Pawley, M. A. Francis, G. R. Warman and A. F. Merry, 'Use of a new task-relevant test to assess the effects of shift work and drug labelling formats on anesthesia trainees' drug recognition and confirmation' (2011) 58 *Canadian Journal of Anaesthesia* 38–47.

[32]   C. Du Chateau, 'Some deaths are never the end' (1998) *New Zealand Herald* A15.

with a number of minor operations under local anaesthetic. The proper technician was temporarily absent, but he shared a workshop with another technician who worked in a slightly different field. This second technician, with the best intentions, to save everyone concerned the delay and trouble of finding the appropriately trained and qualified person, took the initiative of doing the job himself. He did this in the belief that the matter was very straightforward – which on the surface it appeared to be. Regrettably, because of an arcane quirk in the design of the apparatus, his method of repair created an invisible but lethal fault. The apparatus was not properly rechecked before being put back into use. An independent problem subsequently developed in ventilating the first patient to be anaesthetised with the repaired apparatus. This, combined with the fault in the apparatus, caused considerable difficulties for the anaesthetist and the patient died. The degree to which the fault in the apparatus contributed to the cause of death was disputed, but clearly this fault was not helpful to the anaesthetist dealing with a difficult clinical situation. This example provides a good illustration of the way in which a sequence of minor events can lead to disaster. The first violation involved the well-motivated but inappropriate assistance of the wrong technician. There is a similarity between this and the antecedent cause of the Cave Creek example discussed above. It really is very dangerous for people to undertake tasks for which they are not trained in the absence of supervision or instruction – as Lord Finchley found to his cost (in relation to repairing electric lights).[33] This violation was followed by an error – failing to recheck the machine. Although it might be argued that this was also a violation, it is obvious that the machine had been checked at the beginning of the day, and it seems likely that the omission of the recheck was a lapse precipitated by the break in the normal sequence of the day's events. At any rate, the violation and error together had created a situation in which it was much more difficult to deal with a completely independent problem when one arose.

The use of a power tool or outdoor appliance without the precaution of an isolation transformer or equivalent safety device provides another example of the way in which errors and violations may interact to cause harm. In itself, failing to use an isolation device should not be dangerous, but the ability of the system to tolerate subsequent errors is

---

[33] H. Belloc, 'Lord Finchley', in *Hilaire Belloc's Cautionary Verses* (New York, Alfred A. Knopf, 1941), 268–9. See http://allpoetry.com/Lord-Finchley, accessed 24 June 2016.

clearly reduced by this violation, with a consequent reduction in safety. Some years ago, the children of one of the authors offered to clean the family car. Fortunately, an early check was made on progress. This revealed the children hard at work – one with a vacuum cleaner cleaning the inside of the car, the other with a garden hose washing the outside. The use of water at the same time as electricity was an error – a rule-based mistake; the children did know the rule concerning the relationship of water and electricity, but only vaguely, and had not appreciated that it would apply to the activity in question. The vacuum-cleaner cord was plugged into an extension cord, and this pair of connected plugs was lying in a pool of water made by the hose. The combination of a violation (failure to use the isolation transformer, which was available and part of the normal routine of the household in respect of out-of-door appliances) and an error (by which water and electricity were unthinkingly allowed to come together) had created a potentially lethal situation. The proper procedure on the part of the parent in checking on his children's progress offset *his* earlier violation of not supervising the initial steps of the process and ensuring that the isolation transformer was in use. The fact that a disaster was averted was mainly a matter of good fortune. It is interesting to speculate on the analysis of blame that would have ensued if five minutes' additional delay in checking had resulted in the death of a child. An important ground for objecting to even minor violations is that they weaken one layer of the defences that exist in any system, and thereby reduce the margin of safety.

Distinction Between Violations and Errors

Because violations always involve a decision, they most closely resemble mistakes. However, a violation could very easily masquerade as a lapse if the decision involved the omission of an important step in a procedure. For example, the failure to check an anaesthetic machine could be a lapse, but equally it could be a violation. These two categories of unsafe acts are quite distinct, and the difference is very important. We have seen in Chapter 2 that a lapse is something to which all human beings are liable from time to time, on account of the phenomenon of attentional capture. People do not choose to have lapses – they can occur even when every effort is being made to avoid them. On the other hand, a violation involves an active choice. Violations are therefore, to a greater or lesser extent, avoidable, and this raises very different moral questions, to which we shall return in the next chapter. It is not always possible to distinguish an error from a violation, but there are features of each that can assist in making this distinction.

One clue to distinguishing between the two is the track record of the individual concerned, if this is available. If a person is known to be a meticulous checker of anaesthetic machines, then the chances are that a single failure in this process would be a lapse. The other features that would support the diagnosis of a lapse would be the presence of some unusual distraction – the fact that a colleague had interrupted the preparatory process just before the point at which the check would normally have been undertaken, for example. Even more convincing would be a sudden crisis at the critical moment – for example, the sudden onset of a seizure in a patient about to be anaesthetised might lead the anaesthetist justifiably to defer the check, and subsequently forget to perform it later.

The story of the forgotten baby (outlined in Chapter 1) concerned a caring mother trying to do the right thing, but actually doing the wrong thing, so it is the story of an error, not a violation. The relevance here is that it illustrates how similar the two phenomena can be, but also illustrates the sort of objective features that can often assist in making the distinction between error and violation. Many parents do leave children unattended in cars for short periods of time, expecting to get away with this without harming the child. These are violations – these parents are deliberately running a risk that would be impossible to justify if things went wrong. In this context errors cannot be distinguished from violations on the basis of the extent to which the parents love their children – most parents love their children, even those who occasionally take certain risks with them. Similarly, they cannot be distinguished by the level of risk incurred – interestingly, these actions probably incur less risk as violations than as errors, because of the conscious nature of the decision in a violation and therefore an awareness of the necessity to get back to the child quickly. They certainly cannot be distinguished on the basis of outcome – we have discussed the role of *moral luck* in previous chapters, and we will return to this topic in Chapter 7.

Instead, the distinction depends on the evidence (outlined in Chapter 3) that this mother was working from a mental model that had shifted from reality. Notably, it is obvious from her response to the crèche's first text that she was quite convinced she had dropped her baby off at the crèche. Other features characteristic of error in this story are the routineness of the activity of driving to work and dropping the child off at crèche, a track record of doing so on previous occasions, the presence of fatigue, the contribution of distraction (she was 'on autopilot', her mind on her work) and the fact that exactly the same type of error has occurred before, with other people, quite often.

Working While Fatigued – An Example of Violation?

Writing in the *New Yorker*, Atul Gawande observed that 'The real problem isn't how to stop bad doctors from harming, even killing, their patients. It's how to prevent good doctors from doing so.'[34] In Chapter 2 we advanced data that suggest that the level of avoidable harm occurring in hospitals at the present time, worldwide, is substantial. A problem of this magnitude is unlikely to involve only a minority of practitioners. If it is the case, as it seems to be, that most doctors (and other health professionals) cause avoidable harm to a patient at some stage in their careers, this cannot mean that the majority are incompetent or habitually careless. It must mean that Gawande is correct – this is a problem that is affecting the 'good' doctors, nurses and other practitioners as well as those who may be less competent or conscientious.

In Chapters 2 and 3 we argued that every human being is inevitably subject to error at some stage. Can it be that all people are also guilty of violations of one sort or another, from time to time? We turn now to consider in greater depth the issue of doctors (and others) who undertake hazardous activities after working for excessive hours. We suggest that choosing to work while fatigued is an example of a routine violation made by many health practitioners at some stage. Doctors (and at times other health professionals) who have driven themselves to work quite often find themselves in the position of having worked all day and then all night, and then needing to get home to sleep. This is a typical situation for a violation – it is obviously unwise to drive after twenty-four hours without sleep; indeed, the problem of driving while fatigued by long-haul truck drivers, and by the public in general, has been compared to the problem of drinking and driving.[35] An interesting point, though, is that if it is unwise for a tired doctor to drive at 8 a.m., was it acceptable for him or her to be caring for patients at 7 a.m.? In both cases, the pressures to do

---

[34] A. Gawande, 'When doctors make mistakes', *The New Yorker* (1 February 1999), 40–55.
[35] W. C. Dement, 'The perils of drowsy driving' (1997) 337 *New England Journal of Medicine* 783–4.

the wrong thing are strong, and, to make matters worse, insight tends to be less acute in the presence of fatigue.

The violation of doing potentially dangerous things when seriously fatigued has a number of features of particular interest. First, caring for patients while fatigued generally reflects high levels of commitment and motivation on the part of dedicated health professionals, whereas driving while fatigued seems somehow, in general, less edifying, yet these violations are intrinsically very similar. Second, the fact that this problem has largely been eliminated from commercial aviation illustrates the importance of systemic issues to the generation of violations as well as errors. Finally, this example illustrates the diffuse nature of responsibility in relation to certain types of violation. Those in charge of healthcare organisations could do much to deal with both the need to care for patients while fatigued and the need for practitioners to get home safely after situations in which long hours of work are unavoidable, and should share in any associated responsibility related to these issues.

The requirement to work while fatigued has been a striking feature of medical practice and continues to be so for at least some practitioners. For example, in a survey of New Zealand anaesthetists, 71 per cent of trainees and 58 per cent of specialists reported that in the preceding 6 months they had worked longer hours than they considered safe, while 63 per cent and 40 per cent, respectively, had worked longer hours than they considered compatible with their own personal well-being.[36] In 1984 Libby Zion, an eighteen-year-old woman, was admitted to the emergency department of a New York hospital. She died without having been seen by any senior member of staff, and having been in the care of junior doctors who had all been on duty for more than 18 hours continuously at the time. Recommendations for reform of the hours worked by junior doctors in emergency departments were made as a result of this case. Amongst these, a 12-hour limit was placed on emergency room shifts; residents in acute care specialities were to work no more than 80 hours a week averaged over a 4-week period,[37] and no more than

---

[36] P. H. Gander, A. Merry, M. M. Millar and J. Weller, 'Hours of work and fatigue-related error: A survey of New Zealand anaesthetists' (2000) 28 *Anaesthesia and Intensive Care* 178–83.

[37] This still implies some very long weeks indeed. In order to have one week of, say, 40 hours in a four-week cycle, the hours worked in the remaining three would need to exceed 90 hours per week, for example; more probably the hours worked in at least one week in the cycle would be in excess of 100.

24 consecutive hours, and no moonlighting was to be allowed! Obviously, the hours worked previously were even longer, but even the recommended hours of work are hardly compatible with safe practice. Astonishing as it may seem, five years later (after considerable wrangling over various concerns, including the matter of who should pay the increased costs of compliance with these recommendations) many hospitals in New York had failed to implement these recommendations. Many emergency department doctors continued to work hours that by any reasonable standards must be considered excessive.[38] More than two decades later, despite numerous (primarily regulatory) initiatives in various countries to address excessive hours of work by junior doctors, there is substantial evidence to suggest that fatigue is still often at least a potential factor in the generation of errors and that fatigue may be detrimental to the mental and physical well-being of overworked doctors.[39] On the other hand, it has also become clearer that at least some concerns over the downsides of limiting doctors' work hours were at least partially justified, primarily in relation to continuity of care and handovers but also in relation to acquiring adequate experience to become a truly competent independent practitioner.[40]

Anecdotal accounts of heroic feats of endurance are part of the folklore of medicine, and many doctors (particularly older doctors) can recall periods of their training and of their subsequent careers when they worked forty-eight or more hours on continuous duty with little or no sleep. In the past, when there was a world-wide shortage of doctors, such hours may have been justifiable on the grounds that it was better for patients to be seen by a tired doctor than by no doctor at all. Similarly, in a war, many people are called upon to perform marathon efforts of this sort. There may be no alternative. In some low-income areas of the world, this may still hold true, but in peacetime, in most middle- and high-income countries this type of

[38] US Congress Office of Technology Assessment, *Biological Rhythms: Implications for the Worker, OTA-BA-463* (Washington, D.C., 1991), 168–70.
[39] Merry and Warman, 'Fatigue and the anaesthetist'; P. Gander, C. Briar, A. Garden, H. Purnell and A. Woodward, 'A gender-based analysis of work patterns, fatigue, and work/life balance among physicians in postgraduate training' (2010) 85 *Academic Medicine* 1526–36.
[40] N. Spritz, 'Oversight of physicians' conduct by state licensing agencies. Lessons from New York's Libby Zion case' (1991) 115 *Annals of Internal Medicine* 219–22; N. Patel, 'Learning lessons: the Libby Zion case revisited' (2014) 64 *Journal of the American College of Cardiology* 2802–4; D. A. Asch and R. M. Parker, 'The Libby Zion case. One step forward or two steps backward?' (1988) 318 *New England Journal of Medicine* 771–5.

justification should no longer apply.[41] Nevertheless, the fact that this problem persists in healthcare does reflect some genuine challenges in relation to the practice of medicine. We have mentioned continuity of care and the need to gain experience. On the other hand, the relationship between hours worked and money earned can also be a factor in this complex social conundrum, and there may be other factors as well. In the end, though, as with many routine violations, the reality seems to be that many practitioners are less than completely convinced that working while fatigued is necessarily a bad thing to do.

What, then, is the evidence that fatigue really does impact adversely on performance? Ultimately, the answer is obvious and well known: human beings, like all animals, need sleep. Without sleep, their performance will eventually deteriorate, and they will eventually collapse and die. However, the more relevant, and more difficult, question is how much sleep deprivation can be tolerated safely. The answer depends on the individual, the context (adrenaline is a great performance enhancer and boredom may have the opposite effect) and the task. There are certainly data to show that fatigue has an adverse effect on performance in the laboratory, and that the degradation in performance associated with fatigue is progressive and takes place in much the same way as that seen with increasing levels of alcohol in the blood.[42] It is less clear, though, that impaired performance on various psychomotor tests can be extrapolated to particular clinical situations. A number of studies have now examined the question of the impact of fatigue on the performance of doctors in real life: some results have been equivocal, others more compelling.[43] Against this background, and in the face of the attitudes of

---

[41] In fact, in many parts of the world, there seems to be a growing concern over a relative oversupply of doctors, although supply is uneven between specialities and geographical regions, some of which remain short of manpower even in wealthy countries. However, these apparent shortages reflect misdistribution of resources rather than absolute shortage, so solutions should be possible given a genuine will to find them.

[42] J. J. Pilcher and A. I. Huffcutt, 'Effects of sleep deprivation on performance: a meta-analysis' (1996) 19 *Sleep* 318–26; Dawson and Reid, 'Fatigue, alcohol and performance impairment'.

[43] V. Narang and J. R. D. Laycock, 'Psychomotor testing of on-call anaesthetists' (1986) 41 *Anaesthesia* 868–9; E. E. Christensen, G. W. Dietz, R. C. Murry and J. G. Moore, 'The effect of fatigue on resident performance' (1977) 125 *Radiology* 103–5; S. W. Lockley, J. W. Cronin, E. E. Evans, B. E. Cade, C. J. Lee, C. P. Landrigan, … C. A. Czeisler, 'Effect of reducing interns' weekly work hours on sleep and attentional failures' (2004) 351 *New England Journal of Medicine* 1829–37; C. P. Landrigan, J. M. Rothschild, J. W. Cronin, R. Kaushal, E. Burdick, J. T. Katz, … C. A. Czeisler, 'Effect of reducing interns' work hours on serious medical errors in intensive care

many senior doctors whose entire career has been built around a culture of denial of human weakness, it is hardly surprising that change has been slow in coming.

There are many important factors to consider in the interpretation of the results of studies of fatigue in medicine, including the potentially confounding influence of practice effects on psychomotor testing, the influence of circadian rhythms and the fact that different tasks may be impaired to different degrees by fatigue. The results of a study by Howard and colleagues place those of many earlier studies in an interesting light.[44] Traditionally, studies of fatigue in medicine have compared a group of junior doctors who have been on duty the night before with a group who have not. In the Howard study a third group was added to these two traditional samples. In this group of junior doctors, rest was actively promoted for several days. Not only were the members of this group relieved of night duty, they were permitted to arrive later than usual for work, and their early morning duties were covered by seniors. The results were striking, particularly in regard to sleep latency. This test measures the time taken for a subject to fall asleep in a quiet and darkened room with his or her eyes closed. A value of five minutes or less is typical of patients with sleep disorders such as narcolepsy. A normal time is in the order of twenty minutes. In this study, both the traditional groups had sleep latencies of about five minutes (i.e. virtually pathological), with no difference between them, but the third or rested group had significantly longer sleep latencies, much closer to those of normal subjects. The implication is that a single night off duty was not enough for the sleep-deprived doctors to catch up. It is quite likely that, in many previous studies that have attempted to compare tired doctors with rested ones, the members of both groups have been sleep deprived and the failure to show clear differences between them is therefore understandable. Interestingly, in the Howard study, although there was more subjective sleepiness and sleepy behaviour and more impaired psychomotor performance and mood in the sleep-deprived participants than in those allowed extended sleep, no difference was shown between

units' (2004) 351 *New England Journal of Medicine* 1838–48; L. Rosenbaum, Leaping without looking – duty hours, autonomy, and the risks of research and practice'(2016) 374 *New England Journal of Medicine* 701–3.

[44] S. K. Howard, D. M. Gaba, B. E. Smith, M. B. Weinger, C. Herndon, S. Keshavacharya and M. R. Rosekind, 'Simulation study of rested versus sleep-deprived anesthesiologists' (2003) 98 *Anesthesiology* 1345–55.

groups in clinical performance in managing highly realistic simulated cases.[45]

Fatigue has been cited as a contributing factor in a number of major disasters, including the *Challenger* explosion,[46] and in various medical cases. Examples include the case of the 'systems double-bind' discussed earlier in this chapter, and that of a well-regarded junior doctor who made a lethal drug administration error after having worked 110 hours in the preceding week.[47] In the New Zealand survey quoted earlier, 86 per cent of respondents reported making an error that they attributed to fatigue at some stage in their careers.[48] It is likely that certain types of error are more influenced by fatigue than others. For example, in the Australian Incident Monitoring Study, perceived fatigue was overrepresented in drug administration errors.[49] However, there is a difference between the perception that fatigue has been a factor in the generation of an error and hard evidence that it has. A sleep history is more reliable than questions about subjective experiences of being tired. In one large study in which a sleep history was prospectively sought there was no important difference in objective measures of sleep between reports of drug errors in which fatigue was subjectively identified as a factor and those in which it was not.[50] A similar point has been made in relation to the case of Libby Zion – the fact that someone was fatigued does not in itself mean that fatigue was a factor in any error that has been made (although it is appropriate to ask whether it might have been). Both tired and rested people make mistakes.

[45] There may be various reasons for this finding in relation to clinical care: a bigger study may well have shown a difference, but clinical care is complex and quite difficult to assess, doctors who are not fatigued make some mistakes while, on the other hand, most doctors have considerable capacity to compensate for momentary lapses and patients tolerate many forms of error well. Thus the numbers needed in a study of this type to show a difference between groups might be very large indeed. On the other hand even a single mistake by an anaesthetist, attributable to fatigue, *could* be lethal.
[46] S. Coren, *Sleep Thieves* (New York, Free Press, 1996).
[47] R. Savill, 'Tired doctor cleared over patient's death' (1995) *The Daily Telegraph* 3.
[48] Gander et al., 'Hours of work and fatigue-related error: A survey of New Zealand anaesthetists'.
[49] A. L. Garden, M. Currie and P. H. Gander, 'Sleep loss, performance and the safe conduct of anaesthesia', in J. Keneally and M. Jones (eds.), *Australasian Anaesthesia* (Melbourne, Australian and New Zealand College of Anaesthetists, 1996), 43–51.
[50] C. S. Webster, A. F. Merry, L. Larsson, K. A. McGrath and J. Weller, 'The frequency and nature of drug administration error during anaesthesia' (2001) 29 *Anaesthesia and Intensive Care* 494–500.

Nevertheless, we believe that it is at least arguable that the weight of evidence justifies accepting that carrying out *elective* work while excessively fatigued should be viewed as a violation of a principle of safe practice. It is not quite clear how to define the exact number of work hours at which one should draw the line, but it is fairly obvious that many doctors often exceed any reasonable level of fatigue by a substantial margin. The flying hours of commercial pilots have typical monthly limits similar to those worked by some doctors in a week.[51] In the case of the 'systems double-bind' (see Chapter 1) the coroner recognised that fatigue was very probably a contributory factor, but also recognised that the system was more to blame than the individual doctors. He called for the matter to be reviewed by the relevant colleges. Such reviews have been undertaken in various places and at various times, notably by the Australian Medical Association.[52] In Britain, the implementation of the European Working Time Directive (EWTD) has reduced the working week for most doctors to an average of 48 hours, with various other limits and provisions related to hours worked.[53] However, such efforts continue to face opposition, perhaps for good reason. It is interesting that a recent survey of over 8,000 doctors (with a response rate of 54.4 per cent, which is high for a large survey) indicated considerable dissatisfaction over this initiative. Only 12 per cent of respondents agreed that the EWTD has benefited the NHS, 9 per cent that it has benefited senior doctors and 31 per cent that it has benefited junior doctors. Respondents from 'craft' specialties such as surgery, for which (as we have already noted) there is a genuine requirement for extensive practical experience, were particularly critical.[54] The conclusion of the authors of the qualitative arm of this survey is consistent with our observation earlier in this chapter: a balance

---

[51] The actual hours worked exceed the hours of flying, and there are substantial differences between pilots flying long haul for major airlines and those working for smaller companies flying light aircraft over short distances with frequent stops and a greater proportion of other duties. Nevertheless, the limits described above in relation to the Libby Zion case are not unusual for doctors, and in general are far in excess of the hours required of a commercial pilot.

[52] Australian Medical Association Ltd, *National Code of Practice – Hours of Work, Shiftwork and Rostering for Hospital Doctors* (Kingston, 2005).

[53] www.bma.org.uk/support-at-work/ewtd

[54] J. J. Maisonneuve, T. W. Lambert and M. J. Goldacre, 'UK doctors' views on the implementation of the European Working Time Directive as applied to medical practice: a quantitative analysis' (2014) 4 *BMJ Open* e004391; R. T. Clarke, A. Pitcher, T. W. Lambert and M. J. Goldacre, 'UK doctors' views on the implementation of the European Working Time Directive as applied to medical practice: a qualitative analysis' (2014) 4 *BMJ Open* e004390.

is required 'between the need to ensure what is perceived to be a safe working environment for junior doctors, and the needs of patients to experience continuity of care, of trainees to receive adequate training and of all doctors to work in an environment which is conducive to job satisfaction'.

It is likely that in years to come people will look back on the hours worked by doctors in the past (and even today) in amazement. However, if they are surprised at all by the number of harmful events which have occurred in association with fatigue, it may be because they are fewer than one might expect. People seem capable of remarkably successful performance while very tired – most of the time. In an emergency, or the absence of alternatives, working while fatigued may become a necessary violation.

Much has changed in regard to medical practice and fatigue since the first edition of this book was published. Without doubt, progress has been made on reducing the hours worked by many junior doctors from totally insupportable levels to variations on the theme of what is reasonable. In respect of senior doctors, there have been fewer changes in regulation, but we have (anecdotal) evidence of an increasing expectation for, and acceptance of, the exercise of common sense in relation to the management of fatigue.

It seems to us that the way forward lies less in regulation and more in a greater maturity of approach by all concerned (and we think this applies to many examples of violation in healthcare). There is more to impaired performance than hours of work alone. Circadian factors are also very important, so shift work may not be as helpful as one might expect. Also, sleep loss may occur outside the workplace: various social factors may contribute, from partying to having to stay up all night to care for a sick child. In at least some accounts of Flight 447 (see Chapter 1), reference is made to the possibility that the captain had only one hour of sleep on the night before the flight.[55] This was not mentioned as a possible contributory factor to the tragedy in the final accident investigation report,[56] but the possibility that sleep loss might have been a factor in this story

---

[55] 'Revealed: Pilot of Air France jet that crashed in Atlantic Ocean killing 228 people had just ONE HOUR sleep before flight' (15 March 2013) www.dailymail.co.uk/news/article-2293750/Pilot-Air-France-plane-crashed-killing-228-people-slept-just-ONE-HOUR-flight.html, accessed 30 June 2016.

[56] 'Crash du Rio–Paris, la fatigue des pilotes a été cachée [Rio–Paris crash: the pilots' fatigue was hidden]' (15 March 2013) www.lepoint.fr/societe/crash-du-rio-paris-la-fatigue-des-pilotes-a-ete-cachee-15-03-2013-1640312_23.php, accessed 30 June 2016.

illustrates the point that fatigue may be a problem even in an industry that regulates hours of work very effectively. Many people feel obliged to work even when tired or otherwise unwell, particularly if there is no one obviously available to take their place. Again, the motivation here seems laudable rather than reprehensible, but it follows that organisations have a responsibility to provide appropriate practical and moral support for employees who declare themselves unfit to work, for whatever reason, including fatigue.[57] Acute illness is clearly relevant here, and many doctors are notoriously unwilling to take sick leave, although even this is changing, with some hospitals now designating one or two junior doctors as 'relief' staff to cover those who phone in sick.

Somehow an organisation requires a culture that includes willingness on the part of professionals to declare, when appropriate, that they are too tired or too ill to work, without losing the current widespread commitment to going the extra mile when it really matters – in an emergency when no one else is available. This implies supportiveness amongst colleagues and requires administrators who will work with clinicians to find pragmatic locally applicable solutions to the many variations on these challenging themes. Both those who administer healthcare, and those who work in it, should share in accountability for managing fatigue (and other sources of impaired performance) appropriately.

This discussion shows that an apparently simple violation may not be simple at all. Instead, a deceptively complex set of issues may be involved. Many other violations in healthcare reflect similarly complex constellations of factors. As we have already argued, the notion that violations can be adequately understood simply by reference to formal rules does not seem tenable in the context of such complexity. Judgement and personal responsibility are called for on the part of practitioners, within an organisational culture of supportiveness, common sense and collective responsibility for good outcomes for patients.

Design and Violations

In Chapter 2 we discussed the way in which inferior design may predispose to error, and this is equally true for violations. Conversely, good

---

[57] This typically implies the need for some redundancy in staffing – if a pilot or health practitioner calls in sick at the last moment, another has to be found to take his or her place. In the case of Flight 447, having three pilots on an aeroplane that can be flown by two, with facilities for rest, may also be seen as providing a reasonable alternative solution to this problem.

design is a major force in the reduction of violations. In Chapter 2 we discussed Norman's concept of the affordances of things. If something is designed in such a way that its correct use is obvious and easy, while at the same time undesirable practices are difficult, the likelihood of its being used in the appropriate way is greatly increased. If the design of something permits dangerous practices, it is probably only a matter of time before these occur, whether deliberately or in error. The ferry *The Herald of Free Enterprise* sank in 1987, with the loss of 188 lives, when it sailed with both its inner and outer bow doors fully open. In that the order to sail was given in the belief that the doors were closed, this was technically an error, although it was obviously an error that violated an important rule. The assistant bosun, whose job it was to close the doors, was actually asleep at the time, and no one else in the chain of command conducted an explicit check of the doors. There were a number of organisational factors and deficiencies in communication which contributed to this failure, but aspects of the ship's design were also highly relevant. In the first place, the very concept of bow doors that could be flooded if left open is questionable. However, given that such doors have particular advantages and that it had therefore been decided to incorporate them into the design of the ship, it would seem obvious to include within the design of the doors some mechanism to ensure that the ship could not set out to sea unless they were properly closed. At the very least, there should have been an automatic warning system, with indicators on the bridge, to ensure that the master of the boat was aware of their state of openness or otherwise. Neither of these features was present. Apparently bridge indicators of an appropriate type would have cost only about £500 to add to the completed ship, but the real question is why they were not incorporated from the beginning.[58] This was a situation in which simple design improvements would have been far more effective in ensuring proper practice than any number of rules or procedures, although the rules and procedures associated with this disaster seem to have been seriously deficient as well.

A very good example of the same principle is to be found in the design of anaesthetic machines. We have noted that the pre-anaesthetic check of these machines is not always undertaken in the prescribed way, and not always even in an adequate way. In the past there have been several tragic deaths associated with failures to deliver oxygen to patients, either because of an undetected fault in the machine or in the arrangements

---

[58] J. Reason, *Human Error*, 193, 256.

of the pipes carrying different gases to the machine, or because of a failure by the anaesthetist to understand fully the functions of an unfamiliar machine.[59] This was a serious risk, and many more near misses occurred than actual disasters. Reducing this risk has involved several initiatives, but the most effective developments have been in the design of anaesthetic equipment. Today's anaesthetists take advantage of a number of technological developments to make sure that they deliver adequate amounts of oxygen to their patients. Most notably, these include devices that simply will not permit a hypoxic mixture to be delivered from the machine. In general, no mixture of gases with an oxygen content lower than air can be specified by the anaesthetist. As well as this, it is now routine to analyse the composition of the gas mixture coming from the machine and to display it continuously, with alarms set to warn the anaesthetist if certain predefined limits are crossed. As a third tier in this safety network, pulse oximetry is used routinely to monitor the percentage of oxygen in the patient's bloodstream.

We touched on the issue of preventing hypoxia in anaesthesia in relation to error in Chapter 3. The violation of failing to check a machine may be as important in the generation of problems of this type as any error in the conduct of the anaesthetic itself. In the case of violations there is an even stronger tendency to approach problems of this type by focusing on the operator, by exhorting people to behave better, threatening them with harsh punishment if they fail to meet expected standards and by writing increasingly prescriptive regulations to define acceptable procedures. This is not entirely without justification – violations are certainly more amenable than errors to control by initiatives to modify the way in which people carry out their duties. However, taken collectively (and in conjunction with proper standards in relation to the gases which are supplied to the machines and with devices that make incorrect attachments of pipelines and cylinders difficult if not impossible), these safety innovations in respect to anaesthesia have achieved far more to prevent disasters than would any amount of regulation or exhortation. As with errors, the key is to engineer human failure out of the system wherever possible.

Unfortunately advances in design are not universally conducive to greater safety. For example, the increased use of computers (coupled with

---

[59] An example of this is provided in P. D. G. Skegg, 'Criminal prosecutions of negligent health professionals: the New Zealand experience' (1998) 6 *Medical Law Review*, 220–46.

fly-by-wire joysticks) in the Airbus A300 may have contributed to the disaster of Flight 447. On the other hand, these aeroplanes also have many safety features made possible by this increased computerisation, and the overall safety record of the Airbus is very good, so it is difficult to know whether the approach taken by this company has been more or less successful in promoting safety than that taken by other aircraft manufacturers. Similar comments can be made about recent developments in the design of some anaesthetic machines. Increased computerisation has facilitated some useful advances in the safe delivery of anaesthetics, but has come at the price of a more complex user interface and less transparent functionality. Time will tell whether or not the cause of safety has been advanced by this approach.

Promoting Compliance

Systematic and design factors are very important in ensuring that an activity or environment is inherently safe. Unfortunately, safety devices may fail, may generate new problems of their own or may be circumvented by ingenious individuals who consider them a nuisance. The technology exists to limit the speeds on cars, and even to respond to different speed limits in different geographical zones. Devices to measure the alcohol in expired breath can be attached to the ignition systems of cars to prevent the cars from starting until the driver has provided an acceptable sample of breath. Such technology has failed to achieve widespread use. By contrast, devices continue to be sold to detect traffic officers' radar equipment and thereby facilitate the optimising violations of those who choose to drive at unlawful speeds. Each new generation of cars is faster than the one before. Recently, there has been a widespread increase in the interest in passive safety features in the design of cars, and there is clear evidence that these make a considerable difference to outcome in road traffic accidents.[60] Even today, however, features other than those related to safety are deemed more important in the marketing of a new model. The magazines in which motorcars are reviewed devote considerable resources to evaluating their performance. Top speeds ludicrously in excess of any legal limit are extolled as virtues. The road toll is one of the major health problems facing modern societies,

---

[60] NCAP data are available from www.nrma.com.au.index.html, from www.nhtsa.dot.gov ./ncap/nca.cfm, and from other sites. Interestingly, safer cars may result in greater risk-taking on the part of drivers – a recognised revenge effect, called 'risk homeostasis'; see E. Tenner, *Why Things Bite Back* (London, Fourth Estate, 1996), 261–8.

and yet our culture is one of denial and of complicity with violation. Very recently, cars have been developed that are capable of driving themselves with minimal need for human input. It has been suggested that the ownership of motorcars by individuals may give way to collective systems of transport based on cars of this type. These cars will apparently be convenient, economical and completely compliant with the rules of the road. A whole category of violation could become a thing of the past! More development is still needed, but even then it will be interesting to see how long it takes to overcome the current widespread passion for owning and driving cars (and motorcycles).[61]

Increasing the number of rules, and increasing the signs or other notices which promulgate them, is likely to have limited effect on reducing violations unless it is widely perceived that the chances of being apprehended are high and that some punishment will result. The likelihood of routine violations is increased by an environment which seldom identifies and punishes inappropriate behaviour, and which rarely rewards observance of the rules. As already discussed, it is common for violators to believe that no harm will flow from their actions, either to themselves or to other people. Many violations in medicine may be understood on the basis of this insight. The practitioners concerned are simply not convinced that the rules that they violate on a routine basis are important. Their day-to-day experience reinforces the perception that they can get away with these violations. They believe that the risk of harm from such violations to their own patients is negligible. In the same way, the reduction of excessive speed on the roads is more likely to be achieved by ensuring that speeding is highly likely to result in apprehension and a fine than by the thought that it might cause a terrible accident, because most drivers believe the chances of such an accident to be relatively low.

In New York a stricter approach to policing in respect of minor violations appears to have paid dividends in reducing major crime. Most people are more readily influenced by the perception that a moderately undesirable event is likely than by the perception that a terribly serious event is remotely possible – although the factors that lead to an individual's evaluation of any given risk are often far from rational.[62] At the former Green Lane Hospital in Auckland, two

---

[61] J. Harper, 'Self-driving Cars Are No Longer a Thing of the Future', TIME (2015) http://time.com/3661446/self-driving-driverless-cars-ces/, accessed 24 June 2016.

[62] K. Petrie, 'Sum of our fears a bit over the odds', *New Zealand Herald* (17 October 1997), A13.

innovations improved performance with the checking of anaesthetic machines by anaesthetic technicians. First, as discussed above, successive revisions to the relevant protocol have made it easier to do the checks that matter in particular contexts. Second, a logbook was introduced that must be signed by the technician doing the checks. Signing in the absence of carrying out the required checks would be a clear and wilful violation, and could be expected to be discovered eventually through the manifestation of a problem attributable to the lack of checking. This would be viewed by all concerned as a serious matter, and compliance has been excellent. In Colombia, one department of anaesthesia has introduced a system of fines for common minor offences, such as arriving late for the start of a list. Absolute liability applies (i.e. no excuses are accepted), but the fines are reasonable in magnitude and are put into a jointly held account to support discretionary activities for the department, including research. Again, this has proved very successful.[63] To return to the road traffic problem: many countries in recent years have run publicity campaigns to try to change the cultural approach to driving, both by reinforcing the consequences of accidents and by promoting safer behaviour on the roads. To some extent the objective is to increase the acceptance by reasonable and well-motivated people (the majority of society, we believe) of systems of sanction for violations, such as exceeding the speed limit, and lowering the legal limit for blood alcohol while driving. In general, improved performance is more easily obtained than sustained – ongoing effort is required to avoid a gradual drift back to widespread routine violation.

A combination of motivational activity, supported where necessary by minor sanctions, does seem to work with most people, but recidivist violation of established rules on the part of a small minority of individuals seems to be a problem of a somewhat different kind. Observation and anecdote suggests that this is true in general, but, in healthcare, data clearly show that a few individuals generate a disproportionately high number of complaints. Research by Bismark and colleagues demonstrated that nearly half the complaints made against doctors in Australia concerned 3 per cent of the medical workforce. Furthermore (in related research), once a doctor in the State of Victoria had three complaints, there was a greater than 50 per cent chance of a fourth within

---

[63] Ibarra, P. 2015. Personal communication.

two years.[64] These results are likely to apply in most countries. A more definitive approach is warranted to understand and deal with the reasons for repeated complaints: some specialities are associated with higher numbers of complaints for reasons beyond the control of individual practitioners, and illness (including mental illness) on the part of practitioners may sometimes be a factor, but some doctors are clearly just incompetent or otherwise unsuitable for practice. It is possible that personality traits play a part in this, and we return to the role of character in Chapter 9. Whatever the underlying reasons, recidivism of this type should be identified and addressed.[65] We will return to the question of effective accountability in healthcare in Chapter 10.

Violations and the Culture of Organisations

It is natural to expect that properly trained professionals would know the rules and obey them. Examples taken from everyday life probably have little bearing on the work of a specialist doctor, nurse, pharmacist, ambulance officer, fire fighter, policeman, electrician, airline pilot or other professional. It is reasonable to expect a high standard from trained individuals with publically important roles and the privileges that go with these roles. Indeed, it is accepted in law that the standard of care expected of people undertaking dangerous activities should be high. There is no doubt that much of medical training, particularly at a specialist level, is aimed at ensuring that the rules are known.

Violations can be due to the carelessness or laziness of individuals, but most professionals are well motivated and there are probably greater differences between institutions or organisations in the prevalence of certain routine violations, and in the degree to which they are tolerated, than between most well-trained and highly qualified members of a trade or profession within a single institution. A great deal depends on the culture of the institution or organisation. For example, surgical units vary in the extent to which precautions are taken to ensure sterility, and in the extent to which these precautions are enforced. In some, meticulous

---

[64] M. M. Bismark, M. J. Spittal, L. C. Gurrin, M. Ward and D. M. Studdert, 'Identification of doctors at risk of recurrent complaints: a national study of healthcare complaints in Australia' (2013) 22 *BMJ Quality & Safety* 532–40; R. Paterson, 'Not so random: patient complaints and "frequent flier" doctors' (2013) 22 *BMJ Quality & Safety* 525–7.

[65] R. Paterson, *The Good Doctor* (Auckland, New Zealand, Auckland University Press, 2012).

attention is always paid to sterile technique, even in emergencies, to the degree that many of the precautions are probably without scientific foundation. For example, a restriction on the wearing of jewellery in the operating room makes sense if applied to rings for staff who are actually scrubbed and operating or assisting with the operation. It makes less sense if applied to an earring worn by an orderly (which would be unlikely to contaminate a sterile field), and even less if an exception is permitted for wedding rings but not for other types of ring. At least one British unit has, in the past, gone to the lengths of requiring all staff to undergo a full shower with liberal use of antiseptic soap solution before entry into the operating suite. This rule was applied even to people whose function, once in the operating room, had nothing to do with the sterile procedures being undertaken. Other units have a much more casual approach. In some, staff who are not scrubbed and partaking in the actual operation are excused from wearing face masks. What is standard practice in some units would be considered a violation in others. The case for the more rigid and comprehensive approach is that it results in the important things being done, even if this means a great deal of effort is also expended on relatively unimportant activities. An argument for the more relaxed approach is that the best way to make sure the important things are done is to concentrate on those and not waste effort on trivial issues. Another slant on this dichotomy arises from the lack of certainty of much medical knowledge (which we shall discuss again in Chapter 7). In respect of this point, those in the more comprehensive camp may say that, although only half their effort is of value, they do not know which half.

Individuals within an organisation or community may have only limited ability to influence standards, even in the case of those in relatively senior positions: the *culture* of the group or organisation as a whole tends to be more influential than the advocacy of a minority. When US hospitals that ranked in the top 5 per cent in risk-standardised mortality rates for acute myocardial infarction were compared with hospitals in the bottom 5 per cent, there was a substantial difference in organisational culture. Notably, there was a much stronger collective commitment to excellence in the better preforming hospitals.[66]

[66] L. A. Curry, E. Spatz, E. Cherlin, J. W. Thompson, D. Berg, H. H. Ting, . . . E. H. Bradley, 'What distinguishes top-performing hospitals in acute myocardial infarction mortality rates? A qualitative study' (2011) 154 *Annals of Internal Medicine* 384–90.

A key theme of the second edition of this book is that teamwork is critical to success in healthcare, and that the team includes those who fund and administer hospitals as well as those who care for patients directly. When responsibility for accidents is being evaluated, these views should be considered. A well-motivated individual in an organisation whose culture is not strongly oriented towards the promotion of safety is at a considerable disadvantage compared with his colleague in a sister organisation in which the culture is very safety-conscious. Current legal approaches to the regulation of healthcare make it difficult for a court to take such matters into account, but when considering the responsibility of an individual, there should at least be some effort to examine the wider picture and to look at the contribution of factors within the organisation to the generation of any accident. In Chapter 10, we will explore possible alternatives to the regulation of healthcare that would begin from a more collective perspective of accountability.

Violations and Blame

The principal distinction proposed in this and the previous chapter is that between errors, which we regard (in general) as unavoidable and non-culpable, and violations, which are, by contrast, avoidable, and which therefore involve at least some degree of culpability. The basis of culpability within a violation is the fact that a choice has been made to depart from a rule or principle that the actor either knows as an explicit rule or knows to be appropriate in the circumstances. Because of this element of choice, the actor must accept moral responsibility for the consequences of the action. Not all violations are equally culpable. We have identified violations which are appropriate in certain circumstances and which are therefore justifiable. The person who commits such a violation has the defence that it was the best thing to do – a defence that can, if necessary, be translated into the legal defence of necessity.

All other violations involve at least some degree of culpability, but it is important to note that this culpability may rest, at least in part, on persons or organisations other than the individual who performed the act in question. We have seen that there are many cases where violations are made almost inevitable by aspects of the system, and we have discussed the contribution of organisational culture to their generation. If it is impossible for an employee to achieve work targets without committing a violation, the issue of responsibility for this violation becomes a complex one. Some employees may well deliberately choose to violate, but may only do so because they feel unable to carry out their duties in any other way. This would not necessarily exonerate these employees, but may well be a mitigating factor. More importantly, such a situation implies a definite responsibility on the part of the employer for the consequences of the violations. For this reason any allocation of blame should ensure that *all* those involved in the generation of the violation should be answerable and share the liability. Too often the finger of blame is pointed at an individual, who is often relatively junior within the organisation. This has been noted in particular in the prosecution of individuals within corporate bodies in which the relatively junior member of the organisation who actually commits the violation may be blamed while those at a higher level, who bear an overall responsibility, escape liability on the grounds that they were not directly involved. We are not suggesting that the true responsibility is always to be located in the higher echelons of an organisation; in many organisations directors and managers make considerable efforts to ensure safe practice. Our point is that this broader aspect of responsibility must be taken into account.

Even when we have identified a culpable violation and tied it to an individual, it is important to recognise that there may be degrees of blameworthiness. Our discussion of the context in which violations occur and of all the factors that may contribute to their generation reveals that culpability will vary. In a situation in which compliance with regulations or principles of good practice is made difficult by limited resources or other operational factors, the violation may be understandable. This is quite different from a situation in which it is simple laziness or disregard for the safety of others that has led to the violation.

The commission of a violation is a clear wrong in respect of the rights of those affected by it. While we have argued that errors should be accepted as an inevitable concomitant of any complex human undertaking, the same does not usually apply to violations. We have indicated that certain violations ('necessary violations') might be imposed upon individuals by the system, but a person who suffers as a result of a violation has every right to assert that the violation constitutes a direct wrong against him- or herself. How this is translated into rights of complaint, the right to seek compensation or even a call for criminal or disciplinary sanction will depend on the circumstances. In this respect society must seek a delicate balance of rights and interests.

This process involves the elaboration of an acceptable and realistic standard of care. For most practitioners, increased clarity over expectations, support in making compliance as easy as possible, and a system of low-grade sanctions when appropriate is likely to suffice. For a minority, restriction of practice, or even deregistration, may be needed. We will consider the place of criminal liability in Chapter 9.

5

Negligence, Recklessness and Blame

We have argued that certain incidents that lead to harm may, in fact, reasonably be regarded as accidents – in the sense in which we have defined accidents – and not as occasions for blame. We have also suggested that error is an inevitable concomitant of human activity, particularly in complex systems. In practice, however, when things go wrong there is often a call by the community, or by the injured party, for an explanation, and this is frequently accompanied by pressing demands for the attribution of blame. In some cases these demands are justified, but the perceived justification lies not in the mere fact that harm has occurred, but in the fact that it has been caused in a culpable manner.

Theories of moral responsibility based on free choice have traditionally stressed the inextricable link between blame and culpability. Yet this connection has been weakened by the tendency to assume that if there has been a harmful outcome then there is a strong possibility of blame. This claim may be made in the name of accountability, and is a concomitant of the policy of dismantling elitist patterns of professional privilege. The consumerist movement has encouraged this view, arguing that more strenuous efforts to uncover responsibility for mishaps will ensure better protection for the public. There is, of course, some merit in this: it is clearly not in the interest of the public that those providing public services should be able to conceal incompetence or deliberate wrongdoing behind institutional or professional shields. Complaint is an essential part of the process of maintaining quality. The right of reasonable complaint is important. Yet the excessive encouragement of complaint may promote the belief that the attribution of blame, and the identification of a particular offender, whether an individual or an institution, will normally be possible. This leaves little room for acceptance of accidental, or, more generally, less than perfect outcomes (which, as we have argued, may not necessarily be a matter of blame). In such a climate, there may be excessive blaming, with serious consequences for safety and at a high personal cost for those involved in useful but inherently hazardous activities.

The connection between blame and moral culpability has also been undermined by the positivist contention that the law can function as a value-free, mechanistic regulator. In this view, utilitarian considerations allow the invocation of the criminal law as a means of social control, irrespective of the moral status of the targeted offender. What matters in this analysis is that breaches of the criminal law are discouraged by the application of criminal sanctions, even if the offender has not deliberately sought to offend against the law or indeed has been unable to avoid non-compliance. Such a model of criminal justice also allows extensive room for crimes of strict liability, in which the moral innocence of an individual transgressor is subservient to the perceived social value of conviction and punishment. Strict liability allows for prosecution upon proof of prohib-ited conduct without any requirement to demonstrate moral culpability: in the context of the provision of essential services (including healthcare), at least, this seems to us to be invidious.

This demotion of culpability is also evident in the therapeutic approach to crime, which inclines to view criminal offending as a matter of psychopathology rather than individual choice. Sensitivity to the psychology of offending furnishes useful insights into crime and offers, in the long run, considerable possibilities of enlightened crime prevention. On the other hand, there is potential for the abuse of psy-chiatric or psychological explanations, which might destabilise notions of individual responsibility that lie at the heart of the criminal law and indeed of our everyday morality. Herbert Morris has raised objections to this position, which he sees as leading to a demotion of the importance of human agency.[1] Guilt plays a central part in our social lives: without inferences of guilt, moral rules are deprived of their effect and are indistinguishable from other, lower-level precepts or exhortations.

While the role of reason in moral agency should not be discounted, other explanations of moral action stress the role of learned rules, moral metaphor and, indeed, intuition. The sense of guilt plays a part in some of these, not only helping us to identify our own moral failures but also sharpening moral intuitions. Guilt, of course, is capable of being both subjective and objective. We feel it, or we attribute it to others who we consider *should* feel it. To be guilty, then, is to stand in relation to some act or state of affairs that would normally give rise to punishment. But if punishment is visited upon those who are not deemed to merit guilt in

---

[1] H. Morris, 'The decline of guilt' (1988) 99 *Ethics* 62–76. See also C. S. Lewis, 'The humanitarian theory of punishment' (1987) 13 (1) *AMCAP Journal* 147.

this sense, then the moral defensibility of punishment is weakened and, with it, the authority of the criminal law. In such circumstances, the strongest, most practical grounds for obedience to law – our sense that the law represents *fairness* – stands to be undermined. This alone provides adequate reason for preserving the connection between moral culpability and the attribution of liability. Yet, as we have seen in Chapter 4, determining precisely which categories of behaviour are culpable may not be simple. Behaviour that is intended to cause harm needs little discussion. On the whole, there is agreement that acts of deliberate wrongdoing are culpable; any debate tends to focus on the scope of what conduct is legitimate. Such debate is about values; what concerns us is the culpability of particular states of mind in situations in which the values at stake are not the issue. At what point does innocent (even if faulty) behaviour become culpable? At what point does culpability (in the moral sense) become sufficiently serious to merit criminal sanction? These are familiar issues in criminal law theory, yet there still exists surprising uncertainty as to the relationship between these questions and the question of legal liability. At least some of this uncertainty may be because of an insufficient understanding of human cognition and its relevance to the analysis of human action. We address these problems below, starting with an enquiry as to the essential ingredients of a blameworthy state of mind.

Blame

There are two senses in which a person can be blamed for a state of affairs. In the first of these, blame is a matter of mere causal responsibility in which the person who has caused the state of affairs to come into existence is held accountable for it. Conclusions of causal responsibility of this sort – or causal blaming – are reached on the basis of what we understand about the world and its workings. These judgements are not necessarily normative; causal judgements are compatible with the absence of moral culpability, as in a case where damage is caused accidentally. *A* trips over a concealed obstacle and knocks over *B*'s property. The damage to *B*'s property is caused by *A* in this simple, physical sense, but this does not necessarily mean that *A* should be blamed for it in the moral sense. In fact, if there is nothing that could have been done to avoid the obstacle, then it would be quite wrong to blame *A* in this way.

In legal theory this form of causation is referred to as *causation in fact* or *factual causation*.[2] The process of establishing a causal link of this sort between conduct and consequence is usually based on the conclusion that the conduct is sufficient to result in the consequence and that – and this is crucial in legal tests of causation – without the conduct in question the consequence would not have occurred. A factual cause in the law is thus often referred to as a cause sine qua non, or 'but for' causation. If the consequence would have occurred without the conduct, then it is not produced by that conduct, and the actor is not to blame (in this causal sense) for what has happened.

Legal causation is something quite different. Its first requirement is factual causation but, once this has been established, it proceeds to a normative evaluation of the conduct in question. The question that underpins this evaluation is this: does the actor *deserve* to be held accountable – to be blamed, in the normative sense – for what has happened? The causal question at this level thus often becomes indistinguishable from the moral question.

We suggest that it is possible to classify blame into five levels. The first level is pure causal blame, where the agent is identified as the physical cause of an event, but has acted reasonably, has broken no rules and has done nothing wrong in moral terms. The second is blame attributed for an action which unintentionally deviates from or falls short of what can *normatively* be expected of the actor (that is, the way of doing things prescribed in the textbook – the 'theoretical norm'), but where, as we argue below, no moral culpability exists. This may be construed as negligence if conduct is measured against an absolute standard and fails to take account either of the fact that the reasonable person is a human being, with all the limitations that this status implies, or of the state of mind of the individual at the time. The third level is blame attributed for an action which deviates from or falls short of what can *reasonably* be expected of the actor (that is, the way things *are* done by people of reasonable competence in the field – the 'empiric norm'), and where, as we shall argue, moral culpability may exist, even though there is no intention to cause harm. We would argue that people can only be morally accountable for those acts which they have chosen to perform; things which they could not reasonably have avoided doing should not be

---

[2] The issue of legal causation is discussed extensively in H. L. A. Hart and T. Honoré, *Causation in the Law*, 2nd edn (New York, Oxford University Press, 1985). See also A. Norrie, 'A critique of criminal causation' (1991) 54 *The Modern Law Review* 685.

laid to their moral account. The fourth level of blame is appropriate for situations where the actor knows of the existence of a risk and nevertheless proceeds with the action. This is recklessness. Finally, the fifth level (which we have already alluded to above) entails an unambiguous intention to cause harm.

In distinguishing these levels, we must take into account antecedent activity. The conduct of a person prior to an event in which a patient was harmed may have an important bearing on our moral assessment of any error or other failure that contributed to that harm. Antecedent liability, which focuses on the background to an event rather than on the actual event itself, may be based on either a prior act (such as the consumption of alcohol before engaging in a dangerous activity) or a prior omission (such as a failure to attend a safety training session).[3] If something were to go wrong, in a situation where there has been a failure to take all reasonable steps to ensure the safety of a procedure or to minimise risk, culpability may exist, even if the causative action itself fell into category 2 above.

First-level Blaming

To illustrate the first level of blame with a different scenario, we might consider the familiar example of a person who fails to see a child behind him when he reverses a vehicle. He had no reason to believe there might be children in the vicinity. He may have looked in his rear-view mirror and may have taken all the precautions expected of a driver in the circumstances; the child, however, has strayed into the driveway completely unexpectedly and cannot be seen from the driver's position. The driver in this case may be expected to say of himself: *I am to blame for the child having been run over.* It makes sense for him to say this, even if he understands that the incident is not his *fault* – in the sense that, because there was nothing he could reasonably have done to avoid this event, he is not morally culpable. It is interesting to observe here that such a driver may well feel *guilty* about what has happened and may reproach himself for the child's injury. Indeed, not to feel remorse about such an incident would be unnatural and would reveal an astonishing lack of sympathy or ordinary human feeling. But we would be inclined to urge the driver not to reproach himself and not to fall prey to feelings of guilt; and

---

[3] A state of mind may be culpable because of past conduct, as in a failure to acquaint oneself with the facts: see H. Smith, 'Culpable ignorance' (1983) 92 *Philosophical Review* 543–71.

we would do so for the precise reason that we understand that what happened to him is independent of moral fault on his part. There is therefore no sense in which moral opprobrium is appropriate.

The feelings of regret that the driver would experience in respect of the child's injury are very likely to be mirrored in the hostile reactive feelings of the child's parents. Their initial response to the incident is likely to be that the injury is, in all senses, the driver's fault. They may well not distinguish at this early stage between strict causal fault and moral culpability. Again, their feelings of anger are entirely understandable. Indeed, many parents may continue to feel angry and to demand punishment and compensation in the face of a convincing body of evidence as to the driver's lack of *moral* fault, but at least some would be capable of progressing from the crudely reactive state to a more subtle understanding of the issues. At this point, they might accept that the incident is one in which the attribution of blame is simply inappropriate. Whether or not the aggrieved person makes this transition, it is essential that the law should do so. In fact, the ability to distinguish between purely causal blame and morally culpable blame appears at a fairly primitive level of the development of a legal system. Of course, there may be attributions of blame involving other people in this particular case. For example, others may blame the parents for failure to supervise their child, the manufacturer of the vehicle for poor design in respect of visibility or the property owner for failing to fence off the driveway.

This example also illustrates the general difficulty of distinguishing the various senses in which the terms *blame* and *fault* are used. There is a sense in which the driver *is* to blame, just as there is a sense in which the incident is his fault. But we suggest that if these terms are used in this context it should only be in the minimalist sense of *causal* blame and *causal* fault. There is no justification for their use in any moral sense.

In the medical context, further examples would come from adverse events caused by patient-related factors. One example would be a patient who, in the absence of a history of allergy, suffers an unforeseeable anaphylactic reaction to a drug and dies in spite of all reasonable efforts being made to resuscitate her. It could be said that the doctor who administered the drug is causally to blame because if it had not been administered no reaction would have occurred. Few, however, would draw any inculpatory conclusions from that.

Second-level Blaming

At this level of blaming, conduct is measured against a standard that sets out what *ought* to be done in the circumstances in question. This standard should not be unrealistic or impossible to attain. It should also take into account the circumstances in which the action takes place, and any economic and logistic constraints. If conduct fails to reach this standard, then it will commonly be described as negligent. This form of negligence is objective; it does not take into account the subjective state of the actor's mind at the time of the act. Furthermore, it fails to allow for human fallibility. What determines negligence, then, is a disparity between the actual conduct of the actor and the standard of conduct expected.[4]

The prime example in medicine is that of a drug administration error. We have seen that a wrong drug may be given as a result of a momentary lapse caused by distraction. We have also seen that most if not all practitioners make these errors from time to time – they are, in effect, inevitable in the statistical sense; they are entirely analogous to the various slips and lapses made by all people in everyday life. Assuming that there are no contributory or antecedent factors, and that the doctor has indeed been trying his or her best to give the right drug, how is such an error to be judged?

A great deal depends on the question upon which the test relies. If the question is 'is it reasonable to give the wrong drug?', the answer to that would seem to be no. No expert could ever say that giving the wrong drug is the appropriate thing to do – that is, the expected or standard thing to do. The conduct is therefore, in this sense at least, wrong. If, instead, the question is '*could* this have been done by a reasonably skilled and competent practitioner?', then the answer, as we have seen in Chapters 2 and 3, must be yes. In fact, the empirical and theoretical data both lead us to believe that all practitioners make this type of mistake at some time even when trying their best to avoid errors. Phrasing the question in this way places the act in its statistical context as something that is inevitable on an occasional or infrequent basis. The focus is not on the act in isolation from other acts of its type, but on the act as one of a large number of similar events. Thus, one might go one step further and phrase the question as follows: is it reasonable for a practitioner to make one mistake in (for example) one thousand drug administrations?

[4] H. M. Hurd, 'The deontology of negligence' (1996) 76 *Boston University Law Review* 249–72; S. Sverdlik, 'Pure negligence' (1993) 30 *American Philosophical Quarterly* 137–49.

On this basis, it is hard to conclude that such an act should be construed as negligent.

The question, as it is posed in the legal inquiry, is often none of these. In determining whether there has been negligence, the courts may ask the question 'would this have been done by a practitioner who, at the time of the action, was manifesting a reasonable degree of competence?' An important feature of this question is that 'reasonable degree of competence' means that degree of competence to which the practitioner might reasonably be expected to aspire. In other words, it is the *standard* or *recommended* degree of competence or the *standard* or *recommended* way of doing things.

This standard is clearly not unattainable on a single occasion. However, it would be impossible to meet it on *every* occasion over an entire working lifetime in the same way, for example, that it would be impossible for a professional golfer to score par or better on every round of golf. Doctors should certainly try their best to meet the standard on every occasion, but, as we have seen in Chapters 2 and 3, it is inevitable that at some point every doctor will be subject to some form of error and will be unable to do so.

Even if it is agreed that some deviation from the standard is inevitable, this may in practice have little effect on the legal inquiry for the reason that the law is primarily concerned not with overall patterns of behaviour or sequences of acts but with one particular act. This means that the legal assessment of behaviour is artificially detached from the behaviour's context in relation to many similar acts, undertaken over a long profes-sional career. In a medical negligence action, the issue before the court is not whether the practitioner is, in general terms, a negligent doctor (that is, it is not whether he could, on the whole, be described as negligent) but whether *on a particular occasion* he manifested negligence. For this inquiry, questions of statistical likelihood appear irrelevant. A very clear statement of this position was made in the case of Dr Yogasakaran, discussed in Chapter 1. The judge observed that the issue was not whether Dr Yogasakaran was a negligent doctor in general but whether he had been negligent on the one occasion before the court.

The concern of the law with single, isolated events is particularly evident in the way in which criminal law functions. Under current theories of criminal liability, it is the defendant's act rather than his character that comes under the scrutiny of the court. Proponents of character-based theories of liability would argue that we should attribute liability to a defendant on the basis of his general disposition rather than by what he has done on an isolated occasion.[5] In practice, this is not the way in which criminal justice operates. The fact that the act is isolated and 'out of character' does not constitute a defence, although it may mitigate the severity of the sentence. Provided mitigation of sentence is a possibility, the pragmatic requirement for single-act-based liability is acceptable in the case of criminal acts proceeding from a deliberate choice on the defendant's part. Even the criminal law recognises circumstances in which the act is more 'understandable' and less clearly a product of cool-headed deliberation. It is this that underlies the defence of provocation, a defence, which, in those jurisdictions where it is still available,[6] applies where the defendant has been so provoked by the victim as to lose his or her power of self-control. An objection to the application of this 'snapshot' view of action to errors of the type inevitably made by all human beings is that it tends to create an undue risk of liability for those who are professionally required to engage in skilled and hazardous activities. This level of liability may be seen as unreasonable by those upon whom it is imposed, given the inevitability that they will eventually make exactly this type of error. This raises fundamental questions as to the principles underlying civil liability. The question of whether conduct at the second level of blame should be regarded as negligent depends *on the purpose for which one is making the assessment.* If liability is imposed purely for the purposes of loss-adjustment, and no element of moral culpability is implied, then the single-act approach may be appropriate. If, however, the basis of liability includes a moral component, or if there is an element of punishment in the process, then there is an objection to the adoption of this approach at this level of blame. We need, therefore, to examine civil liability with a view to ascertaining the degree to which the objectives underlying the whole system of tort law dictate the grounds upon which such liability will be attributed.[7]

---

[5] An example of a theory of liability which would give greater weight to character is that supported by N. Lacey, *State Punishment: Political Principles and Community Values* London, Routledge, 1988). See also N. Lacey, 'The resurgence of character: Responsibility in the context of criminalization', in R. A. Duff and S. P. Green (eds.), *Philosophical Foundations of Criminal Law* (Oxford, Oxford University Press, 2011) 151–78. For further discussion, see P. Arenella, 'Character, choice and moral agency: the relevance of character to our moral culpability judgments', in E. F. Paul, F. D. Miller and J. Paul (eds.), *Crime, Culpability, and Remedy* (Cambridge, MA, Blackwell, 1990) 59–83.

[6] The defence of provocation has been removed in some countries; for example, it was repealed in New Zealand by s4 of the Crimes (Provocation Repeal) Amendment Act 2009.

[7] We will consider the implications of this to the question of criminal liability in Chapter 9. For a discussion of the objectives of tort law, see the illuminating treatment of the topic by

Blame and the Purposes of Tort Liability

The primary purpose of tort liability is to ensure that those who suffer injury, whether to their property or to their person, are compensated and, in so far as is possible, returned to the position they were in prior to the injury. This is a system of loss redistribution: where appropriate, loss is not left to lie where it falls, but is transferred by the law to the person who caused it – provided, of course, that he or she *deserves* to bear it. This is clearly the main function of the law of torts, but, in addition to this compensatory goal, the law of torts is widely credited with a deterrent role. In this view, the prospect of legal liability has the effect of discouraging unsafe practices across the whole range of human activity. It is argued, for example, that the degree of caution exercised by manufacturers would be considerably reduced if they were not faced with the possibility of substantial damages claims in respect of faulty products. In the medical context, the argument is that hospitals and individual doctors would place a lower priority on patient safety – and patient interests in general – if the threat of legal action were removed. Would the medical profession have given so much attention to the need to obtain informed consent if this had not been brought home by a number of high-profile civil suits? It is impossible to say, but it seems likely that litigation acted as the spur in this area, although other devices might have been equally effective. In New Zealand, for example, the role of the Health and Disability Commissioner and the Code of Patient Rights, backed by disciplinary sanctions, seems to have achieved much the same result.

A further function served by the law of torts is that it provides access, effectively of right, to a forum in which an injured person can obtain a thorough airing of his or her complaint.[8] Almost all other systems of redress, including criminal and disciplinary processes, involve some screening as to merit. In the latter case, the possibility exists of 'professional capture' at the screening stage. Even if this does not occur, the perception that it might do so is a major drawback. There are various reasons why people take an issue to court, but a powerful one in this

---

J. L. Coleman, 'The goals of tort law', in *Risks and Wrongs* (New York, Cambridge University Press, 1992) 197–211.

[8] Financial considerations may limit access to the civil courts for many people. This is an important problem, but it is slightly different in nature from processes that might preclude a patient from getting a hearing, whether or not he or she can afford to pay. This and other limitations of tort law are discussed in more detail in Chapter 9.

context is the need for explanation and, in many cases, for tangible acknowledgement that something went wrong. For many, an explanation and an apology is all that is wanted. These patients and families also want to ensure that the same problem does not occur to anyone else. A smaller proportion appear to be searching for retribution or even revenge, in the sense that they either want the wrong 'annulled' by punishment or, in the case of revenge, they seek the satisfaction of seeing the wrongdoer suffer.[9]

It is important to acknowledge that all these objectives are, to a greater or lesser extent, achieved by tort law, and indeed this is one of its attractions and strengths. However, many of these objectives are secondary or are achieved as incidental effects. Furthermore, the support that they lend to the case for the continuation of the traditional system is weakened by the fact that some of these purposes could be more reliably and efficiently achieved by other means. Perhaps the most important of these objectives is that of promoting safety. Over the last decade it has become increasingly obvious that this end is likely to be better served by a broadly based systems-oriented focus than simply by reliance upon random tort actions. Regulation has an important role to play in ensuring that appropriate standards of structure and process are met, but there is now much greater emphasis on the need for proactive continuous quality *improvement* as well as quality *assurance*,[10] and of a culture of openness in which lessons can be learned from things that go wrong. At the same time, some means of ensuring accountability is required,[11] and also of compensating patients when appropriate.

We will return to these themes in later chapters (notably Chapter 9), but in the meantime it is relevant that the civil law does not succeed in adjusting all loss. Tort liability is not a system of universal insurance: it identifies certain categories of loss as being within its purview and excludes others. In particular, it excludes those losses that are produced by factors outside human agency, such as acts of God (earthquakes, lightning strikes, etc.).[12] Similarly excluded are those losses that result

[9] For an interesting discussion of the relationship between tort and revenge, see S. Hershovitz, 'Tort as substitute for revenge', in J. Oberdiek (ed.), *The Philosophical Foundations of the Law of Torts* (Oxford, Oxford University Press, 2014) 86–102.

[10] D. M. Berwick, 'The science of improvement' (2008) 299 *Journal of the American Medical Association* 1182–4.

[11] R. M. Wachter and P. J. Pronovost, 'Balancing "no blame" with accountability in patient safety' (2009) 361 *New England Journal of Medicine* 1401–6.

[12] The 2001 Australian comedy film, *The Man Who Sued God*, provides a fascinating exploration of some implications of the concept of an 'act of God'.

from natural processes, such as disease or decay. These are the inescapable misfortunes of life that the victim is expected to bear.

Tort liability requires that an act that causes harm should satisfy certain criteria of wrongfulness. In western jurisprudence this has traditionally been defined as *fault*. Liability depends on the fact that the defendant was at fault in acting as he or she did. The legal definition of fault is clearly crucial. Does it mean *moral* fault, or is it fault in a non-moral sense?[13] If we examine the development of the law of torts in modern times, it will be seen that a strong moral element has rooted itself in the civil concept of fault. The exposition of the law of civil liability undertaken by the natural lawyers of the seventeenth century injected a strong overtone of moral wrongdoing into the concept of *culpa* embodied in the received Roman law then applying in Western Europe. *Culpa* in earlier times may have had some moral significance, in that it was applied in situations where there may well have been moral fault, but the moral nature of the duty to compensate had not previously been made explicit. To a considerable extent, English common law developed in isolation from continental legal theory, but it too gradually moved from strict liability to notions of liability based on moral wrongdoing. In strict liability all that had been required was that the defendant should have caused the damage. The more modern view required that the conduct of the defendant demonstrate wrongfulness in the moral sense – in particular, a failure to show sufficient care. In this way, moral considerations came to permeate the very fabric of the law of negligence and the language used to express the duty of care. The essential philosophical foundation of this branch of the law of torts was that the right to damages depended on showing that the defendant *deserved* to pay for the damage that he or she had caused. This was expressed in the concept of negligence: negligent actors should make good the damage they have caused because it was their fault (in the moral sense) that the damage had occurred. This is in accord with basic ideas of fairness in human transactions. By the end of the nineteenth century, fault was established as the basis of negligence liability, with the criterion of fault being a failure to meet the requisite standard of care. This standard was defined as that degree of care that was *reasonable* in the circumstances.

---

[13] Whether blameworthiness (in the moral sense) should play a role in the law of torts is a matter of persistent debate. Useful contributions include D. G. Owen, 'The fault pit' (1992) 26 *Georgia Law Review* 703–23; Coleman, *Risks and Wrongs*; J. C. P. Goldberg and B. C. Zipursky, 'Tort law and responsibility', in J. Oberdiek (ed.), *Philosophical Foundations of The Law of Torts* (Oxford, Oxford University Press, 2014) 17–36.

The role played by moral considerations in liability for negligence is subtle and uncertain. It is clear that the obligation to compensate is based on a moral conviction, namely, the idea that a person who causes harm to another ought to compensate the victim.[14] This is not incompatible with strict liability, in which the duty to compensate flows from the mere fact of causing the loss. However, considerations of justice led to a refinement of the law and to the replacing of strict liability in many areas of the law of torts with liability based on moral fault.[15] At a later stage – most markedly in the second half of the twentieth century – the pendulum began to swing in the opposite direction, at least in respect of products liability and certain other forms of injury, and strict liability notions began to displace fault-based negligence.[16] For many personal injury matters, however, liability has continued to be based on negligence, even if strict liability has made marked inroads in the area of product-related injuries.

The development of negligence was propelled by notions of fault in the moral sense, and this entailed imposing liability only for those acts which would normally be regarded as morally wrongful. The typical example of this would be a case where there was a failure to show proper care not to harm others – usually a matter of moral failing. However, the inquiry was not directed to the state of mind of the actual defendant but *to his actions*. The question was not whether the individual defendant had manifested any morally culpable state of mind such as indifference to the interests of others. All that was required was that he or she should have acted in a way that would *normally* be indicative of a morally blameworthy attitude. The moral judgement, then, had become focused on the externals of the action, with the question being asked: is the conduct in question of such a type as would *normally* be morally reprehensible, at least to the extent that a failure to take appropriate care to avoid harming another is morally reprehensible? It is important to note that, in spite of the objective nature of this standard, the terms used to describe liability continued to be redolent of subjective moral wrongdoing: *fault*, for example, suggests actual subjective culpability, and *negligence* similarly implies morally

---

[14] This is essentially the notion of corrective justice, which many tort law theorists see as the basis of tort liability. For discussion, see E. J. Weinrib, *The Idea of Private Law* (Cambridge, MA, Harvard University Press, 1995); J. Gardner, 'What is tort law for? Part 1. The place of corrective justice' (2011) 30 *Law & Philosophy* 1–50.

[15] G. E. White, *Tort Law in America: An Intellectual History* (New York, Oxford University Press, 1980).

[16] The embracing of strict liability in the United States is discussed in G. Schwartz, 'The beginning and possible end of the rise of modern American tort law' (1992) 26 *Georgia Law Review* 601–702.

culpable failure. In fact, as we have seen, a conclusion of objective liability says nothing about the moral culpability of the actual defendant. It may be that the defendant was morally culpable – in that his or her attitude was one of culpable carelessness or disregard for safety – but this is not necessarily so. This distinction has led to considerable confusion, and judges occasionally find it necessary to stress that when they talk about negligence or fault on the part of the defendant, they are not necessarily implying moral culpability. Indeed, the very name of the entire branch of law has been detached from moral connotations; in the landmark case of *Overseas Tankship* v. *Morts Dock*,[17] an Australian appeal to the Privy Council, the court observed: 'The words "tort" and "tortious" have, perhaps, a somewhat sinister sound but, particularly when the tort is not deliberate but is an act of negligence, it does not seem that there is any more moral obloquy in it than a perhaps deliberate breach of contract.'

The proposition that negligence liability is quite distinct from moral culpability is supportable, but only to a degree. In fact, the bringing of a claim based on negligence amounts to an allegation of failure on the part of the defendant. For strictly legal purposes, this failure can be seen to have no moral overtones, in that it is merely a failure to meet what may be recognised by lawyers as an arbitrary standard of care. However, such an action is almost always viewed, both by the public and by the defendant, as an allegation of culpable conduct. For practical purposes, all the objectives listed above are served: the defendant feels that he is put on trial and if the case goes against him he will feel that he is the object of a punitive process. Lawyers who argue that the civil justice process should not be seen in this light – that it should be seen as doing no more than adjusting loss – ignore persuasive evidence of the effect of such litigation on a defendant, particularly when the latter is an individual rather than an organisation. There is evidence of a considerable impact on doctors and other health professionals of malpractice actions.[18] This should be taken into account in any assessment of the tort system: the efficacy of the system in achieving compensation for the injured person is one factor in

---

[17] [1967] 1 AC 617.
[18] M. J. White, 'The value of liability in medical malpractice' (1994) 13 *Health Affairs* 75–87; B. A. Liang, 'Assessing medical malpractice jury verdicts: a case study of an anesthesiology department' (1997) *Cornell Journal of Law and Public Policy* 121–64; J. Thomas, 'The effect of medical malpractice' (2010) 19 *Annals of Health Law* 306–15. In the context of complaints in general, rather than malpractice actions in particular, see also W. Cunningham, 'The immediate and long-term impact on New Zealand doctors who receive patient complaints' (2004) 117 *New Zealand Medical Journal* U972.

the equation (and here the data reveal a picture of inefficiency in the medical context); other factors must include the system's impact on medical personnel and on the way in which medicine is practised.

An Example

The case of Dr Yogasakaran will be remembered from Chapter 1. In Chapters 2 and 3 we reviewed the specific problem of drug administration error in medicine and saw that these events are often slips or lapses, a form of skill-based error inevitably made by everyone at some time. We saw that distraction is a key precipitating factor for these errors, and reviewed the evidence that the vast majority of anaesthetists have given the wrong drug at some time in their careers. To reiterate the key features of Dr Yogasakaran's case: at the end of an anaesthetic an emergency developed for which Dr Yogasakaran wished to administer intravenously a drug called dopram. Unbeknown to him, a second person had incorrectly substituted dopamine for dopram in the appropriate section of the drug drawer. Under the distracting influence of the emergency and under acute pressure to react, Dr Yogaskaran drew up and administered the incorrect drug. This ultimately resulted in the patient's death. No suggestion was made that any other aspect of Dr Yogasakaran's management of the case was deficient. Dr Yogasakaran did not even know that he had given the wrong drug until he himself discovered the empty ampoule some time later. In Chapter 3 we showed the difficulties involved in classifying the act of giving the wrong drug in this case. We also referred to doubts as to whether or not, in the actual case, he looked at the label on the ampoule. In our analysis below, we shall consider these events from the point of view of allocating blame, and suggest solutions based on whether his actions can be considered to represent an error or a violation in the strict sense in which we have defined these terms in Chapters 3 and 4. We identify three possibilities, the first two involving second-level blame, and the third involving blame at the third level:

(a)   The Label Is Read Incorrectly

For the reasons given under (b), it is entirely plausible that this would represent a problem of 'mindset', by which Dr Yogasakaran interpreted the label as saying what he expected it to say. This would be a variety of slip, a skill-based error and would involve no choice on his part. The culpability of this is discussed below.

(b)   There Is an Unintentional Failure to Read the Label

Given the pressure of time and the distracting nature of the emergency, the possibility of a lapse by which Dr Yogasakaran unintentionally failed to read the label is plausible. The empirical evidence presented in Chapter 4 makes it clear that this does happen to anaesthetists from time to time and expert evidence to this effect should have been readily forthcoming. It is hard to see what steps Dr Yogasakaran could have taken to ensure avoiding ever making a lapse of this type, particularly taking into account that he did not even know that he had made an error until later. We have seen in the previous chapters that simply trying harder will not avoid errors of this type, and that the solution lies in a systemic response to the underlying error-prone process of drug administration.[19]

Blame in (a) and (b)

The interpretation of the facts in both (a) and (b) opens Dr Yogasakaran's action to second-level blame only. The failures in these two instances are both skill-based errors, and we consider them morally indistinguishable but, as we shall see below, quite distinct from (c). Under current tests of civil liability the outcome would be uncertain, but it is likely that a finding of negligence would be made in at least some jurisdictions. Whether such a finding is defensible depends on one's view of the purposes of tort law. If the goal is compensation irrespective of culpability, then this finding would seem to be acceptable. However, is this really any more than strict liability?

From the perspective of our understanding of the nature of human cognition and error, we have already noted that this type of error is unintended. In addition, although it is foreseeable in a general sense that such errors will be made from time to time, it would have to be said that the complete elimination of this type of error is essentially impossible. Furthermore, it would seem inescapable that any competent practitioner

---

[19]   In this case, a purely systemic response turns out to be relatively illusive (see, for example, A. F. Merry, C. S. Webster, J. Hannam, S. J. Mitchell, R. Henderson, P. Reid, K. E. Edwards, A. Jardim, N. Pak, J. Cooper, L. Hopley, C. Frampton and T. G. Short, 'Multimodal system designed to reduce errors in recording and administration of drugs in anaesthesia: prospective randomised clinical evaluation' (2011) 343 *British Medical Journal* d5543), and there is a compelling argument for expecting people to engage in systemic initiatives to improve safety (see Wachter and Pronovost, 'Balancing "no blame" with accountability in patient safety'). At the time of Dr Yogasakaran's case, however, no substantive initiatives of this type had been advanced and it was never argued that his practice fell short of the standards pertaining at the time.

would occasionally make errors that, on the basis of the cognitive processes involved, are identical. The outcome of the error would depend more on chance than on any other factor, and is not relevant to our assessment of the standard of care, although it is obviously very important in other respects.

It is therefore very hard to see how any moral culpability can be attributed to Dr Yogasakaran for this error under interpretations (a) and (b). If there is culpability, it is possibly better located in the decision to place a relatively inexperienced doctor in circumstances where he might be required to undertake anaesthesia for a high-risk case without the supervision that he might have needed. The central argument concerns the error itself, and any antecedent issues in this case are unrelated to the actual error and probably not of Dr Yogasakaran's making.[20] In particular, he had conducted an otherwise adequate and attentive anaesthetic, he was present in the operating theatre at the time of the crisis and no criticism has been made concerning any other aspect of his management of the problem when it arose.

This last point raises an important issue. Many theories of culpability – and this is notably true of legal theories – focus on human acts in isolation from those acts preceding and following them. We have already alluded to the wider issue of a doctor's performance over many years. In this case the judge made the point that Dr Yogasakaran's honesty, on discovering his mistake, in drawing the attention of all concerned to the true nature of the patient's problem was irrelevant to the question of guilt. This view makes perfect sense in the context of most criminal offences, and will strike the criminal lawyer as unexceptional. Yet there are powerful reasons why it should be considered a very dysfunctional approach in the context of medical errors. We have seen that errors are endemic in medicine. It is commonly taught that one important aspect of such errors is to identify them, disclose them openly and then take all reasonable steps to limit or correct their consequences. This ethos pervades good medical practice and is very much in the interest of patients.

---

[20] The question of antecedent events is a generic point about the wider matter of organisational responsibility: there has never been any suggestion that lack of experience contributed to this particular error. However, raising this point does illustrate the difference between a legal analysis of the events, focused on a specific action and its consequences, and a more systemic analysis that seeks to identify ways to improve safety in general, which should include identifying and addressing latent weaknesses in the system even if they have not yet contributed to harm. From the latter perspective it makes little sense to put a doctor deemed to need supervision into a setting in which adequate supervision is not available.

It could be argued that the error and the subsequent response by the maker of the error are two separate issues, each of which needs to be dealt with in isolation. Each act – the making of the error and the reaction to it – is to be assessed on its own merits. Thus, if there was culpability at the stage of making the error, even exemplary behaviour at a later stage – let alone the absence of culpability at that point – does nothing to alleviate the culpability attached to the first stage. An example from the criminal law might be where one person steals property from another, but then discovers that the property was of great sentimental value. He immediately returns it and does his best to make up for his wrongdoing. He is guilty of theft in the same way as if the property had not been returned, although his action in returning it would no doubt be taken into account in assessing the measure of punishment. This seems straightforward, and in most cases there is no alternative but for the criminal law to take this view of human conduct. However, when applied to more complex issues of culpability, the weakness of this approach becomes apparent. A particular objection to this way of regarding human action focuses on the fact that assessments of culpability are contextual. We make such judgements *with a purpose in mind*, and this purpose may determine the way in which we choose how to draw the boundaries of action.

A well-known Australian case demonstrates this. In *Ryan* v. *The Queen*,[21] Ryan had decided to commit armed robbery. In the course of the robbery he told his victim to stand with his hands behind his back, in such a position that he could be tied up. Unfortunately, while the rifle was pointed at him, the victim made a sudden move. This caused Ryan's finger to squeeze the trigger in what he claimed was a reflex movement. However, the nature and effect of a 'reflex action' are matters of uncertainty. On one view reflex actions do not 'count' as actions in respect of which there can be criminal liability. Ryan therefore argued that the act of killing the proprietor was an involuntary act for which he could not be held liable, and was, therefore, not guilty of murder.

The court took a contextual view of the reflex action, pointing out that events cannot be 'sliced up' in this way. There was an overall act – the act of robbing the filling station – and this was overwhelmingly voluntary, even if there was a single, momentary act within the sequence that could be described as involuntary. Culpability lay in the voluntary nature of the overall sequence of action – the bigger act, so to speak – and it is this that

[21]   (1967) 121 CLR.

had to be judged. Ryan's appeal against conviction for murder was therefore rejected.

The problem of complex sequences of actions is one that has attracted the attention of philosophers of action, who talk of the *individuation of events*. Such analyses stress the importance of how acts are described. It is possible to adjust the boundaries of an act by choosing a broader or narrower act-describer, according to what seems to be most suitable for the purpose in hand. This technique has been aptly described by the legal philosopher Joel Feinberg as the 'accordion effect'.[22] The term used to describe an act may be 'extended' to embrace a whole series of events and actions. Thus *winning the war*, which is described here as one action, involves perhaps twenty individual battles (twenty actions), each of which involves possibly twenty individual conflicts, and so on down the action tree. These ideas are consistent with processes of human cognition in general, which we outlined in Chapter 2, and our discussion of outcome in relation to the definition of error in Chapter 3.

The typical process of assessing conduct for the purposes of establishing negligence takes a highly individuating approach. This involves looking at each component of a cognitively integrated sequence of actions as if it had been performed in isolation. In terms of cognitive psychology, we have seen how quite complex sequences of actions can be understood as an integrated whole: tying one's shoelaces or driving to work are examples. The intention of each individual component is subsumed under the overall intention of the larger identifiable cognitive unit. It is difficult to justify singling out one act within that unit for separate evaluation unless it can be shown that a separately cognised intent applied to that act. Thus, in the case of errors which are by definition unintentional, it is difficult to see logic in an approach which judges them as if they were separate or individuated intentional events. By contrast, violations in which the deviation from the normal procedure is actually intended can be separately delineated, and there is, therefore, at least some logical foundation for the position that requires such violations to be judged on their own merits. Even in this type of situation, however, acts immediately before and after the violation are relevant and cannot be discounted altogether.

In situations (a) and (b) above, it is hard to see a rational basis for treating an action, which we have characterised as an unintentional error,

---

[22] J. Feinberg, *Doing and Deserving: Essays in the Theory of Responsibility* (Princeton, Princeton University Press, 1970).

as if it warranted status as a self-standing morally significant act. This is particularly true in the context of the circumstances in which it took place and the exemplary behaviour immediately following it, by which every effort was made to deal with the consequences of the error. We shall deal below with the third possible interpretation, in which there is greater foundation for individuating the act. Even then, at least some cognisance should be taken of the context and of the response.

This shows that the assessment of negligence is strongly dependent upon where the boundaries of an act are set. Traditionally this has been done in a somewhat arbitrary manner, allowing for a conclusion of negligence that challenges our intuition as to the overall moral quality of the conduct involved. A powerful indication of this is our sense of the appropriateness of language. If it seems counter-intuitive to describe a painstaking and highly competent person as *negligent* simply on the basis of a momentary lapse, to which we can all relate on the basis of our own fallibility, it is precisely because of our inherent sense that assessment ought to be a contextual matter.

The taking of a contextual view of action, which should incorporate our knowledge of cognitive psychology, does not preclude focusing on highly individualised segments of conduct where appropriate. What it does is to increase the precision with which we can appropriately define the boundaries of the segments that need to be evaluated. The effect will by no means always be to excuse behaviour: the court's decision in *Ryan* shows how the appropriate drawing of act boundaries may lead to inculpation rather than exculpation. Indeed, in the majority of instances in which this is done in criminal law, precisely this result is achieved.

We accept, of course, that a highly atomistic analysis of events may be necessary to identify causes in the non-moral or scientific sense. Even here, as we have seen in Chapter 2, a range of antecedent influences, including those of other actors, may be more important than the final identified human failure that led to a particular outcome.

Dr Yogasakaran's conduct as interpreted in (a) and (b) should be classified as blameworthy at the second level. It does not appear to involve moral culpability; whether it should be considered negligence for civil liability purposes depends on how the standard of care is set. This will be discussed in Chapter 6.

Third-level Blaming

The case of Dr Yogasakaran is subject to a third interpretation:

(c)   The Label Is Intentionally Not Read

Expert evidence led by the defence confirmed that some attempt should always be made to identify any drug before it is administered, even in an emergency. If we were to accept that Dr Yogasakaran *chose* not to read the label, then this was not an accident. Because the making of a choice would have been involved, it follows that an alternative, safer option would actually have been available to him. This allows us to attribute at least some degree of moral culpability to his failure. It should be noted that we would not accept that this was an error of judgement, in which his decision was an understandable choice to save time. This is because no expert evidence was advanced to support such a position. It would, of course, not be necessary for all experts to agree with this interpretation, but, at the minimum, at least a responsible body of such opinion would have to take this view (the *Bolam* test).

This view of the facts would place Dr Yogasakaran's action – a violation – into the sphere of our third level of blaming. At this level, there would be a strong case for a finding of negligence and consequent liability. (The actual context of this case was a prosecution for manslaughter, under the simple negligence test then applied in New Zealand – in effect the test typically applied under civil law. We will return to the role of the criminal law in cases of this type in Chapter 9, but for now we will simply state that we do not accept a simple negligence test as appropriate for criminal conviction.)

In this interpretation we are assuming that Dr Yogasakaran considered that the non-reading of the label was acceptable in the circumstances. This, however, does not reduce his blameworthiness below this third level of blame. Had he deliberately omitted to read the label in full knowledge that the risks involved were unacceptable, then his blameworthiness would have been higher, and he would have qualified for the fourth level of blame (discussed below). The fact that one does not appreciate the wrongful implications of an action is not of itself sufficient to excuse a conscious decision to carry out the prohibited action; the test is whether other reasonable doctors would have appreciated the wrongfulness of the course of action. As we have seen, the expert evidence in his case was clear: doctors should read the label of a drug, even in an emergency.

Level Four Blaming

There was never any suggestion that Dr Yogasakaran knew of an unacceptable risk and nevertheless chose to take it. Such conduct would amount to recklessness, which has been defined as acting with the knowledge that one's action involves a risk. This risk is usually, although not always, a risk of harm to another. It is also important to make a distinction between subjective and objective recklessness. Subjective recklessness requires that the risk-taker should be aware of the existence of the risk; objective recklessness may be inferred where the risk-taker acts in circumstances in which a reasonable person would have been aware of the existence of the risk. There has been an animated debate in the criminal law as to which form of recklessness is more appropriate. English courts have adopted subjective recklessness for the purposes of some crimes, but in respect of others they have been prepared to convict on the basis of objective recklessness, although the current approach of the courts favours subjective recklessness.[23] A greater attachment to notions of subjective guilt has also been evident in the practice of the Canadian courts.[24] Whichever form of recklessness is preferred for legal purposes, for purposes of the attribution of moral culpability, subjective appreciation of risk is essential.

An extraordinary degree of confusion appears to dog the distinction between recklessness and negligence.[25] This is understandable when an objective test of recklessness is used. In level three blame, the only distinction between negligence and objective recklessness appears to be the degree of risk. If a high degree of risk is entailed in negligent behaviour, the tendency has been to characterise it as reckless (in the objective sense), because in this way the riskiness is stressed. This reflects ordinary linguistic usage but it blurs the important distinction between the two concepts and deprives the concept of recklessness of its strong moral connotations. We must have a term for the deliberate taking of dangerous risks. Recklessness serves to do this work, provided we retain the subjective element.

---

[23] A. Ashworth, *Principles of Criminal Law* (2nd edn, Oxford, Clarendon Press, 1995). See *R. v. G* [2004] 1 AC 1034, [2004] 1 Cr. App. R 21 (HL).

[24] For discussion of the subjectivist/objectivist positions in Canadian criminal law, see B. Rolfes, 'The golden thread of criminal law – moral culpability and sexual assault' (1998) 61 *Saskatchewan Law Review* 87–126; D. Stuart, *Charter Justice in Canadian Criminal Law* (Scarborough, Carswell, 1991); *R. v. Sansregret* [1978] S.C.J. No. 59, [1978] 2 S.C.R. 1299.

[25] For discussion of the distinction, see J. B. Brady, 'Conscious negligence' (1996) 33 *American Philosophical Quarterly* 325–35.

An example might help to illustrate the distinction. There are frequently reports of boating incidents in which people fail to carry life-jackets in the boat. In many of these instances, this failure occurs in the presence of full awareness of the risk involved. Such conduct is unquestionably reckless. On occasions, however, particularly when the boat journey is made by persons with little experience or knowledge, such people may genuinely believe that the omission to carry life-jackets involves no significant risk. It could be argued that they *ought* to appreciate the degree of risk, and if the term 'objective recklessness' were to be used, this is a situation in which it might be applied. We would suggest that the concept of gross negligence would be more appropriate, because it retains the key distinction between negligence and recklessness – namely, awareness of risk.

Neither negligence nor recklessness is a monolithic concept. In reality, there is a spectrum of behaviour that runs from correct or acceptable behaviour at one end to intentional harm-doing at the other. Within this spectrum there are bands. The traditional bands are: blameless behaviour, negligence, recklessness and intentionally wrongful conduct. Our description of five levels of blame is an attempt to clarify and refine the last three of these. It seems better to qualify negligence and recklessness in terms of degree – for example, gross negligence – than to blur the distinctions between the bands. For this reason, unless otherwise stated, our use of the term 'recklessness' corresponds to subjective recklessness.

Risk-taking: A Medical Example

In the case of the Bristol cardiac surgeons,[26] the key element for our purposes is that at least one of the surgeons concerned continued to carry out complicated heart operations in the face of repeated warnings that it would be unwise to do so. To say that one does not know of a risk after one has been warned by an appropriate person that the risk exists does not allow one to disclaim responsibility for the materialisation of the risk. Risk-taking may in some circumstances amount to recklessness. This will be the case if the risk is sufficiently major and the actor knows of the existence of the risk. It would be acceptable to set aside such advice only if one could show that a suitable review of the risk had been undertaken and the conclusion reached that the advice was unfounded. The conduct of the surgeon in continuing to operate in circumstances where the

---

[26] See Chapter 1.

mortality rate was unconscionably high, even if well-intentioned, was considered unacceptable.

Recklessness and Culpability

The moral culpability of recklessness is not located in a *desire* to cause harm. It resides in the proximity of the reckless state of mind to the state of mind present when there is an intention to cause harm. The intention in reckless conduct is focused on the action, not the possible outcomes of the action. Nevertheless, there is a clear appreciation that harm of some type may well ensue from the action. There is, in other words, a disregard for the possible consequences. Or, putting it another way, there is an appreciation of the risk that some harm may occur, and that the risk is an unreasonable one to take. The consequences entailed in the risk may not be *wanted*, and indeed the actor may hope that they do not occur, but this hope nevertheless fails to inhibit the taking of the risk. As we saw in Chapter 4, certain types of violation, called 'optimising violations', may be motivated by thrill-seeking. These are clearly reckless.

The culpability of recklessness lies in the moral offensiveness of the attitude of relative indifference to consequence. This links the actor to the consequence; he or she pursues a gain at the cost of another, implicitly valuing that gain above the interests of the person who stands to be harmed.

Level Five Blaming

This is appropriate to cases where there is a deliberate attempt to do harm. The culpability of this conduct is apparent; the only possible debate here is about the meaning of harm. It is beyond the scope of our enquiry to consider the defensibility of rules relating to, say, euthanasia or abortion.

Accidents and the Levels of Blame

In Chapter 1 we proposed a strict definition of the word 'accident', one which would preserve the exculpatory connotation of the term. Under this definition, to qualify as an accident, an event must meet the following conditions: (i) that it was unintended; *and either* (ii) that it was reasonably unforeseeable *or* (iii) that it was foreseeable (in a general or statistical sense at least) but could not realistically have been prevented. Incidents associated with blame at levels one and two meet these criteria. At level three, because there is an element of choice associated with violation, an incident could be said to be foreseeable and preventable, and therefore not an accident. The boundaries between each of the levels described (including levels two and three) will of course be blurred – in reality we are dealing with a continuum.

Conclusion

This analysis has been concerned with clarifying culpability. We have set out to identify the various ways in which the language of blame is used. As we have seen, this usage is often loose, both in the popular arena and in the more specialised context of the law. It is notoriously difficult to tie language down. In some cases, this will matter little: we shall never agree on the precise meaning of a whole range of terms in our daily discourse, but the consequences here often do not extend beyond minor misunderstandings. However, when it comes to serious issues of culpability, in both the legal and the moral sense, terminological confusion is highly undesirable because the terms themselves exert considerable influence on the process of attributing liability. The term 'blame' is a prime example, but there are others, including 'negligence' and 'recklessness'. The use of one of these terms implies a judgement as to the quality of the conduct to which it is being applied. This judgement should be based on careful evaluation rather than on a superficial assessment based on the *external features* of action. In many cases, the allocation of an act to a particular category of blameworthy behaviour, such as negligence or recklessness, is fairly straightforward. Problems arise at the boundaries between categories and with actions in which the link to culpability is relatively subtle. Increasing the depth of the enquiry may not remove the need for judgement at these boundaries, but it will increase the precision with which these difficult cases can be allocated to their appropriate level of blame.

Where does negligence fit into this scheme of blame? Negligence, as understood by the courts, is conduct which fails to meet the required standard of care, defined as the standard of care of the reasonable person. Some instances of negligence, as determined by the courts, will involve morally blameworthy conduct, but some will not. There may therefore be a finding of negligence even where there is no moral culpability, as in a case where a defendant makes an error that the court considers a reasonable person should not have made, but which, as we have shown, might easily have been made by any reasonable person. Other instances of conduct currently regarded as negligent for civil liability purposes may indeed be blameworthy, in that they involve a violation, as in a case where there is deliberate and unjustifiable disregard of a rule or principle. There will also be cases where conduct found to be negligent is in fact really recklessness; here the defendant will have acted in the face of a risk of harm that he or she knows to be unreasonable.

Our interim conclusion, then, is that negligence, as it currently operates in tort law, does not always follow the contours of blame. In Chapters 7 and 8 it will become increasingly clear that the problem lies not so much in the way the law is stated but rather in the way in which it is applied.

6

The Standard of Care

How are we to decide when an act is negligent? As is often the case with complex questions, the answer to the question may depend on the reason for asking it in the first place. If the question is asked when one is seeking to determine liability in tort, then the definition of negligence will be framed in such a way as to grasp those situations where it is thought that loss should be shifted from plaintiff to defendant. If the question is framed in the context of criminal punishment, or as part of an inquiry into moral blame, negligence may be given a very different definition. In this chapter we shall be concerned primarily with civil liability and with the way in which negligence should be defined for those purposes. We will consider negligence in the context of the criminal law in Chapter 9.

A central question in tort theory in recent decades has been that of how we are to identify a satisfactory justification for transferring loss through the medium of civil liability. A prominent trend in this analysis has been the championing of economic theories that have sought to establish a broadly utilitarian basis for the attribution of liability.[1] In these theories, the aim of the law of torts is to shift loss where to do so will satisfy the economic interests of society. This was most famously stated in 1947 by Judge Learned Hand in *United States* v. *Carroll Towing Co.*,[2] in which he proposed that conduct will be deemed to be unreasonable (and therefore negligent) where

$$P \times L > B$$

where P is the probability of injury, L is the magnitude of the injury and B is the benefit to be expected from the conduct in question. Later

---

[1] G. Calabresi, 'Some thoughts on risk distribution and the law of torts' (1961) 70 *Yale Law Journal* 499–553; W. M. Landes and R. A. Posner, *The Economic Structure of Tort Law* (Cambridge, MA, Harvard University Press, 1987); G. P. Fletcher, 'Fairness and utility in tort theory' (1972) 85 *Harvard Law Review* 537–73.

[2] 159 F 2d 169 (1947).

theorists have attempted to abandon what they see as the crude utilitarianism of the economic theory of tort liability, preferring to invoke an ostensibly Kantian view in which the interests of others must be treated as of equal value to one's own – a position which gives rise to an obligation to ensure that one does not take risks which will threaten those interests. The duty to take care, then, is a moral duty, which springs from respect for those who might be affected by one's acts. Reasonableness, in this analysis, need not be based on utilitarian considerations of the maximisation of benefit but on the equality of interests, and it is the objective of corrective justice to address imbalances resulting from a failure to give adequate attention to the interests of others. In one view, the apparent contrast between the utilitarian and deontological approaches to tort law may be reduced. Coleman, for example, defends a 'mixed theory' in which corrective justice is based on both economic and moral considerations. The moral justification of the duty to annul the harm one has caused is based on an idea of wrongfulness – the actor has caused harm by offending a community norm. This is because he or she has taken a risk defined as unacceptable by the norm, or, in the absence of deliberate risk-taking, his or her actions fail to meet an expected safety standard. In each of these cases, the negligent actor's conduct fails to meet a standard of care set out for the sort of behaviour in question.

Where is the morality in this? In the case of deliberate risk-taking, the moral wrongfulness of the conduct is principally located in the attitude of disregard which the actor has for the welfare of the person who is placed at risk by his or her conduct: if I pursue my interests even at the cost of potential injury to you, then, in the absence of any justification for doing so, I fail to treat you as my moral equal. But if I do not deliberately place you at risk, my defective conduct is not necessarily indicative of moral wrongdoing. There *may* be moral wrongdoing on my part – in that I may fail to exert myself sufficiently to avoid harm to others – but subjective wrongdoing will be absent where I think that I have taken all the necessary precautions (and have not), or where I try, but fail, to conduct myself to a sufficiently high standard.

In a system of completely objective liability, the standard by which conduct would be measured could be set by purely utilitarian criteria. The question of liability would be determined by reference to what conduct promoted disutility, causing harm that, in the circumstances, could reasonably have been avoided. The setting of this standard need have nothing to do with the subjective capacity of the actor. Indeed, it could be achieved with reference to checklists of the most mechanical sort. One might say, for example, that if circumstances x prevail, then precautions a, b and c need to be taken; any failure to do a, b and c will amount to a departure from the necessary standard of care. The fact that the actor was unaware of the need to do c would be no excuse; nor would it be an excuse to say that he or she tried to do c but failed because of some incapacity on his or her part.

The law has never been this mechanistic. Not only would such a system seem unjustifiably arbitrary, it would also fail to capture the essential morality underlying the obligation to compensate for harm caused. The standard of conduct expected is expressed in terms that provide *in themselves* a purported moral justification for the founding of the obligation. The law eschews, then, a purely arbitrary standard, and expresses the failure to meet the standard in terms of fault. You are liable for the consequences of your harmful act because you acted in a way that was *faulty*. Inevitably, this notion of faulty conduct carries with it a suggestion of culpable failure, a phenomenon, which, as we have already pointed out, was already present in the notions of *culpa* developed by the natural lawyers of the seventeenth century.

Because of the moral element implicit in the standard of care, this standard should, in theory, be one that the actor whose conduct is being evaluated could have achieved had he or she been conscientious. If the standard is pitched at too high a level, then it becomes unattainable and failing to meet it loses its flavour of fault. Liability, under these circumstances, is to all intents and purposes strict. The law seeks to prevent this result by employing the notion of the reasonable. We have a duty to take steps so as to avoid causing harm to those who might reasonably be foreseen as being at risk from our actions. This is the language of the classic tort case, *Donoghue v. Stevenson*,[3] in which the court expresses the essence of liability in negligence, using language that is clearly moral in tone. Not only is the notion of what is reasonable a moral one, but foreseeability itself has moral overtones in that it is the justification for requiring a precaution. By declaring that a consequence is foreseeable, the court is effectively making a judgement as to the defendant's capacity to avert the occurrence of that consequence.

The standard of care, then, is best seen as an adjustable criterion by which the law infers liability. The moral backdrop against which it is defined dictates that the standard should be couched in terms of what can

---

[3] [1932] AC 562.

reasonably be expected of people. In so far as one cannot be blamed for a failure to achieve the impossible, the standard is couched in the language of culpable failure. In its application, however, questions of moral culpability may be overshadowed by utilitarian considerations, the effect of which is to impose an objective enquiry. In the end, the question before the court is not 'was the state of mind of this particular defendant a careless one?' but, rather, 'was the behaviour of this defendant below the standard which can be expected by the plaintiff in the circumstances in question?' Ultimately, then, the law imposes civil liability in those cases where the defendant has risked harm, whether or not there was intent to place others at risk, and whether or not the defendant was actually capable of acting to a higher standard. This appears to be a form of objective liability, but, significantly, the objective standard is not plucked out of the air without reference to what is humanly possible. The courts do not set out to impose an insupportable burden in respect of the taking of precautions; their aim is, as they have repeatedly stated, to set the standard at such a level that most people might reasonably meet it. The standard, then, is pegged to a sense of the possible and, furthermore, the reasonable.

In this chapter, we ask whether the standard of care, as it is applied in common-law systems of tort law, is pitched at an acceptable level, or whether it has been raised excessively. If the latter is true, then the effect will be twofold. First, the extent of civil liability will be expanded, in much the same way as the extent of liability is expanded when a duty of care is imposed in circumstances where previously no duty of care was deemed to exist. Second – and this is a consideration which has been given scant attention – the raising of the standard of care may impose on individuals a burden of anxiety which may, in the end result, have a deleterious effect on safety standards. We have suggested elsewhere that the protection of the public is not necessarily achieved by encouraging a punitive culture. Yet the effect of applying an unrealistic standard of care may be to do just that, in that the connection between subjective culpability and blame is lost, and liability is imposed on those who could not reasonably have avoided it.

Occurrences of Subjective Fault in the Traditional Definitions of the Standard of Care

A truly objective system of civil liability would require no more than the externals of action on the part of the defendant. In fact, more than this is required: in the absence of a minimum mental element in the action in question, the defendant may escape liability, a fact that is suggestive of a moral fault requirement. An example of this is provided by the case of *Mansfield* v. *Weetabix Ltd.*[4] In this case a driver suffering, without knowing it, from malignant insulinoma lapsed into a state of hypoglycaemia while driving his vehicle. As a result of the impairment of his consciousness, he drove into a shop front, causing the death of one of the occupants of the building. In the subsequent civil action, the defendants (the driver's employers) argued against liability on the grounds of absence of fault. This argument was upheld by the court of first instance, where the judge stated the law in the following terms:

> The position is ... that if the driver suffers a sudden, unexpected, onset of some condition which then and there affects his ability to drive, and because of that sudden onset he has an accident which he is unable to prevent by the exercise of all reasonable care and skill, there is no liability, because it is that sudden disabling event that causes the accident in question.

This view was endorsed in the Court of Appeal, where it was accepted that, in the absence of fault on the part of the driver, there could be no liability. There is an interesting contrast here with cases in which a driver has gone to sleep at the wheel. In these cases, the courts have tended to hold that there is liability – civil and criminal – on the grounds that the driver must have received some warning, through drowsiness, of the fact that he or she was about to go to sleep. In fact, sleep experts say that this may not always be so: a tired person may not be aware of his or her state and sleep can overcome a person without any warning. Either way, a point of similarity is the emphasis on fault: if there were no warning of the onset of sleep, by inference, there should be no liability.

A similar result has been reached in cases where a defendant is suffering from mental disorder. In the past, the common law provided for strict liability in respect of damage caused by the insane; a more recent line of authority recognises mental disorder as a defence to liability. In the case of *Canada (Attorney General)* v. *Connolly*,[5] the defendant, who suffered from severe bi-polar disorder, caused serious injury to a police officer by driving his car while the latter's arm was trapped in the window. The court held that he was not liable in negligence on the grounds that his illness prevented him from being able to foresee the consequences of his action. The court admitted that this was a departure from the

---

[4] [1998] 1 WLR 1263.   [5] [1989] 64 DLR 4th 84.

objective test usually applied in negligence, but said that 'the foresee-ability of the reasonable person is normally the measure of liability in an action for negligence', continuing: 'negligence, perhaps more than most other torts, is about fault and mental state'.

The mental disorder cases give a role to subjective fault. The mentally disordered defendant may not be held to the same standard of care as the normal defendant, but are there other instances in which the courts are prepared to take into account individual characteristics of a defendant that may have the effect of moderating the standard of care? There are two categories of case in which this issue becomes a live one: the liability of children and the liability of novices. In each of these the law is faced with a defendant who might claim, with some justification, that it would be inappropriate to be judged against the normal standard of care. In the case of children, one of the most influential decisions is *McHale* v. *Watson*,[6] in which the High Court of Australia considered the question of the liability for personal injury damages of a boy of twelve. The defendant had been throwing a piece of sharpened welding rod at a target but hit a nine-year-old girl in the eye instead. The court was faced with a dearth of modern authority on the liability of children. It accepted that, in general, the standard of care by which a defendant's conduct would be measured was an objective one which would not afford a defence in respect of his being 'abnormally slow-witted, quick-tempered, absent-minded or inexperienced'. It did not follow, however, that this would exclude the taking into account of a limitation in capacity relating to foresight and prudence which was not personal to the defen-dant but which was, in the language of the court, a 'characteristic of humanity at his stage of development and in that sense normal'.

By bringing such limitations into account, the court went on,

> [the defendant] appeals to a standard of ordinariness, to an objective and not a subjective standard. In regard to the things which pertain to fore-sight and prudence – experience, understanding of causes and effects, balance of judgement, thoughtfulness – it is absurd, indeed it is a misuse of language, to speak of normality in relation to persons of all ages taken together. In those things normality is, for children, something very dif-ferent from what normality is for adults.

The standard of care for children, then, is subjective in the sense that it takes into account the *capacity* of typical defendants of that age; it is objective in that the extent to which that particular defendant deviates

---

[6] [1966] ALR 513.

from the norm for his age group is not taken into account. In Canadian law, a further twist has been added to the matter by those decisions which have imposed on children liability in those circumstances where they engage in activities of an 'adult' nature (such as driving a snowmobile).

Inexperience is obviously one of the reasons why a lower standard of care should be applied to children, and yet the fact that the defendant is a novice is not in general taken into account in determining the standard of care. Here the objective principle is firmly applied, as the court made clear in *Nettleship* v. *Weston*,[7] one of the leading decisions on the matter. In this case a learner driver caused personal injury to the person who was teaching her to drive. The defendant's driving fell below the standard to be expected of a competent driver, but it was claimed on her behalf that she should be assessed by the standards of the reasonable learner driver rather than by those of the reasonable licensed driver. The court rejected this argument, pointing out that it would be an impossible task for a court in every case to assess the level of competence to be expected of an individual driver. It suggested, too, that to apply such a variable standard in the context of driving would lead to demands to apply it to other activities, asking – rhetorically – whether an inexperienced surgeon would be held to a lower standard of care than an experienced one.

The refusal of the court in *Nettleship* v. *Weston* to lower the standard of care in order to take inexperience into account has been widely accepted in common-law countries, with only one major court venturing a contrary view, and that in a case in which very special factors were operating.[8] In the medical context, the issue arose in the case of *Wilsher* v. *Essex Area Health Authority*,[9] in which injury was caused to a patient being treated by a team of several persons of differing medical rank. The case is principally of interest in respect of what it says about causation, but the court observed that the standard of care to be applied in such cases was determined by the post occupied by the defendant rather than by the defendant's rank. This is consistent with the argument that a major reason for not departing from an objective test is the public's entitlement to rely on a certain level of competence from those engaged in potentially hazardous activities. We are entitled to expect a certain level of care from

---

[7] [1971] 3 All ER 581.

[8] The Australian High Court's decision in *Cook* v. *Cook* [(1986) 162 CLR 376] applied a lower standard of care in a case where a totally inexperienced driver injured the person who had persuaded her to attempt to drive. The court was likely to have been influenced by the fact that the plaintiff brought her own misfortune upon herself.

[9] [1988] 1 All ER 871 (HL).

the drivers, pilots, lifeguards, nurses or doctors whom we encounter, not least because our own affairs are planned on the basis that such a level will be met.

This is another important factor in the philosophical underpinning of tort law. Increasingly, in cases concerned with the scope of the duty of care (the issue which determines the *boundaries* rather than the *level* of liability), courts have acknowledged that one of the main grounds for the attribution of liability will be considerations of justice and equity. This test, which has most notably been articulated by the House of Lords in cases such as *Caparo* v. *Dickman Industries*[10] and *Marc Rich*,[11] asks whether it would seem *just* to transfer the loss from the defendant to the plaintiff. The debate in the duty of care cases has usually taken place around the notion of economic loss, which admittedly is different from cases involving personal injury, but the frank recognition by the courts in *Caparo* and in other cases of the role of considerations of justice involved in determining these issues might be extrapolated to the whole range of tort liability. One factor in this process of equitable balancing is the notion of reliance, which has played a very important role in founding liability in duty of care cases. The fact that one person has relied on another may be grounds for constructing a legally recognised duty of care between them, but it may also be relevant in determining the standard of care expected. If *A* relies on *B* to perform to a particular level, then *A*'s expectation may go some way towards defining the level which the law will regard as the appropriate standard of care. This is a matter of entitlement flowing from the relations between the parties, although the reliance which *A* places on *B* must be deemed to be reasonable (*B*, for example, must be aware that *A* is relying on him).

Patterns of reliance within society will therefore have some bearing on the development of legally recognised standards of care. The standard of care is not defined purely in terms of what the court, as detached arbiter, thinks will be appropriate; the standard will reflect general social expectations and the general social sense of what is equitable. This general expectation is that, in relation to hazardous or specialised activities, a minimal level of competence will be required as people cannot investigate in every case the actual level of competence of the person with whom they come into contact. But social expectations may play another, more subtle role. If it becomes widely believed in society that we are entitled to expect the highest possible standards, and if this

10 [1990] 2 AC 605. 11 [1995] 3 WLR 227.

expectation is expressed in terms of reliance, the courts will in due course interpret the standard of care in such a way as to reflect that reliance. The effect of this may be to drive up the standard of care from that which is reasonably attainable to that which is expected of a flawlessly functioning system. If social expectations are unrealistic – and we have argued in Chapters 2 and 3 that this is indeed the case in respect of many mishaps – there is a risk that the legal standard will in due course reflect these expectations and become unrealistic too.

Setting the Standard

Our enquiry so far has revealed that the law of negligence applies what is, for the most part, an objective standard even if its legitimacy relies on expression in terms redolent of fault and culpability. But how is this standard actually articulated? A distinction must be made here between the formal test and what the formal test means in practice. In what follows, this gap between theory and practice will be explored at greater length and the conclusion reached that the standard of care as often applied by the courts has departed to a significant extent from what might reasonably be expected of a conscientious and competent person of only average ability.

There is no shortage in common-law systems of judicial explanations of the standard of care expected of a defendant. A classic, and frequently cited, exposition of this is to be found in *Glasgow Corporation* v. *Muir*,[12] in which Lord Macmillan begins his account of the standard of care by stating that legal liability 'is limited to those consequences of our acts which a reasonable man of ordinary intelligence and experience so acting would have in contemplation'. This is the foresight test, which defines the standard in terms of a failure to avoid *foreseeable harm*. This restricts liability to a certain identifiable category of risks and excludes liability for the materialisation of other risks. It should be remembered that the test is not what the defendant actually foresaw, but what was *foreseeable* in the circumstances, which is effectively what he ought to have foreseen.

Some judicial definitions of the reasonable person are more complete. In the Canadian case of *Arland* v. *Taylor*,[13] for example, the judge observed that the reasonable person

> is not an extraordinary or unusual creature; he is not superhuman; he is
> not required to display the highest skill of which anyone is capable; he is

[12] [1943] 2 All ER 44.   [13] [1955] OR 131 at 152.

> not a genius who can perform uncommon feats, nor is he possessed of
> unusual powers of foresight. He is a person of normal intelligence who
> makes prudence a guide for his conduct. He acts in accord with general
> and approved practice.

To foresight, then, is added a certain degree of skill and a willingness to adhere to recommended practices, both of which can be explained in terms of risk. The unskilled operator poses a risk to others, even if he or she is not aware of the fact; the person who departs from the approved way of doing things may also create a risk, in this case a risk that exceeds the acceptable level of risk tolerated in the 'normal' or recommended way of doing things.

The writer A. P. Herbert, whose parodies of legal obfuscation are still capable of striking a chord, described the reasonable man as an 'odious individual'. Priggish he may seem, but there are other reasons for challenging the concept. Prominent amongst these is the argument that the 'reasonable person' test is no more than a cipher: the real decision is based on the judge or jury's perception of acceptable risk. In this view, the reasonable person is no more than a justification for a decision that is taken on other grounds. In an attempt to find out how people determined negligence, Green distributed a set of 'facts' to a wide sample of research subjects, asking them to assess negligence in relation to a hypothetical swimming-pool accident.[14] The results disclose that factors playing a part in this process include suggestion from judicial instructions and the magnitude of injury risked. The inclusion of a reasonable person test in the jury instruction did not appear to influence the outcome to any great extent.

We have seen how central to the notion of the reasonable person is the role of foresight. If the reasonable person would have foreseen a risk of harm, then it becomes negligent not to have done so. Yet how are we to tell whether the reasonable person could have foreseen that risk? The person making such a decision – whether it be a judge or a jury-member – must surely imagine himself in the position of the defendant, even if he is consciously attempting to imagine how the hypothetical reasonable person would have viewed the situation in which the defendant found himself. The difficulty with this exercise, of course, is that it is an after-the-event process, and the person who makes the appraisal is in possession of facts that the defendant would not have been in possession

---

[14]   E. Green, 'The reasonable man – legal fiction or psychosocial reality?' (1968) 2 *Law and Society Review* 241–57.

of at the time when he or she was actually faced with the circumstances in question. It is easy to say, today, that the *Challenger* space shuttle should not have been launched when it was, but this is because we know what happened when the O-rings failed. We know that crucial information about the state of the seals was available prior to the launch and we are therefore inclined to say that the decision to go ahead with it should not have been taken. This is the wisdom of hindsight, a wisdom that often leads us to conclude that we would have foreseen disaster even if those who acted did not themselves foresee it.

The hindsight factor has been extensively studied by psychologists. The first major study of the distorting role played by hindsight was that undertaken by Fischhoff, who argued that people frequently exaggerate the extent to which outcomes could have been anticipated once they know what the actual outcome was.[15] Fischhoff tested his supposition about hindsight bias on a group of student subjects, giving them an account of an obscure nineteenth-century British colonial war. Some subjects were informed of the actual outcome; others remained in ignorance of it. When asked to rate the probability of each of four possible outcomes occurring, those who knew what the actual outcome was tended to rate the probability of its occurring much more highly than those who were ignorant of it. Numerous subsequent studies have also tested the effect, using a range of different situations.[16] Fischhoff's conclusions have been consistently supported: once we know what happened, we are much readier to state that such an outcome was predictable.

Various explanations have been suggested for the existence of hindsight bias. One of the more promising of these involves what Fischhoff termed 'creeping determinism', whereby people tend to attribute a narrative pattern to past events in order to make sense of them.[17]

---

[15] B. Fischhoff, 'Hindsight ≠ foresight: the effect of outcome knowledge on judgement under uncertainty' (1975) 1 *Journal of Experimental Psychology: Human Perception and Performance* 288–99. See also S. A. Hawkins and R. Hastie, 'Hindsight: biased judgments of past events after the outcomes are known' (1990) 107 *Psychological Bulletin* 311–27; R. A. Caplan, K. L. Posner and F. W. Cheney, 'Effect of outcome on physician judgments of appropriateness of care' (1991) 265 *Journal of the American Medical Association* 1957–60.

[16] Examples include: D. C. Pennington, 'The British firemen's strike of 1977/78: an investigation of judgements in foresight and hindsight' (1981) 20 *British Journal of Social Psychology* 89–96; N. E. Synodinos, 'Hindsight distortion: "I knew-it-all along and I was sure about it."' (1986) 16 *Journal of Applied Social Psychology* 107–17.

[17] Hawkins and Hastie, 'Hindsight'.

We all have a desire to see the world as coherent rather than as unpredictable and uncertain. If we feel that we can interpret the world correctly, then it is a less threatening place. So we impose order on events that might actually be beyond our capacity to interpret correctly. Closely connected with this is a tendency to attribute blame. The attribution of blame fulfils an explanatory role: if we can identify somebody to carry the blame, then the uncertainty of an event is removed. The random nature of the outcome, which is potentially threatening, is 'domesticated' by our being able to lay the event at another's door. A bad outcome is not a question of fate – of hazard – but the responsibility of an identified individual.

Blaming brings into focus another form of bias, which, like hindsight, has been the subject of psychological enquiry. *Outcome* bias causes us to attribute blame more readily when the nature of the outcome is serious than we would do when the outcome is comparatively minor. This must be distinguished from a mere failure to enquire as to responsibility: where damage is slight, it seems reasonable not to bother to ascertain who caused it. What is the point, one might ask, in making the enquiry in such a case? By contrast, where the damage is substantial, we feel more inclined to identify the person responsible because there are pragmatic reasons to do so: the identification of the person responsible may help to prevent such a thing from happening again. But blaming is more than a mere pragmatic exercise in the prevention of future harm: it satisfies a psychological need to find an object of punishment. By punishing another we feel that we annul the wrong; we lessen the hurt.

The significance of outcome bias is that if the harm or suffered loss is great, then the desire to find somebody to blame may mean that we may find wrongdoing or negligence in those circumstances in which, were we to examine the situation dispassionately, there is none. It may also obscure the fact that responsibility for an outcome is, in fact, multifactorial. Thus, a search for a single wrongdoer who can be blamed may mean that we pay insufficient attention to the role played by other actors in the event and by system factors. The possibility that harm is accidental may also be obscured. We may accept a minor injury, for example, as being an inevitable concomitant of the operation of a complex system. 'Something is inevitably going to go wrong', we may say when the loss is slight, but when it is considerable we are much more likely to say 'Somebody must be to blame for this death: people don't just die for no reason at all.'

Is the Standard of Care Excessively High?

We have seen that the courts have set out to define the standard of care in terms that suggest that it is well within the reach of the 'average' person. If this is how the standard is applied in the courts, then it is probably not too high. Yet there are grounds for arguing that in some areas of activity the standard has risen to a point where levels of litigation are counter-productive, distorting the relationship between providers and recipients of services and, in some cases, preventing providers from discharging their duties in a way which they consider ethical. So-called 'malpractice crises' in medicine are examples of this distorting effect. If these crises exist, then the social purpose of the law of torts is not being served. The same argument may apply in other areas such as product liability: if the prospect of liability deters innovation in the development of products, then the public suffers. It is a matter of getting the balance right.

But why would the courts allow the standard of care to be raised above an appropriate level? One way in which this may happen is through the operation of pro-plaintiff views on the part of jurors. This is always a possibility in systems in which civil juries determine liability, although the evidence for perverse verdicts of this sort is uneven. The raising of the standard of care is also, however, a feature of systems in which judges, rather than juries, make decisions as to liability – pro-plaintiff prejudice is therefore not always going to be an explanation of the phenomenon. To understand why the standard of care has a tendency to impose unduly on the defendant, we might examine how it operates in the context of medical negligence. In what circumstances will a doctor be adjudged to have failed to achieve the necessary standard of care?

The general standard of care is that of the reasonable person. This suffices for many activities, but the exercise of a special skill calls for something more – the standard of skill of the person performing those professional or skilled functions. The surgeon, therefore, is judged not by the standards of the reasonable amateur trying his hand at surgery but by the standards expected of a surgeon. This is trite law, but the issue becomes more complicated as we enquire further into the question of how this special standard is to be determined.

In English law, the classic case on this point, even if beleaguered by academic criticism, is *Bolam* v. *Friern Hospital Management Committee*,[18] a case which continues to be applied by the courts more

---

[18] [1957] 2 All ER 118.

than forty years after its hearing. The plaintiff in this case had suffered a fractured hip after electro-convulsive therapy had been administered to him without his having been given a relaxant drug and without having his convulsive movements restrained. The defendant argued that he had acted in accordance with good practice, and that there was therefore no negligence. This was accepted, the judge ruling that there could be no finding of negligence if a doctor acted in accordance with 'a practice accepted as proper by a responsible body of medical men skilled in that particular art'. Negligence would not be inferred merely because other responsible medical experts took a contrary view.

The judge in *Bolam* was echoing a test that had articulated a slightly earlier Scottish medical negligence case, *Hunter* v. *Hanley*,[19] where the judge observed:

> In the realm of diagnosis and treatment there is ample scope for genuine difference of opinion, and one man clearly is not negligent merely because his conclusion differs from that of other professional men, nor because he has displayed less skill or knowledge than others would have shown. The true test for establishing negligence in diagnosis or treatment on the part of a doctor is whether he has been proved to be guilty of such a failure as no doctor of ordinary skill would be guilty of if acting with ordinary care.

The *Bolam* test, as it has come to be known, has been criticised on the grounds that it will allow the defendant to escape a charge of negligence if he or she can show that what was done was in accordance with an established and professionally approved practice within the medical profession. This, it has been argued, is to allow the medical profession to set its own standards irrespective of whether the practices adopted by the profession provide an adequate level of protection for patients.

Bolam is an instance of what has become known in the law as the 'custom test' of negligence. Its status in the law of torts is well established, although there are now chinks in its armour. Under the custom test, expert evidence establishes what the reasonably skilled and prudent person in a particular profession or trade would do in the circumstances, and the defendant's conduct is then measured against this. In the medical context, a robust (and, by the standards of today, somewhat unsophisticated) defence of the test can be seen in the judgement in *Marshall* v. *Lindsey County Council*.[20] In this case the judge said:

---

[19] [1955] SLT 213.   [20] [1935] 1 KB 516.

An act cannot, in my opinion, be held to be due to a want of reasonable care if it is in accordance with the general practices of mankind. What is reasonable in a world not wholly composed of wise men and women must depend on what people presumed to be reasonable constantly do. Many illustrations might be given and I will take one from the evidence given in this action. A jury could not, in my opinion, properly hold it to be negligent in a doctor or a midwife to perform his or her duties in a confinement without mask and gloves, even though some experts gave evidence in their opinion that was a wise precaution. Such an omission may become negligent if, and only if, at some future date it becomes the general custom to take such a precaution among skilled practitioners.

The recognition of the legitimising force of custom, supported in *Bolam*, was to be further entrenched in *Maynard* v. *West Midlands Regional Health Authority*.[21] This was a decision of the House of Lords in a case in which there was a difference of expert opinion as to the reasonableness of conducting a diagnostic operation on a patient who suffered vocal cord paralysis as a result of this procedure. According to expert medical evidence adduced for the plaintiff, the carrying out of this operation was inappropriate, a view which was ultimately preferred by the trial judge. On appeal, it was held that the judge was not entitled to prefer one view to another: on the basis of *Bolam*, if what the defendant did was in accordance with an accepted body of medical opinion – which it was – then he could not be held to be negligent simply because another body of opinion held otherwise.

The privilege accorded to customary practice has not gone unchallenged in the courts, and there are cases in which judges have asserted that the ultimate arbiter of whether a professional practice is acceptable will be the courts themselves, rather than expert witnesses from the professions. The customary conveyancing practice of Hong Kong solicitors was rejected by the court in *Edward Wong Finance Co. Ltd* v. *Johnson, Stokes and Master*.[22] The court said that the fact that what the defendant did was in accordance with what was normal amongst her professional colleagues was not conclusive evidence that it was prudent, and the fact that other solicitors did the same did not make the risk 'less apparent or unreal'.

A number of courts have directly challenged customs of the medical profession. The Supreme Court of South Australia considered the matter in *F* v. *R*,[23] an action for damages brought by a patient who had undergone sterilisation by tubal ligation and who claimed that she

---

[21] [1985] 1 All ER 635.   [22] [1984] AC 296.   [23] [1983] 33 SASR 189.

had not been warned of the possibility of subsequent failure of this method to prevent conception. The court accepted that there will be many cases where evidence of professional practice will be decisive, but cautioned that

> professions may adopt unreasonable practices. Practices may develop in professions, particularly as to disclosure, not because they serve the interest of the clients, but because they protect the interests or convenience of members of the profession. The court has an obligation to scrutinise professional practices to ensure that they accord with the standard of reasonableness imposed by the law.

The ultimate question, the court said, was not whether the defendant's conduct conformed with the practices of the profession but whether it conformed with the law's standards of reasonableness. A similar willingness to reserve to the court the question of whether a customary practice is reasonable emerged in the decision of the High Court of Australia in *Rogers* v. *Whittaker*,[24] another case of failure to disclose a risk to the patient. The adoption of a 'patient-oriented test' in the face of evidence of medical custom was greeted with enthusiasm by opponents of the custom test. But the English courts were still bound by *Bolam* – until the decision in *Bolitho* v. *City & Hackney Health Authority*[25] appeared to question at the highest level the particular authority accorded professional custom.

The litigation in *Bolitho* followed a hospital doctor's failure to intubate the trachea of a child who was experiencing respiratory distress. Expert evidence was given to the court to the effect that a reasonably competent doctor would have intubated the trachea in the circumstances, but there was also evidence from the defendant's expert that not doing so was a clinically justifiable course of action. The issue of *Bolam* arose: if a practice was in accordance with a responsible body of medical opinion, then there should be no liability – or so *Bolam* suggested. However, in *Bolitho* the judge qualified this by saying:

> In particular, in cases involving, as they so often do, the weighing of risks against benefits, the judge before accepting a body of opinion as being responsible, reasonable or respectable, will need to be satisfied that, in forming their views, the experts have directed their minds to the question of comparative risks and benefits and have reached a defensible conclusion on the matter.

[24] [1992] 67 ALJR 47.   [25] [1997] 4 All ER 771 (HL).

This would appear significantly to restrict the effect of *Bolam*. However, there is a caveat: the court in *Bolitho* was clearly of the view that any challenge to professional custom would be rare. As the judge said:

> In the vast majority of cases the fact that distinguished experts in the field are of a particular opinion will demonstrate the reasonableness of that opinion. But if, in a rare case, it can be demonstrated that the professional opinion is not capable of withstanding logical analysis, the judge is entitled to hold that the body of opinion is not reasonable or responsible ... I emphasise that, in my view, it will very seldom be right for a judge to reach the conclusion that views genuinely held by a competent medical expert are unreasonable.

Even if the decision in *Bolitho* is interpreted conservatively, it demonstrates a position for which there is a consistent line of authority over the years, a position that, moreover, is attuned to recent decisions in Australia and Canada. In view of public sensitivities over the exercise of professional power, the likelihood of the courts endorsing purely professional setting of standards is slight. However, there are inherent difficulties with this approach, particularly when one asks whether a defendant can reasonably be expected to meet a purely court-determined standard when he or she is operating within the context of a profession that *expects* its members to comply with what it identifies as the appropriate standard.

Imagine that A is a doctor who is trained to carry out a medical procedure in a specified way. The reason for following the recommended course of action may be one of patient safety, but it may also relate to considerations of resources. In the latter case, it may be that resources simply do not permit the carrying out of a particular diagnostic test; an expensive test may be thought to be unjustified in that it will deprive other services of funds. Every health service must make such choices unless it operates within the context of patient payment for the full cost of treatment. If A carries out the procedure in accordance with the practice recommended by the profession itself, he cannot be negligent under a *Bolam*-type test. He will also be aware – or should be aware – of what is required of him. By contrast, if his conduct is to be assessed by another, external standard, how will he be able to assess whether his conduct satisfies the expected standard of care? It is surely exceptionally difficult for a person engaged in a technically complex activity to imagine how his conduct will be viewed by a future court. Inevitably the question 'how should I do this?' is answered by imagining how professional colleagues – and, in particular, those who give professional training – would do it.

This is the basis of much medical training; the neophyte learns by working with and observing others. It is impossible to develop medical skills on the basis of first principles alone. Experience must be gained and procedures learned from assisting or being supervised by more senior colleagues. If the law fails to recognise this, then it misses an essential feature of medical practice.

A move from the *Bolam*-type *reasonable doctor* test to a *Rogers and Whittaker*-type *reasonable patient* test will present particular difficulty for defendants in cases involving informed consent. The traditional approach of some doctors who may have thought it adequate to tell a patient only what they thought the patient *ought* to be told was unacceptably paternalistic. Under the *Rogers* v. *Whittaker* approach, the doctor must disclose to a patient those risks that a *reasonable person in the position of that patient* might wish to know. On the face of it this is perfectly acceptable, but there are some practical difficulties created by expressing the test in this way. How is the doctor to know what information an individual patient would wish to have? The problem is compounded by the fact that a patient cannot necessarily be expected to know what questions he or she should ask. It has been shown that patients' assessments of the appropriateness of the information provided to them change in the light of knowledge subsequently gained. Once the patient knows in detail about a risk, he or she is likely to think this information should have been imparted before the procedure.[26] A patient who suffers a particular complication is likely to become very well informed concerning that complication. After the event, that patient may understandably feel that inadequate disclosure took place in respect of the harm that actually occurred. What, however, of all the other possible complications which did not in fact occur and concerning which the patient does not possess the same level of information? For the doctor to provide enough detail about a complication that does occur to ensure that a patient is satisfied *after the event* with the adequacy of the disclosure would imply giving equal quantities of information about all the possible risks of a procedure. In some cases, before a procedure, the risk of possible adverse events may be very long indeed, although the chances of any one of these occurring may be very low. There is a real risk that the conscientious doctor will overload the patient with information and actually create a situation in which the patient's decision is rendered

---

[26] A. L. Garden, A. F. Merry, R. L. Holland and K. J. Petrie, 'Anaesthesia information – what patients want to know' (1996) 24 *Anaesthesia and Intensive Care* 594–8.

unnecessarily difficult. Ultimately, each doctor will assess his or her own conduct in terms of what a hypothetical conscientious doctor in the same position would do. This standard, of course, is quite capable of taking into account the expressed or implicit desire of a particular patient to know certain information, but there is no escaping the fact that the doctor must use his or her judgement to work out what this is. There is no doubt that the doctor should try to see the situation from the patient's point of view, but the professional standard is quite capable of allowing for this and of embracing the evolution of patient expectations as society changes. The fundamental problem with the decision in *Rogers* v. *Whittaker* lies not in the implication that doctors should perhaps tell patients more than they have done in the past – a perfectly acceptable proposition; the problem lies in the uncertainty that it creates. Under this test the doctor cannot rely on his understanding of what a reasonable *doctor* in his or her position would think the patient would wish to know. It disregards the principle of peer guidance. It is hard to see on whose advice or evidence the court is going to come to an informed decision as to what a reasonable patient would wish to have known in the circumstances. Under *Bolam* it is open to both the plaintiff and the defendant to call experts, and the court may have to decide which expert evidence it prefers. Under *Rogers* v. *Whittaker,* presumably the court will have to decide this matter on the basis of its own assessment of materiality of risk, and will view such expert advice as irrelevant. Apart from any other objection, the court's view will inevitably be highly subject to the influence of outcome bias.

This objection to attacks on the *Bolam* standard, of course, is based on the perspective of the defendant rather than the plaintiff. The latter might be expected to respond by pointing out that he or she is entitled to the protection of a system that allows for external review – by the courts – of standards developed by the profession. The issue appears, then, to be one of conflicting claims or interests. The plaintiff has an interest in protection; the defendant has an interest in not being put into a position of uncertainty as to what is the right thing to do. Which side of this conflict of interests is to be preferred depends on one's view of the role of the law of torts. This must be to achieve some sort of balance. We do not accept strict liability in this context, and it is therefore legitimate to balance the plaintiff's interest in compensation with the requirement that an impossible burden is not placed on the defendant. It does seem that a movement away from the custom test could place some defendants in a position of unacceptable uncertainty. Furthermore, to impose liability when a person has conscientiously followed recommended practices strikes at fairness, which, as we have seen, remains a goal of the law of torts.

Room for Human Error?

In Chapter 3 we examined the role which human error played in many mishaps. The argument we advanced then was that a degree of human error is inevitable, and that much of this error does not involve culpability. We now turn to the issue of whether the standard of care allows adequately for human error.

Mistakes are inevitable, and even the most careful person can be expected to make mistakes. The reasonable person can therefore be expected to make mistakes, although the reasonable person may be expected to commit violations less frequently than the unreasonable person, who, by definition, cannot be relied upon to take adequate precautions. How far does the standard of care, as it is applied under the reasonable person test, allow for the making of errors? The standard of care is not portrayed as being a standard of perfection, as is apparent in the definitions of the reasonable person we cite above. In his judgement in *Whitehouse* v. *Jordan*,[27] an obstetric negligence case, Lord Denning observed that an error of judgement in a professional context did not amount to negligence. To test this, he said, 'one might ask the average competent and careful practitioner: "Is this the sort of mistake that you yourself might have made?" If he says: "Yes, even doing the best I could, it might have happened to me", then it is not negligent.' At the House of Lords, however, this passage was 'corrected'; Lord Fraser courteously suggested that what Lord Denning had *meant* to say was that an error of judgement was not *necessarily* negligent. Lord Fraser said:

> The true position is that an error of judgment may, or may not, be negligent; it depends on the nature of the error. If it is one that would not have been made by a reasonably competent professional man professing to have the standard and type of skill that the defendant held himself out as having, and acting with ordinary care, then it is negligent. If, on the other hand, it is an error that a man, acting with ordinary care, might have made, then it is not negligence.

What Lord Denning probably meant to stress is that errors are inevitable, and that a perfectly competent practitioner is likely, at some stage, to

27 [1980] 1 All ER 650.

make them. The occurrence of such errors does not necessarily reflect on the level of competence of the person who makes them. Indeed, increased expertise may predispose to certain types of error.[28] This is surely correct; Lord Fraser, however, was right to refine the proposition, pointing out that whether or not an error of judgement will or will not be negligent depends on whether it *demonstrates a lack of care* on the part of the person making it. If the error is compatible with the taking of due care, then it will not be negligent.

In theory, then, some mistakes will be permissible. In practice, though, most errors will be viewed as incompatible with the exercise of due care because of the perception that due care, at the time, would have prevented them. In Chapter 3 we showed that errors can occur even when a person is acting with full care. Furthermore, a reasonably competent person will, *over a period of time*, manifest a lack of care for short spells, simply because it is humanly impossible to satisfy a requirement of full care all the time. Unfortunately, the assessment of such a person will not be based on his or her record over time but will look at a particular moment. In the examples that we have considered there seems to have been some variability in the way in which this is actually done in different cases. It is therefore misleading to talk about the reasonably competent person being the yardstick, because the way in which reasonableness is defined is neither clear nor consistent. All too often the yardstick is taken to be the person who is capable of meeting a high standard of competence, awareness, care, etc. *all the time*. Few such people exist.

One response to the difficulties posed by this essentially normative approach is to resort to an empirical definition of reasonableness and to suggest that the yardstick should be the *average* person. This would permit the courts to take account of inevitable human errors, but in fact confuses two issues. One of these issues is that individuals vary considerably in their levels of skill, knowledge and ability. It is an obvious but easily overlooked fact that, given a normal distribution, half of those performing a particular task will be below average in its performance.[29] The other issue is that all people are subject to error, and that certain types of error are made more likely by increased levels of skill. Thus, slips or lapses are more likely with highly practised practitioners than with those who are less familiar with the task in question, although the converse applies to many other forms of mistake.

---

[28] See the discussion of slips and lapses in Chapter 3.
[29] More generally, half the people will be below the *median* of any particular measure.

The truth is that a simplistic empirical approach is also unsatisfactory. We know that the required standard for any activity is not that which is attainable by half the people by whom it is undertaken. Rather, it is a standard that produces an acceptable result with acceptable safety. In general, most individuals who are trained should be able to achieve this standard. For example, the vast majority of people can learn to drive with an adequate level of skill. It is possible to define a minimal level of accomplishment that is acceptable, and in reality it is this standard that we all expect of one another. In other words, we have returned to a normative definition, but one that takes for its reference the task under consideration and the minimal level of knowledge, skill and care that is generally considered reasonable by society. To take an example, consider the situation in which a child runs into the road unexpectedly in front of a car. There will be some circumstances in which the distance between the child and the oncoming car is such that no driver would be able to stop in time to avoid impact. In such circumstances, no blame could be attached to a failure to avoid hitting the child. How do we determine the distance reasonably required before blame should be attributed to the driver who fails to stop in time? Some drivers will be able to stop more quickly than others. A highly expert driver with the fast reactions of comparative youth may be able to stop within a shorter distance than a less skilled and perhaps older driver. It would be at least theoretically possible to determine the distance which would be required by the average driver: in other words, the distance in which half of all drivers would be able to stop. However, to set the standard at that point – that is, at the average level – would be to set a standard that 50 per cent of drivers would fail to achieve. Clearly this would not be reasonable. If 50 per cent is too high, as it obviously is, then is 10 per cent a better figure? We would certainly be more comfortable at this level because we should not be surprised to learn that one in ten drivers fell below a standard that we would endorse. In fact, it is impossible to express this standard in terms of the precise percentage of the population in question who can be expected to meet it. The best we can say is that the standard should be one that most people, with the exercise of care, could meet.

In addition, however, this standard must make allowance for occasional human errors. In a sense this approach is still normative, but in a sense it is also empiric. We know empirically that such errors are inevitable, and it would therefore be unrealistic to set an expected (or normative) standard that we knew to be unattainable. Also, to a degree, the level of skill that we would define as acceptable on normative grounds (for the purposes of granting a licence, for example) would be strongly influenced by our empirical experience of the attainable. To some extent, defining a minimal acceptable standard also addresses the question of whether any distinction should be made between the learner driver or trainee surgeon and the fully qualified person. The answer is that the required standard, being a minimum, must be met by all who undertake the activity, and that appropriate supervision or assistance must be available when necessary to ensure that it is met.

Within the context of healthcare, the onus to ensure that appropriate supervision or assistance is available is only part of a wider organisational responsibility that extends to the provision of adequate resources (equipment and medications) and reasonable working hours, credentialing, monitoring of competence and so forth. We discussed the importance of teamwork on the outcomes of patient care in Chapter 2. These outcomes, assessed collectively (as annual rates of mortality, for example), will certainly depend on the culture of the organisation as a whole and the way in which individuals within it interact at multiple levels.[30] There is a strong argument for considering the standard of care in relation to the standard provided by a given institution rather than in relation to a single practitioner within that institution on a single occasion. There are times when a failure to meet an acceptable standard of care will be the sole responsibility of one person, but there are many situations in which the responsibility for such failures extends far beyond the individual actually involved in a particular incident.

We have seen that judicial direction plays an important role in determining the outcome of a jury's deliberations. It is likely that the precise phrasing used in explaining the concept of reasonableness is very important. There is a key difference between asking whether an event (such as an error) represented a reasonable standard of practice and asking whether it was something that could have happened to the reasonable and conscientious person. The latter is much more likely to facilitate a judgement which is in accordance with the facts of real life and normal human cognition.

In this chapter we have argued that the standard of care is not as consistently and clearly defined as it should be. Often it seems to have

---

[30] L. A. Curry, E. Spatz, E. Cherlin, J. W. Thompson, D. Berg, H. H. Ting, . . . E. H. Bradley, 'What distinguishes top-performing hospitals in acute myocardial infarction mortality rates? A qualitative study' (2011) 154 *Annals of Internal Medicine* 384–90.

been defined without reference to what is practically possible or, on the other hand, statistically inevitable. Because of this, there is often a tendency to set the standard at too high a level. In this way the balance of interests between plaintiff and defendant may be tipped too far in the direction of the plaintiff. At times, there may also be a tendency to focus exclusively on the responsibility of an individual without adequately considering the wider organisational context and the possible contribution of others within this context to the generation of situations in which avoidable patient harm is made more likely. This is unlikely to be in the interests of the individual defendant, the plaintiff or the wider public.

The issues discussed in this chapter relate to theoretical concepts underpinning the standard of care. In practice, there are many features of the tort system that may confound the outcome. We are of course aware of the difficulties that plaintiffs may experience in seeking compensation for injury. These difficulties, including those related to establishing causation, have been widely acknowledged in tort scholarship. At times, problems related to the practical conduct of the case may disadvantage the defendant. In the next chapter we shall examine some of these influences. In particular, we shall consider the importance of expert witnesses in placing flesh on the conceptual bones of the standard of care.

7

Assessing the Standard – The Role
of the Expert Witness

The central thesis of this book is that many incidents currently defined as negligent – in both a criminal and a civil context – do not, on close analysis, reflect significant blameworthiness. Our discussion of the standard of care concluded that this standard will tend to be driven up by the way in which it is applied in negligence litigation. The expert witness plays an important role in this process.

The court is the trier of fact in any legal action. In jury-based systems, it will be the jury that performs this role; in non-jury systems, it will be the judge. Whichever system is favoured, the task will be the same – that of deciding whether a particular fact existed. To do this, courts will listen to the evidence of those who witnessed or participated in the events under dispute. The law of evidence is designed to ensure that the court considers only that evidence that will enable it to reach a reliable conclusion. Opinion evidence – evidence about what people *thought* about a matter – is usually excluded,[1] as is evidence of knowledge that is indirectly obtained (*the hearsay rule*).[2] Opinion evidence, however, may be allowed where the opinion is necessary to enable the trier of facts to understand the facts in question. So, for example, a witness may be asked whether, in his opinion, a person was intoxicated at the time of his observation, or whether he was in a state of distress. Another form of opinion evidence that is admissible is expert evidence, and it is here that one finds the most significant exception to the general inadmissibility of statements of opinion.[3]

There are several important requirements which expert evidence must satisfy if it is to be admissible in court. The first, and most important, of these is that it must be necessary to hear expert evidence. This means that the expert's evidence must address a matter that the

---

[1] A. A. S. Zuckerman, 'Relevance in legal proceedings', in W. Twining (ed.), *Facts in Law* (Wiesbaden, Steiner Verlag, 1983), 145–55.

[2] *R. v. Sharp*, [1988] 1 WLR 7.

[3] T. Hodgkinson, *Expert Evidence: Law and Practice* (London, Sweet and Maxwell, 1990).

trier of fact (the judge, or a member of the jury in a jury trial) cannot determine for himself or herself. The test here is whether the evidence relates to matters that are outside the knowledge and experience of the layperson. In many cases, there will be little doubt about whether evidence falls into this category: scientific questions will normally be assumed not to be within the court's knowledge, and therefore it will be necessary to hear expert evidence where there is, for example, a medical or engineering issue to be settled. A matter of, say, the stress-bearing capability of a construction material will need to be explained by an expert in civil engineering as a judge or a jury cannot be expected to be able to pronounce on such a matter. Expert evidence will often be concerned with issues of cause and effect. Could a particular injury, for example, have been caused by a particular chemical agent? This is the day-to-day activity of expert witnesses involved in toxic tort cases where plaintiffs have been exposed to allegedly harmful substances. The determination of such questions may be far from simple, particularly where a condition may be multi-factorial in its aetiology, and experts may be called upon to commit themselves to causal judgements of considerable subtlety.[4]

In cases where the science involved is highly specialised, and perhaps even esoteric, there may be little disputing the central role of the expert witness. There are areas, however, where the issue is less clear-cut, and where there may be some dispute as to the admissibility of the expert opinion. Human psychology is one such area, and in this context there has been considerable tension between the courts, jealous to guard their role as the triers of fact, and psychologists, who claim professional insights denied the layperson.[5] In general, courts have tended to hold that matters of normal psychology – how the average person reacts to situations – are questions for the judge or jury to decide, based on common sense and their ordinary experience of life, whereas matters of abnormal psychology may be commented upon by forensic psychologists.[6] This debate is relevant to

---

[4] The question of what scientific evidence will be acceptable has been the subject of considerable debate. In the United States, the Supreme Court addressed this controversial issue in its decision in *Daubert* v. *Merrell Dow Pharmaceuticals*, 113, Sup. Ct., 2786 (1993). For background and discussion, see L. Loevinger, 'Science as evidence' (1995) 35 *Jurimetrics* 153–90.

[5] R. D. Mackay and A. M. Colman, 'Equivocal rulings on expert psychological and psychiatric evidence: turning a muddle into a nonsense' (1996) *Criminal Law Review* 88–95 (discussing, inter alia, the decisions in *R.* v. *Turner* [1975] QB 834 and *R.* v. *Graham* (1982) 74 Cr. App. Rep. 235).

[6] D. Sheldon and M. D. MacLeod, 'From normative to positive data: expert psychological evidence re-examined' (1991) *Criminal Law Review* 811–20.

our current theme, in that matters of error, in relation to which psychologists profess expert knowledge, may be viewed by the court as a matter of ordinary knowledge, and thus within the trier of fact's competence to determine. The reality is, in fact, quite different. There is a substantial body of specialist knowledge relevant to the analysis of the cognitive processes that underlie unsafe acts. A number of concepts must be understood, and some of these are actually counter-intuitive. It should be obvious from the material presented in Chapters 2, 3 and 4 that this is, without doubt, a field in which the courts should seek expert evidence. Similarly, expert evidence may well be relevant, in some cases, in relation to the elements of teamwork in the delivery of healthcare, the factors that contribute to the success and failure of the *coordinated* care required in the management of complex problems and the boundaries of responsibility when things go wrong.

The other requirements for the admissibility of expert evidence are that the expert must speak within a recognised field of expertise, that the evidence must be based on reliable principles, and that the expert must be qualified in that discipline.[7] Of these requirements, the one that is of greatest interest for our current discussion is the reliable principles requirement, because it is against the background of this need for a principled basis to the expert opinion that expert pronouncements on the standard of care may be assessed. It is this basis of principle that gives expert evidence its authority and promotes an opinion into a normative conclusion. But how far does an expert pronouncement on a standard of care issue actually have scientific weight behind it? In other words, if an expert witness says that it is not reasonable to do *x*, is this statement based on *knowledge as to the practice of the hypothetical reasonable practitioner* (who is, as we saw in Chapter 5, the yardstick against which conduct is measured), or is it based on what the expert himself or herself would do? If it is the former, then does the statement satisfy the requirement normally made of expert evidence that it is based on a body of theory which is susceptible to testing and indeed has been subjected to testing? If it is based – as we shall argue below to be the case – on the actual practice of an appropriate doctor from a comparable background, then obviously, in the case of a reputable expert, it will satisfy these criteria and will have been subjected to the objective scrutiny provided by peer review and publication. But this, we suggest, is not necessarily always the case.

---

[7] Hodgkinson, *Expert Evidence: Law and Practice.*

The Selection of Expert Witnesses

Before expert evidence can be led it is necessary to establish the qualifications of the expert witness. Counsel for the other side may challenge these qualifications, especially if the opinion given is thought likely to be unhelpful to that side's case. Furthermore, such unhelpful opinion is likely to be countered by contrary expert evidence, and one of the factors influencing the weight given by the jury or judge to two conflicting expert opinions will be the relative standing of the experts involved. A prominent international authority on a subject may well be thought more reliable than a junior consultant[8] from the defendant doctor's own department, for example. In reality, however, the latter may have a much better idea of the prevailing standard of care in relation to the issue in question.

Bona fide expert witnesses are therefore likely to be selected in the first instance on account of their eminence in general. Such eminence is usually achieved by extensive research and numerous publications. Often the expert will hold a senior academic position and perhaps a senior administrative position as well. It is also unlikely that individuals of this standing will be of average or below average age in relation to all specialists in their field.

The second factor leading to the selection of genuine experts is their standing in relation to the specific issue in question. For example, if the case is about a central venous catheter (CVC) insertion, a specialist who has not only performed many such procedures but has also written and lectured on the specific issue of the use of CVCs is likely to be seen as more credible than a practitioner whose practice involves only an occasional CVC insertion, even if the latter's experience is much closer to that of the defendant.

The third factor in the selection of experts relates to their ability to communicate and to think rapidly under pressure. The expert is there not only to inform but, from counsel's point of view, also to persuade. There is, furthermore, little value in an expert who can easily be discredited by aggressive cross-examination.

There is much to be said in favour of this approach to selecting an expert. Assuming the person selected is honest (and we shall consider the alternative possibility in due course), a well-informed, articulate and confident person of some standing is likely to provide high-quality

---

[8] 'Consultant' is primarily a British term; in the United States, the equivalent would be an 'attending physician' (or more colloquially, just an 'attending'), and in Australia and New Zealand the term 'specialist' would be more common.

evidence and unlikely to be easily influenced by either side into modifying his or her genuine opinion to suit a particular point of view. Whether such a person has much in common with the majority of practitioners who carry out most of the day-to-day clinical work within the particular speciality is another matter altogether. More importantly, some such super-specialists may have relatively little sympathy for the difficulties faced by the journeyman who must turn his or her hand to a range of procedures, who may undertake some of these only occasionally and who may be familiar only with the basic literature on any given procedure – and in some cases only with rather out-of-date literature at that. Obviously it would be better if all practitioners who undertake procedures or care for patients with a given condition are as well informed and current in their understanding as the super-specialist just described. Unfortunately, the majority are not. Much medicine is, of necessity, carried out by individuals who are broadly trained and able to cope with a wide range of situations. Inevitably, their knowledge and skill in relation to any given situation will be adequate rather than outstanding.

This, after all, is the assumption on which qualifying examinations in medicine are based, even at the specialist level. The knowledge of the new medical graduate must encompass the whole of medicine, but only in broad terms. The specialist orthopaedic surgeon, for example, is able to forget most of his or her basic obstetrical knowledge but must still cover the whole range of acute and elective orthopaedic surgery. The expert who has gone on to spend ten or more additional years working in the sub-speciality of (let us say) elective spinal surgery has been able to forget about hip replacements, acute fractured femurs and shoulder repairs. This type of sub-specialist may even have refined his or her knowledge in one or two specific aspects of spinal surgery to the point where he or she has achieved recognition as an international authority. The general orthopaedic practitioner, who may have to undertake some spinal surgery, will be expected to have sufficient knowledge and skill to undertake such surgery adequately and safely, as well as the core procedures in hip surgery, knee surgery, shoulder surgery, hand surgery and so on. Notwithstanding the fact that specialist examinations are very rigorous indeed, the expectations of training and examination are of general all-round competence rather than focused brilliance.

This too is the stated expectation of the courts in reference to the standard of care. We repeat the comments from the Canadian case of

Arland v. *Taylor,*[9] quoted in Chapter 6. The judge said that the reasonable person

> is not an extraordinary or unusual creature; he is not superhuman; he is not required to display the highest skill of which anyone is capable; he is not a genius who can perform uncommon feats, nor is he possessed of unusual powers of foresight. He is a person of normal intelligence who makes prudence a guide for his conduct . . . He acts in accord with general and approved practice.

It seems, however, that the expert retained to assist in determining the standard of care is often possessed of something very like the characteristics discounted by this judge.

The gap between the knowledge of the expert (in court, after the fact) and the practitioner faced with his or her next patient in routine practice is even greater than the above facts would lead one to expect. Having been selected, the expert is not likely to offer an opinion without first revising his or her knowledge of the topic in question to ensure that this is indeed completely up to date and properly founded in the medical literature. The more conscientious and cautious experts may supplement this process by discussion with colleagues of the issues at stake, although the courts do not necessarily encourage this very useful precaution. Such revision and discussion will probably be undertaken after a review of the specific facts of the case, and it will therefore be possible for the expert to focus on those aspects of the topic that are relevant and spend less effort on those that are not. This is a very different situation from that facing the practitioner treating a particular patient. Such a person will need a very broadly based knowledge that covers all aspects of the management of the patient and all possible eventualities, some of which will be rare. Thus, this person may know only enough about any complication that may arise during a procedure to identify it and undertake the basic preliminary steps of management if it occurs. The risk of certain rare complications of a procedure and the incidence of certain unusual medical conditions may be so low that the average practitioner is unlikely ever to be confronted with such a problem. After the event, an expert selected because he or she has made a special study of the particular rare complication or malady is then able, at leisure, to refresh his or her knowledge of this very narrow subject. This, then, is the 'peer' who will comment on the standard of care to be expected from the clinician who, having had the misfortune of actually meeting this complication, was perhaps required

[9] [1955] OR 131 at 152.

to respond to it immediately, with no opportunity for consultation or reference to the literature. Although this discussion has focused on doctors, very similar comments apply to other disciplines. For example, a professor of nursing or pharmacy called as an expert witness in a particular case may bring a very different level of expertise to a particular problem from that of a generalist in these fields, and probably a different perspective as well.

We saw in Chapter 6 that a trainee who undertakes a procedure is likely to be expected to meet the standards of any competent practitioner undertaking that procedure. Equally, the qualified specialist will be expected to undertake any given procedure or care for a patient with any given condition in the so-called 'correct' way. The sub-specialist is certainly likely to know more about this than the generalist, but is the standard of the sub-specialist really the standard one should expect of all practitioners in the field? We recognise that the question put to the expert would be: 'What could be expected of the ordinarily competent practitioner practising in that particular speciality at the level he or she professes to practise?' However, it is entirely understandable that the expert, in answering this question, is liable to describe what *ought* to be done rather than necessarily what *is* commonly done. Even if he or she makes reference to differences between common practice and preferred practice, some bias towards high standards rather than average (let alone minimally acceptable) standards is likely. The same sub-specialist conducting a seminar for generalists would teach the ideal approach, and would encourage aspirations to perfection. That is appropriate. Every effort should be made to promote the best possible standard of practice. Whether this role can be separated from the role of the expert in describing the true current standard of the ordinarily competent practitioner is less certain. Counsel for the plaintiff is not likely to phrase questions in such a way as to encourage such an emphasis. Even if the expert acknowledges such differences, or even if concessions are subsequently obtained in cross-examination, it is very likely that the court will at least hear a description of a standard of care that is very high indeed, presented as the 'right way' of managing the case.

An example may help to illustrate this. A specialist anaesthetist working in a small centre was asked by a surgical colleague to insert a CVC into a patient who needed ongoing intravenous feeding. He used a CVC that had been given to his department as a free sample. He had therefore not used this type of CVC before. In a position such as his, an anaesthetist might be required to insert a CVC a few times a year. In training, he might have inserted a number of CVCs under supervision, but the exact number varies from person to person, and this particular specialist had been fully qualified for more than ten years so that experience would have been fairly distant.

The CVC in question turned out to be longer than the recommended size for insertion into the internal jugular vein via the neck – the route used by this specialist. It was in fact 30 cm long, whereas the usual length is not more than 20 cm, and ideally only 15 cm. This was because the CVC was primarily designed for insertion by a different route. Typically, a CVC placed via the internal jugular vein should be inserted to a depth of about 13 cm, although this varies a little from patient to patient. The anaesthetist failed to recognise that his CVC was too long for the purpose and inserted it to its full length of 30 cm. This resulted in a malposition of the CVC and subsequent complication. There were other points of practice which were subject to criticism as well: notably, a chest radiograph to check the position of the CVC tip was not obtained within a reasonable period of time, as it should have been.

The expert called to give evidence in the disciplinary proceedings that followed was a cardiac anaesthetist.[10] In this capacity he inserted several CVCs per week – sometimes two or more in one day. It would have been immediately obvious to him that a 30 cm catheter was far longer than the CVCs he normally used. In his hospital the process of obtaining chest radiographs after the insertion of a CVC was routine. Before appearing before the tribunal, this expert took great care to refresh his knowledge of the recommendations concerning the depth to which a CVC should be inserted, as well as various other related matters, including details of the use of radiographs to confirm the placement of CVCs.

The expert was very conscious of the differences between his practice and that of the anaesthetist concerned. Obviously the baseline expertise of a practitioner whose practice includes inserting several CVCs a week would usually exceed that of a more typical practitioner who inserted only a few CVCs each year. In addition, the recently refreshed knowledge that he brought to his role as an expert actually exceeded his normal level of knowledge. Had he been approached without warning, he would have been far less certain of all his facts than he was when appearing before the disciplinary tribunal. It is also likely that the generalist in a situation such as this will have a broadly based knowledge, which would exceed that of

[10]   The details of this case are directly known to one of the authors (Merry), who assisted with the proceedings. See also R. V. Trubuhovich and A. F. Merry, 'Pericardial tamponade: a complication of central venous cannulation' (1994) 107 *New Zealand Medical Journal* 252.

the expert in many other areas of practice.[11] The expert was very well aware of all this. However, he was obliged to outline his view of the correct procedures in relation to CVC insertion. In dealing with details of the management of CVCs, this witness could hardly fail to convey a picture of competence and knowledge that would contrast strongly with the picture conveyed by the details of what the defendant had actually done. Inevitably, the latter would tend to look incompetent, although in truth he was probably at least as competent as most of his peers in relation to the insertion of CVCs, and quite possibly as competent (or perhaps even more competent) overall than the expert. An attempt to present the tribunal with a perspective that placed the defendant's failure into this sort of perspective would probably have less impact than the description of what ought ideally to have been done.

The case is of even greater interest because of a subsequent study[12] published in the medical literature from which two facts emerged. First, about half the anaesthetists in a cardiac surgical unit were found to be in the habit of inserting CVCs somewhat deeper than the depth recommended by the expert on the basis of the published literature at the time – although still nowhere near as far as 30 cm. In other words, many highly experienced practitioners were breaking the rules in this regard. The main implication of this would probably be that these practitioners were not convinced of the importance of the rule in their practice – an issue we discussed in relation to violations in Chapter 5. Yet this was the very rule that had been evoked in evidence against the defendant. Second, this new study showed that the conventionally accepted method by which a chest radiograph was used to determine the depth to which a CVC had been inserted was in reality unreliable, and its authors proposed new and better landmarks for this purpose. In other words, some of the information conveyed by the expert, although accepted at the time, was actually wrong. Yet the defendant who had failed to use this unreliable method could not have failed to look incompetent on account of this failure and in light of the evidence presented.

This leads us to the question of the source of an expert's knowledge, and of its reliability.

---

[11] The court, of course, is interested only in the particular incident – not in the overall standard of practice of the defendant.

[12] J. S. Rutherford, A. F. Merry and C. J. Occleshaw, 'Depth of central venous catheterization: an audit of practice in a cardiac surgical unit' (1994) 22 *Anaesthesia and Intensive Care* 267–71.

The Source and Reliability of an Expert Witness's Knowledge

Expertise is developed over years. In Chapter 2 we made the point that expertise involves the possession of a substantial base of knowledge. An expert's knowledge is derived from teachers, textbooks, refereed journal articles, the guidelines and other documents of the medical colleges, from colleagues and from personal experience. We emphasised the importance of the last of these sources – experience – in the development of expertise, particularly in the context of building up a store of schemata to draw upon in diagnosing particular clinical situations, and a corresponding store of rules for responding once a diagnosis has been made. We explained that experience is particularly important when time is limited.

In part because experience varies considerably between individuals, it turns out that the level of agreement between physicians asked to review the quality of care of particular cases may be very low.[13] Another reason relates to the mass of often conflicting information from all these sources that must be synthesised into a coherent whole. Data not only have to be learned, they need to be interpreted. A hierarchy of evidence is recognised, in which personal experience stands rather low and the well-designed, prospective, randomised, double-blind clinical trial much higher. In reality, however, randomised controlled trials are only suitable for answering certain questions, and surprisingly few aspects of medical practice can be supported with this sort of evidence. Furthermore, even prospective randomised clinical trials may be badly flawed, or may be wrong on the basis of chance alone.[14] Even when sound data from relevant clinical trials do exist, the phenomenon of bounded rationality in human cognition (discussed in Chapter 2) may come into play. One manifestation of this is the tendency to give undue weight to personal experience, particularly experience which is recent and which has made a powerful impression on the individual. Taking all of this into account, it is not surprising that there are different views on many issues in medicine. In fact, the extent of variation in practice is astonishing. There are many examples in which patients going to one reputable institution will receive very different care from those attending another. One such example pertains to the operation of carotid endarterectomy, where the

---

[13]   R. L. Goldman, 'The reliability of peer assessments of quality of care' (1992) 267 *Journal of the American Medical Association* 958–60.

[14]   For a discussion of this issue, see: A. F. Merry, J. M. Davies and J. R. Maltby, 'Editorial III. Qualitative research in health care' (2000) 84 *British Journal of Anaesthesia* 552–5.

rate in different parts of the United States varies ten-fold,[15] but there are many others, some of which have been captured in atlases of healthcare variation.[16] The astonishing thing about this variation is that much of it has nothing to do with differences between individual patients, or in resources available for healthcare (although the latter factor is also a source of variation, particularly internationally); instead, much of the variation relates to differences in philosophy of care between institutions and even between individual practitioners within the same institution. The correct rate is not obvious from the ten-fold variation in rates of carotid endarterectomy in the United States, but clearly the two extremes of this range cannot both be correct.

The emergence of many clinical practice guidelines, which attempt to reflect current evidence on particular issues, is one of the many responses to this variation in practice. The aforementioned atlases of healthcare variation to highlight the problem and promote greater consensus in approaches to common conditions are another. Sackett, widely held to be the father of evidence-based medicine, has defined this as

> the conscientious, explicit, and judicious use of current best evidence in making decisions about the care of individual patients. The practice of evidence-based medicine means integrating individual clinical expertise with the best available external clinical evidence from systematic research.[17]

It will be seen that there is no mention of randomised controlled trials in this definition, although such trials would be an important part of 'current best evidence'. It will also be seen that variation that recognises differences between individual patients is explicitly expected – evidence-based medicine is not about applying a 'cook book' approach. Rather, the idea is that if the same patient sees two doctors, or goes to two institutions, he or she should expect to be managed in a substantially similar way, whereas if two patients with the same medical problem but different

[15] J. D. Birkmeyer, S. M. Sharp, S. R. Finlayson, E. S. Fisher and J. E. Wennberg, 'Variation profiles of common surgical procedures' (1998) 124 *Surgery* 917–23.

[16] M. M. Cooper, 'The Dartmouth Atlas of Health Care: what is it telling us?' (1996) 29 *Health Systems Review* 44–5, 7; J. Wennberg, 'Wrestling with variation: an interview with Jack Wennberg [interviewed by Fitzhugh Mullan]' (2004) Suppl Variation *Health Affairs* VAR 73–80; L. Newman, 'New Dartmouth Atlas: improving US cardiac care?' (2000) 356 *Lancet* 660; R. Hamblin, G. Bohm, C. Gerard, C. Shuker, J. Wilson and A. F. Merry, 'The measurement of New Zealand health care' (2015) 128 *New Zealand Medical Journal* 50–64.

[17] D. L. Sackett, W. M. Rosenberg, J. A. Gray, R. B. Haynes and W. S. Richardson, 'Evidence based medicine: what it is and what it isn't' (1996) 312 *British Medical Journal* 71–2.

values, desires and other background conditions see the same doctor, it might be quite appropriate for them to be treated differently. An important point inherent in this approach is a recognition that much that is contained in textbooks, taught in medical schools and used as a basis for medical practice has very little scientific basis, and at times is actually in conflict with the best evidence. Evidence-based medicine seeks to build expert consensus from this uncertainty.

The main tool for building expert consensus is the systematic review. Traditional or narrative reviews of the medical literature have long been used as a means for producing coherent recommendations from the conflicting mass of information on a topic. However, these may be prone to bias because there is little to restrain the reviewer from including whatever references suit his or her point of view, and excluding those that do not. Systematic reviews bring an explicit and repeatable procedural approach to this task and, when relevant, use the statistical method of meta-analysis to synthesise the data of the various studies on a given topic. The Cochrane Collaboration has established standards for the conduct of such reviews and has established a web site to make reviews that meet these standards ('Cochrane reviews') readily accessible.[18] This approach should improve the quality of the information available for expert witnesses, but it is important to understand the limitations of systematic reviews and of the guidelines derived from them (and other sources of information). As explained, the principal advantage of a systematic review is its repeatability and its formalised approach to dealing with the possibility of bias in a narrative review. There is likely to be a greater consistency between two systematic reviews than between two narrative reviews. For example, two narrative reviews published within months of each other in the journal *Pain* on the same subject (the efficacy of epidural steroids in low back pain and sciatica) came to rather different conclusions.[19] While this would still be possible with systematic reviews, the reasons for any differences would be clearer and more easily evaluated. However, it does not follow that systematic reviews will always give the right answer, or that narrative reviews will necessarily be unreliable. Any review can only be as good as the studies on which it is based, and as good as the interpretative acumen of the

---

[18] www.cochrane.org/, accessed 26 March 2016.

[19] E. R. Kepes and D. Duncalf, 'Treatment of backache with spinal injections of local anesthetics, spinal and systemic steroids: a review' (1985) 22 *Pain* 33–47; H. T. Benzon, 'Epidural steroid injections for low back pain and lumbosacral radiculopathy' (1986) 24 (3) *Pain* 277–95.

reviewer. In particular, negative findings may simply mean that no benefit has been shown, which is different from saying that no benefit exists.

All of this may be summarised by saying that medicine continues to be an art as well as a science. Attempts to formulate firm guidelines and protocols do find fertile ground in a number of areas, but are defeated by the complexity and diversity of information and opinion in many others.

A review of any type, or a chapter in a book (which often constitutes a type of review), amounts to a document describing evidence from research, the author's interpretation of this evidence and the author's recommendation of what he or she thinks ought to be done in a given situation. Even if the message conveyed is correct, very few book chapters or reviews contain a description of what actually *is* done. When surveys are undertaken to establish the answer to this question, the results are disconcerting. The consistent message is a widespread failure to meet the standard of practice as defined on the basis of what ought to be done. Practitioners give the wrong drugs, insert CVCs further than the accepted guidelines dictate, work considerably longer hours than is sensible, fail to wash their hands between examining different patients in intensive care rooms, construct records that are unreliable, inadvertently inject micro-organisms into patients, fail to follow accepted guidelines surprisingly often and make numerous errors and mistakes in every field of medical practice.[20] We have examined some of the reasons for this in Chapters 2, 3 and 4.

Consider the implications of this for expert evidence. We have seen that the expert may be unusually knowledgeable and highly skilled in

[20] W. B. Runciman, T. D. Hunt, N. A. Hannaford, P. D. Hibbert, J. I. Westbrook, E. W. Coiera, ... J. Braithwaite, 'CareTrack: assessing the appropriateness of health care delivery in Australia' (2012) 197 *Medical Journal of Australia* 100–5; E. McGlynn, S. Asch, J. Adams, J. Keesey, J. Hicks, A. DeCristofaro and E. Kerr, 'The quality of health care delivered to adults in the United States' (2003) 348 *New England Journal of Medicine* 2635–45; L. Rowe, D. C. Galletly and R. S. Henderson, 'Accuracy of text entries within a manually compiled anaesthetic record' (1992) 68 *British Journal of Anaesthesia* 381–7; A. F. Merry and D. J. Peck, 'Anaesthetists, errors in drug administration and the law' (1995) 108 *New Zealand Medical Journal* 185–7; Rutherford, Merry and Occleshaw, 'Depth of central venous catheterization'; A. F. Merry, C. S. Webster, J. Hannam, S. J. Mitchell, R. Henderson, P. Reid, ... T. G. Short, 'Multimodal system designed to reduce errors in recording and administration of drugs in anaesthesia: prospective randomised clinical evaluation' (2011) 343 *British Medical Journal* d5543; D. A. Gargiulo, S. J. Mitchell, J. Sheridan, T. G. Short, S. Swift, J. Torrie, ... A. F. Merry, 'Microbiological contamination of drugs during their administration for anesthesia in the operating room' (2016) 124 *The Journal of the American Society of Anesthesiologists* 785–94.

relation to the issue on which he or she has been called. In addition to this, it should by now be apparent that this knowledge may be substantially derived from sources which are theoretical, based on ideas of what should be done rather than what actually is done, and at times even unreliable. Given that some experts may, on account of their senior positions, spend more time on research and administration than in actual clinical practice, this gap between the theoretical and the actual may at times be very great indeed. In some cases the expert will have actually written the relevant review or textbook chapter. It is relatively unusual for such chapters to dwell on the sad failure of practitioners to achieve perfection. That is not the purpose of such communications. As with teaching, textbooks, guidelines and reviews are intended, quite rightly, to set high standards and to encourage the best possible practices.

Amongst the various documents available to the expert, formal guidelines are unusual in that they are directly concerned with describing appropriate clinical practice in defined situations. They are therefore an attractive source of evidence as to whether or not there has been a departure from acceptable practice. There is a real possibility that they will be accepted on face value as the norm to be followed in all cases.

This will not be problematic in cases where the guideline is widely accepted, based on firm knowledge, and does indeed embody what might be described as universal practice. However, this is not always so, and as guidelines proliferate, increasingly they will deal with situations where there is not necessarily an established consensus and where the information underpinning the guidelines is equivocal. The quality of guidelines will vary. Some may be local in their effect and may represent no more than the preferences of a particular department or even individual. Others will be formulated with great care and wide consultation and will certainly reflect at least a section of authoritative opinion. Yet even such well-supported guidelines may fail to indicate the existence of alternative opinion. When they are used to support expert opinion, the impression may easily be created that they represent the only proper approach to a given situation. The insertion of a standard or general disclaimer may not adequately offset this effect.

Guidelines emanating from learned institutions such as the medical colleges will have considerable authority, but they will naturally tend to represent a particular section of medical opinion – that precise section which is likely to be put forward in court. There will be considerable overlap between expert witnesses and people who write this type of guideline. Guidelines are a powerful force in the promotion of advances in practice, and it has been shown that they may have a beneficial effect on patient care.[21] Indeed, they are at times used deliberately to support innovations – the introduction of pulse oximetry being an example. Guidelines from the Australian and New Zealand College of Anaesthetists were very helpful in persuading hospitals throughout the region to meet the cost of introducing this technology. Pulse oximetry is widely held to have made an important contribution to increased safety in anaesthesia and has been almost universally adopted in the western world. The use of pulse oximetry in anaesthesia is now accepted as the standard of care in well-resourced parts of the world. As part of an initiative to improve anaesthetic care in low- and middle-income countries, where mortality associated with anaesthesia is high and pulse oximetry is often not available, international standards endorsed by appropriate world bodies have been promulgated. However, there is a considerable gap between the promulgation of standards and their implementation. In this initiative, work to provide affordable and fit-for-purpose pulse oximeters has gone hand in hand with the promulgation of standards. Many anaesthesia providers (including many who are not medically qualified) must still provide care for patients who need essential surgery without these monitors, and without many other important but unavailable resources. Nevertheless, progress has been made, and continues to be made.[22] This is a good example of the way in which medical practice evolves. This is at the heart of the rationale for guidelines. During the development of these international standards, some concern was expressed that they might be used to support legal actions against practitioners who had no choice but to work in ways that fall short of the expected care. This risk was thought to be low, and was

---

[21] J. E. Pelly, L. Newby, F. Tito, S. Redman and A. M. Adrian, 'Clinical practice guidelines before the law: sword or shield?' (1998) 169 *Medical Journal of Australia* 330–3. For discussion of the potential impact of such guidelines on medical malpractice actions in the United States, see A. J. Rosoff, 'The role of clinical practice guidelines in health care reform' (1995) 5 *Health Matrix* 369–96.

[22] I. A. Walker and I. H. Wilson, 'Anaesthesia in developing countries-a risk for patients' (2008) 371 *Lancet* 968–9; A. F. Merry, J. B. Cooper, O. Soyannwo, I. H. Wilson and J. H. Eichhorn, 'International standards for a safe practice of anesthesia 2010' (2010) 57 *Canadian Journal of Anaesthesia* 1027–34; L. M. Funk, T. G. Weiser, W. R. Berry, S. R. Lipsitz, A. F. Merry, A. C. Enright, ... A. A. Gawande, 'Global operating theatre distribution and pulse oximetry supply: An estimation from reported data' (2010) 376 *Lancet* 1055–61; I. A. Walker, A. F. Merry, I. H. Wilson, G. A. McHugh, E. O'Sullivan, G. M. Thoms, ... D. K. Whitaker, 'Global oximetry: An international anaesthesia quality improvement project' (2009) 64 *Anaesthesia* 1051–60; Lifebox, http://www.lifebox.org /about-lifebox/faq-2/what-is-the-pulse-oximetry-gap/.

further mitigated by the fact that the standards are stratified to align with different levels of available resources, but the important point is that standards and guidelines are designed to improve the standard of medical practice. For this reason standards are often, to some extent, aspirational, and are not usually written with an eye to assisting the courts in setting the standard of care.

We have seen that experts tend to be selected from amongst those doctors who may be at the forefront of medical research and therefore probably working in leading institutions. A problem may arise where an expert has strong views that are ahead of those of many other medical practitioners. Innovations are not implemented overnight, and there are many reasons why some practitioners may be slow to adopt new approaches to practice, including a justifiable degree of conservatism. Future developments may or may not vindicate a particular position, but if an expert is persuaded of the merits of his particular view and has the moral support of a guideline (which he or she may well have written, or at least contributed to) there is a risk that the standard presented to the court will be unrealistically high, or at least may differ from the standard practised by a substantial group of responsible, well-motivated and reasonable clinicians. It is exactly this point that the *Bolam* test implicitly recognises.[23] A move away from *Bolam* could result in the courts pre-ferring the apparent authority of guidelines to alternative but nonetheless supportable approaches.

Of course, a defendant whose practice has conformed to a guideline will find the guideline very helpful in justifying his or her actions. One who has deliberately chosen to deviate from a guideline, whether because of limited resources or for sound clinical reasons related to some unusual feature of a particular situation, should be able to defend such a departure. This will be easier if the reasons have been documented, and even more so if it has been possible to obtain endorsement for the decision by a colleague beforehand. More difficulty will be encountered if the practitioner simply was unaware that the guideline existed. As more and more guidelines are promulgated from an increasing variety of sources, this possibility is becoming inevitable. In the same way that it is already quite impossible for any practitioner to keep up with all publications related to a particular speciality, the number of guidelines will soon defy even the most conscientious efforts to remain abreast of them.

[23] For further details on the *Bolam* test, see Chapter 6.

The Gap Between Practice and Preaching

Thus far we have considered the possibility that the standards advanced by an expert witness may be higher than those prevailing in general, and we have advanced a number of reasons to support this contention. There is an additional possibility – namely, that the standard described by the expert might at times exceed that actually practised even by the expert him- or herself.

We have seen that experts are likely to be unusually well informed on the specific matter before the courts. There is a flattering aspect to being called as an expert witness. Even the word 'expert' conveys a certain sense of pre-eminence, although the term is of course simply a technical one in law. Having described how practice ought to be conducted, some experts may not be entirely comfortable about admitting the ways in which their own practice actually falls short of this. Even more worryingly, some may have restricted clinical workloads, which are furthermore not strictly comparable with that of the defendant. Not only may some become quite out of touch with the standards in their own departments, they may also practise in very narrow fields and very circumscribed circumstances. Some may even be retired. Some may come from different specialities of medicine, or different disciplines in healthcare (a doctor, for example, might be called to give evidence on a matter concerning the practice of a nurse, or a pharmacist to comment on prescribing standards in a case involving a doctor). This is not to say that an authority from one field may not make a useful contribution to the evidence in a case concerning a defendant from another field. It is important, however, that the standard of care is not defined in a court by such a person's idea of what *should* be done rather than by evidence describing what usually *is* done by competent practitioners in the defendant's position, and what could therefore reasonably be expected to have been done.

The Changing Nature of Professional Knowledge and Practices

As in any area of modern scientific endeavour, the boundaries of medical knowledge have been expanded in modern times at a much faster rate than at any point in the past. This has had two main effects. The sheer amount of knowledge in any given area has increased to the point where it will be impossible for any one person to master more than a portion of it, and, even when knowledge has been mastered, it may quickly become outdated as further developments take place in the field. The resulting challenge for the person engaged in any professional activity – but particularly for those engaged in medicine – is one of keeping abreast of a rapidly changing, complex body of knowledge if professional competence is to be maintained. This challenge is further compounded by the fact that continuing professional education must be undertaken at precisely the time when other pressures have made the discharge of day-to-day professional responsibilities increasingly arduous.

The reasonable practitioner standard undoubtedly requires of any clinician that he or she should not be out of date. This seems simple enough, but obviously a great deal depends here on what is meant by not being out of date. It will be impossible for any specialist to be aware of every development in his or her field. The volume of publications generated in every area of medicine today would make it humanly impossible for any person to read, or even to skim through, every report of every piece of research published in his field.[24] Many practitioners may manage to keep up with two or three journals in their speciality and therefore to be familiar, at some level at least, with the matters reported in the columns of those journals. However, the mere reading of articles may be of limited use. What is really required is thoughtful evaluation of their contents and of their implications for practice. Given the level of research activity within all specialities today, this task will make major demands on the increasingly limited time of each practitioner.

There are other ways by which one may attempt to keep up with developments. Most doctors would be expected to attend a certain number of meetings or courses at which new developments are discussed. In many countries there are now formal requirements for continuing professional education, which need to be fulfilled to maintain licensing. But even this level of activity may not be enough to ensure that practitioners are comprehensively aware of *everything* that is happening in their speciality, and there will almost certainly be matters which the expert witness may be aware of which may have passed the ordinary practitioner by or which may not yet have attracted his or her attention.

---

[24] As one example of the challenges in 'keeping up with the literature', a search of the PubMed medical publication database (www.ncbi.nlm.nih.gov/pubmed) undertaken on 2 July 2016 on the keyword 'anaesthesia' produced 13,523 references in this single medical field for a publication date of 2015 alone – 36 for each day of the year. Of course, the relevance of each of these publications to any anaesthetist's practice will vary, but given that anaesthetists are concerned with many aspects of the perioperative care of patients, it is also true that numerous relevant and important publications will have been missed by this search.

Will such ignorance amount to a failure to meet the standard of care? If the expert witness concludes that a particular procedure could have been used at the time, but that the defendant did not know of the existence of this option, does this mean that the defendant was not a reasonably competent practitioner?

It is clear that the courts accept the changing nature of the corpus of medical knowledge and have also recognised the difficulty of dissemination of this knowledge. A decision of the Supreme Court of Canada illustrates this. In *ter Neuzen* v. *Korn*,[25] the appellant had participated in an artificial insemination programme run by the defendant (an obstetrician and gynaecologist). The period during which this treatment was provided ran from 1981 until January 1985. On the last of these procedures, she became infected with HIV. She had not been informed of this risk by the defendant. In the resulting litigation, the question before the court was whether the defendant's failure himself to be aware of this risk, together with his failure to screen his donors in such a way as to reduce the level of risk, amounted to negligence. The appellant argued that he could have been expected to know of the risk, even if the majority of medical practitioners might not have been aware of it at the time.

Reports of heterosexual transmission of HIV were first published early in 1983. It was not until October 1983, however, that the first mention was made in the medical literature of the possibility of transmitting sexually transmitted diseases through the medium of artificial insemination. This came in the form of a letter published in the influential (and widely circulated) journal, the *New England Journal of Medicine*. However, this journal, in spite of its general pre-eminence, was not widely read by obstetricians and gynaecologists. In September 1985 a medical journal published a report of a case in which HIV had been transmitted through artificial insemination. This was not mentioned in obstetric literature, and it was not until 1986 that an article appeared in which a complete list of known risks of artificial insemination was published.

At this stage of the HIV pandemic, information was sketchy and there were significant regional differences in respect of what was known about the virus. The issue of transmission through artificial insemination had been a matter of some discussion in Australia, where, in 1984, it had been established that a number of babies had become HIV-positive as a result of blood transfusion. The discussion in Australia, it appeared, was not

---

[25] [1995] 3 SCR 674.

widely reported in North America, and it was not until later in 1985 that it became generally known amongst doctors in North America that these events had occurred in Australia. Finally, in September 1985, an article appeared in *The Lancet* reporting cases in which Australian women were found to have contracted HIV through artificial insemination. It was at this point that the defendant halted his artificial insemination programme and recommended to his patients that they be tested for the virus.

It is clear that the defendant *could* have been aware of the risk in question when he administered the final insemination in January 1985. It also became apparent on the basis of evidence put before the court that the defendant's practice in relation to artificial insemination was in line with such practices in Canada at the time. In holding that the defendant was not negligent, the court recognised that, in spite of the theoretical availability of this knowledge, the defendant could not reasonably be expected to have discovered it. This suggests an acceptance of reasonable limitations on the extent to which a practitioner, even in a fairly specialised area of activity such as artificial insemination, may be expected to follow international developments. The use of electronic dissemination of medical information is changing the precise nature of the problems associated with keeping up to date, but it is unlikely to eliminate them, and, paradoxically, it may even be making the problem worse by accelerating the rate of increase in the volume of information that is accessible if one only had the time to read it.

In this case not only were the difficulties of keeping up with medical developments acknowledged, but the court also heeded Lord Denning's advice in *Roe* v. *Ministry of Health*[26] that 'we must not look at the 1947 accident with 1954 spectacles'. As a general rule the courts will try to ensure that judgements are made according to the knowledge, practices and resources prevailing at the time of the incident. This is not always easy to do, as change in all three of these factors tends to occur gradually over a period of time. In this sort of situation individual practitioners do not all change abruptly at the same moment. For example, attitudes to internal or other intimate examinations have changed markedly over the last thirty years. The training of doctors who qualified at the beginning of this period usually placed great emphasis on the importance of conducting such examinations in any circumstances in which there was the remotest possibility that they could be helpful. It is still considered just as important as ever that the clinical information elicited from such

---

[26] [1954] 2 All ER 131 (CA).

examinations be obtained. However, several factors have contributed to a change in approach. New technology has allowed doctors to obtain images of the internal organs in ways not previously possible, and often more comfortably for patients. There is now also a more ready availability of specialists who could be expected to conduct internal examinations more skilfully than their generalist colleagues. Some of the latter would therefore see less point in subjecting a patient to an uncomfortable and embarrassing examination that they knew would need to be repeated later by someone else. Most significantly, there has been a striking change in awareness of the sensitivities of patients, and in the importance placed on these. Obviously, patients still need to have internal examinations carried out, and at times it will be quite appropriate for this to be done by a general practitioner. Indeed, it would often be negligent to omit such an examination. However, a practitioner who continued to follow the previous practice in this regard, on patients for whom the examination could be justified only on the grounds of completeness, might well be open to criticism of sexual impropriety in a way that would not have been likely when he or she first qualified. In New Zealand an otorhinolaryngologist was subject to prolonged disciplinary proceedings precisely in this context, in relation to the examination of lymph nodes in the groins and axillae of female patients whose complaint related to the throat or nose.[27] Another example of change of this sort is provided by the highly publicised inquiry into practices at the National Women's Hospital in Auckland in the 1980s. During this inquiry it emerged that a common practice in this major teaching hospital involved the permitting of medical students to conduct vaginal examinations on patients who were undergoing gynaecological procedures under anaesthetic. The lack of consent in regard to this training exercise was the central point of criticism. However, one of the outcomes of the affair was the implementation of clinical surrogates. These are women who agree to undergo vaginal examinations in a teaching context and on a paid basis, in order to satisfy the requirements of training without necessarily having to seek the participation of patients. Once again, there is a substantial change between the earlier and later approaches. Many of the doctors involved in the inquiry argued that their practices were standard and ethically acceptable, and some commentators have supported the view that, at that period in time, they were not alone, internationally, in this belief. The presiding judge left

[27] '"No need" to touch genitalia' (28 November 1995) *New Zealand Herald*.

no doubt that she considered the practices unacceptable, not only at the time of the inquiry, but for a considerable period prior to it.[28]

The argument here is not about the need for change. What we want to illustrate is how, when practices change over a period of time, some practitioners may unwittingly find themselves out of kilter with the new consensus. It may be very difficult to distinguish knowingly inappropriate activity from insensitivity (possibly associated with arrogance), and insensitivity from conscientious compliance with rules emphasised as extremely important during a doctor's training but now no longer always (or perhaps ever) applicable.

It may be even more difficult to establish the appropriate standard at the time if events of this sort are brought before the courts many years after they occurred. It is not suggested here that failure to adjust to more enlightened practices should be condoned. We simply draw attention to the difficulty a court might have in determining whether a given incident would have been acceptable at the time it occurred. This is particularly so when the change involves human considerations rather than scientific or technological developments. The assessment of past practices in relation to informed consent provides a particularly pertinent example of this difficulty. This is an area that has undergone progressive evolution over the last decades, and in which it is difficult to establish a precise chronology of change. Not only has the norm changed, but, as discussed in Chapter 5, concepts of what is legally acceptable have changed as well.

Outcome Bias – Looking Beyond the Individual Accident

In Chapter 5 we mentioned the work of Fischoff, which showed that knowing what did in fact happen makes people much more likely to state that such an outcome was predictable. Caplan, Posner and Cheney have shown that knowledge of outcome has, in a similar way, an important confounding influence on physician's judgements of appropriateness

---

[28] S. R. Cartwright, *The Report of the Committee of Inquiry into Allegations Concerning the Treatment of Cervical Cancer at National Women's Hospital and into Other Related Matters* (Auckland, Government Printing Office, 1988). See also S. Coney, *The Unfortunate Experiment* (Auckland, Penguin, 1988); L. Bryder, *A History of 'The Unfortunate Experiment' at National Women's Hospital* (Auckland, Auckland University Press, 2009); R. W. Jones, 'National Women's Hospital deserves a fair and balanced history–with response by Linda Bryder' (2010) 123 *New Zealand Medical Journal* 130–2; author reply 2–3.

of care. One hundred and twelve practising 'anesthesiologists'[29] were asked to judge the appropriateness of care in twenty-one cases involving adverse anaesthetic outcomes. For each case two outcomes were provided: one involving temporary harm and one involving permanent harm. A significant inverse relationship was observed between the severity of the outcome and the judgement of appropriateness of care in 71 per cent of the matched pairs of cases.[30] Being informed that permanent harm occurred made it much more likely that the reviewer would be critical of the appropriateness of care than being told that the harm was only temporary – although the facts were identical in each case. In a situation such as that involving Dr Hugel (discussed in Chapter 1), in which an essentially healthy child undergoing a relatively minor procedure died, this influence is very powerful. The tragedy of the outcome demands a response. Reviewing such a case, even the most conscientiously objective expert witness could not help but feel deeply moved by the loss of a young and promising life. Emotionally, the sense that such a disaster simply should not have occurred would be almost overwhelming. The truth is that disasters of this type do occur, not only in medicine; it is by no means always the case that they are avoidable, or that someone is to blame, but it may be very difficult to remain dispassionate. Simply framing the question in such a way that it focuses on the care provided rather than the outcome which resulted – as the courts would do – is not enough to prevent outcome bias; that is the precise message of Caplan et al.'s study.

It may be useful to consider once again the example of drug error discussed in Chapter 2. Clearly, the defendant in a case where a wrongly administered drug has caused harm to a patient may have been no more negligent than the majority of his or her colleagues, who will themselves have made very similar errors at some time that did not contribute to harm. Thus, the defendant is to some degree the victim of two influences beyond his or her control. The first relates to outcome bias. The second, well recognised within the law, is often referred to as *moral luck*;[31] had no

---

[29] In the United States, an 'anesthesiologist' is medically qualified and distinguished from a nurse 'anesthetist'. In British practice (and in Canada, Australia and New Zealand), nurse anaesthetists are very unusual (or completely absent), and the term 'anaesthetist' is equivalent to the American term 'anesthesiologist'.

[30] R. A. Caplan, K. L. Posner and F. W. Cheney, 'Effect of outcome on physician judgments of appropriateness of care' (1991) 265 *Journal of the American Medical Association* 1957–60.

[31] Alternatively, the phrase 'outcome lottery' is sometimes used in this context; we have touched on the concept of moral luck previously, in Chapters 1, 2 and 5.

harm occurred, it is almost certain that no case would have been brought. It has not escaped us that the patient is also a victim of this lottery and has usually paid an even higher price for this misfortune. In judging the degree of negligence involved, however, it is instructive to compare the difference between the opinions that might be expressed in this situation and in the situation in which exactly the same slips or lapses produced no harm. In the latter case, most practitioners would probably be inclined to accept the errors as inevitable, and worthy only of minor comment or discussion. In the former, harsher criticism would be likely. We think neither position is entirely correct. The former tends to place undue responsibility for a systems problem onto an individual practitioner; the latter discounts the importance of the problem. In our opinion events which are hazardous but which do not cause harm should be taken very seriously indeed. Every effort should be made to identify the factors that predispose to them, and to find ways to make their occurrence less likely. This type of approach has been gaining greater acceptance in medicine in recent years,[32] but, as we discussed in Chapters 2 and 3, there is still room for improvement. For the purposes of the assessment of the standard of care, it is important to distinguish between two different issues. The fact that serious harm may result from errors is one issue, and implies that errors are important whether that harm occurs or not. It also implies that the standard of care *required* is high. The fact that there is a risk of serious harm must place a considerable onus on practitioners, *and on institutions*, to ensure that considerable care is taken. This principle is well established in the law of negligence, where the courts have frequently stressed that the more serious the possible harm that can be caused, then the higher will be the standard of care expected. The classic statement of this proposition in English law is to be found in the case of *Paris* v. *Stepney Borough Council*,[33] in which a workman to whom the council owed a duty of care had only one eye. It was held that the seriousness of any eye injury to such a plaintiff meant that a much higher degree of care than normal was required. The second issue is the level of care actually *observed*. The fact that harm actually has occurred in a particular case does not necessarily imply that the high level of care *required* was not actually *observed*. The distinction could be expressed as follows. The possibility of a harmful outcome may raise the standard of care

---

[32] L. L. Leape, 'Error in medicine' (1994) 272 *Journal of the American Medical Association* 1851–7; D. Blumenthal, 'Making medical errors into "medical treasures"' (1994) 272 *Journal of the American Medical Association* 1851–7.

[33] [1951] AC 367.

required; the actual occurrence of a bad outcome says nothing about whether the appropriate degree of care was or was not taken.

In assessing the standard of care it may sometimes be more relevant for the expert to examine the contribution of general or systemic factors to the prevailing standard of practice within an institution rather than to focus on the individual. In a case of a drug administration error, for example, the individual will probably have been practising at the same standard as many of his or her colleagues in the same institution. The contribution of rostering systems to fatigue is an obvious example of an institutional factor that might be relevant to the generation of an error – and there are many others.

Unfortunately, liability depends (amongst other things) on proof of causation. It is usually easier to prove that a certain doctor administered an identified drug, which harmed a patient, than to show that general aspects of an institution's organisation were important in the generation of the error. Once again, it is apparent that the standard that comes to be expected of the individual practitioner may at times be rather higher than that which prevails in practice.

Statistical Approaches to Assessing Acceptable Standards of Technical Performance

In Chapter 3 we noted that the case of the Bristol cardiac surgeons raises the question of defining acceptability in relation to performance in a technical sense. Typically, this arises in the context of measurable outcomes such as mortality, postoperative infection rates or rates of perioperative myocardial infarction after coronary surgery.

This is a complex subject and numerous methods have been developed to assist the audit of practice standards. Often these involve comparing the results of an individual with those of a group – all the cardiac surgeons in Britain, for example. This may be done on an ongoing basis, using cumulative outcome plots, and might make use of certain percentiles (such as the 10th percentile) to set limits which reflect the practice of the group as a whole. Variations in patient risk factors ('case mix') must be taken into account, and random variation must also be allowed for.[34] The appropriate use of these methods is not simple, and as

---

[34] J. Poloniecki, O. Valencia and P. Littlejohns, 'Cumulative risk adjusted mortality chart for detecting changes in death rate: observational study of heart surgery' (1998) 316 *British Medical Journal* 1697–700. N. Kang, V. T. Tsang, S. Gallivan, C. Sherlaw-Johnson,

yet they have not been widely adopted into medical practice. Typically, the approach is normative: performance is considered acceptable provided it is better than that of a certain percentage of the group. Being in the top two-thirds might be considered reassuring, for example, and being the worst member of a department might be cause for concern – but is this valid? A moment's reflection will show that it is a matter of statistical inevitability that, in any group, someone will be the best and someone the worst. The worst can only improve his or her ranking at the expense of others, but improvement on the part of the worst individual is not evidence of deterioration on the part of those he or she has passed. Surely the important question relates to whether all or any of the group are good enough? However, the alternative of defining acceptable limits from first principles raises the issue of what is achievable, and in the end this can only be determined from results obtained in actual practice. One factor may nevertheless assist: for most procedures it may well be that the distribution of results is skewed, with the majority of competent surgeons achieving relatively similar results, and a small number of less competent operators performing at a markedly different level. Thus, it may be possible to establish a national standard for a procedure, with the expectation that such results will be achievable by any competent and well-trained practitioner.

The larger the group, the more reliable normative approaches will be. Comparing across a country will be more robust than comparing across a unit. Even then, allowance will be needed for differences in the mixtures of cases. It must also be realised that the numbers needed to show statistical differences are often very large. For example, two deaths out of twenty cases may seem very high – a mortality rate of 10 per cent. In fact, the 95 per cent confidence limits for this rate are 1.2 per cent, 31.7 per cent (i.e. there is a 95 per cent chance that this result reflects a true performance within these limits). This result (two deaths out of twenty) is in fact not significantly different from a result of two deaths out of 100 (Fisher's exact test: $P = 0.13$).[35] This may be important if a review is carried out on a relatively small sample of a practitioner's cases. Inquiries may (quite reasonably) be precipitated by a short run of deaths in close succession. Often the approach is to focus on just those cases in which the patient died or had major complications. It would be much more

T. J. Cole, M. J. Elliott and M. R. de Leval, 'Quality assurance in congenital heart surgery' (2006) 29 *European Journal of Cardio-Thoracic Surgery* 693–7.

[35] G. E. Dallal, 'PC-Size: Consultant – a program for sample size determinations' (1990) 44 *American Statistician* 243.

appropriate to review a large body of work – five years' worth, for example – but this may be more difficult and more expensive. A further problem arises from the interpretation of any criticism. An audit or review may identify problems without the reviewers necessarily intending to imply a degree of negligence. In exactly the same way as expert witnesses, those conducting audit are likely to focus on any areas where improvement might be possible. There is a grave risk that such constructive criticism will precipitate legal or disciplinary proceedings in which the chance of a balanced view of the statistical significance of an isolated problem is even less likely.

In some countries, notably the UK and the United States, selected data related to outcome and other aspects of practice are published for individual surgeons in certain specialities (notably cardiac surgery, which is characterised by relatively standardised and common procedures and relatively high mortality rates). The question of whether New Zealand should follow this lead was debated and reviewed in detail recently. The statistical issues outlined above are relevant even to cardiac surgeons, but apply overwhelmingly to other specialities. Actually, in some, such as neurosurgery, serious disability may be a more common complication of surgery than death, but this is more difficult to quantify (death has the convenient features that it is objective and that its measurement is binary). However, another aspect of the problem that seems to have been widely overlooked emerged from the discussions. As we discussed in Chapter 2, the outcomes of surgery are heavily and increasingly dependent on teams rather than on individual surgeons (or individual anaesthetists, nurses, intensive care physicians or any of the other practitioners or support staff critical to good outcomes with complex, high-risk procedures). At the same time, the publication of results is an important element of transparency, and the evidence does suggest that this practice is associated with improvement in results over time, at least at the level of institutions. For all these reasons it makes much more sense to publish results by institution, with proper attention to risk adjustment and the numbers needed for meaningful statistical analysis – and this view seems to have found traction in New Zealand.[36] When used appropriately and with proper allowance for the complexities of different situations, statistical methods can be very helpful in monitoring performance and

---

[36] We will return to these important matters in Chapter 10, but the arguments have been extensively reviewed: see R. Hamblin, C. Shuker, I. Stolarek, J. Wilson and A. F. Merry, 'Public reporting of health care performance data: what we know and what we should do' (2016) 129 *New Zealand Medical Journal* 7–17.

identifying substandard care. However, these methods are no more than tools, and their use requires considerable expertise and judgement.

The Unethical Expert

Up to this point we have confined our discussion to ethical, well-motivated experts who are genuinely trying to give fair and balanced opinions. We have argued that even highly qualified, honest and sympathetic experts may at times provide an opinion that describes an unrealistically high standard.

Not all expert witnesses are completely ethical. We have discussed the variability that may occur between experts in their honest assessment of the care given to a patient. In practice it is often necessary to approach only three, or perhaps four, individuals in order to find one whose opinions are genuinely helpful to a particular point of view. However, if the stakes are high, experts may be found who are willing to express a certain view even if such a view is essentially untenable. There are individuals who have made a career out of this sort of activity, and there may be those who are particularly skilled in developing certain fundamentally dishonest lines of evidence.[37] While it is hard to assess how widespread this type of behaviour actually is, it does not seem that such unethical witnesses are often a major problem, although they may occasionally be the direct cause of a profound injustice, equally for a plaintiff or a defendant.

The Subtle Nuances of Complex Evidence

The evaluation of complex issues in medicine and other technical activities is very demanding. It is probably beyond the ability of many members of an average jury to undertake this task adequately. A particular risk is that juries will be more swayed by an expert who is a skilled and arresting speaker with a clear, one-sided and well-presented message than one who is conscientiously determined to present a balanced viewpoint. Again, this problem may be thought to apply

---

[37] This problem has been most acutely felt in the United States, where concern over the standards of highly partisan expert evidence has led to demands for professional disciplining of unscrupulous medical witnesses: see C. Terhune, 'Beset by suits, doctors target enemy within' (29 April 1998) *Wall Street Journal*. This article is a commentary on the attempt by the Florida Medical Association to subject testimony to peer review and to resort to professional sanctions against unethical conduct by expert witnesses.

equally to defendant and plaintiff, but in reality the emotional aspects of a case tend to be on the plaintiff's side, and it is these that lend themselves to dramatic presentation. The argument that because there has been injury there must have been negligence is easily run from the starting point of a manifestly bad outcome for the patient. The loss of a teenage boy's life during a minor procedure in the Hugel case (mentioned earlier in the context of outcome bias) is a classic example of the concept of *res ipsa loquitur*, but in such cases it is typically the prosecutor who can argue that 'the facts speak for themselves,' while it is more often the defendant's expert who has the task of conveying facts to the contrary, which may be both difficult to grasp and perhaps somewhat uninteresting.

The Importance of Appropriate Expert Evidence

The medical profession has been grappling with a rapid transition for some time – the pace of change is increasing but the clarity promised by early protagonists of evidence-based medicine is proving surprisingly elusive. Many traditional views of what constitutes good medicine have been challenged, and continue to be. A shift in emphasis from the over-riding importance of the individual to the critical contribution of team-work has introduced new dimensions to the pursuit of accountability, and to the nature of expert evidence required in any particular circumstance. The skilled use of sophisticated statistical and scientific techniques, which has been integral to medical research for several decades, is applying, increasingly, to everyday practice as well. Many doctors are struggling with the demands for increased rigour in their decision-making, and it is not always easy to make sense of different views of the same information. However, the fact is that much progress has been made by the medical profession in understanding how to reach a valid conclusion about a complicated issue. It is important that the courts take cognisance of these advances in the approach to sorting out conflicting or inconclusive evidence. To some extent this is happening. The retention of an expert by the court rather than, or in addition to, one side of a dispute or the other, and the expectation that experts called by the plaintiff and the defendant should confer and together identify points of agreement and disagreement have been sensible innovations in England and Wales, and deserve to be more widely used.[38] It is highly ironic and totally

[38] J. Woolfson, 'Medical liability reform: the British approach' (2010) 115 *Obstetrics & Gynecology* 1120–4.

unacceptable that inquiries (or other proceedings) into alleged failures on the part of an individual or institution to meet an appropriate standard should themselves fall short of an appropriate standard of process – and yet it is clear that this does occur from time to time.[39] In addition to insisting on proper legal process, it seems reasonable to expect courts, disciplinary bodies and those who run inquiries to embrace, if not the sort of scientific rigour that would be expected of modern medical research, at least the basic messages of statistics, cognitive psychology and the empirical data concerning the nature of expert evidence. Appropriate expert advice is needed not only on the facts of a case, but also in relation to the structure and conduct of the proceedings. We have discussed the sources of an expert's knowledge; in our view, the presentation of opinion in court frequently places too little emphasis on those sources. We have presented the concept of a hierarchy of evidence; in this hierarchy, anecdote and personal opinion rank relatively low. It does seem unsatisfactory, therefore, for a viewpoint to be accepted as expert evidence on the basis that the witness begins a statement with a phrase such as 'In my opinion' without thorough justification. In a medical forum, explicit reference to research and clinical experience would be required before much credence was placed on an individual's opinion. Certainly, reference to sources and authorities are permitted in court, but there may be a case for arguing that they should be *required*. This would be very helpful for evaluating the quality of each of two conflicting opinions, and would provide at least some assurance that claimed expertise was based in fact.

A key message of this book relates to the importance of expert evidence in evaluating adverse events in medicine, particularly evidence concerning the cognitive and systemic factors that underlie errors and violations. In this chapter we have discussed some of the difficulties related to expert evidence in general. This is not to diminish the value of expert evidence. On the contrary, we would emphasise the importance of ensuring that the required expert evidence is obtained and that it is of a high standard. It should relate not only to the theoretical ideals of the textbook, but also to the realities faced by normal human beings (albeit highly trained and often very able human beings), working with limited resources, often in teams, adapting to increasingly rapid technological and social changes over time, in real hospitals or in real communities, to treat real people who, in many instances, are very ill indeed.

---

[39] R. Smith, 'Inquiring into inquiries' (2000) 321 *British Medical Journal* 715–16.

8

Beyond Blame: Responding to the Needs of the Injured

Our concern in this book has been to assess how we respond to accidents – with a focus on accidents in medicine. We have indicated that many events that are judged to constitute instances of medical negligence are, in fact, the inevitable concomitant of human limitations in the face of demanding situations. We have argued for a re-examination of the process of the allocation of blame in such cases and suggested that an excessive focus on fault may be unjust and counter-productive to the improvement of safety. Such claims, though, may easily be misinterpreted. It might be thought that to argue against an undue emphasis on blame is to favour the practitioner and pay inadequate attention to the plight of the injured patient. After all, our argument is not merely a matter of academic interest but concerns real people who have suffered injury.

One might recall at this stage the studies reviewed in Chapter 2, which show just how extensive the harm from error and negligence in medicine may be. As we pointed out, estimates of incidence vary, but the central conclusion is clear: too many patients are being harmed in this way, often quite seriously. Behind these statistics there exists substantial suffering, not only in the shape of the pain and discomfort of physical injury, but also in financial terms, with loss of earnings and costs associated with disability. In general, however blameless the doctor, the patient is even less to blame for the injury. Furthermore, it is perhaps asking too much to expect the majority of injured patients to weigh the concepts outlined in this book and concur with our conclusion that certain types of error are not necessarily culpable, particularly under pressure of work and when time is limited. Even those who accept the point that errors of the type made by everyone are, in a statistical sense, inevitable, may understandably feel less than comforted by this insight. It is worth remembering that the objective of medical treatment is usually to cure or alleviate a patient's illness. It is hardly surprising, then, that a patient, who instead of being helped, has been made worse, might feel aggrieved. It is even less surprising that the publication of the statistics reviewed in Chapter 2 has led to much adverse comment. For many, the question might seem to be not why so many doctors face litigation or criminal prosecution, but why so few? A balanced response to the problem of medical injury must include consideration of the claim of its individual victims to compensation for misfortune for which they regard the medical system as being responsible. It must also take into account the pressing need to improve safety within the healthcare system as a whole. There can be no doubt that these are primary and central concerns. However, there are other considerations that also need to be taken into account, but which have often been ignored. We have argued that tort-based compensation is an unreliable and inefficient means of compensating injured patients, may often produce unjust results, has placed undue and unproductive pressure on doctors and has not turned out to be particularly effective in improving safety. In the wider sense we have attributed at least some of these drawbacks to the climate of blame that pervades modern society. But a critique of current approaches should also address the issue of alternatives.

If there were no viable alternative to a fault-based tort system, then it could be argued that these negative consequences should be accepted as inevitable. In such a view, any human activity, and especially any high-risk area of activity such as medicine, will involve pressure and conflict; this being the case, the distress implicit in the issue of compensation simply cannot be wished out of existence. Ultimately it is better, in this view, for as many people as possible to be compensated, even if the result is an increased burden on providers of services. At present, the proportion of those who suffer medical injury and who actually receive compensation is small; indeed, that is one of our criticisms of the tort-based system. To reduce this number further, by making the burden of bringing a personal injury action greater without providing alternative means of compensation, would be an altogether socially undesirable consequence of relieving some of the burden on providers. Not only would this be economically unjust – at least from the viewpoint of social risk-sharing – but it would also lead to a sense on the part of many victims that they had been badly treated by both the medical and the legal systems.

Against the background of these considerations, the question to ask is whether there is any reasonable alternative that is compatible with the major goal of this book: that there should be a fundamental re-evaluation of the way in which we think about accidents and blame. There are alternatives to the current system of fault-based compensation, which would not only deal with the human costs that flow from excessive readiness to infer fault but which might also prove more cost-effective in providing compensation and more successful in advancing the cause of safety for future patients. Economic and practical problems do present a formidable barrier to change, but these difficulties may be overstated. The real barrier may be cultural, and lie in an excessive readiness to respond to misfortune by blaming others, combined with the lack of will on the part of substantial segments of society to assume collective financial responsibility for a socially adequate and equitable approach to compensating injury. So long as the focus is on finding some individual to blame every time things go wrong, and making that person pay, it is unlikely that much progress towards a system that is safer, more effective and more equitable will be made. That does not mean that nothing can be done. Reforms are possible within the framework of tort law that could remove some of the adverse effects of the current system. Indeed, in some jurisdictions, examples of such reform are already in place. In addition, there are more radical possibilities, such as the approaches adopted in the Nordic countries and New Zealand.

The Elements of Quality in Healthcare

Before considering the merits and limitations of existing legal and regulatory approaches to the assurance of safety in healthcare, it is worth reflecting on the overall objectives of healthcare. For the most part, healthcare is a response to disease and injury, and its purpose is the relief of suffering and the saving of life. It is possible to avoid harming patients simply by not providing any service at all, but this sort of restriction of healthcare will not usually result in a net gain for any population. In fact, in high-income countries, healthcare is one of several factors that have been critical to the substantial improvements to the length and quality of the lives lived by most people today, compared with (say) one or two hundred years ago. Those who doubt this assertion need only compare data on relevant metrics between (for example) the Nordic countries, Canada or the UK with any number of low-income countries. For many people, the primary risk is one of inadequate access to health-care in the first place, and, in many parts of the world, patients who need essential care would see the services provided in the former example countries as amazingly safe and also of very high quality. We do not suggest that there is no room for improvement in even the best performing healthcare systems of the world – indeed, we have provided plenty of evidence to the contrary. Rather, our point is that safety should not be considered in isolation from other important objectives of healthcare.

The elements of quality in healthcare have been defined as safety, timeliness, efficiency, efficacy, equity and patient-centredness. The term 'access' is often included as an element of quality because this concept is not fully captured by the ideas of timeliness and equity.[1] In many parts of the world access is a major problem for patients, with barriers to accessing healthcare professionals locally, transport to facilities that can manage problems once diagnosed and obtaining safe and effective treatment once the nearest institution has been reached.[2] The affordability of healthcare is of increasing concern everywhere, particularly when cost is left to lie with individual patients, but also when dealt with collectively through insurance schemes or taxation – the costs of healthcare have escalated markedly over recent decades in most countries. With these general issues in mind, The Institute for Healthcare Improvement has articulated a 'Triple Aim' for healthcare systems: improving the patient experience of care (including safety, quality and satisfaction), improving the health of the populations and reducing the per capita cost of healthcare.[3] Finally, measurement is widely recognised as integral to improving and assuring quality in healthcare.

A key assumption in this book is that most of the things that go wrong in healthcare are the consequence of errors (which by definition are inadvertent) on the part of people who are generally very competent and well motivated, but are working in an imperfect and highly complex system. Given this assumption, we can see no reason to apply less worthy objectives to the legal responses to iatrogenic harm than to any other

---

[1] Institute of Medicine, *Crossing the Quality Chasm: A New Health System for the 21st Century* (Washington, D.C., National Academy Press, 2001). The acronym 'STEEEP' serves as a mnemonic for these elements. See also B. Runciman, A. Merry and M. Walton, *Safety and Ethics in Healthcare: A Guide to Getting It Right* (Aldershot, Ashgate, 2007).

[2] J. G. Meara, A. J. Leather, L. Hagander, B. C. Alkire, N. Alonso, E. A. Ameh, . . . W. Yip, 'Global Surgery 2030: evidence and solutions for achieving health, welfare, and economic development' (2015) 386 *Lancet* 569–624.

[3] 'The IHI Triple Aim', Institute for Healthcare improvement (2012). www.ihi.org/offer ings/Initiatives/TripleAim/Pages/default.aspx, accessed 7 August 2015; D. M. Berwick, T. W. Nolan and J. Whittington, 'The triple aim: care, health, and cost' (2008) 27 *Health Affairs* 759–69. See also C. Shuker, G. Bohm, D. Bramley, S. Frost, D. Galler, R. Hamblin, . . . A. F. Merry, 'The Health Quality and Safety Commission: making good health care better' (2015) 128 *New Zealand Medical Journal* 97–109.

aspect of investment in the health of populations. It is also true that at least some of this harm is attributable to incompetence or indefensible lack of care (often as much on the part of employers and supervisors of individual practitioners), but, whatever approach is used, the cost of its regulation is part of the cost of healthcare: money spent on legal processes, on compensating injured patients, and on preventing harm cannot be spent directly on providing essential treatments. It is, surely, just as important to ensure that the best value is obtained from resources directed to these ends as it is from direct expenditure on the provision of patient care.

The best way, and certainly the most cost-effective way, to respond to the problem of avoidable harm in healthcare is to focus on avoiding it – by ensuring that safe and appropriate care is provided to all patients in the first place. It follows that, whatever else they aim to do, legal and regulatory responses to iatrogenic harm should promote this end.

The Merits of Tort Law

Tort lawyers are accustomed to suggestions for radical reform. Broadside attacks on tort-based compensation were common in the second half of the twentieth century, either focused on particular areas of the problem – such as motor accident compensation – or concerned with compensation for all forms of personal injury. Such criticisms have met with a broad measure of support, but just as often the conclusion has been reached that, for all its faults, tort works and that schemes for its replacement in the area of personal injury are unjustified.[4] This was the conclusion of the Pearson Commission, which, in the 1970s, considered possible reform in the law of England and Wales and recommended against fundamental change in the way in which such injury was compensated.[5] Even when recommendations have been made for the replacing of tort with a system of no-fault compensation – as was the conclusion of the Woodhouse Report in New South Wales, Australia – these have tended not to be implemented. New Zealand was one exception, with the central recommendations of a Royal Commission, chaired by the same Sir Owen Woodhouse, being introduced as one of the few comprehensive no-fault

---

[4] See, for example, the conclusions of the Tito Report in Australia: Law Reform Committee of Victoria, *Legal Liability of Health Service Providers, Final Report* (Melbourne, Parliament of Victoria, 1997).
[5] *Report of the Royal Commission on Civil Liability and Compensation for Personal Injury* (London, HMSO, Cmnd 7054, 1978).

systems of compensating injury in the world. Overall, however, tort law appears tenacious, and in most countries has survived a continuing barrage of academic and political criticism.[6] One explanation for this survival is that the cost of radical reform is just too great to be attractive to governments; another possibility is that, for all its faults, the current system of tort-based compensation has merits, which justify its retention. As a result, efforts at reform have often tended to confine themselves to speeding up the process of compensation and to removing some of the most glaring deficiencies. This was the approach adopted in the wide-ranging review of civil justice in England and Wales undertaken in the late 1990s by Lord Woolf, who had identified medical negligence claims as being the area where civil justice was 'failing most conspicuously'.[7] It was also the approach adopted by the Law Reform Commission of Victoria in its investigation of the issue.

Justifications of tort-based compensation may be made on both theoretical and pragmatic grounds. The theoretical justification of the tort system is that considerations of justice require fault-based compensation to be sought from the person who is causally responsible for a loss or injury. In this view, the denial to an injured party of the right to bring a legal action amounts to a condonation of a wrong. The motivation to sue a defendant may go beyond a desire to recover a loss or to seek monetary compensation for pain and suffering: an explanation of what happened may also be wanted, and often some form of public accountability, and at times even retribution.[8] To remove this opportunity to have the nature and circumstances of a wrong aired in open court is likely to cause resentment and frustration. In addition, this may also face objection on constitutional or human rights grounds.

There may also be defendant-oriented justifications for the retention of the tort system. A system of automatic compensation, which makes an

---

[6] For a general review, see P. Cane (ed.), *Atiyah's Accidents, Compensation and the Law*, 7th edn (London, Butterworths, 2006). Medical calls for no-fault liability include: British Medical Association, *Report of the BMA No Fault Compensation Working Party* (London, BMA, 1987).

[7] Lord Woolf, *Access to Justice: Final Report to the Lord Chancellor on the Civil Justice System in England and Wales* (London, HMSO, 1996), 15. 2.

[8] See F. A. Sloan, K. Whetten-Goldstein, S. S. Entman, E. D. Kulas and E. M. Stout, 'The road from medical injury to claims resolution: how no-fault and tort differ' (1997) 60 *Law and Contemporary Problems* 35–70; C. Vincent, M. Young and A. Phillps, 'Why do people sue doctors? A study of patients and relatives taking legal action' (1994) 343 *Lancet* 1609–13; S. Hershovitz, 'Tort as substitute for revenge', in J. Oberdiek (ed.), *The Philosophical Foundations of the Law of Torts* (Oxford, Oxford University Press, 2014).

award to the injured party irrespective of whether the defendant was at fault in causing a harm, may well be objected to by the person who is implicitly blamed for what went wrong. A defendant may wish to protect his or her reputation from a suggestion of incompetence or negligence, and this is one reason why insurers at times refuse to settle certain claims. Again, the assertion of a right to defend oneself against an imputation of negligence is entirely understandable, and denial of this right is equally likely to give rise to a feeling of resentment. The tort system, for all its imperfections, at least allows a defendant to mount a vigorous defence with a view to establishing that an injury is not due to incompetence but instead reflects no more than an inevitable concomitant of an inherently risky procedure.

Arguments Against Tort

The Importance of Caring for Patients

One of the consequences of the tort system is that those who are unable to establish that their injury was caused by the fault of another are expected to accept that some risk of injury is an inevitable part of life, and that they must therefore be prepared to bear the cost of their injury themselves. Other than in special circumstances, such as workplace injuries, very few societies have embraced the contrary position and enshrined the right of a person to be compensated on the sole basis that an injury has occurred, regardless of the cause of that injury. On an analogous basis, most societies place the primary burden of an *illness* on the individual affected, and at best provide support only for those who are unable to meet that burden. In general, there is no one to blame for the contraction of an illness. Even when it is clear that a patient has contracted an illness from an identifiable second person, it is unusual to hold that person accountable.[9] The risk of contracting an illness is held to be part of the background risk of life. Similarly, many injuries are considered to be part of that background risk. In general, it is only the identification of fault on the part of another that justifies the transfer of loss from the injured person to the person who caused the injury. In the absence of fault, it is

---

[9] In particular, doctors who become infected by patients are generally expected to accept this as a risk of their profession. On the other hand, patients who become infected by a doctor may at times hold the doctor responsible and argue that some response is required. There are other exceptions, such as in relation to liability for the sexual transmission of disease.

usual to leave the loss where it lies. Thus, the doctor who has been the direct cause of a patient's injury but who can mount a defence that he or she was nevertheless not at fault can argue that it is perfectly reasonable to leave the entire burden of the injury to be borne by the patient. Obviously this result may be seen as very unsatisfactory by the patient or the wider public, who may have strong expectations of a more sympathetic approach. It is a result that sits poorly with the notion of medicine as a caring and responsible profession.

A particular reason for sympathising with the viewpoint of patients in this regard is that their injuries have taken place in the context of the special relationship that exists between doctor and patient. The purpose of healthcare is to help patients, specifically in relation to their personal health and well-being. In this respect healthcare differs from many other activities in which people may be injured. Doctors in particular tend to have a very direct relationship with individual patients. This is in contrast to those situations such as the accidental injury of a pedestrian by a motorist in which no such relationship exists. It is inappropriate, when medical treatment goes wrong, for the patient to be deserted simply on the grounds of a moral argument that no fault was involved. The health system should not abandon the ill, and there is certainly no justification for abandoning those who are injured by medical treatment. To do so diminishes the role of the doctor and of the hospital. The needs of patients injured in accidents associated with little or no blame are no less than those of patients injured negligently. It is in the interests of the patient, the doctor, the healthcare organisation and society to find a way of providing for the needs of all those who are injured during healthcare, whatever the cause.

The relationship between patient and doctor (and, more generally, patient and institution) is important not only because of this greater measure of accountability when accidental injury occurs, but also because the relationship itself may well be of considerable value to the patient, and worth preserving. A patient who has been injured by medical treatment needs practitioners more than ever. If the process of responding to the injury is open and honest and meets the injured patient's reasonable needs for compensation and ongoing care, established relationships can be strengthened. Many people understand that things can go wrong even in the best of hands: however, the response to unintended harm matters a great deal. A defensive response characterised by a reluctance to acknowledge that something has gone wrong and a retreat into communication through legal representatives will destroy trust and damage or end the relationship. If the only way for patients to obtain an adequate explanation and reasonable compensation is through a lawsuit, this type of defensive response from practitioners and the institutions they work in may be more likely. It is noteworthy that, even in societies with a strong culture of suing, some institutions have chosen (as a matter of policy) to respond proactively when patients are injured, with open disclosure and appropriate compensation on a negotiated basis. This approach seems often to have been successful in meeting the needs of many patients cost-effectively. It is likely to preserve relationships as well and perhaps even to strengthen them. In general, it does seem that any response to harm that promotes openness and an engagement in putting things right would be more helpful in this regard, particularly if underpinned by access to appropriate compensation without the need to sue.

Accepting the proposition that a patient should be compensated even for injuries in which no fault can be established does not necessarily imply that the process of compensation, with its attendant element of blame, should be focused on an individual practitioner or institution, even if the real financial burden is borne by insurers. This raises the question of a role for the state, and of whether it is justifiable to identify medical injuries as a special case deserving special treatment.

There are a number of situations where the claims of a specific category of injured persons are given particular consideration irrespective of fault. Workman's compensation schemes are one example; the victims of road traffic injuries and product liability cases are others. In all of these categories society has decided that compensation is appropriate whether fault is involved or not, because there are reasons to underwrite the risk. For example, the social consequences of leaving workplace injuries uncompensated have been deemed unacceptable. Admittedly, this is to privilege such victims over those, for example, whose injuries do not fall into one of these special categories: such victims may say that there is no justice in singling out certain categories of injury and that what really matters is the need of the victim rather than the source of the accident. In a typically thought-provoking contribution to the debate, Harris has argued that there is a fundamental unfairness in paying awards to the victims of medical injury even when fault can be established, given that there are other pressing demands being made on the same funds.[10] He

[10] J. Harris, 'The injustice of compensation for victims of medical accidents' (1997) 314 *British Medical Journal* 1821–3.

suggests that, although victims of negligence may have a claim, this claim should not have priority over the needs of those whose claim is for treatment for a medical condition. This idea has attracted little support,[11] but it serves as a vivid reminder of the fact that compensation claims are, in fact, competing for scarce resources, and are given priority in the process (because they are, after all, legally enforceable as opposed to moral claims). The point applies equally to no-fault systems of compensation such as that which operates in New Zealand. If social need is to be the criterion of allocation of resources in the public sector, there is a case for arguing that the claim of one who has been injured through negligence is not necessarily morally stronger than the claim of one in urgent need of an organ transplant (for example). Similarly, it is difficult to see why a person paralysed through an accident should have a stronger claim to compensation than one paralysed through a medical condition (such as transverse myelitis). The argument advanced by Harris is stronger when applied to cases in which no negligence can be established. The issue of fairness becomes particularly acute when alternative resources are inadequate for those whose injuries (or illnesses) do not qualify for compensation. A system seems unsatisfactory if it provides inadequate funds for potentially life-saving coronary artery surgery while at the same time providing relatively generous access to operations for the repair of tissue damage in shoulders simply because the latter arose during accidents, yet this seems to have been the case in New Zealand at the turn of the century.[12]

Some societies are in fact prepared to provide a high level of social support for all who need it, but in others economic arguments result in more stringent limits on resources and in greater pressure to identify which needs should be recognised. This matter is often discussed within the framework of rationing or even of triage. In fact, there are limits to the available resources in every society, and no society is able to ignore these considerations completely. In addition, there are those commentators who point to perceived disadvantages of excessive welfare support and argue that there are merits in promoting at least some degree of self-reliance. In the extreme form of this view it is no

---

[11] For discussion, see Letters (1998) 316 *British Medical Journal* 73–4.

[12] J. Neutze and D. Haydock, 'Prioritisation and cardiac events while waiting for coronary bypass surgery in New Zealand' (2000) 113 *New Zealand Medical Journal* 69–70. At the same time that access to cardiac surgery was being restricted, surgery to treat injuries was freely available through New Zealand's system of accident compensation.

business of the state to compensate the victims of accidents; such claims are left to the individual to pursue as best possible, using the courts if appropriate.

In reality few, if any, countries will be prepared to provide for all meritorious claims and some process of selection will usually be necessary. This being the case, is it reasonable to privilege some claims, or would it be better to follow the more equitable argument and leave the same requirement to establish fault on all who have been injured? This fundamental question has already been answered by most societies, in that, as we have seen, they already recognise categories such as workers' compensation as special cases. This is because the pragmatic consequences of not compensating in such cases would be too disruptive or divisive for society. As we have already argued in this chapter, a strong case can be made for treating medical injuries as another special category, justifying compensation even in the absence of fault. One challenge in those cases associated with little, if any, fault is to provide compensation without invoking for the practitioner or institution the adverse consequences associated with inappropriate blame. A parallel challenge is to provide compensation equally readily in cases which do involve some element of fault: after all, these are the situations in which there is no dispute that compensation is appropriate – the only question is how it should be provided. What then of accountability? Compensation is an important part of accountability, but other elements are also important, including acknowledgement of error and an apology when appropriate. Sanction may be called for in some cases, but more often (and more importantly) a clear plan to avoid recurrence is essential. Such a plan should address deficiencies in the system, where relevant, but it might also need to address problems in the capability, behaviours or attitudes of one or more practitioners, or even of the institution's senior management. Since effective avoidance of recurrence will often depend on a combined and coordinated approach between many people, improvement will often require initiatives that involve whole institutions or at least whole units (or teams) within the institution. The challenge, then, lies in breaking the link between compensation and the other elements of accountability without losing the latter.

Compensatory Inefficiency

One of the most powerful criticisms of the tort system is that it is strikingly inefficient in delivering compensation to injured patients.

Bismark and Paterson[13] have summarised what they call 'the trouble with torts': most patients who suffer adverse events in healthcare do not qualify for compensation because their injuries were not negligently caused; even negligently harmed patients are unlikely to sue, particularly those who are elderly or poor; paradoxically, most lawsuits arise out of appropriate care; and there is little evidence that the threat of litigation is effective as a deterrent to negligence, although defensive practices by some doctors might be increased. These observations suggest that tort is not serving the public well, particularly if one accepts that the focus should be on promoting excellence rather than just avoiding care that falls below the standard expected of reasonable practitioners (a minimum acceptable standard, in effect).

Tort fails many deserving patients altogether: in the Harvard Medical Practice Study, for example, only a small proportion of negligently injured patients received compensation through successful litigation. Even for those that it does serve well in the end, the process is often prolonged, costly and stressful. In the first place, it may be difficult to establish negligence and causation – requirements for a successful claim. Then, even if a causally significant breach of the standard of care is established, the slow and expensive nature of the legal process absorbs a great deal of the total cost of the system, resulting in the injured parties receiving in damages only a small part of the overall cost.

This criticism is made from the point of view of the patient; a similar criticism may be made from the point of view of overall social efficiency. Compensation for medical injury may come from various sources. In a system of state-financed medical care, it is ultimately the state that will pay for such compensation: even if individual hospital authorities place the risk with private insurers, the state pays the insurance premiums. In a system of private medicine, the cost of legally compensated medical injury will be borne by the insurers of doctors and hospitals, but the costs of the premiums are usually passed on to patients. In either model, the public ultimately pays, although in the private system the cost

[13] M. Bismark and R. Paterson, 'No-fault compensation in New Zealand: harmonizing injury compensation, provider accountability, and patient safety' (2006) 25 *Health Affairs* 278–83. See also T. Douglas, 'Medical injury compensation: beyond "no-fault"' (2009) 17 *Medical Law Review* 30–51; M. S. Sekhar and N. Vyas, 'Defensive medicine: a bane to healthcare' (2013) 3 *Annals of Medical & Health Sciences Research* 295–6; O. Ortashi, J. Virdee, R. Hassan, T. Mutrynowski and F. Abu-Zidan, 'The practice of defensive medicine among hospital doctors in the United Kingdom' (2013) 14 *BMC Medical Ethics* 1–6.

is more narrowly focused: only the users of private medicine contribute to the insurance cost. In the United Kingdom, until 1995, health authorities and, later, National Health Service Trusts shared the costs of awards with doctors' insurers: employees' premiums were paid for by the trusts. After that date, all claims in respect of treatment by the NHS were met from its general funds. Either way, the cost of such awards is covered by the money that has been allocated for treatment, but the link is now more direct. If damages become payable, then that means that there is a correspondingly reduced amount available for the maintenance of wards and equipment, the purchase of drugs, or the provision of treatment. A medium-sized award, therefore, may be crudely translated into ten fewer hip replacement operations.

As we have indicated, whatever system pertains, the cost of managing medical accidents is an integral part of the overall cost of healthcare, and in the end is borne by the public. Therefore the case for efficiency is very strong.

The Limitations of Tort Liability as a Deterrent

The formal justice argument in favour of tort law holds that it is a legitimate function of civil liability to encourage people to take care in their dealings with others. According to this argument, the possibility of legal action acts as a deterrent against lack of care. This claim is difficult to assess but it remains unproven that the level of care adopted by people engaged in hazardous activities will necessarily be affected by the likelihood or otherwise of a personal injury action. Dewees and Trebilcock, for example, pointed out in 1992 that doctors in the United States were five times more likely to be sued for malpractice than their Canadian equivalents, yet there was no reason to believe that Canadian doctors were less careful than their professional colleagues in the United States.[14] On the other hand, there may be some connection between careful driving and levels of concern over being sued for damages in respect of road injury. In one Australian study, it was found that after the introduction of a no-fault system of compensation for injuries sustained in road accidents, the level of fatal accidents on the road increased by 16 per cent.[15] Similarly, successful actions for failure to obtain adequately

---

[14] D. Dewees and M. Trebilcock, 'The efficacy of the tort system and its alternatives: a review of empirical evidence' (1992) *Osgoode Hall Law Journal* 57–138.

[15] R. Ian Mcewin, 'No-fault and road accidents: some Australasian evidence' (1989) 9 *International Review of Law and Economics* 13–24.

informed consent have been associated with the spending of more time by doctors in communicating with their patients. In a study of the influence of a seminal informed consent case on the practice of Canadian physicians, Robertson found that, even if there was not widespread medical understanding of the precise legal implications of the judgement, the court's decision was still understood as having a symbolic function in underlining the importance of effective communication between doctor and patient.[16] This suggests that the medical response may be a very generalised one; the precise features of the law may not be what prompts a change in medical behaviour so much as an understanding that there is a 'medico-legal threat'.

We showed in Chapters 3 and 4 that deterrence is unlikely to be effective in preventing errors, but may produce worthwhile changes in behaviour in the case of violations. In this regard there may be particular value in actions against organisations or the management of organisations. Civil actions against employers in respect of harm caused by employees who have been required or permitted to work excessive hours are a case in point.[17] For example, in a non-medical criminal case, two directors of a transport company were convicted of manslaughter after ignoring the excessive working hours of one of their drivers, who caused a fatal crash after falling asleep at the wheel.[18] If hospitals were held accountable for errors made by junior (or any[19]) doctors after they had worked even longer hours than the 60 per week attributed to this driver, the likelihood of change would be considerable. It is neither just, nor likely to produce change, to punish a doctor forced by the system to work while tired. Similarly, it is pointless to focus on junior doctors who make mistakes when they are unsupervised without at least considering the responsibilities of the absent supervisors and of the hospital for failing to implement policies to ensure that adequate supervision is the norm. If the objective is to deter unsafe practices, it is very important to include within the scope of that deterrence those who actually have the authority

---

[16] G. Robertson, 'Informed consent ten years later: the impact of *Reibl* v. *Hughes*' (1991) 70 *Canadian Bar Review* 423–47.

[17] *Faverty* v. *McDonald's Restaurants of Oregon*, 892 P 2d 703 (1995).

[18] A. Leathley, 'Firm's directors convicted over fatal crash' (20 November 1999) *The Times*.

[19] M. Hashmi, 'As a consultant, I worked longer hours than current junior doctors when I trained. Here's what I think of the strike' (6 February 2016) *Independent* www .independent.co.uk/voices/as-a-consultant-i-worked-far-longer-hours-than-current-junior-doctors-when-i-trained-heres-what-i-a6855831.html, accessed 27 March 2016.

to change those practices as well as those directly involved in caring for patients.

In Chapter 1 we alluded to work that argues convincingly that there is no foundation in the principles of any school of psychological thought to support the belief that tort law will be effective in promoting greater care by individuals – even in the case of most violations.[20] The point here is that remote but serious consequences are less effective in this regard than sanctions, which are less serious but more likely to occur. In Chapter 4, we discussed the example of motorcycle helmets: the thought of death or serious injury appears to be less effective in promoting their use than a well-enforced policy of fines. Proactive measures to promote and enforce high standards on a day-to-day basis are much more likely to improve safety and quality than the threat of litigation. Furthermore, the effect on behaviour of threats perceived as very serious may often be perverse, leading, for example, to the practice of defensive medicine. Instead of focusing exclusively on individual practitioners, it might well be more effective for the courts or other authorities to hold to account those responsible for the governance of medical services (hospital boards, for example) in the expectation that they in turn will hold their staff to account and will also ensure that all appropriate policies, facilities, equipment and staff are in place.

The Association of Tort Liability with the Practice of Defensive Medicine

The connection between high levels of personal injury litigation and the practice of defensive medicine continues to play a major role in the debate over tort law reform. In one view, a fear of being sued encourages doctors to practise defensive medicine, in which inappropriate investigations are carried out to exclude every possibility, however unlikely. Defensive medicine, it is argued, subjects the patient to unnecessary extra expense, inconvenience and sometimes risk, and distorts the doctor's exercise of clinical judgement.

Attempts to verify whether defensive medicine does, in fact, result from a fear of litigation have tended to confirm anecdotal accounts that this is indeed happening. An important collection of empirical data on the effect of liability on medical practice is that which was gathered in

[20] D. Shuman, 'The psychology of compensation in tort law' (1994) 43 *Kansas Law Review* 39–77.

Canada by the Review on Liability and Compensation Issues in Health Care (the 1990 Prichard Report[21]). The Prichard studies were focused on anaesthesia and obstetrics and gynaecology, two areas of medicine that had been particularly associated with a high level of legal claims. The studies looked at the way in which doctors working within the specialities in question viewed and responded to legal threats. It is irrelevant that the real risk of litigation might have been misunderstood by some doctors; what mattered was how a *perceived* threat affected clinical practice. A wide range of responses was obtained, but a substantial proportion of those doctors canvassed indicated that their practice had changed as a direct result of their understanding of the medico-legal situation. In some cases, areas of practice had been abandoned out of concern over a heightened medico-legal risk; general practitioners, for example, reported a reduced offering of obstetric and anaesthetic services. There was also evidence of increased use of tests. Various other studies have added evidence to support the general point that at least some doctors do sometimes practise defensive medicine.[22] However, caution should be exercised in attributing changes in practice solely to medico-legal factors. For example, improved record keeping and increased numbers of investigations may, at least in part, be responses to developments in recording technology and diagnostic tools. By the same token, greater care to communicate risk may be a result of a growing awareness of the general moral claims of patients to be informed of medical procedures rather than a fear of being sued should there be a failure to impart adequate information.

One of the difficulties in this argument relates to knowing the difference between defensive medicine and appropriately increased care. For example, it may be safer for general practitioners to withdraw from potentially risky fields (as has tended to happen over recent decades

---

[21] J. Robert and S. Pritchard, *Liability and Compensation in Health Care* (Toronto, University of Toronto Press, 1990).

[22] Submission of the Working Group on Obstetrics and Gynaecology, 9–10, quoted at 186 in B. Dickens, 'The effects of legal liability on physicians' services' (1991) 41 *University of Toronto Law Journal* 168–233. See also D. P. Kessler, 'Evaluating the medical malpractice system and options for reform' (2011) 25 *Journal of Economic Perspectives*; G. Ogunbanjo and D. Knapp van Bogaert, 'Ethics in health care: the practice of defensive medicine' (2014) 56 *South African Family Practice* S6–8; W. Cunningham and H. Wilson, 'Republished original viewpoint: complaints, shame and defensive medicine' (2011) 87 *Postgraduate Medical Journal* 837–40. In recent years there have been moves away from excessive testing, characterised by initiatives such as Choosing Wisely': see www.choosingwisely.org/.

in anaesthesia in many countries, for example) provided an adequate number of more highly trained specialists is available.[23] Thus, litigation can have desirable effects on medical practice as well as undesirable ones, but it is an uncertain and unpredictable means of achieving sensible and rational change.

The Effect of Litigation on Doctors and Other Practitioners

The Prichard Review in Canada considered in some depth the adverse consequences of litigation on the morale of doctors. Doctors gave evidence of the profound effects which being sued had on their psychological health and their ability to do their job. In his analysis of the Prichard findings, Dickens quotes the account of a Canadian doctor who describes his experience in the following vivid terms:

> First of all, I experienced 'denial'... A nasty part of the denial reaction was the way it scrambled up my memory of the events so that what I believed had happened did not actually happen... Worse still, it blinded me to the fact that I was blameless... The part which was very hard to take was that I felt very badly about myself and my fitness to act as a physician. I lost faith in my judgement.

Dickens comments on these feelings:

> This anecdotal narration of a legal suit inducing feelings of denial, confusion of events, self-blame, anger, unworthiness, hesitancy, and insecurity is graphic not simply in itself, but also because it is so closely identifiable with the grief reaction following bereavement. It appears that being sued may be like suffering a death in the family, the more stressful because the death may not be sensed to be of the defendant's self-image, self-esteem, and self-confidence.[24]

Other studies have reached conclusions similar to those of the Prichard Review.[25] Working under a threat of litigation creates

---

[23] It is important to remember that many countries are seriously under-resourced in these disciplines. The Lancet Commission has recently reported on a global crisis in surgery, anaesthesia and obstetrics: see Meara et al., 'Global Surgery 2030'. This raises complicated questions of how best to regulate practitioners who are providing essential services with limited training and resources, but of course many countries in which this applies also have poorly resourced legal and regulatory systems.

[24] See pages 181–2 in Dickens, 'The effects of legal liability on physicians' services'.

[25] D. P. Kessler and M. B. McClellan, 'The effects of malpractice pressure and liability reforms on physicians' perceptions of medical care' (1997) 60 *Law and Contemporary Problems* 81–106; W. Cunningham and S. Dovey, 'The effect on medical practice of disciplinary complaints: potentially negative for patient care' (2000) 113 *New Zealand*

a climate of fear, which cannot be conducive to the best use of human resources within the medical system. Moreover, the impact on a doctor (or any health professional) once a complaint has been made is likely to be deleterious to the subsequent discharge of his or her professional duties. The adverse effect of excessive stress on performance is well known,[26] and a person experiencing the trauma of litigation is therefore likely to be a greater safety risk than one who is not under such personal pressure. Furthermore, in the same way as an injury to a patient has implications for that patient's family, friends and colleagues, the effects of a civil or disciplinary action will extend beyond the doctor concerned to those who are closely associated with him or her. In both cases, the spouse and children are likely to be the most affected, but, beyond that, it can be very demoralising to observe the impact of medico-legal proceedings against a close colleague, particularly if the colleague is respected and the proceedings are seen from a medical perspective as unjust.

It may be thought that many of these problems can be alleviated by timely out-of-court settlements. Such settlements might also be seen as solving the problem of the patient who has a serious injury but where no fault is involved. However, there are difficulties with this approach. The insurers argue that a reputation for readiness to settle will quickly result in a huge increase of unmeritorious claims. In addition, there are difficulties for the doctor, whose reputation will be damaged by the settlement. Many medical institutions (particularly in the United States), as part of employment screening, enquire into a candidate's history of settled claims, and might be almost as reluctant to employ a doctor with a track record of out-of-court settlements as one who has been successfully sued. Thus, an element of punishment is present even though the terms of the settlement may expressly state that no fault is acknowledged.

Medical Journal 464–7; W. Cunningham, 'The immediate and long-term impact on New Zealand doctors who receive patient complaints' (2004) 117 New Zealand Medical Journal U972; W. Cunningham, 'The impact of complaints on medical professionalism in New Zealand' (2005) 118 New Zealand Medical Journal U1592; T. Stuart and W. Cunningham, 'The impact of patient's complaints on New Zealand dentists' (2015) 111 New Zealand Dental Journal 25–9.

[26] R. Yerkes and J. Dodson, 'The relation of strength of stimulus to rapidity of habit formation' (1908) 18 Journal of Comparative Neurology and Psychology 459–82; J. W. Rudolph and N. P. Repenning, 'Disaster dynamics: understanding the role of quantity in organizational collapse' (2002) 47 Administrative Science Quarterly 1–30.

Of course, everything that is said here about the doctor could equally be said about the injured patient, who in addition must contend with the direct physical consequences of injury. In serious cases these may be death, brain damage or paraplegia. We do not suggest that the adverse effects for the doctor usually equal those faced by the patient, although in some cases they may well do. At a psychological level, the traumatic effects of unanticipated injury and the stress involved in making a claim and pursuing it through a tortuous legal process will also entail a considerable level of distress. Irrespective of outcome, both plaintiffs and defendants are affected, sometimes profoundly, by the adverse psychological consequences of litigation with its adversarial nature and its delays. For both parties, plaintiff and defendant, the whole experience is a highly fraught one. Reform directed solely at the alleviation of the defendant's position would be correctly subject to the criticism that it ignored the difficulties faced by the plaintiff and thereby worsened the position of disadvantage in which the victims of medical injury find themselves.

Such criticism would be justified, if the correction that was made in the system were to result in an *unfair advantage*. If it were merely designed to restore balance between the parties, or, better still, to improve the outcome for both parties and for society overall, then it could be defended against such criticism. In theory, the elements of a successful claim for damages – duty, breach and causation – adjudicated before an impartial tribunal would seem to satisfy criteria of fairness. In practice, one might argue that it is inherently unfair on plaintiffs that, for example, they should have to establish causation according to stringent legal criteria. Similarly, defendants could argue that an inherent unfairness of the system is that it may attribute enormously burdensome consequences in respect of a momentary lapse on their part and that account should be taken of an overall record of competent and conscientious practice. The current system of tort-based liability is overwhelmingly one-dimensional. It looks at a single decision or act and imposes, on that basis, consequences that may be quite out of proportion with the degree of wrongdoing. Thus, a doctor who carries out 1,000 complex procedures may make an error in respect of one part of one of them; this single error may result in months or years of anxiety and stress and, at the end of the day, loss of professional reputation or self-esteem. The fairness of this, in terms of overall desert, might well be questioned. It is also relevant and must be stressed that the outcomes of healthcare typically depend upon complex paths of care and the coordinated efforts of a wide range of practitioners and support staff functioning as a team. Thus, from the perspectives of both the plaintiff and the defendant, it is often unfair to confine the focus of the legal response to just one individual, let alone to just one inadvertent action by that individual. This argument is particularly compelling when all the blame is placed upon a junior practitioner, without reference to those responsible for the relevant processes of training, oversight, appointment, credentialing and so forth. Surely most defendants would wish all those responsible for a failure in treatment to be included in the process of accountability and reparation, including the senior clinicians, managers and directors of the institution in question? This is not only a matter of justice. These, after all, are the people with the ability to implement change. As we have discussed earlier in this book, a tendency to concentrate on the isolated actions of a single individual in this way is not only a failure in justice: it is also unlikely to promote sustained improvements in safety.

Politically, any adjustment of the current system of compensation that made it more difficult for a successful negligence action to be brought against a practitioner would be treated with suspicion. Contemporary attitudes towards professional privilege tend to be hostile, particularly in respect of the medical profession. Patients' groups and advocates of easier access to civil justice are likely to take exception to the notion that the doctor's position in medical injury should be given special treatment in the legal system. As we emphasise in Chapter 9 (in relation to the criminal law), any arguments supporting such privilege would also apply to other health professionals, and to those who work in other essential, challenging and hazardous occupations, such as ambulance and fire services.

The difficulty is that there are actually three objectives that need consideration in the response to accidental injury: compensation, accountability (including accountability for ensuring safer practice) and, where appropriate, punishment. Problems arise from attempts to achieve all of these objectives by a single mechanism – that of the law of torts. As long as the compensation of injured patients is linked to accountability and punishment of individual practitioners, it is only to be expected that they will defend themselves on the latter two fronts, and little progress will be made towards alleviating the difficulties of the patient. Ideally, safety should be assured, but, as we have seen, despite considerable efforts to this end, patients continue to be harmed. Once an injury has occurred, high priority should be given to addressing the medical, rehabilitative and financial needs of the patient. It follows that one important objective of reform should be the provision of speedier compensation for a larger proportion of claimants, but consideration must also be given to the need for a more discriminating evaluation of culpability and of the lessons to be learned from the event with a view to preventing recurrence.

Options for Reform

Although the existing system of tort-based compensation has its defenders, the extent of dissatisfaction over its failings cannot be ignored. Broadly speaking, two options present themselves, one being the retention of tort, subject to the carrying out of various reforms, and the other being the introduction of a radically different system of no-fault compensation. Examples are to be found in New Zealand and Nordic countries, notably Finland, and, in respect of birth injury, in Virginia and Florida.[27]

Adjusting the System: Making Tort More Responsive

One of the main arguments for the reformist approach is that, since considerations of cost and political opposition to no-fault compensation seem to have prevented the introduction of such schemes in more than a handful of jurisdictions, the most productive approach might be to retain the main features of the tort-based system but to improve it through reforms which address its shortcomings. These measures have included the introduction of screening methods to ensure that only serious cases succeed in getting into the courts, the encouragement of mediation and alternative dispute resolution procedures, the development of case management techniques designed to ensure the speedy passage of cases through the courts and the capping of damages. In each case, the reform must be tested according to the criteria that have been established by critics of the current system. Does it diminish the level of confrontation and help the meritorious plaintiff to overcome the hurdles of obtaining information and proving negligence? Does it provide reasonably quick compensation to the injured patient? Does it ensure rapid identification of those doctors whose degree of negligence or incompetence requires an uncompromising response? Does it

---

[27] Virginia: Birth-Related Neurological Compensation Act (Virginia Code, s. 38. 2–5000–21); Florida: Birth-Related Neurological Injury Compensation Act (Florida Statutes Annotated 766).

discourage frivolous actions? Finally, but importantly, does it provide a less blame-oriented environment in medical practice?

Screening

Screening devices, which are designed to stop unmeritorious claims at an early stage, were introduced in a number of jurisdictions in the United States as a legislative response to what was widely seen as a 'malpractice crisis'. Under these arrangements, a person seeking to establish medical negligence is required to satisfy a sifting panel that there is a prima-facie case against the defendant. Failure to do this would not preclude further action in the courts, but obviously would act as a deterrent. Although there is an advantage to the patient in obtaining early advice on the strength of the claim, there are critics of this approach. In the view of some, this sort of device merely serves to create a further hurdle for the plaintiff. Constitutional challenges to these measures have usually been unsuccessful.[28]

Mediation and Alternative Dispute Resolution

Many victims of medical injury claim that one of the main reasons why they pursue a claim in the courts is the desire to find out what happened. They report considerable difficulty in obtaining an explanation from the doctor or hospital, and the decision to sue is then taken to reveal the truth as to the circumstances of the injury. Whether or not such stated motives represent the real reasons of those who profess them, it is probable that the desire to find out the truth does assume a very important role in the minds of many prospective litigants. Certainly, the possibility that frank communication, and an apology, may defuse an otherwise fraught situation is widely recognised, and any system that facilitates this might be expected to reduce the incidence of litigation and improve the satisfaction of patients. In fact, there is some dispute over whether the overall risk of litigation will be reduced by proactive open disclosure alone,[29] but

---

[28] *Di Antonio* v. *Northampton-Ammomack Memorial Hospital*, 628 F 2d 287 (1980). For a useful history of the use of medical-legal screening in relation to medical malpractice claims, see R. L. Winikoff, 'Medical-legal screening panels as an alternative approach to medical malpractice claims' (1972) 13 *William and Mary Law Review* 693–723.

[29] D. M. Studdert, M. M. Mello, A. A. Gawande, T. A. Brennan and Y. C. Wang, 'Disclosure of medical injury to patients: an improbable risk management strategy' (2007) 26 *Health Affairs* 215–26.

there are compelling ethical and therapeutic reasons for this approach. On balance, experience seems to suggest that substantial reductions in the costs of litigation can be achieved if disclosure is managed well and linked to effective dispute resolution processes, including courteous and communicative response to patient complaints and a culture in which mediation can flourish.[30]

Considerable attention has been paid to mediation in both the United Kingdom and the United States. In the UK, two National Health Service regions carried out a study between 1995 and 1999 of mediation procedures, comparing the outcomes to a cohort of cases in which conventional tort-based measures were used.[31] The sample examined was fairly small, owing to a low rate of uptake of mediation, but the patients who were involved in the process appeared to be satisfied by the results (which included financial settlements). Significantly, mediation was seen by patients as being a very satisfactory way of obtaining objectives which they regarded as very important – namely, an explanation and an apology, as well as assurances to the effect that steps would be taken to ensure that such incidents would not happen again.[32] In New Zealand, a positive development in this direction has been the establishment of the office of the Health and Disability Commissioner, with an emphasis on accessibility for patients and on mediation as a first step towards resolution of disputes. Some Australian states have similarly sought to encourage mediation, whether or not the parties agree to it: in Victoria and Queensland, for example, the court may order mediation at any point in the proceedings.

---

[30] L. L. Wilson and M. Fulton, 'Risk management: how doctors, hospitals and MDOs can limit the costs of malpractice litigation' (2000) 172 *Medical Journal of Australia* 77–80; R. Lamb, 'Open disclosure: the only approach to medical error' (2004) 13 *Quality & Safety in Health Care* 3–5; A. J. Finlay, C. L. Stewart and M. Parker, 'Open disclosure: ethical, professional and legal obligations, and the way forward for regulation' (2013) 198 *Medical Journal of Australia* 445–8; R. Iedema, C. Jorm, J. Wakefield, C. Ryan and S. Dunn, 'Practising Open Disclosure: clinical incident communication and systems improvement' (2009) 31 *Sociology of Health & Illness* 262–77; K. Mullen, 'Patient's right to information under the New Zealand Code of Rights' (2015) 23 *Journal of Law & Medicine* 218–42; D. H. Sohn and B. S. Bal, 'Medical malpractice reform: the role of alternative dispute resolution' (2012) 470 *Clinical Orthopaedics & Related Research* 1370–8. In the literature review by Sohn and Bal, early apology and disclosure programmes report over 50 per cent success in avoiding litigation as well as significant reductions in the amount paid per claim. Open disclosure is discussed further in Chapter 10.

[31] L. Mulcahy, *Mediating Medical Negligence Claims: An Option for the Future?* (London, HMSO, 1999).

[32] C. Dyer, 'Patients, but not doctors, like mediation for settling claims' (2000) 320 *British Medical Journal* 336.

Reference to arbitration is becoming an increasingly popular way of ensuring the resolution of a dispute outside the framework of litigation. This has been little used in healthcare, but its attractions would be speed and financial efficiency, the costs of arbitration usually being considerably lower than the costs of court-based litigation. A further advantage of arbitration and mediation is that they are both considerably less confrontational approaches to disputes, and they do not involve the same element of blame which formal litigation involves for the defendant who is found liable. We referred above to the difficulty for the doctor whose record now includes a settled claim. This seems to be a genuine problem in the United States, where prospective employers ask about such settlements, but it appears to be less of an issue elsewhere, and if this type of mediation were to be facilitated it would be important that a reasonably enlightened attitude be maintained in respect of those doctors who willingly take part in the process.

The Case Management Approach

Reforms of this sort may seek to combine features of mediation with measures designed to ensure openness and adequate dispatch in the preparation and conduct of legal actions. Major reforms of this sort have been implemented in England and Wales following the report of Lord Woolf into access to civil justice.[33] This report acknowledged that civil proceedings were frequently slow, costly, uncertain and frustrating for the parties, and that this was particularly so in medical negligence actions. In this area, Lord Woolf was of the view that the civil justice system was failing badly, and that the need for reform was pressing. The resulting reforms, which came into force in 1999, constitute a major remodelling of the way in which civil justice is administered, with a strong emphasis on the power of the court to ensure that actions proceed without undue delay. In the revised system, parties are given major incentives to resort to mediation and to settle actions. They are also encouraged not to proceed to court without thorough preparation and agreement amongst themselves as to the issues that the court will be asked to determine. There are also major changes in the role played by expert witnesses: the new Civil

---

[33] Lord Woolf, *Access to Justice.*

Proceedings Rules stress the role of the expert, not as a partisan witness, but as one who has an overriding duty to the court to assist it to discover the truth. The effects of the Woolf reforms on medical litigation have been significant. For example, all NHS staff now enjoy Crown Indemnity, although most doctors maintain membership of a defence society because of potential liability arising from private practice or disciplinary proceedings. However, the basic nature of the process has remained and negligence is still determined according to the same substantive rules of law. Furthermore, the costs of litigation against the NHS are still very high. The cost of providing appropriate compensation to injured patients can be expected to reflect the large numbers of patients harmed by healthcare, whatever system is used to achieve this. However, a substantial part of the costs to the NHS seems to be attributable to legal fees. Furthermore, the fact that these legal costs are usually confidential is interesting in light of the increasing emphasis on transparency in most other aspects of healthcare.[34]

Controlling Damages

The capping of damages is designed to keep down the cost of medical malpractice insurance and thus to control medical costs in general. In principle, too, it may be prudent to exclude juries from the setting of damages and leave this task to judges. Control of the level of damages is also intended to reduce the difficulty of ensuring specialist cover in those areas of medicine where the risk of liability is sufficiently high to make insurance prohibitively expensive. Such an approach has been tried in a number of states in the United States, most notably in California, where the Medical Injury Compensation Reform Act of 1975 introduced a variety of measures, including a cap on non-economic damages; a study by the American Academy of Actuaries in 1996 confirmed that the reforms had led to a substantial fall in medical malpractice costs in California. Furthermore, in their study 'Do doctors practise defensive medicine?', Kessler and McClellan found that reforms of this type result in a reduction of 5–9 per cent in the costs of treating cardiac disease,

---

[34] See, for example, J. Woolfson, 'Medical liability reform: the British approach' (2010) 115 *Obstetrics & Gynecology* 1120–4, and for a more general overview of the changes, N. Andrews, 'The three paths of justice court proceedings, arbitration and mediation in England', in M. Sellers and J. Maxeiner (eds.), *Ius Gentium: Comparative Perspectives on Law and Justice* (Dordrecht Heidelberg London New York, Springer, 2012).

a reduction which was not accompanied by any significant effects on mortality or other medical complications.[35] However, the reforms have not had a marked effect on the frequency of medical negligence claims. In general, such schemes address the financial implications of the growth of medical litigation, rather than changing in any substantial way the litigious climate.

No-fault Compensation[36]

It is not our purpose to provide a detailed review of all (or any) existing approaches to the compensation of accidents in and out of the workplace. There are aspects of the approaches used in the Netherlands, Britain, Switzerland, several states in America and Canada, and no doubt many other countries, which could illustrate the points we wish to make. However, the experiences in New Zealand and Nordic countries are particularly relevant to our concerns. The New Zealand scheme is the only comprehensive system which has attempted to provide compensation for all forms of accidental injury on a no-fault basis, in which the common-law right to sue for compensation of negligently caused harm has been abolished by legislation. For this reason we shall discuss it in some detail. Notwithstanding several changes to the name of this scheme, it is known to most New Zealanders as 'the ACC', an abbreviation for the Accident Compensation Corporation, which emerged from the former Accident Compensation Commission in 1981. The ACC was the result of the 1967 Report of the Royal Commission of Inquiry for Personal Injury in New Zealand, chaired by Sir Owen Woodhouse. This report was a response to many of the deficiencies discussed above in the systems of tort and workers' compensation, which preceded the ACC. The report identified five principles. These were:

---

[35] D. Kessler and M. McClellan, 'Do doctors practice defensive medicine?' (1996) 111 *Quarterly Journal of Economics* 363–90. See also T. Keren-Paz, 'Liability regimes, reputation loss, and defensive medicine' (2010) 18 *Medical Law Review* 363–88.

[36] I. B. Campbell, *Compensation for Personal Injury in New Zealand: Its Rise and Fall* (Auckland, Auckland University Press, 1996); R. Harrison, *Matters of Life and Death: The Accident Rehabilitation and Compensation Insurance Act 1992 and Common Law Claims for Personal Injury* (Auckland, Legal Research Foundation, Publication 35, 1993); S. A. M. McLean (ed.), *Law Reform and Medical Injury Litigation* (Dartmouth, Aldershot, 1995); K. Wallis, 'New Zealand's 2005 "no-fault" compensation reforms and medical professional accountability for harm' (2013) 126 *New Zealand Medical Journal* 33–44.

1) community responsibility;
2) comprehensive entitlement;
3) complete rehabilitation;
4) real compensation; and
5) administrative efficiency.

In other words, the community was to share the costs of providing realistic levels of compensation for all injuries (not just those occurring in the workplace) and rehabilitation of the injured (so far as possible) to their former position, in a way that was efficient in time and costs. On the face of it, these principles would meet many of the objectives for a system of compensation identified in our discussion so far.

The introduction of the ACC amounted to an implicit social contract between the state and its citizens by which people set aside their common-law right to sue for compensatory damages for negligently caused personal injury for the provisions of the scheme, which included lump sums for pain and suffering, and realistic levels of earnings-related compensation on an ongoing basis. The scheme was intended to provide for the fair and sustainable management of personal injury. Importantly, it covered all types of injury. Medical injuries were not differentiated in any way, and the right to sue doctors was lost along with the right to sue anyone else for injuries resulting from accident, whether or not a claim is made to the ACC, or compensation granted.

The loss of the right to sue doctors for negligently caused injury was to become highly contentious. It was not long before commentators were alluding to the loss of tort as a means of ensuring accountability by the medical profession and other health professionals. Much of this commentary highlighted the loss of the right to sue doctors without necessarily acknowledging the general nature of the loss of the right to sue anybody on the grounds of personal injury. In particular, the critics often failed to acknowledge that a specific concomitant of losing the right to sue others in this context (be they doctors or not) was that those others had also lost the right to sue them. Thus, if they – the critics – were accidentally or negligently to cause an injury, they would enjoy exactly the same level of immunity from a civil action as anyone else. This part of the 'contract' is often overlooked, and yet it is central to the discussion. Even if the ACC has failed to fulfil other aspects of its obligations, it has created in New Zealand a haven from the risk of litigation for negligence arising from accidents. The right to pursue exemplary damages remains, but only in very limited circumstances. In New Zealand exemplary damages are reserved for exceptional cases, and the threshold for an award is very high, requiring proof of intentional misconduct or subjective recklessness. There are other exceptions to the prohibition on the right to sue, but in effect it is very difficult to bring an action against another for personal injury in New Zealand and such actions are extraordinarily uncommon. As a result, a whole legal industry around the hearing of civil cases for treatment injury has gone from New Zealand. The courts, the judges, the administrative staff and the tort lawyers, which would have existed had the 1972 Act not been introduced, are simply not there. In its place, however, a substantial bureaucracy has been created, generating its own frustrations and barriers to access and justice.

The New Zealand scheme has been subjected to many reviews since the Accident Compensation Act came into force on 1 April 1974. Its purpose, at the time of enactment, was held to be to promote distributive justice rather than corrective justice 'by spreading the economic consequences of negligent conduct over the whole community and to provide compensation for injury (regardless of fault)'.[37] Amongst many minor changes, there have been several landmark reforms. The Accident Compensation Act 1982 replaced the 1972 Act and came into force in 1983. This extended the definition of 'accident' to include heart attacks and strokes, set limits on lump-sum payments and reduced the first week's compensation for work accidents to 80 per cent of earnings. The inequity of compensating disability from accidents more generously than disability caused by illness has always been a criticism of the scheme, and the 1982 revisions made some small progress towards reducing this gap. In the 1989 government budget, plans were announced to take this further and extend ACC to all forms of incapacity. Unfortunately, the Accident and Rehabilitation and Compensation Insurance Act 1992 turned the scheme in the opposite direction. This Act introduced the words 'insurance-based', a quite different emphasis from Woodhouse's concept of 'community responsibility'. It also used the phrase 'financially affordable', shifting the scheme's priority from Woodhouse's desire to provide 'real compensation' to that of limiting expenditure. New and narrower definitions of the term 'accident' were introduced, and lump sums were abolished. The scheme had become significantly more restrictive than on its introduction.

---

[37] *Accident Compensation Corporation* v. *Ambros* [2007] NZCA 304, [2008] 1 NZLR 340 at [25], per Glazebrook J.

From the point of view of the present discussion, the most significant feature of the 1992 Act was the identification of medical injuries as different from all others. One reason for this was the difficult problem of differentiating injuries that warrant compensation from the normal consequences of treatment. For example, it would not normally be reasonable to pay compensation for the scar of a healed surgical wound, or for the losses of important parts of the body associated with a planned mastectomy or amputation of a limb to treat cancer. More cogently, most surgical procedures are associated with a 'normal' rate of mortality. For example, this is a little more than 1 per cent for many cardiac operations today. Few people would suggest that these deaths should be compensated. In New Zealand, the approach taken in 1992 was to specify that, to be compensable, an injury had to be a 'medical misadventure' – either a 'medical mishap' or a 'medical error'. A medical mishap was defined as a consequence of properly given treatment that was rare (occurring in fewer than 1 per cent of cases) and severe (a disability or prolonged hospitalisation). 'Medical error' was defined (with caveats) as 'the failure of a registered health professional to observe the standard of care and skill reasonably to be expected in the circumstances.

This definition re-instated the concept of fault. As can be seen, it was, in effect, a definition of civil negligence. Unfortunately, the usual safeguards of tort law were missing. The Act required 'Medical Misadventure Committees' to determine whether or not medical error had occurred and, if so, to refer the case to the appropriate authority, which usually meant the Medical Council, the Health and Disability Commissioner or the police. Health professionals were permitted to respond in writing to the allegations against them, but not to appear before the Committees or to be represented. In some cases doctors felt (with good reason) that they had been denied their rights to natural justice.

It appears that these provisions were intended to address the public perception that the loss of the right to sue had left a serious gap in medical accountability. Where medical error was found, discipline would now be considered as part of the process by which compensation was awarded. This reintroduced fault, but only for injuries involving health professionals.[38]

---

[38] There was also a plan to introduce a Medical Misadventure Account, funded by registered health professionals.

These changes were widely criticised over the ensuing years. The concept of 'medical mishap' accounted for the majority of accepted claims, and did allow injuries arising from healthcare to be compensated without the need to prove negligence. However, the definition was seen as difficult to interpret and, anyway, too arbitrary. For one thing, the incidence of many complications of surgery is not precisely known. For another, it was not obvious why a normal consequence of surgery should be compensated simply because it is rare. In practice, many patients who would previously have received compensation now failed to qualify, so in circumstances which did not amount to negligence they were no longer covered. This, of course, is where the second category – that of 'medical error' – came in, but the process of establishing medical error drew considerable criticism. So did the concept itself, on the grounds that it was inconsistent with the original intent of 'no fault' compensation and defeated the main attraction of the ACC as a response to the problems we have discussed above.[39] In 2002 an interagency review of the scheme was undertaken, and on 1 July 2005 these terms were replaced with a new concept of 'treatment injury'.[40] This change returned the scheme to its 'no fault' origins. Since then, cover includes all personal injuries suffered as a consequence of healthcare (a causal link between the treatment and the injury is required). Necessary, ordinary consequences of treatment are not covered. As previously, consequences arising solely from the way resources are allocated are not covered. An important objective of the overall changes brought in by the new Act was to facilitate ready access to early treatment of injury. A second expectation was for ACC to analyse data from claims and work with the health sector on initiatives to improve patient safety. The question of accountability was addressed by a requirement to report any 'risk of harm to the public' to the appropriate authorities, and for claimants to be informed about the processes available for resolving concerns about the quality of their care. Importantly, these processes are independent of the ACC.

One important lesson to be learned from this experience is that the removal of the right to sue must be accompanied by some acceptable alternative to ensure that reasonable complaints against doctors can be heard, and dealt with. This point has been made within New Zealand and in other countries contemplating a move to similar arrangements. In the

[39] See, for example, the discussion in the first edition of this book.
[40] Injury Prevention, Rehabilitation and Compensation Amendment Act (No.2) 2005. In 2010 this Act was renamed the Accident Compensation Act 2001. See Accident Compensation Amendment Act 2010, s 5.

period between the introduction of the scheme and the legislative changes in 1994, this concern was understandable in New Zealand: the gap created by the abolition of tort law had been left unfilled. However, following a major inquiry into events at a leading hospital in the early 1980s,[41] the New Zealand government established the office of the Health and Disability Commissioner to address this deficiency.[42] By the time of the reforms of 2005 the success of this office was widely acknowledged. There were critics, but it was widely perceived to be providing easy and affordable (i.e. free) access to any patient who felt a need for answers to questions over the standard of care he or she had received. Also, while holding practitioners and organisations to account when necessary, the Commissioner was attempting to focus on a systems-oriented response to improving safety – in respect of individual complaints, but more importantly, in respect to emerging patterns from multiple complaints over time.

The Nordic countries (Finland, Iceland, Norway, Sweden and Denmark) have, in turn, all moved away from tort law to systems that provide compensation for personal injury arising from healthcare without the need to demonstrate negligence. The term 'The Nordic Model' is sometimes applied to the general approach taken in these countries.[43] The underlying notion is that compensation should be provided through a collective mechanism rather than sought from individual practitioners, but unlike the New Zealand system, which is (in effect) tax based,[44] the Nordic model achieves this through compulsory insurance. The following comments apply primarily to the Swedish scheme,

---

[41] S. R. Cartwright, *The Report of the Committee of Inquiry into Allegations Concerning the Treatment of Cervical Cancer at National Women's Hospital and into Other Related Matters* (Auckland, Government Printing Office, 1988).

[42] The office of Health and Disability Commissioner was established by the Health and Disability Commissioner Act 1994

[43] Kachalia et al. conducted interviews with administrators and stakeholders in Sweden, Denmark and New Zealand, and have published a detailed discussion of the Swedish and Danish schemes and of the New Zealand scheme prior to its reform in 2005: see A. B. Kachalia, M. M. Mello, T. A. Brennan and D. M. Studdert, 'Beyond negligence: avoidability and medical injury compensation' (2008) 66 *Social Science & Medicine* 387–402; V. Ulfbeck, M. Hartlev and M. Schultz, 'Malpractice in Scandinavia' (2012) 87 *Chicago-Kent Law Review*, 111. We are indebted to Rolf Gunnar Jørstad, Director General of Norsk Pasientskadeerstatning for very helpful comments and advice on this section (see also note 40).

[44] The funding of the New Zealand System is embedded in the country's overall accident compensation scheme. Levies are specific to the scheme and not part of general tax, but they are raised and administered by the Government.

but the concepts and principles appear to apply to a greater or lesser extent in all of these countries.

The introduction of the Nordic schemes seems to have reflected a desire to provide appropriate compensation more comprehensively and efficiently and to avoid the adversarialism and excessive costs characteristic of torts. In Nordic countries, compensation is explicitly separated from processes of discipline and the deterrence of unsafe behaviours. Information collected during the processes of compensation is protected from disciplinary processes. Patients are entitled to complain through procedures that differ between countries. Except in Denmark, patients are allowed to sue as an alternative to using their country's scheme. There is seldom any advantage in doing so, and tort law is not often used except, occasionally, when an injury is not covered under a scheme.[45]

If the element of negligence is discarded as essential for compensation (while retaining causation, the other essential element under tort law), the affordability of any scheme, and its success in compensating the 'right' people, depends on the criteria used to determine whether a claim is compensable. In the Swedish scheme, injuries associated with healthcare are divided into five categories: (1) treatment injury; (2) diagnostic injury; (3) material-related injury; (4) infection-related injury; and (5) accident-related injury. The last of these categories covers injuries not directly related to medical care, such as falls within hospital, and illustrates an interesting distinction between the Swedish and New Zealand schemes: the latter starts from the compensation of all accidents, so events of this sort are automatically part of the wider scope of the scheme

---

[45] Rolf Gunnar Jørstad (see note 41) explained the situation in Norway as follows: 'In Norway the right to sue public hospitals/owners of these hospitals (the four regional health authorities), the counties and the municipalities has been removed (with one exception: claims for compensation due to gross negligence). This removal does not include the right to sue doctors, other healthcare personnel or privately owned hospitals. But in such cases the patient will have to prove negligence on the part of the doctor/health care personnel or privately owned hospital. This means that the act on Patient Injury Compensation does not apply to such cases. Because of this, it is very rare that patients sue a doctor/health care personnel or a privately owned hospital. The most important reason for this must be that their interests are better served by using the Patient Compensation Scheme. But one has to bear in mind that when the patient has had his claim handled by NPE and – if he disagrees with NPEs decision – the Patient Injury Compensation Board within the administrative scheme, he then may take the Board to the courts of law. This year NPE will receive in all c. 5800 claims, and of these c. 220 (c. 4%) will be brought before the courts of law by way of suing the Norwegian State c/o the Patient Injury Compensation Board.'

and don't require separate consideration. Specific criteria apply to categories 3 and 4 of the Swedish scheme, but the vast majority of claims fall into the first two categories, and these are of the greatest relevance to the present discussion.

In the Swedish scheme, injuries from healthcare are compensated if a panel of neutral experts deems that they were 'avoidable' by an 'experienced specialist' – in effect not a 'reasonable' practitioner, but the 'best' level of practitioner in the particular field. As with negligence, this requires an assessment of quality of care. However, the standard is that of excellent care rather than acceptable care, and captures a wider range of injuries.[46] There are differences between Nordic countries in the nuances of clauses that refine this definition by dealing with things such as whether the wisdom of hindsight is allowable, or whether alternative treatment options should be considered.[47] Nevertheless, this central principle seems to provide a reasonable means of differentiating between the normal or expected consequences of treatment and injuries that reflect failures in care. As with the New Zealand scheme, it seems that more injured patients receive compensation sooner and more cost-effectively than through civil litigation in the United States (for example).[48]

In all Nordic countries, and in New Zealand, the schemes are underpinned and supported by well-developed social welfare and public health and disability systems. Overall, as with New Zealand, these systems appear to work well in the Nordic countries, with low levels of confrontation between doctors and patients.

---

[46] The resources available in the specific situation must be taken into account – much in the same way as New Zealand law precludes compensation on the basis of the allocation of resources. In Nordic countries, compensation would be awarded if referral was possible and could have avoided the injury. An injury meeting this criterion would probably qualify for compensation in New Zealand as well, on the grounds that it would not be a normal consequence of treatment.

[47] In the Danish and Finnish systems a 'reasonableness' rule extends compensation to injuries that are out of proportion to the underlying disease and the consequences that might reasonably be expected of it. This rule seeks a balance between the idea, on the one hand, that all injured patients should be compensated and the reality, on the other, that some injuries should be accepted by the patient: the more serious the disease or more major the operations, the greater the extent of associated harm that should be accepted. In the Norwegian scheme a patient is entitled to compensation if the damage to his or her health is caused by 'failure in connection with the providing of health services, even if no one is at fault'. This means that compensation will usually be provided, regardless of whether negligence played a role in causing the harm, but still carries the assumption that something irregular has occurred.

[48] See Table 1 and Figure 1 in Kachalia et al., 'Beyond negligence'.

One of the criticisms often raised about schemes of this type is that they are too expensive. In fact, it is the cost of healthcare-associated injury itself, and of the rehabilitation and support of the injured people, that is expensive. It is true that the New Zealand and Nordic schemes involved many administrators, case managers and other staff in the place of the lawyers, administrators and other people that would be required under tort law (the reduction in the latter group has presumably been somewhat greater in New Zealand than in Nordic countries). Nevertheless, in New Zealand, administrative overheads have been estimated at about 10 per cent of the total cost of the scheme compared with more than 50 per cent for tort law in the United States.[49] Furthermore, although patients regularly appeal against the decisions of the ACC, sometimes through the courts, these processes are not of a frequency or magnitude that would offset this difference to any great extent. Also, these appeals seldom create or even contribute to conflict between practitioners and patients. The efficiency of the Nordic schemes is less clear,[50] but there is nothing to suggest that they are more expensive than tort-based alternatives. Perhaps the best answer to this criticism is the observation that, after nearly fifty years of operation, the ACC is in good financial heart (as of 2015) and is widely held to be serving the people of New Zealand well. In 2013, Wilson and colleagues reported that most of the financial costs of injury were being met by the ACC.[51] There is no apparent desire on the part of the legal profession, the public or politicians to replace the ACC, and certainly no enthusiasm for a return to tort law as an alternative. Similar sentiments seem to prevail in Nordic countries.

Reporting and the Need to Promote Safety

When considering possibilities for legal reform it is easy to lose sight of the fact that the real problem is the continuing occurrence of avoidable adverse events in medicine. Errors and violations will never be completely eliminated from any complex system of human endeavour, but there is room for improvement in healthcare. The fewer the patients who are harmed during treatment, the lower the cost of dealing with that harm. In a safe system the tensions between doctors and patients are minimised.

---

[49] Bismark and Paterson, 'No-fault compensation in New Zealand'.
[50] Ulfbeck, Hartlev and Schultz, 'Malpractice in Scandinavia'.
[51] R. Wilson, S. Derrett, P. Hansen and J. D. Langley, 'Costs of injury in New Zealand: Accident Compensation Corporation spending, personal spending and quality-adjusted life years lost' (2013) 19 *Injury Prevention* 124–9.

Ultimately, the overriding legal, regulatory and medical objective should be the reduction of the human cost of iatrogenic harm.

A great deal is already being done by health professionals to reduce errors and improve the standard of care given to patients. Sight of this fact is all too readily lost in the glare of publicity associated with figures such as those reported by the Institute of Medicine.[52] There is no doubt that iatrogenic harm in healthcare is a very important issue but, in Chapter 2, we advanced a more cautious interpretation of its true extent. The reality is that outcomes from healthcare are steadily improving.[53] Even when one considers adverse events in isolation from the overall context of the ill health in which they occur, there is much greater engagement today in acknowledging these events and addressing them. Voluntary incident reporting is well established in the culture of anaesthesia, is gaining strength in other specialities and has led to a number of important advances in safety.

Reporting is a fundamental requirement for the continuous improvement of quality and safety in any complex system. Much of the information in this book arises directly or indirectly from reports of one sort or another. There are various approaches to reporting. For example, in voluntary incident reporting, as practised in anaesthesia, a practitioner (usually the anaesthetist, but occasionally a nurse or other person involved with patient care) fills in a form anonymously and forwards it to a central agency for inclusion in a large database. Usually, this is done in two stages. A departmental database forms the basis for local feedback and quality control. The information is then forwarded to a national or international centre for amalgamation with reports from other departments, in order to create a much larger database. An incident is defined, in effect, as any event that does or could reduce safety for a patient.[54] In some cases, harm will have occurred, and this is reported. In others,

---

[52] L. T. Kohn, J. M. Corrigan and M. S. Donaldson (eds.), *To Err Is Human: Building a Safer Health System* (Washington, D.C., National Academy Press, 1999); T. A. Brennan, 'The institute of medicine report on medical errors – could it do harm' (2000) 342 *New England Journal of Medicine* 1123–5; see also M. A. Makary and M. Daniel, 'Medical error – the third leading cause of death in the US' (2016) 353 *British Medical Journal* i2139.

[53] See Chapter 2, footnote 10. In addition to improving rates of perioperative mortality, outcomes from acute myocardial infarction, many forms of cancer and numerous other conditions are much more favourable today than they were two decades ago.

[54] W. B. Runciman, A. Sellen, R. K. Webb, J. A. Williamson, M. Currie, C. Morgan and W. J. Russell, 'The Australian Incident Monitoring Study. Errors, incidents and accidents in anaesthetic practice' (1993) 21 *Anaesthesia & Intensive Care* 506–19.

although no harm has occurred it is obvious that it might have done. The information collected typically includes a description of the incident and an opinion on factors that predisposed to its occurrence, factors that facilitated its avoidance or the minimisation of the consequences of the incident, and other relevant details. An example of this type of reporting is the Australian Incident Monitoring Study (AIMS).[55] Information from the AIMS database resulted in numerous publications in medical journals, and has influenced practice in a number of important areas. For example, the introduction of pulse oximetry as a routine standard of monitoring in anaesthesia in Australasia by anaesthetists in the face of scepticism (if not outright opposition) from fund holders was greatly facilitated by reference to these data.

A different approach to reporting involves specific, prospective projects looking in detail at particular problems. Thus, the practice of central venous cannulation was the subject of a study at the former Green Lane Hospital in Auckland, which identified that, in a high proportion of catheters, tip placement was deeper than ideal.[56] In the event of a rupture of the catheter through the wall of the central vessel, or heart chamber, this suboptimal placement increases the risk of death (by pericardial tamponade). This was addressed in several ways, including the simple systems-related measure of shortening the length of the central venous catheters for routine use. The study also raised awareness of the issue in the department, and promoted greater care. A subsequent study showed a much improved incidence of this problem.[57] This example illustrates the concept of 'closing the loop'. There is little point in reporting unless action is taken on the reported data. Furthermore, it is important to confirm the value (or otherwise) of any changes made. The 'loop' may be summarised as *data–action–data*.

---

[55] R. Holland, J. Hains, J. G. Roberts and W. B. Runciman, 'Symposium – The Australian Incident Monitoring Study' (1993) 21 *Anaesthesia & Intensive Care* 501–5; see also Chapter 1 footnote 56.

[56] J. S. Rutherford, A. F. Merry and C. J. Occleshaw, 'Depth of central venous catheterization: An audit of practice in a cardiac surgical unit' (1994) 22 *Anaesthesia and Intensive Care* 267–71; see also the more extensive discussion of the issue of the depth of insertion of central venous catheters in Chapter 7.

[57] A. F. Merry, C. S. Webster, I. C. Van Cotthem, R. L. Holland, J. S. Beca and N. G. Middleton, 'A prospective randomized clinical assessment of a new pigtail central venous catheter in comparison with standard alternatives' (1999) 27 *Anaesthesia and Intensive Care* 639–45. See also the third study in this series of quality improvement projects: C. S. Webster, A. F. Merry, D. J. Emmens, I. C. Van Cotthem, R. L. Holland and N. G. Middleton, 'A prospective clinical audit of central venous catheter use and complications in 1000 consecutive patients' (2003) 31 *Anaesthesia and Intensive Care* 80–6.

In both the New Zealand and Australian examples, reporting is anonymous, participation is voluntary, and the identity of individuals is protected. This usually results in ready compliance, open and comprehensive communication and worthwhile information. However, there are many who criticise the confidential nature of the exercise and suggest that any adverse events identified in such studies should be disclosed to the authorities and subject to formal inquiries and possible discipline or litigation. It is important to understand that confidential or privileged reporting does not in any way inhibit alternative means of identifying and responding to the same events. Thus, if a patient is injured, the information in the notes is available, the participants can be asked for reports, and all the normal mechanisms for investigating and dealing with the problem can be pursued. All that is protected is the information provided voluntarily and confidentially to the study or audit activity. It is reasonable to expect honest professionals to provide all the facts to any appropriate authority. However, as part of the adversarial nature of litigation and most disciplinary systems, individuals facing potential legal action are not required to give an opinion or to incriminate themselves.[58] In both Australia and New Zealand the privilege against self-incrimination allows a witness, including a medical expert, to object to answering questions on the grounds that to do so may expose the witness to the risk of criminal or other proceedings.[59]

People facing possible legal or disciplinary action are also entitled to legal counsel and adequate time for the preparation of their responses. The advantage of confidential, privileged voluntary reporting is that the same individual can with confidence provide a timely and frank account of what went wrong, including his or her opinion of the causes of the event, even if this opinion is damaging to any defence. Thus, information is readily gathered, which in some cases might never be elucidated by an adversarial system, or in others be discovered only after prolonged proceedings. In addition, this information is collated into large and useful databases from which general conclusions can be drawn and recommendations made for safer practice in the future. The early gains of the Australian Incident Reporting scheme have not been followed with the same momentum of success in identifying and improving outcomes for

[58] The issue of the right to silence has become a controversial one in criminal law, where pressure has grown in some jurisdictions to allow adverse inferences to be taken from the accused's silence. This is not currently the case in New Zealand, where the right to silence is preserved by s23 of the Bill of Rights Act 1990.

[59] See Evidence Act 1995 (Cth); s 128 Evidence Act 2006, s60 (NZ).

patients, and, as with most good ideas, adequate investment, engagement and attention to detail are all important for sustained progress. Considerable efforts are continuing in both Australia and New Zealand to ensure the effectiveness of incident reporting in anaesthesia.[60]

Provisions exist in many countries for the protection of information collected on a voluntary basis for the purposes of improving safety and quality, but they are not universal, and there are often exceptions, which reduce the level of protection they provide. The Institute of Medicine has recommended that such protection be provided throughout the United States, and has endorsed the value of voluntary reporting systems. However, it has gone further and recommended nationwide mandatory reporting as well. At present, mandatory reporting systems exist in twenty states in the United States. Other countries have also indicated an interest in establishing mandatory systems of this type following the report of the Institute of Medicine and its associated publicity. The report describes the objectives of mandatory reporting as follows: 'Such systems ensure a response to specific reports of serious injury, hold organizations and providers accountable for maintaining safety, respond to the public's right to know, and provide incentives to health care organizations to implement internal safety systems that reduce the likelihood of such events occurring.'[61]

In themselves, these objectives seem laudable. In so far as reporting is confined to factual information, there can be little objection to such an initiative. There is great value in knowing accurate rates of death and injury in healthcare. However, a recommendation for the public disclosure of information about serious adverse events should at the least differentiate between ascertainable facts and subjective opinion. Requiring individuals or organisations to set aside their legal rights to avoid self-incrimination is only likely to result in the suppression of useful information. This point has been made by Brennan in the *New England Journal of Medicine*.[62] In the UK, the Department of Health

---

[60] I. Mitchell, A. Schuster, K. Smith, P. Pronovost and A. Wu, 'Patient safety incident reporting: a qualitative study of thoughts and perceptions of experts 15 years after "To Err Is Human"' (2015) *BMJ Quality & Safety*; P. J. Guffey, M. Culwick and A. F. Merry, 'Incident reporting at the local and national level' (2014) 52 *International Anesthesiology Clinics* 69–83.

[61] See p. 8 in Kohn, Corrigan and Donaldson (eds.), *To Err Is Human: Building a Safer Health System*.

[62] T. A. Brennan, 'The institute of medicine report on medical errors – could it do harm'. (2000) 342(15) *New England Journal of Medicine* 1123–5.

report *An Organisation with a Memory*[63] also stressed the importance of reporting culture, which moves away from blame and sets out to develop an appreciation of the underlying causes of these incidents. The importance of incident reporting, and the potential for more 'to be made of this important source of information', is also mentioned in the Francis report into the events at the Mid Staffordshire NHS Foundation Trust.[64]

Even in respect of factual information, a requirement for mandatory reporting raises difficult issues. Obviously, it is to be hoped that the honest doctor will be completely open and frank in his or her disclosure to any authority concerning an injured patient, but equally there will be those whose approach is understandably more oriented to self-preservation. Does this mean that the requirement for mandatory reporting is placing the honest doctor under unreasonable pressure to set aside personal considerations? The answer to this question depends a great deal on the extent to which blame pervades the response of society to those who honestly disclose errors and mistakes of the type that, as we have seen, will be made by all practitioners at some stage of their careers. We will return to these questions in Chapter 10.

Professional Self-regulation and Harm to Patients

Reporting of errors and the creation of a responsive system of safety procedures certainly help to minimise the incidence of iatrogenic harm. Yet once the system identifies doctors whose ability to perform competently is in question, there must be an adequate way of protecting the public from such practitioners. Here the medical profession has been criticised on the grounds that the system of medical self-regulation adopted in many countries has failed to provide patients with an efficient method of monitoring performance and of weeding out those practitioners who are a danger to the public. Typical criticisms of such systems were that they did not prevent a closing of professional ranks, that they

---

[63] Department of Health, *An Organisation with a Memory – Report of an Expert Group on Learning from Adverse Events in the NHS* (London, Stationery Office, 2000).

[64] R. Francis, *The Mid Staffordshire NHS Foundation Trust. Report of the Mid Staffordshire NHS Foundation Trust Public Inquiry. 3 vols* (London, Stationery Office, 2013) www.midstaffspublicinquiry.com, accessed 2 July 2016, p. 71; see also D. Berwick, 'A promise to learn – a commitment to act: improving the safety of patients in England', Department of Health (2013) www.gov.uk/government/publications/berwick-review-into-patient-safety, accessed 3 December 2016.

were cumbersome and tardy in their response and that their thresholds for intervention were too high. In the United Kingdom, criticism of this sort, which had been levelled against the regulatory body of British medicine, the General Medical Council, became politically irresistible after the conviction of Dr Harold Shipman for the murder of fifteen of his patients.[65] This conviction, which followed shortly after the Bristol case, significantly affected public trust in the medical profession's ability to regulate itself. The public trust in health services, in the UK and elsewhere, has been eroded further by more recent scandals, notably that which occurred in the Mid Staffordshire NHS Foundation Trust.[66] In fact, it may be surprisingly difficult to identify clinicians whose competence falls short of acceptable standards,[67] and even more difficult to identify the homicidal practitioner. It is clear that medical self-regulation has been far from perfect, but what may not be quite so obvious is the considerable degree to which the profession has in fact been successful in ensuring high standards of medical care for the public.[68] The postgraduate college-based systems for the selection, training and examination of specialist doctors (including, more recently, those who specialise in general practice) have become increasingly rigorous over time – so much so that established doctors are at times accused of setting standards too high in order to protect themselves from competition. Charles Bosk provided an account of how surgeons in a North American teaching hospital recognise and deal with surgical mistakes, and particularly with trainees who make them.[69] Bosk,

---

[65] B. O'Neill, 'Doctor as murderer' (2000) 320 *British Medical Journal* 329–30. It was subsequently found that the total number of patients killed by Harold Shipman was well over 200: see R. Baker and B. Hurwitz, 'Intentionally harmful violations and patient safety: the example of Harold Shipman' (2009) 102 *Journal of the Royal Society of Medicine* 223–7.

[66] B. Jarman, 'Quality of care and patient safety in the UK: the way forward after Mid Staffordshire' (2013) 382 *Lancet* 573–5. See also R. Francis, *The Mid Staffordshire NHS Foundation Trust. Report of the Mid Staffordshire NHS Foundation Trust Public Inquiry*. 3 vols (Stationery Office, London, 2013): www.midstaffspublicinquiry.com, accessed 2 July 2016; see also D. Berwick, 'A promise to learn – a commitment to act: improving the safety of patients in England', Department of Health (2013) www.gov.uk/govern ment/publications/berwick-review-into-patient-safety, accessed July 2016.

[67] R. Hamblin, C. Shuker, I. Stolarek, J. Wilson and A. F. Merry, 'Public reporting of health care performance data: what we know and what we should do' (2016) 129 *New Zealand Medical Journal* 7–17.

[68] See footnote 51.

[69] C. Bosk, *Forgive and Remember: Managing Medical Failure* (Chicago, University of Chicago Press, 1979).

a sociologist, spent eighteen months working with and observing a surgical service. He made the interesting observation that hesitation and mildness, which may often surround such controls, related in part to the uncertainties that frequently existed in pinpointing the cause of a therapeutic misadventure. Partly for this reason, perceived deficiencies in a trainee doctor's honesty and integrity tended to be seen by senior colleagues as more important, and tended to be dealt with more harshly, than issues of technical competence. Bosk made the further observation that, unfortunately, trainee doctors found wanting in one institution often found employment in another, perhaps less prestigious, hospital.

Even when it has been accepted that professional self-regulation at all levels has been associated with some spectacular failures, it has yet to be shown that alternatives, which depend more on external agencies and the involvement of lay people in the processes of professional regulation, will be any more effective in identifying dangerous doctors. There is a real risk that well-intentioned responses to events, such as the scandal of Harold Shipman, may do little more than add to the burden of the majority of honest practitioners without improving either their standards of practice or the chances of avoiding the occurrence of similar types of disaster in the future.[70] It is interesting that, in an era that stresses the importance of evidence-based medicine, changes in approach to the regulation or management of healthcare are made with little if any serious attempt to conduct a proper evaluation of their impact. There is good reason to retain those aspects of self-regulation that have merit, and to ensure that doctors continue to have a substantial role in committees dealing with ethics, discipline and regulation. There is certainly value in much greater involvement of lay people in such activities, to represent the perspective of the public (or particular segments of the public). In addition, certain non-medical people, such as lawyers, have a training or background that may be of great value in managing the process of dealing with adverse events. Nevertheless, doctors and other practitioners are better placed than lay people to understand and identify unacceptable behaviour in the context of the complexities of healthcare, and there is a risk that an excessive reduction in their involvement in the process of regulating medicine might produce a result which is less satisfactory with respect to the needs of the public. The professional regulation of medicine is not a simple matter; it is important that the need for a well-informed and

[70] D. Haines, 'The legacy of Dr. Harold Shipman' (2015) 83 *Medico-Legal Journal* 115.

balanced appraisal of adverse events in healthcare is recognised, and that new measures aimed at improving the situation should build on the strengths of the past and not simply replace one imperfect system with another, possibly an even less effective one. Yet the public may not be sensitive to these difficulties. There may be increasing demands for external controls in healthcare, associated with an expectation that incidents of the Shipman, Bristol and Mid Staffordshire sort can be prevented by a rapid, draconian system of suspension from practice at the first suggestion of incompetence, or the first occasion on which harm has occurred to a patient. Demands for action are understandable, but responses to them need to be sophisticated, and their effects should be carefully evaluated to ensure that progress is being made in the pursuit of better and safer healthcare.[71]

The General Medical Council was not particularly well placed to defend itself in the face of criticism arising from the Shipman scandal that it had failed to protect the public. It is only since 1995 that the Council has been able to take action in respect of incompetent doctors; prior to that the Council responded only to the professional misconduct of doctors. In 1995 Parliament passed the Medical (Professional Performance) Act, which came into force in late 1997. This legislation gives the Council the power to respond, through disciplinary proceedings, to those doctors whose performance of their duties was seriously deficient. There was some debate as to what this level should be, but in the event proposals to allow for sanctions for 'unacceptable performance' or for merely 'deficient' performance were rejected in favour of the higher level of deficiency. This did not satisfy the demands of organisations that had been campaigning for a more severe response. In a contribution to the *British Medical Journal*, for example, the chief executive of Action for Victims of Medical Accidents wrote:

> Patients who are on the receiving end of poor performance are more concerned with the accountability of those who were responsible than with the definition of seriously deficient performance. If a patient has suffered injury as a result of treatment by a doctor, or as a result of a failure to treat, then surely he or she must have been at risk. If the patient was at risk then there must be a danger that others will be at risk in the future. The problem is that the new procedures are aimed solely at a pattern of

---

[71] Shuker et al., 'The Health Quality and Safety Commission: making good health care better'; R. Hamblin, G. Bohm, C. Gerard, C. Shuker, J. Wilson and A. F. Merry, 'The measurement of New Zealand health care' (2015) 128 *New Zealand Medical Journal* 50–64.

behaviour. How many ureters must a surgeon divide before a pattern is established? How many babies must suffer asphyxia? What patients want to know is whom doctors will be held accountable to after the first occasion that they cause such a serious injury.[72]

This comment demonstrates the nature of the blaming response that we have sought to appraise in this book. In this view, the making of a single error appears to raise a presumption of incompetence; in fact, as we have argued, the making of a certain number of errors is a statistically inevitable feature of any career in medicine. It does seem reasonable to monitor every substantive failure in practice made by a medical practitioner, but the insistence that a clear pattern should be demonstrated before harsh action is taken at least distinguishes between the normally competent doctor who makes errors and the doctor who repeatedly falls below a reasonably attainable level of competence. It is very important to understand that the truly malign doctor, such as Harold Shipman, is a completely different matter again. Such a person may be highly competent and may be well liked by many of his or her patients, as was Shipman. A truly criminal doctor may be very skilled at concealing harm deliberately caused to patients and may not be readily identified by either approach, again as was Shipman. Such individuals are in fact uncommon, and, deplorable though the failure to identify them may be, the issue of genuinely criminal behaviour on the part of a healthcare professional must be seen as separate from that of competence. The events at Stafford Hospital make clear the wider importance of institutional culture and the need to broaden the scope of accountability for the safety and quality of healthcare to include those responsible for the governance of healthcare as well as those responsible for its actual delivery to individual patients.

The use of professional discipline to minimise harm to patients will provide some security against the incompetent doctor, but in many countries disciplinary processes tend only to deal with the more egregious cases.[73] There has been increasing recognition over the last two decades that the price of continued professional self-regulation is the

---

[72] A. Simanowitz, 'Performance procedures for seriously deficient professional performance are flawed [letter]' (1996) 313 *British Medical Journal* 562.

[73] There are exceptions. As we have discussed above, in New Zealand the threshold for the investigation of complaints arising from healthcare, with the possibility that disciplinary findings at the lowest level will follow, is quite low, perhaps in part because of the absence of the option to sue a doctor: see, for example, Bismark and Paterson, 'No-fault compensation in New Zealand'.

installation of additional means of ensuring that levels of competence are maintained and the incidence of medical injury contained. For example, in the UK, the General Medical Council has introduced a system of revalidation, which will require all doctors – at junior and senior levels – to submit every five years to a process of assessment of competence,[74] which is a substantial change from the previous system, which allowed for a doctor to continue to practise indefinitely once he or she had been registered. The United Kingdom comes relatively late to this system, as do Australia and New Zealand, but recertification has long been an established feature of speciality practice in the United States, where a certificate in a speciality has to be renewed every seven to ten years. Various processes addressing similar objectives are well established in Canada and in many other countries.[75] Such approaches have much to recommend them, but there is ongoing debate about their value and about the best way to achieve two distinct (and arguably conflicting) objectives: making good doctors better, and identifying bad doctors.[76] Greater insistence on continued professional development, along with programmes of clinical governance designed to raise clinical standards, is one of a number of measures that may be expected to have an impact on reducing the incidence of patient injury, particularly when operated in conjunction with effective reporting systems and audit arrangements. The picture that this suggests is one of more highly regulated medical practice with less room, perhaps, for what used to be described as 'clinical freedom'. There are considerable financial costs to increased regulation, and to such measures as increasing the levels of supervision provided to junior doctors, limiting the hours worked by any doctor (junior or senior), and introducing initiatives to address the numerous latent conditions in the system (poor ampoule labelling, for example).

---

[74] S. Carter, 'Government announces start of revalidation' (2012) 345 *British Medical Journal* e7092; V. Nath, B. Seale and M. Kaur, 'Medical revalidation. From compliance to commitment', The King's Fund (2014) www.kingsfund.org.uk/sites/files/kf/field/field_ publication_file/, accessed 2 April 2016.

[75] Recertification (similar in concept to revalidation) was introduced in New Zealand in 2001; maintenance of competence (MOC) is well established in the United States, as is Maintenance and Enhancement of Professional Performance (MEPP) in Canada; in Australia the cost benefit of such measures is still being debated, although continued professional development (CPD) is now compulsory; See J. J. Norcini, 'Recertification in the United States' (1999) 319 *British Medical Journal* 1183–5; K. J. Breen, 'Revalidation – what is the problem and what are the possible solutions?' (2014) 200 *Medical Journal of Australia* 153–6; L. J. Roberts, 'Revalidation: implications for Australian anaesthetists' (2015) 43 *Anaesthesia & Intensive Care* 652–61.

[76] Nath, Seale and Kaur, 'Medical revalidation. From compliance to commitment'.

However, this increased cost in the provision of treatment is likely to be more than offset by the savings in respect to the current costs of iatrogenic harm – in both financial and human terms. Overall, there is no doubt that improvement is needed in ensuring that the care received by all patients is of at least an adequate standard, and the important matter is that this entire approach should be preventive and improvement-oriented. It is also important that the system of healthcare is considered as a whole, and that many other systemic factors (some of which have been discussed in previous chapters) are also addressed. We will return to these themes in Chapter 10.

Conclusions

Various possible reforms have the potential to improve the situation for injured patients and to reduce unproductive conflict between patients and practitioners. A good system should address the following objectives:

1) Patients who have been injured during healthcare should have timely access to adequate support, rehabilitation and compensation without the burden of having to prove negligence.
2) The improvement of the safety of healthcare must be a priority, but the other elements of quality must also be promoted.
3) There must be effective systems for the early identification and control of those doctors (and other health professionals) who are grossly negligent, incompetent or impaired.
4) At the same time there should be a more sophisticated understanding of the nature of error, and a less punitive approach to those conscientious and competent practitioners who, in the course of their careers, will inevitably make a mistake at some time.
5) The adversarial response to accidents needs to be replaced with a climate in which trust between practitioners (particularly doctors, where the loss of trust seems to have been most marked) and patients is re-established, the role of blame is reduced and the focus is placed on co-operation: the concept that care should be patient-centred should also apply to the legal and regulatory response to harm.
6) The overall costs of healthcare, including legal and regulatory costs, must be affordable.

How are these objectives to be achieved? It is unlikely that a single model will be universally acceptable. A great deal will depend on the economic, political and social environment of the society concerned.

Thus (for example), Nordic countries, with their long tradition of social welfare, might be expected to favour communitarian approaches, while the United States, with its attachment to notions of individual responsibility, is more likely to prefer a greater role for the tort system. In general, adjustments to improve whatever system is already in place will probably be more acceptable and successful than attempts at far-reaching and radical reform. The experience of the United States, where tort law reform has been a politically contentious issue, demonstrates the difficulties associated with substantial changes in direction. Nevertheless, there is considerable room for improvement in many countries. In particular, there is a strong case for the wider implementation of no-fault systems of compensating injured patients, backed up by appropriate means of ensuring the accountability of health professionals, including improved approaches to professional regulation. If these work well, there will be little need for patients to resort to litigation, as is the case in Nordic countries. Whatever system is adopted, the value of reporting and of sophisticated approaches to monitoring the performance of practitioners should be borne in mind, and preserved. One advantage of no-fault systems of compensation is that effective reporting of errors and mistakes may more readily be achieved. However, prohibition of the right to sue in respect of personal injury, medical or otherwise, is probably undesirable: tort has its advantages. In particular, it provides an established and useful resort when other approaches prove unsatisfactory. It would be reasonable to require that alternatives be used first, and that settlements and sanctions arising from these alternatives be taken into account in the civil process. Yet, after the less adversarial possibilities have been exhausted, for an individual who feels the alternatives have not worked well, the opportunity to bring a civil action is an important right. For a community that believes other methods are failing in a general sense, tort provides a mechanism for asserting dissatisfaction. A substantial increase in the rate of litigation would signal widespread dissatisfaction with, for example, a no-fault system that was not working well. Sound alternatives to tort should be capable of preventing the excesses that have characterised civil litigation in the past.

A better understanding of the objectives of health services, the elements of quality, the causes of medical accidents, the factors which underlie errors or promote violations and the theoretical basis of safety in complex systems is essential if reforms in the way we regulate healthcare are to be effective in achieving their primary objective: improved patient safety and a more acceptable response to the needs of injured patients. In this chapter we have focused on approaches that have been implemented in one form or another in different parts of the world. In Chapter 10 we will extend our analysis of ways in which these principles could be applied and include some possibilities that have yet to be tried.

9

The Place of the Criminal Law in Healthcare

In the majority of cases in most countries of the world, legal responses to harm inadvertently caused by healthcare involve either the civil law or some form of disciplinary process. The disciplinary processes may be administered by national bodies set up for that purpose[1] or by the organisations employing the practitioners involved with the incident. In some countries, when a patient dies there might often be a coronial inquiry or review in addition to any other processes that follow. Sometimes, however, the response to a patient's death is a criminal prosecution.

The criminal law is seldom invoked in relation to inadvertent harm that falls short of death. This is an interesting observation. It seems that if a clinician makes errors and commits violations in patient care, a criminal charge is much more likely if the patient dies in consequence of those actions than if he or she is simply injured (e.g. rendered paraplegic). It follows that prosecution in most cases in this context relates to charges of one form or another of homicide. A conviction for murder (as in the case of Harold Shipman) requires, amongst other elements, intent, but intent to cause harm is very unusual in the context of healthcare. Thus, the majority of cases involve some variant on the theme of manslaughter. This has led to the coining of the term 'medical manslaughter'. This term has no standing in law, and simply serves to emphasise a very particular social and professional context. Manslaughter is a generic offence with potential application to any capacitated adult responsible for doing dangerous acts or performing dangerous omissions that result in another's death.

Manslaughter is a term that covers a notoriously broad range of moral culpability. Nevertheless, it is strongly pejorative. What are we really saying when we say that a doctor or a nurse is a 'manslaughterer'? The term certainly carries connotations of criminality. To fully

---

[1] These bodies may also have other purposes, such as the registration of practitioners, for example.

understand the implications of this, it is worth contrasting the process typical of a criminal prosecution for manslaughter with that which surrounds a civil action for negligence. In the case of a criminal prosecution all of the following apply:

1) A charge is laid by the police; this involves going to the police station and having photographs and fingerprints taken.
2) The continuing liberty of the charged person is dependent on the provision of bail. In most cases of 'medical manslaughter' this is likely to be granted, but it is not a right.
3) The charged person is often required to surrender his or her passport and freedom to travel outside his or her country is typically removed.
4) The name of the charged person will often be included in lists alongside the names of other people who are also facing criminal charges; these charges will typically include crimes such as rape, murder, theft and assault.
5) During court proceedings the charged person will typically be accompanied by a prison officer at all times and may be held in custody in some form of cell during periods of remand.

These are not accompaniments of civil proceedings. In Chapter 5, we discussed the idea that civil actions in negligence are primarily intended to adjust loss rather than punish any individual (although the latter may occur incidentally, or in some cases through the explicit award of exemplary damages). It is illuminating to imagine explaining matters to a family member, such as one's grandmother (in effect, what one might call 'the granny test'). In a civil case one might reasonably say that something unfortunate has happened, an accident, which has led a patient to commence a lawsuit. Financial and reputational consequences may follow, but life is likely to continue much as before once the case is over. In many societies civil cases are common, and people (including family members) are likely to understand that this sort of thing might well happen to anyone. In a criminal case, by contrast, it is the State that has acted, by laying, arguably, the second most serious charge available, with the potential, in a worst-case scenario, for a long custodial sentence. It would be hard for one's grandmother (or anyone else) to escape the implication that one is believed to have done something very bad indeed.

This may not always be the State's intention, when manslaughter charges are laid. Perhaps the intention is only to say that the charged person is responsible for having permitted a bad outcome to occur. There may be no intended judgement as to his or her essential character. Unfortunately, the criminal law is a blunt instrument, and a prosecution for manslaughter, whatever the context, is inextricably embedded in everything that the criminal law implies. It involves holding a human agent publicly accountable for a very serious offence, falling short of murder, but nevertheless carrying a very strong social stigma, and other collateral social judgements.

In this chapter we explore the role of manslaughter in the context of healthcare in order to gain a better understanding of its true character and its social utility as a means of regulating medical errors and violations in healthcare. Our position can be stated simply. We accept that there is a role for the criminal prosecution of a health professional whose wilful or egregiously reckless conduct causes the death of a patient, but such an approach should be a course of last resort, to be used only in cases of wantonly bad behaviour. Prosecution for manslaughter should not lightly be initiated against a well-intentioned individual who makes a single, but lethal, causal error, particularly in the context of highly complex and rapidly evolving medical situations, and particularly in situations where many other people are also at least partially responsible.

We begin with some general observations on the status of medical manslaughter prosecutions in a number of different jurisdictions. In summary, the rate of such a prosecution is very low in most judicial systems that have their origins in the common law of England. New Zealand was an exception towards the end of the last century, but a change in the law in 1997 returned the situation to that of most comparable countries. At the time the first edition of this book was written, it seemed that the topic was of little practical interest in any part of the world. Doctors, nurses and other health professionals had little to fear from the criminal law unless they chose to harm patients deliberately, or to engage in more conventional (and typically extramural) criminal practices, such as fraud, drunken driving, assault, burglary or the like. Any unintentional shortcomings in their practice would be dealt with under the civil law, or perhaps become the subject of disciplinary proceedings. However, the rate of prosecutions in the last two decades in England and Wales has increased enough to justify some level of anxiety on the part of health professionals. It is quite possible (albeit still unlikely) in England or Wales today that simply going to work with the full intention of caring conscientiously for patients could lead to criminal charges through nothing more than the combination of an error (of the type that all humans make from time to time) and the unhappy influence of chance. It is these recent events that make this topic worthy of careful consideration in the present edition of this book.

The rate of prosecution may reflect the process by which prosecutions are initiated, so we consider that process next, including the question of prosecutorial discretion. We then discuss some key terms and reflect on how errors are characterised for the purposes of a criminal investigation. We examine different modes of assessing criminal responsibility, and discuss the problems of *moral luck*, which we have referred to previously (in Chapters 1, 2, 4 and 7), as well as some of the other vagaries of prosecutions, notably the tendency to focus on outcomes rather than the character of the conduct that leads to these outcomes. We deal with the fault requirement in cases of medical negligence, and the important distinction between subjective and objective requirements. We suggest that the concept of 'gross' negligence has outlived its usefulness and ought to be replaced by the subjective fault standard of advertent recklessness.

Our concern, ultimately, is to affirm the idea that the innocent must not be made to suffer punishment.[2] Those whose state of mind is reckless or malign are another matter, but, in the context of healthcare, these are exceptions. It is our view that the current legal approach in England and Wales allows for the real possibility of innocent men and women suffering punishment for medical outcomes *that do not reflect serious moral culpability*. We conclude that better ways are needed to ensure that the innocent do not suffer punishment while protecting the public from the consequences of both intended and unintended harm.

Overview of Medical Manslaughter

Prosecutions for manslaughter arising from medical negligence are exceedingly rare, compared with other forms of crime, but there is some variation in both law and policy across comparable common-law jurisdictions.

England and Wales

England and Wales share a common legal system. In the early part of the nineteenth century, prosecutions for manslaughter in these

---

[2] J. Hall, 'Negligence and the general problem of criminal responsibility' (1972) 31 *The Yale Law Journal* 949–951.

countries required only a failure to meet the civil standard of using reasonable skill, knowledge and care when undertaking dangerous activities. In time the harshness of this approach was appreciated, and criminal sanctions came to be reserved for cases involving gross negligence.[3] On the other hand, recklessness is not a requirement for a conviction of manslaughter. This point appears to have been settled in *Adomako*,[4] when the House of Lords confirmed that in cases of manslaughter by criminal negligence involving a breach of duty, it is a sufficient direction to the jury to adopt the gross negligence test previously established by the Court of Appeal in *Bateman*.[5] Prosecutions of healthcare practitioners were infrequent in Britain before the later part of the last century. Subsequent developments will be discussed later in this chapter.

Scotland

In Scotland, manslaughter by gross negligence is not a recognised crime. The closest equivalent is the crime of culpable homicide. The required mental state is 'wicked negligence', which is a very high threshold. In particular, 'culpable homicide' in Scotland requires proof of a particular mental element, characterised as 'gross, or wicked, or criminal negligence, something amounting, or at least analogous to a criminal indifference to consequences'.[6] Scottish courts have held that it is wrong to suppose that the actual state of mind of a person accused of culpable homicide can be ignored, and guilt or innocence can be determined solely on the basis that proof that the conduct in question fell below an objectively set standard.[7] Accordingly, prosecutions for culpable homicide for a death resulting from medical negligence, or from a breach of health and safety, are very rare. While there have now been at least eleven convictions for corporate manslaughter under the Corporate Manslaughter and Corporate Homicide Act 2007

---

[3]   A. M. McCall Smith and A. Merry, 'Medical accountability and the criminal law: New Zealand vs the world' (1996) 4 *Health Care Analysis* 45–54.

[4]   *R* v. *Adomako* [1994] 3 WLR 288.

[5]   *R* v. *Bateman* (1925) 10 Cr App Rep 8; however, see also, *Akerele* v. *R* [1943] AC 255, 263 (PC), where Their Lordships 'stress the care which should be taken before imputing criminal negligence to a professional man acting in the course of his profession'.

[6]   *Paton* v. *HM Advocate* 1936 JC 19, per Lord Justice-Clerk Aitchison, at p22.

[7]   *Transco PLC* v. *Her Majesty's Advocate*. High Court of Judiciary, Appeal No XC392/03 at 38.

in England and Wales, as at 30 March 2015 there had been no such convictions in Scotland.[8]

New Zealand

New Zealand has a criminal code, the relevant sections of which were based on the draft criminal code of Sir James Fitzjames Stephen. Until 1997, the requirement for criminal negligence was expressed in terms of simple or civil negligence.[9] After some interesting early cases,[10] it was not until 1982 that a health practitioner was convicted of manslaughter for negligence causing a patient's death. This case involved the inadvertent administration of carbon dioxide instead of oxygen to a child during anaesthesia under circumstances in which the anaesthetist was using unfamiliar equipment. Eight more practitioners were charged with manslaughter in the 1990s. Of these, another anaesthetist (Dr Yogasakaran, see Chapter 1) and a nurse were convicted and discharged, and a radiologist (Dr Morrison, see Chapter 1) pleaded guilty and was discharged, after patients died following inadvertent drug administration errors. A dentist was charged with manslaughter after a patient died under sedation, but these charges were dropped. A highly reputed cardiac surgeon faced lesser criminal charges after inadvertently leaving a clamp in place for longer than intended on a critical artery during complicated congenital heart surgery in a baby, but these charges were also dropped (see footnote 36 on p. 124). Another cardiac surgeon was convicted of manslaughter after three deaths following technical problems in surgery, in which the level of incompetence appears to have been considerable. In a pivotal case, a third anaesthetist was dismissed by the judge before trial, following the death of a very sick elderly patient. Some air had inadvertently been allowed to enter the patient's circulation during an emergency operation but the cause of death was far from clear. Indeed, inoperable dead bowel had already been discovered and the patient's cardiovascular state was highly unstable). Hammond J made the following comments: 'Further,

---

[8] S. Tombs, 'Corporate Killing with Impunity', International Centre for Comparative Criminological Research, The Open University https://oucriminology.wordpress.com /tag/gross-negligence-mans, accessed 28 November 2016.

[9] *R v. Storey* [1931] NZLR 417.

[10] Anon, 'Dr Wilkins's case – charge of manslaughter' (1901) II *New Zealand Medical Journal* 133; Anon, 'Medico-legal etc. A Bogus Doctor' (1902) II *New Zealand Medical Journal* 304–5; Anon, 'Surgeon's liability' (1902) IV *New Zealand Medical Journal* 15. We are grateful to Dr Leona Wilson for drawing our attention to these cases.

a mistake or error of judgment does not necessarily constitute a failure to take reasonable care';[11] and 'A conviction for manslaughter is, of course, in and of itself a very harsh penalty for harm inadvertently caused.'

This particular case assisted the cause of the New Zealand Medical Law Reform Group, whose advocacy led to a legislative amendment to the Crimes Act 1961 (NZ) in 1997. This amendment resulted in a lifting of the threshold for establishing negligence to a 'major departure' from the expected standard of care.[12] In effect this established a requirement for gross negligence before a person could be convicted of manslaughter, but focused on the extent to which practices departed from the expected standard rather than suggesting that a lower standard was acceptable.

Interestingly, a fourth anaesthetist (Dr Hugel, see Chapter 1) then underwent trial after she failed to save the life of a teenage boy who developed the dangerous complication of negative pressure pulmonary oedema after a relatively straightforward operation in circumstances that included the late development of a blocked filter in the breathing circuit. This trial was conducted after the change in the law, but under the previous provisions, on the grounds that they were the provisions pertaining at the time of the event. The jury found her not guilty.

Some commentators have suggested that these cases illustrate how difficult it was to obtain a conviction, even when it was not necessary to prove gross negligence.[13] Given that five out of these nine cases resulted in convictions, we prefer an alternative view. In eight of these cases the prosecutions clearly arose out of errors made by competent practitioners in the course of their normal clinical work. The low level of blameworthiness associated with these errors is reflected in the light sentences, and in some of the comments made by the judges, notably the comments of Hammond J quoted above and that of Anderson J in the case of Dr Yogasakaran, quoted in Chapter 1. It is also worth emphasising that New Zealand is a small country – at the time, its population was less than 4 million. Thus, these 9 cases would equate to approximately 135 in a country the size of the UK.

Even in the remaining case, that of the convicted cardiac surgeon, it is debatable whether the criminal courts are the best place to deal with allegations of incompetent practice. The circumstances of this case

[11] Long v. R [1995] 2 NZLR 691.
[12] See s 150A Crimes Act 1961 inserted, as from 22 November 1997, by s 2(1) Crimes Amendment Act 1997 (NZ).
[13] P.D.G. Skegg, 'Medical acts hastening death' in P. Skegg and R. Paterson (eds.), Health Law in New Zealand (Thomson Reuters, Wellington, 2015) 636.

reflected a much more general failure in the training and certification of this surgeon in the UK. Nevertheless, in the circumstances prevailing at the time, criminal prosecution in this case may have been the only effective way to bring about a prompt end to this practitioner's ongoing pursuit of a career in cardiac surgery. (Indeed, he never practised again as a cardiac surgeon.) In New Zealand, at that time, it was almost impossible to bring a civil action against a doctor in circumstances of this sort, and the office of the Health and Disability Commissioner had only recently been established, so there really was a dearth of options.[14] It is certainly not our position that incompetence should be tolerated, and we will return to this theme later in this chapter and in Chapter 10. In the other cases, though, we agree with the comments of the judge in the case of Long: in our view, few, if any, of these *criminal* charges should have been laid in the first place. Similar comments have been made more recently in the English context.[15] It should be noted that not all of these cases involved doctors, and it is relevant that a few cases that had nothing to do with healthcare were also prosecuted under the same provisions of the New Zealand law – for example, in relation to deaths associated with the use of farm machinery or inadequate safeguarding of swimming pools. In at least some of these cases, mistakes were made, but the level of negligence appears to have been low. The change in the law rightly applied across the board, not only to medical practitioners.

Criminal prosecutions of health practitioners have now become rare in New Zealand. A midwife was charged over the death of a baby in Dunedin, but found not guilty by the jury. A cosmetic surgeon was convicted of the lesser charge of 'criminal nuisance' in relation to a death, involving the injection of phenol under sedation, in which several (ongoing) aspects of his practice were called into serious doubt. At about the same time a farmer was charged under the same provisions of the New Zealand law after his young child died while riding a four-wheeled motor-bike (a 'quad bike') – a practice that apparently was

---

[14] The Medical Practitioner's Disciplinary Tribunal was one option, and proceedings through this body could have resulted in the loss of the surgeon's licence to practice, but public confidence in this process might not have been very high. After all, it might have been thought that the registration process had already failed by allowing this doctor to practice beyond his level of competence for some considerable period of time.

[15] R. E. Ferner and S. E. McDowell, 'Doctors charged with manslaughter in the course of medical practice, 1795–2005: a literature review' (2006) 99 *Journal of the Royal Society of Medicine* 309–14; S. E. McDowell and R. E. Ferner, 'Medical manslaughter' (2013) 347 *British Medical Journal* f5609; P. McDonald, 'Doctors and manslaughter' (2014) 96 *Annals of the Royal College of Surgeons of England (Suppl)* 112–113.

(and probably still is) quite common on New Zealand farms. He was also found not guilty by the jury.[16] Since then, no patient death has resulted in a manslaughter prosecution.[17] It seems that such prosecutions have 'all but ceased'.[18]

Australia

The Australian situation is somewhat complicated by the Federal nature of its legislature. Victoria, New South Wales, South Australia and the Capital Territory operate under the common law, in which the requirement is for recklessness, as encapsulated in the following passage from *R* v. *Gunter*.[19]

> Negligence which is essential before a man can be criminally convicted must be culpable, exhibiting a degree of recklessness beyond anything required to make a man liable for damages and civil action. It must be such a degree of culpable negligence as to amount to an absence of that care for the lives and persons of others which every law abiding man is expected to exhibit.

Queensland, Western Australia, Tasmania and the Northern Territory have criminal codes. Their codes, like those of New Zealand and Canada, were based on the draft criminal code of Sir James Fitzjames Stephen. Like that of New Zealand before 1997, the requirement for criminal negligence is expressed in terms of simple or civil negligence. However, in *R* v. *Callaghan*[20] the High Court of Australia ruled that the section had to be construed in the context of a criminal code dealing with major crimes involving grave moral guilt:

> [T]he expression 'omission to perform the duty to use reasonable care and take reasonable precautions' which in effect is that of [the statutory sections] must be regarded from the point of view of the context where it occurs. It is in the criminal code dealing with **major crimes involving grave moral guilt**.

(Emphasis added)

---

[16] 'Farmer found not guilty over daughter's quad bike death' (25 March 2006) *New Zealand Herald*.

[17] R. Paterson, 'From prosecution to rehabilitation: New Zealand's response to health professional negligence.' in D. Griffiths and A. Sanders (eds.), *Bioethics, Medicine and the Criminal Law* (Vol 2) (Cambridge, Cambridge University Press, 2013) 244.

[18] Skegg, 'Medical acts hastening death', 636.

[19] *R* v. *Gunter* (1921) 21 SR (NSW) 282; see also *Nydham* v. *R* [1977] VR 430, 435 (Supreme Court of Victoria, Full Court).

[20] *R* v. *Callaghan* (1952) 87 CLR 115.

For this reason, the civil standard of negligence was rejected and the Australian common law standard was applied.

The Australian situation illustrates how difficult it can be to identify past criminal prosecutions of a particular type. Dobinson drew attention to the paucity of relevant literature, but suggested that only three doctors and a dentist have been charged with negligent manslaughter in the context of healthcare since the prosecution of Dr Valentine in 1843.[21] More recently, by searching media archives, Carter uncovered a further thirty-three prosecutions of this type, including that of Dr Durie in 1839 as the earliest case now known.[22] Carter emphasises the limitations of media sources for information of this type, and he indicates that it is by no means certain that all cases have been identified.

Perhaps the best known Australian case is that of Dr Jayand Patel, a surgeon who had relatively recently immigrated to Queensland. In 2009 he was prosecuted on three counts of manslaughter relating to the deaths of patients under his care. This prosecution resulted in a retrial because of a miscarriage of justice as a result of prejudicial evidence being admitted at the trial. He was acquitted on one count at a retrial, and on another retrial the jury failed to reach a verdict. The Queensland Director of Public Prosecutions decided not to pursue any further charges, although Patel was later barred by Queensland's Civil and Administrative Tribunal from ever practising medicine in Australia again.

Canada

In Canada, Fiona McDonald found only one physician charged with manslaughter between the years 1900 and 2007, although fourteen others faced lesser charges. This physician was convicted, following a guilty plea, for criminal negligence causing bodily harm.[23] McDonald concluded that very few physicians face serious criminal charges in Canada as a result of negligence in their clinical practice,[24] and also that, even taking

---

[21] I. Dobinson, 'Medical manslaughter' (2009) 28 *University of Queensland Law Journal* 101–12.

[22] D. J. Carter, 'Correcting the record: Australian prosecutions for manslaughter in the medical context' (2015) 22 *Journal of Law and Medicine* 588–609. See also N. Tuckett, 'Balancing public health and practitioner accountability in cases of medical manslaughter: Reconsidering the tests for criminal negligence-related offences in Australia after R v Patel' (2011) 19 *Journal of Law and Medicine* 377–95.

[23] F. McDonald, 'The criminalisation of medical mistakes in Canada: a review' (2008) 16 *Health Law Journal* 1–25.

[24] McDonald, 'The criminalisation of medical mistakes', 13.

population differences into account, English physicians were more likely to face serious criminal charges and be convicted for errors in practice than their Canadian counterparts.[25] McDonald suggests that a possible explanation for the low rate of successful prosecutions against doctors in Canada is that 'Canadian courts ... do not appear to be conflating the seriousness of the consequences with the culpability of the actions'[26] or assigning blame where none exists. The conservative position in Canada is in fact long established, with the criminal code specifying a requirement for 'wanton or reckless disregard'.[27]

We discuss recent prosecutions in England and Wales later in this chapter. The difference in frequency of prosecution between England and Canada in recent years may well reflect prosecution policy more than differences between their laws. It seems plausible that several high-profile events involving patients who have died as a result of negligent acts and omissions (or even been murdered by their doctor), media calls for accountability and a loss of trust in medical professionals have all combined to increase public pressure on prosecutorial authorities to see that justice is done and make health professionals in England and Wales more vulnerable to criminal prosecutions.[28] Other than a brief outline of the situation in France, we have not widened our analysis to consider in any depth countries whose legal systems are rather different from those that have originated in English common law, but in jurisdictions of the latter type it does seem that England and Wales, since the turn of the millennium, and New Zealand during the 1990s, have been exceptions to a general reluctance to prosecute doctors for serious crimes where evidence of moral culpability is low.

The United States

In the United States, criminal prosecutions of doctors have again been uncommon historically. Formulations vary between states, but, in effect, at least gross negligence is required. There have recently been some criminal

---

[25] McDonald, 'The criminalisation of medical mistakes', 13.
[26] McDonald, 'The criminalisation of medical mistakes', 15–16.
[27] R v. Rogers [1968] 65 WWR 193; R v. Tuppen (1989) 48 CCC (3d) 129; R v. Baker [1929] 2 DLR 282.
[28] McDonald, 'The Criminalisation of Medical Mistakes,' 14. See also O. Quick, 'Prosecuting "gross" medical negligence: manslaughter, discretion and the Crown Prosecution Service' (2006) 33 Journal of Law and Society 421–50, and J. Holbrook, 'The criminalisation of fatal medical mistakes' (2003) 327:7424 British Medical Journal 1118.

prosecutions for manslaughter based on reckless endangerment. However, the rate is still very low given that the American Department of Health and Human Services estimates that there are about 700,000 physicians in North America and evidence that the number of deaths arising from preventable errors during healthcare may be larger than previously appreciated.[29] [30]

France

In a balanced and thoughtful paper, Kazarian, Griffiths and Brazier have drawn attention to France as a possible 'exemplar of a much broader role for the criminal process in holding doctors for [sic] account for clinical negligence'. Perhaps the greatest advantage of the French law in this context is its inquisitorial nature. It does seem that an inquisitorial approach would be more likely than the adversarial process of English common law to facilitate the elucidation of a comprehensive picture of any failure in the care of a patient. These authors note, furthermore, that France has a greater range of potential criminal charges where personal injuries, short of death, have been caused by negligence.[31] Victims of such injury are able to choose the criminal process as a *partie civile* in order to get compensation for injury instead of having to pursue the equivalent of a civil action in tort for clinical negligence. Kazarian et al. suggest that this might have merit for victims of such injury seeking to hold negligent medical practitioners accountable. We certainly agree that there is no good reason to restrict the use of the criminal law to those cases where death occurs. Our primary reservation is that the threshold for prosecution should be appropriately high. Kazarian et al. make a similar point, citing the position of Professor Brazier that only recklessness should transform a civil wrong into a crime.[32] They also

---

[29] See 'Death by physician' The Patriot- News, November 2006. See also '10 Things you want to know about medical malpractice', Forbes, 16 May 2013.

[30] It has been suggested that, in 2013, 250,000 Americans died as a result of preventable mistakes: see M. A. Makary and M. Daniel, 'Medical error – the third leading cause of death in the US' (2016) 353 *British Medical Journal* i2139.

[31] M. Kazarian, D. Griffiths and M. Brazier, 'Criminal responsibility for medical malpractice in France' (2011) 27 *Journal of Professional Negligence* 188–99 (quotations all at p. 6); this paper derives from a major Arts and Humanities Research Council funded project, 'The Impact of the Criminal Process on Health Care Ethics and Practice', based at the universities of Manchester, Lancaster and Birmingham.

[32] M. Brazier, 'Criminalising medical malpractice', in C. Erin and S. Ost (eds.), *The Criminal Justice System and Health Care* (Oxford, Oxford University Press, 2007).

acknowledge that there is no evidence that greater use of the criminal law makes healthcare safer: 'Report after report indicates that blame cultures and fears of civil claims and disciplinary proceedings inhibits health professionals from being open about their own errors and those of colleagues.' Nevertheless, we have some sympathy with their position that there may be some 'untapped potential' to use the criminal law to achieve accountability for non-fatal injury. For example, they refer to the Mid Staffordshire scandal and suggest that wilful neglect would warrant criminal prosecution, and, as a general point, this seems sensible. They note that 'strong feelings can be generated when harm to a patient is seen to result from truly "bad" medical negligence' prompting pressure on the Crown Prosecution Service to prosecute health professionals for mal-practice. In such circumstances, they suggest, the French model could be emulated. We agree that the criminal law as currently applied in England and most similar jurisdictions is too narrow in scope to serve the popula-tion well. However, this is only one of the many limitations of the criminal law, and it would still be our position that, in most cases, the entirely justifiable public desire for greater accountability in healthcare could better be served by other means. If major reform were to be proposed to improve accountability in healthcare, we think effort would be better expended in other directions. For example, Oliver Quick has emphasised the importance of candour at both organisational and individual levels,[33] and we discuss some more proactive possibilities in Chapter 10. It is worth emphasising that we find the fact that there is no requirement in French criminal law for subjective fault particularly concerning, and we do not seem to be at odds with Kazarian et al. on this point.

A Special Case for Doctors?

It should be self-evident that the issues discussed in this chapter are applicable to all professional and occupational groups whose activities carry the risk of causing injury or death to others. Any person who causes death by an omission without lawful excuse to fulfil a particular statutory,

---

[33] O. Quick, 'Regulating and legislating safety: the case for candour' (2014) 23 *BMJ Quality & Safety* 614–18. Under the Criminal Justice and Courts Act 2015, s20, an offence of ill-treatment or neglect by a care worker has been created in England and Wales. It carries a prison term of up to 5 years for an indictable offence and up to 12 months or a fine for conviction for a summary offence. There is also a separate offence of ill-treatment or wilful neglect by a care provider. This offence, applicable to corporations, carries a fine together with a 'remedial' order as possible penalties.

or common law duty, may be guilty of 'culpable homicide'.[34] Typically, this will amount to manslaughter, unless there is credible evidence of an intent to kill, in which case a charge of murder may be appropriate.

A pre-requisite for charges of manslaughter is a dead person, and death is part and parcel of many fields of medical practice. The difficulty for medical professionals is that the nature of their work necessarily involves a duty to act in clinical situations that are often fraught with risk and considerable uncertainty. As we discussed in Chapter 3, the mortality rate for the emergency surgical repair of Type A dissection of the aorta is 11 per cent in good units, but without intervention death would be virtually certain.[35] In many, but not all, other occupations, the option not to proceed is often available. This may often also be true in healthcare, but with many patients who are acutely ill the best chance may lie in an intervention that is difficult and hazardous. Even with elective care, many treatments have inherent perioperative mortality rates that are actually quite high. For coronary artery surgery, for example, overall average rates of about 2 per cent are fairly typical[36] yet the average length and quality of life of appropriately selected groups of patients will be increased by this type of surgery. Anaesthesia and intensive care are integral to these interventions, and many of the drugs and techniques used in these specialities are inherently very hazardous. The combination of risk, complexity and tight coupling between actions and their consequences (see Chapter 2) may explain the apparent over-representation of anaesthetists and cardiac surgeons in the New Zealand cases. Except in times of war or major disaster, it is difficult to think of other occupations in which everyday work is associated with mortality rates of anything close to this magnitude. Similar comments apply in other specialities, but in some, such as neurosurgery, the risk of serious permanent disability may be more prominent than the risk of death. As discussed earlier, there is no less reason for serious non-fatal harm, such as damage to the brain or spinal cord, to evoke the interest of the police than death.

These considerations mark the working environment in which doctors, nurses and other health professionals must function as quantitatively

---

[34] See Crimes Act 1961, s 160 (2)(b) (NZ).

[35] K. Suehiro, P. Pritzwald-Stegmann, T. West, A. R. Kerr and D. A. Haydock, 'Surgery for acute Type A aortic dissection: A 37-year experience in Green Lane Hospital' (2006) 15 *Heart, Lung & Circulation* 105–12.

[36] POMRC, *Perioperative Mortality in New Zealand: Fourth Report of the Perioperative Mortality Review Committee* (Wellington, Health Quality & Safety Commission, 2015).

different from many other professional work contexts. Furthermore, perhaps because of the uniquely invasive character of some aspects of their work, and the trust bestowed on them, bearing, as they do, the deepest secrets of their patients' minds and bodies, doctors seem to be more readily singled out for prosecution even than nurses when things go wrong.

Thus, we think there are good reasons to be concerned if the law, or even prosecutorial policy, impacts unjustly on those who work in healthcare, but we do not think this implies that the solution lies in legislation that singles healthcare out for special treatment. As we have said, equivalent considerations apply to many situations and occupations. In its advocacy during the late 1990s the New Zealand Law Reform Group developed a firm position that there should be no special case for doctors. We agree with this position. The law should apply to all, in an even handed fashion, but in doing so it should reflect the reality that some people, for various reasons, provide intrinsically dangerous services or undertake intrinsically dangerous activities. In many cases, society needs these services. The fact that an activity is hazardous creates a duty to exercise considerable care, but the law should recognise the reality that all people make mistakes, even when trying, conscientiously, to be careful, and that the consequences of a mistake may be quite out of proportion to its moral culpability.

The Impact of a Prosecution

The impact of a criminal prosecution is unlikely to be good for any person, whether or not he or she is ultimately acquitted of a charge. As discussed above, there is a unique and substantial stigma associated with criminal prosecution. Equally importantly, criminal prosecution is often less helpful for patients than might be expected. The principles of criminal prosecution, including a strong focus on single events, the need to prove causation beyond reasonable doubt and questions of degrees of negligence whose definitions often seem circular must often lead to a bewildered sense of frustration, particularly when a doctor is found not guilty. Anecdotally, and from comments to the media, there is little doubt that many people who have lost loved ones end up feeling that the interests of justice have not been well served. Furthermore, there is unlikely to be any financial compensation for the families of victims, even if conviction occurs, and public acknowledgement of the losses that may have been suffered is also not guaranteed, particularly when a doctor is acquitted of criminal charges.

Of course, these concerns would not apply in the context of genuinely egregious behaviour. In such circumstances a conviction will rightly be seen by the patient's supporters as evidence that justice has been done, and may serve an important role in alleviating grievances, at least to some extent. Therefore, a great deal hinges on the decision to prosecute in the first place.

The Initiation of Criminal Charges

In most jurisdictions the initial decision to prosecute lies with the police. Criminal proceedings are started once a charging document has been filed in the lower court. In serious cases involving homicide, in most jurisdictions based on English common law, prosecutions are conducted by professional Crown Prosecutors who operate independently from, though often in conjunction with, the police. In some countries, the police have this responsibility, but this function is administratively distinct from both the investigation and uniform divisions of the force. In England, the Code for Crown Prosecutors, issued by the Director for Public Prosecutions, is a public document which lays out the general principles to be considered by prosecutors when deciding whether to charge a person. As in other jurisdictions based on the English common law system, there are two principal questions to be asked:

1) Is there enough evidence against the defendant? (The Evidential Test).
2) Is it in the public interest for the prosecution to be brought? (The Public Interest Test).

Crown Prosecutors are required to consider first whether there is sufficient reliable and credible evidence that can be used in court. There must be a reasonable expectation that an impartial jury (or judge), properly directed in accordance with the law, will be satisfied beyond reasonable doubt that the individual who is prosecuted has committed a criminal offence.[37]

Where a prosecutor is satisfied there is sufficient evidence to provide a reasonable prospect of conviction, he or she must then exercise his or her discretion in deciding whether prosecution is required in the public interest.[38]

---

[37] See, for example the New Zealand Crown Law *Solicitor-General's Prosecution Guidelines* 1 July 2013, at para 5.1.
[38] Crown Law *Solicitor-General's Prosecution Guidelines* at para 5.5.

The Role of the Coroner

At present, it seems that the usual sequence of events in many countries is for the coroner's inquiry to follow the conclusion of criminal proceedings. For example, in New Zealand a coroner may only report on a person's death and identity, and the causes and circumstances of the death. A coroner cannot determine civil, criminal or disciplinary liability,[39] but, as part of his or her role, must receive a report of a death from the New Zealand Police.[40] This would appear to prevent the possibility of a coronial inquiry being held *before* the police investigation occurs, and there may be sound reasons for this. However, a coronial inquiry is an inquisitorial investigation, not concerned to assign blame, but rather to determine the cause of death. An argument could be made that this is a process better suited to meet public expectations for appropriate accountability when things go wrong, and could be an ideal way of deciding which cases should be referred for prosecution. This would preserve the doctor's integrity in a non–stigmatic and non-adversarial manner, at least up to the point that clear evidence of seriously blameworthy behaviour had been established, and in most cases would allow a full investigation of causal factors outside the blaming culture that is typically implicated in a police prosecution.

The Frequency of Prosecution

While there is no rule that suspected criminal offences must automatically be the subject of prosecution, there is a presumption that the public interest *requires* prosecution where the criminal law has been contravened. Where there has been a sudden death involving apparent human agency, and where negligence in some form is implicated, prosecution is almost inevitable.

That there are prosecutions for medical manslaughter should, therefore, not surprise us. Harm from healthcare is a significant risk. In Chapter 2, we outlined evidence suggesting that the number of adverse events in healthcare is remarkably high, and that some of these events do contribute to the deaths of patients. To what extent, then, do the many errors that occur in healthcare result in prosecutions for manslaughter?

As we have explained, patterns of prosecution for medical manslaughter vary from jurisdiction to jurisdiction and from time to time. For our

---

[39] Coroner's Act 2006, s 4 (1)(e) (i) (NZ).   [40] Coroner's Act 2006, s 4 (1)(a).

purposes the experiences of New Zealand and the UK are illustrative. Such prosecutions have at certain times occurred at a much higher rate in the UK and in New Zealand than in most other comparable jurisdictions. The New Zealand experience has been outlined earlier in this chapter. In a well-known study published in 2006, Ferner and McDowell found that, since 1795, a total of eighty-five doctors had been charged with manslaughter in Britain, of which sixty were acquitted, twenty-two convicted and three pleaded guilty. However they also found a disconcerting increase in the numbers of doctors charged with manslaughter in England and Wales since 1990.[41] It is also worrying that, where doctors have been convicted, there seems to have been a trend towards quite severe sentences, including the use of imprisonment.[42] In three English cases since 2012, medical professionals, including a GP, a urologist and a general surgeon, were sentenced to imprisonment for manslaughter for periods ranging from two to two-and-a-half years.

An even greater concern lies with the nature of the conduct for which prosecutions were commenced. Ferner and McDowell observed that while most of the cases from the nineteenth century related to obstetrics, most cases in the twentieth century involved errors in the administration or prescribing of medicines. The introduction, in the twentieth century, of powerful, sometimes dangerous, medicines was suggested as the explanation for the majority of prosecutions during this period. While some cases during this period involved drunkenness, or 'brutal lack of skill,' many were attributable to mistakes or slips. Yet, as the authors correctly note:

> Slips are inherent to human cognition and are more likely to occur when an individual is tired, distracted or interrupted. They can only be prevented or minimized when the systems and processes in which doctors work are made safer. This is most likely to happen when practitioners are candid about their errors.[43]

In fact, in 37 of the 85 cases of doctors charged with manslaughter, the predisposing cause was a mistake (an 'error in the planning of the action'). Seventeen cases were classified as slips (errors 'in the execution of an action that often occur as a result of distraction or momentary failure of

---

[41] Ferner and McDowell, 'Doctors charged with manslaughter'.
[42] S. Edwards, 'Medical manslaughter: a recent history' (2014) 96 *Annals of the Royal College of Surgeons of England (Suppl)* 118–19.
[43] Ferner and McDowell, 'Doctors charged with manslaughter', 309–14.

concentration'). Three cases involved technical problems (failures 'to carry out an action successfully even where the plan of action and technique were appropriate'). About one-fifth of the cases (16) involved alleged violations.

A survey at about the same time as the Ferner and McDowell study, undertaken by Quick, and spanning the period from 1966–2005, revealed a total of sixty-four cases of manslaughter arising from the practice of healthcare in some form. The vast majority of these cases involved doctors. The bulk of the incidents identified (40) occurred between 1996 and 2005.[44]

In a more recent study, Ferner and McDowell report a subsequent apparent fall in the numbers of doctors tried for manslaughter on the basis of negligence, with a corresponding fall in the number of convictions.[45] Using media reports and data provided by the General Medical Council, the authors identified eight trials in England and Wales and three convictions in the years 2006–12, compared with twenty-three trials and eight convictions in the preceding seven years. They suggest that the fall in prosecutions is unlikely to be a consequence of fewer cases of patients being harmed through healthcare, but may reflect the difficulties with current English law on criminal negligence manslaughter. We will examine this claim as the chapter proceeds.

We have already outlined the situation in New Zealand. Professor Ron Paterson has suggested that, since the law change in 1997, there is 'no realistic prospect of revival of the use of the criminal law in this area'.[46] Paterson further suggests that most New Zealand patient advocacy groups, doctors and lawyers now agree that the criminal law should only be used in healthcare settings in cases of deliberate harm or gross negligence – for example, where a doctor is absent without leave while on call, or where the doctor is drunk on duty or where the physician 'blindly continues with a risky procedure without proper regard for the consequences'.

However, it is sometimes difficult to decide whether a failure in care has been so serious that a criminal conviction should be accepted as a possible consequence.[47] Dieneke Hubbeling discusses the role of moral

---

[44] Quick, 'Prosecuting "gross" medical negligence'.

[45] McDowell and Ferner, 'Medical manslaughter'.

[46] R. Paterson, The Good Doctor (Auckland, Auckland University Press, 2012) at p. 51. Our own view is that the law may well be used occasionally in the future, but only in cases that clearly meet the new 'major departure' threshold for negligence.

[47] D. Hubbeling, 'Criminal prosecution for medical error' (2010) 103 (6) Journal of the Royal Society of Medicine 216–18.

luck in determining whether a person gets punished or not. She notes that criminal prosecution is possible where there has been a clear objective rule violation – for example, where the person has consumed alcohol before driving. One can make an argument for prosecuting violations but not simple errors, but moral luck often determines the outcome of either an error or a violation, and it is outcome that also tends to trigger a prosecution. Hubbeling refers to the 'intuition' model, arguing that intuition suggests that because somebody has died, someone must have committed a criminal offence and, by implication, ought to be prosecuted. This is a form of *outcome bias*, which we discussed in Chapters 6 and 7. Clearly, moral luck, of itself, is not a reasonable basis for decision-making about errors in healthcare that contribute to a fatal outcome. It is simply too capricious a foundation for proceeding with a prosecutorial decision. Something more is needed.

Assigning Responsibility for Major Crime

By general agreement, criminal punishment is based on notions of subjective fault, in order to give proper expression to common perceptions of fairness. The subjective element is rooted in the common law idea of *mens rea*, or guilty mind, which tells us that, to be truly culpable, criminal conduct must be accompanied by a particular state of mind. This is usually expressed in terms of intention, knowledge, foresight or recklessness. The idea is that in order to be truly guilty of a crime, a person must have acted with a measure of subjective awareness or intentionality, so that it can be said that his or her mind went along with what was allegedly done. This state of mind may also be broadly described as *advertent* wrongdoing. Importantly, for the purposes of this discussion, it is generally agreed that criminal responsibility in most English common law jurisdictions is founded in a certain set of capacities, having both cognitive and volitional elements. In order to be responsible for crime, people must be in possession of, or be capable of being in possession of, 'the relevant knowledge or beliefs about the context in which they acted or omitted to act, and who had a fair opportunity to act otherwise than they did'.[48] While the *cognitive* conditions for responsibility typically include *actual knowledge* of facts, or *foresight* of consequences, it has always been a matter of some controversy whether it is enough that a 'reasonable

---

[48] N. Lacey, 'Responsibility and Modernity in Criminal Law' (2001) 9 (3) *The Journal of Political Philosophy* 249–76, at 255 (hereafter 'Responsibility').

person' could have acquired such knowledge or realisation, provided the defendant actually had the capacities of a reasonable person. The reasonable person standard, which is a test of *objective* liability, is the threshold indicator for negligence liability. Because the negligence standard invokes an objective test, it is generally eschewed as a basis for assigning criminal responsibility for serious crimes. Human beings, and the *subjective* attitudes they hold, are central to the theory of responsibility applied in most modern systems of criminal justice.[49]

Elements of Manslaughter

The crime of manslaughter is a serious offence, which, in many jurisdictions, carries life imprisonment as a maximum penalty.[50] This marks it as amongst the most serious of crimes, despite the very broad range of criminal conduct it potentially encompasses. New Zealand criminal law provides an interesting example in this regard, in part because it is codified. In New Zealand Law manslaughter is a form of *culpable homicide*, which may be committed by an unlawful act, or an omission, without lawful excuse to perform or observe a legal duty, or by both combined.[51] An 'unlawful act', at least for purposes of New Zealand law, must be a criminal offence, and is defined to mean a breach of any Act, regulation, rule or bylaw.[52] Generally, though not exclusively, an 'unlawful act' relates to public safety. To be unlawful, a relevant act must be accompanied by the mental state (*mens rea*) to make it an offence, and it must be done without lawful justification or excuse.

As an example of the sort of context in which unlawful-act manslaughter might operate in a medical context, consider the situation where ventilatory support is withdrawn from a patient who cannot breathe unaided. Provided the doctors are not in breach of any legal duty, and have a lawful excuse for discontinuing ventilation, turning off the ventilator may not amount to an unlawful act for the purposes of s160 (2)(a) of the Crimes Act 1961. For example, in *Auckland Area Health Board* v. *A-G*,[53] the New Zealand High Court held that there was 'lawful excuse' to discontinue ventilation when there was no medical justification for continuing that form of medical assistance. The Court held that it was not unlawful to discontinue if the discontinuance accorded with good medical practice.

---

[49] See Lacey, 'Responsibility', 255.   [50] See, e.g., Crimes Act 1961 (NZ), s 177.
[51] Crimes Act 1961 (NZ), s 160 (2).   [52] Crimes Act 1961 (NZ), s 2(1).
[53] [1993] 1 NZLR 235, 250.

As we have noted, in 1997 the Crimes Amendment Act added a new s150A to the Crimes Act 1961. This meant that liability for manslaughter by failure to perform a legal duty thereafter required proof of a 'major departure' from the standard of care expected of a reasonable person. Since 2012, where an unlawful act is based on proof of negligence, under New Zealand law a person performing that act will be criminally responsible only if the act is a 'major departure' from the standard of care expected of a reasonable person.[54] This law change reflects the decision of the New Zealand Court of Appeal in R v. Powell[55] whereby the 'major departure' test was held to apply not only to manslaughter by omission to perform a legal duty, but also to manslaughter under s160 (2)(a) by an unlawful act involving either carelessness or negligence.

As we have seen, prosecutions for medical manslaughter are currently rare in New Zealand, although since 2010 there have been at least sixteen unreported cases of manslaughter, encompassing a wide spectrum of manslaughter prosecutions in contexts other than healthcare, where the 'major departure' standard has been implicated. Nevertheless, experience with the 'major departure' test is still limited, and it seems that it may still contain some difficulties.

The Problem of Gross Negligence

However characterised, negligence involves a *failure* do what is required of a person. A person, P, is negligent if he or she fails to do what it would be *reasonable* to expect someone, placed in similar circumstances to P, to have done. It implies an *objective* standard, in that P's conduct is *objectified* and attributed to an impersonal reasonable person, who has no corporeal existence but who becomes a sort of litmus test as to whether P acted properly on this occasion. It means we do not have to try to look into P's mind to assess his or her motivations, intentions or knowledge. It is enough to know that the reasonable person would, or would not, have acted as P did to cause the harm or risk of harm that has occurred, whether or not P actually had a culpable mental state.

While such a distal objective assessment may be appropriate in some areas of the law (e.g. in assessing culpability for a minor driving infringement, where there is minimal stigma and public condemnation involved)

---

[54] See Crimes Amendment Act (No 3) 2011, in effect from 19 March 2012.
[55] [2002] 1 NZLR 666 (CA).

it is less clear that such a standard is appropriate for major crimes. These often carry a high risk of condemnation and loss of liberty where there is a conviction.

The problem is that objective negligence liability, sometimes termed 'culpable inadvertence', 'loses sight of the notion of blame which is the proper foundation of criminal law'.[56] Some commentators argue that negligence should *never* be the basis of criminal culpability because on a strict view a teleological construction of penal theory (means-end, conduct-harm) necessarily excludes negligence.[57] Because negligence implies inadvertence, and complete unawareness by the defendant of the dangerousness of his or her behaviour, it is doubtful whether negligence is a state of mind to which criminal culpability can properly attach.

Assuming, however, that the adoption of negligence as a standard of culpability in criminal law is now ubiquitous, and probably irreversible, what are we to make of 'gross' negligence, or its New Zealand counter-part, the 'major departure' test? Does that addition of the qualifier 'gross' give us breathing space, or is it as problematic as the expression it qualifies? Quick has noted that the term 'gross negligence' is notor-iously vague, to a degree that it leaves prosecutors struggling to apply the test to medical cases.[58] He suggests that prosecutors are reduced to using synonyms such as 'absolutely disgraceful', 'extra bad', 'totally unacceptable' or 'pretty abysmal' in the absence of any obvious or objective system for classifying the negligence associated with events as 'gross' or 'not gross'. This indicates 'prosecutorial unease' with gross negligence, and may be pushing some prosecutors towards working to the subjective recklessness standard.[59]

As Quick has pointed out in his magisterial study on medical man-slaughter prosecutions,[60] looseness of definition of the concept of 'gross negligence' has often left medical experts in disarray as they have endea-voured to assign an operational meaning to the term and to align that meaning with the facts of particular cases.[61] Indeed, the imponderable

[56] O. Quick, 'Medicine, mistakes and manslaughter: A criminal combination?' (2010) 69 (1) Cambridge Law Journal 186–203, 192.

[57] J. Hall, General Principles of Criminal Law (2nd edn) (Bobbs- Merrill, Indianapolis/ New York, 1960) 114.

[58] Quick, 'Medicine, mistakes and manslaughter', 193.

[59] Quick, 'Medicine, mistakes and manslaughter', 193.

[60] Quick, 'Prosecuting "gross" medical negligence', 421

[61] Quick, 'Prosecuting "gross" medical negligence', 446.

problems associated with defining what gross negligence actually means has led Quick to recommend that the offence of medical manslaughter be abolished.[62] In Quick's assessment the offence is too broad for prosecutorial judgement to be applied consistently, and this means that prosecutions impact very harshly on those 'operating in error-ridden activities who are exposed to risk of prosecution by virtue of their socially vital work, and often at the mercy of moral luck'.[63] What is true of 'gross negligence' may turn out to be equally true of the 'major departure' test, despite the view expressed that '[t]he major departure' is a 'good formulation and avoids any difficulties which might be thought to apply to the term "gross negligence"'.[64] While it is true that the 'major departure' test focuses on the behaviour rather than the result, it is arguably plagued by the same uncertainties and vagueness that bedevil the 'gross negligence' model.

In New Zealand, the prosecution of a Dunedin midwife for manslaughter in 2006 was said by Paterson to have had the effect of 'casting a chilling shadow over the health sector'.[65] The manslaughter charge resulted from the midwife's involvement as the lead maternity carer in the death of a baby following a vaginal breech delivery. As we explained, this case arose some years after the law change, which was expected to reduce the frequency, though not the importance, of such prosecutions, in appropriate cases. Paterson has argued that the prosecution was a backward step for the regulation of negligence by health practitioners in New Zealand for reasons of prosecutorial inconsistency, frustration of normal channels of accountability and the negative ripple effect of manslaughter prosecutions upon health practitioners' peer review processes. Of particular interest is that Paterson, a former highly regarded Health and Disability Commissioner and New Zealand Health Ombudsman, believes that a manslaughter conviction is an unhelpful form of accountability for a careless health practitioner whose acts or omissions have caused a patient's death. He says:

[62] Quick, 'Prosecuting "gross" medical negligence', 449.

[63] Quick, 'Prosecuting "gross" medical negligence, 449.

[64] New Zealand Medical Law Reform Group Submission to Justice and Law Reform Select Committee, Crimes Amendment Bill (No 5) 1996, 'Medical Manslaughter,' submission 5.n.

[65] Paterson, 'From prosecution to rehabilitation', 244. See also R. Paterson, 'Doctors in the dock,' *Medical Council News*, June 2006, 4. It is worth noting, however, that some observers, including ourselves, would only have been concerned if the result of the case had indicated a failure to recognise the new threshold of negligence; in fact, the verdict added to evidence that this new threshold is a reasonably high one.

If the rationale is to punish a wrongdoer, professional disciplinary processes seem better designed to that end. If the purpose is to recognise the
value of human life, and the tragedy of preventable death, that is better
achieved through coronial mechanisms designed for that very purpose.
If the aim is deterrence (to prevent the deaths of other patients in similar
situations), manslaughter prosecutions are an ill-conceived intervention,
as shown by the continuing deaths from administration of the anti-cancer
drug vincristine, notwithstanding highly publicised English prosecutions
of doctors who mistakenly administered it. If the goal is to provide
answers for grieving families, mediations or investigations by independent public officials such as a commissioner or coroner are more effective
to that end.[66]

Given the developments in New Zealand law, and the fact that the
position regarding prosecutions for medical manslaughter has now
remained stable in New Zealand for many years, why is the position
different in England and Wales, where medical manslaughter prosecutions seem, by contrast, to have increased over the earlier part of the same
period and still continue to occur on a regular basis? To understand why
this might be, it is necessary to consider broader patterns of attribution of
responsibility that may throw some light on the rationale for the urge to
punish errant physicians. What emerges from this discussion is not
a simplistic need to punish 'wrongdoers' but, rather, a set of complex
and nuanced rationalisations that have to do with the ways in which
criminal responsibility is attributed in particular circumstances and to
particular social groupings. This may be influenced by historical patterns
of attribution and by contemporary social influences, which dictate the
ways in which society evaluates the conduct of discrete types of offenders.

Character

In recent writing, Quick has commented on how the resurgence in the
relevance of character to questions of criminal liability may have consequences in the context of well-motivated health professionals who
make mistakes.[67] Quick suggests that this is likely to arise in practice
where knowledge and assessment of general character act as a 'natural
filter' for such cases in the first instance. On this basis, families, colleagues, investigators, prosecutors and experts 'may be swayed by evidence

---

[66] Paterson, 'From prosecution to rehabilitation', 246.
[67] O. Quick, 'Medical Manslaughter and expert evidence: the roles of context and character',
in Griffiths and Sanders, Bioethics, Medicine and the Criminal Law.

of what they perceive as good or bad character traits of the individual under suspicion'. It is suggested that, in addition to the nature of any failure in care, 'general impressions about character are likely to play a part in the construction (or not) of a criminal case'.[68] According to this analysis, assessments of character may influence prosecutorial decisions in two ways:

1) as judgements of a particular doctor's character *disposition* (i.e. whether he or she is arrogant, dishonest, unwilling to admit error, unapologetic, obnoxious, or the opposite of these vices); or
2) as a judgement of that doctor according to a particular racial and cultural profile.

Quick observes that using character perceptions to inform the assessment of gross negligence is problematic, in that '[e]valuating character is complex and character theory is arguably too rich and potentially unfair in the context of investigating fatal medical error'.[69] Equally, the use of racial and cultural background as an arbiter of character is highly problematic because of the danger of unfair discrimination against doctors from other jurisdictions based on issues as diverse as perceptions of language skills to ability to gain employment and better supervision in 'superior' hospitals. Quick's justifiable concern is that some experts who testify in medical manslaughter cases may be at risk of applying racist stereotypes where there has been an 'illegitimate blurring of ethnic origin on the one hand and character/conduct on the other'.[70]

Nicola Lacey has also noted the resurgence of 'character' attribution of responsibility in English criminal law. Character assessments of criminal responsibility focus on the *quality* of an offender's disposition as distinct from his or her *conduct*. Of particular relevance to the present discussion is the survival of 'status' as a basis for criminalisation founded upon character attribution. Although generally the criminalisation of status is eschewed in modern criminal law,[71] modern examples, including vagrancy and prostitution and 'regular recreations of "dangerousness" categories, show that the impulse to organize

---

[68] Quick, 'Medical manslaughter and expert evidence' 111.
[69] Quick, 'Medical manslaughter and expert evidence' 113.
[70] Quick, 'Medical manslaughter and expert evidence' 115.
[71] Though Lacey doubts that the history of status criminalisation in English law can simply be told as a story of decline. See N. Lacey, 'The resurgence of character: responsibility in the context of criminalization', in R. A. Duff and S. P. Green (eds.), *Philosophical Foundations of Criminal Law* (Oxford, Oxford University Press, 2011), 151–78.

responsibility-attribution along status lines is a pervasive one in the history of criminal law'.[72] In this regard it may be argued that the persistent tendency over the last thirty years to criminalise the accidents and errors of 'bad' doctors is simply a further manifestation of the dimension of character in attribution of criminal responsibility. Like inebriates and the feeble-minded in Victorian England, 'bad' doctors are persons of bad character and the 'good' public need special protection from their particularly pernicious form of evildoing. The essential reasoning, drawing on Lacey's analysis of character attribution, is that in addition to doing acts that are socially dangerous – making errors and committing violations – there is 'something additionally . . . wrong about being a certain kind of person, engaged in a certain kind of activity', namely, 'an aggravation of blameworthiness which justifies a special criminalization regime'. This form of 'character essentialism' operates on the assumption that there is a finite number of 'bad people' who are doctors who harm patients, and if we are able to 'take out' enough of them, 'the world will be a safer place for those of "good character", who alone deserve the full protections of the rule of law'.[73] While Lacey's analysis was undertaken with particular regard to the use of character responsibility in the context of terrorist prosecutions, her approach resonates with the criminalisation of errors and violations that contribute to patients being harmed.

Outcome Responsibility

Another theory of attribution of responsibility that may have relevance to this discussion is the idea of 'outcome responsibility'. The notion that being a cause of a particular outcome may under certain circumstances be a basis for attributing criminal responsibility has long exercised the thinking of legal philosophers.[74] Assigning responsibility on the basis of outcome stands in for concern with the social harms caused by crime.[75] The idea is that people are truly responsible for the outcome of their actions 'even when they are "accidental" in the sense that we could not

---

[72] Lacey, 'The resurgence of character', 161.

[73] Lacey, 'The resurgence of character', 164–165.

[74] See e.g. T. Honoré, 'Responsibility and luck: the moral basis of strict liability' (1988) 104 Law Quarterly Review 530–53.

[75] Lacey, 'The resurgence of character', 155.

have done otherwise than we did'.[76] According to this approach the results of our actions become part of our sense of identity, of who we are, so that while we may be related to 'unintended outcomes' differently from 'intended' ones, they still engage our agency in a morally relevant way. The issue, it seems is that there is an *emotional* need to attribute responsibility to *someone*, even if injury genuinely does occur accidentally. The proffered rationale in such cases is revealing. Lacey says: 'In the distinctive context of criminalisation, this identification with harmful outcomes which we cause is attendant on the pursuit of a *voluntarily assumed and risk creating activity*' (emphasis added).[77]

Adopting this analysis, it could be argued that the prosecution of medical professionals for medical manslaughter in cases of errors and slips are clear examples of outcome responsibility principally because these events occur within the context of a 'voluntarily assumed risk-creating activity' (VARA). It might be argued that VARA has thus become the paradigmatic basis of criminal responsibility in cases of medical manslaughter, often, it would seem, with only a marginal concessions being made towards actual evidence of moral fault.

In more recent writing, Lacey suggests why this might be. She suggests, on the basis of an hypothesis she has developed of criminal responsibility–attribution since the late nineteenth century, that 'patterns of responsibility-attribution relate to the *roles and needs* of a criminal justice system: to a political need for legitimation, and to a practical need to specify and co-ordinate the sorts of knowledge which can be brought into a court room' (emphasis added).[78]

As many writers have pointed out, attributing causation in medical misadventure is a complex and professionally demanding task, so focusing on outcome, regardless of the vagaries of 'moral luck', thwarts a more nuanced examination of causal factors and a proper evaluation of liability on the basis of the state of mind and the cognitive processes involved in the act in question. Not differentiating between different errors and violations eases probative problems for the courts, problems that might otherwise be seen as obstructing the law's broader purposes – namely, protection of the public against social harm.[79]

---

[76] N. Lacey, 'Space, time and function: intersecting principles of responsibility across the terrain of criminal justice' (2007) 1 *Criminal Law and Philosophy* 233–50.

[77] Lacey, 'Space, time and function', 239.

[78] See N. Lacey, 'Psychologising Jekyll, demonising Hyde: the strange case of criminal responsibility' (2010) 4 *Criminal Law and Philosophy* 109, 116.

[79] Lacey, 'Space, time and function'.

All this points to another factor. The increasing use of outcome-based practices of attribution applied to the prosecution of health professionals may be a product of a decreasing confidence in the ability of judges to manage attribution of criminal responsibility on the basis of subjective capacity-based judgements. As Lacey observes, in the context of 'increasingly complex, sophisticated and technical developments in the natural and human sciences, it may be that the compatibilism of criminal law judgments of capacity or opportunity is being increasingly unsettled by the suspicion that incontrovertible proof of the causally determined nature of much criminal conduct is not far in the future'.[80] Thus far, claims of deterministic causal reasoning have not significantly engaged the courts in relation to attributions of criminal responsibility. In a context as difficult as unintended but lethal harm in healthcare, where deterministic science has made little headway, it may be less demanding for legal professionals to simply rely on heuristic reasoning in resolving difficult problems of causation and scientific analysis, as has clearly been evident in attempts to assign meaning to concepts such as 'gross negligence' and what is 'reasonable'. This will lead some legal professionals to rely instead on 'ordinary common sense' as an 'unconscious animator of legal decision-making',[81] rather than doing the 'hard yards' associated with establishing relevant fault.[82]

Although the common law of crimes has long recognised a substantive defence of mistake of fact, this is seldom a relevant consideration in the context of fatal harm, where the threshold test is based on an objective standard of gross medical negligence, regardless of the offender's actual mental processing of the relevant facts. This is a curious anomaly, given the commonly draconian penalties available upon conviction for manslaughter in most common law jurisdictions. As Quick has rightly observed, the use of the notion of gross negligence is unusual among serious offences. It is 'a contested and controversial concept challenging the orthodox subjectivist demand for intention or recklessness as the appropriate form of *mens rea*, and criticised as inappropriate' despite the

---

[80] Lacey, 'Space, time and function', 248.

[81] M. L. Perlin, *The Hidden Prejudice: Mental Disability on Trial* (American Psychological Association, Washington, D.C., 2000) 16.

[82] Quick has noted that while 'medical' manslaughter is based on an objective standard of 'gross negligence', and is not dependent on evidence of a state of mind of conviction, prosecutors are often uneasy with the objective framing of the law and look for subjective fault. See Quick, 'Prosecuting "gross" medical negligence', 444.

substantial academic support for the idea that negligence should some-times be a basis of penal liability.[83]

Discretion and Prosecutorial Intuition – A Postmodern Problem?

A substantial element in Quick's study concerns the nature and exercise of prosecutorial discretion in medical manslaughter cases. This discretion is described as 'mandated flexibility' but, as Quick observes, discretion is also about power, accountability and justice.[84] Decisions to prosecute are influenced by decision makers' 'structure of knowledge, experience, values and meanings' and may be shaped by subjective values, in particular personal views about blame and desert, and good and bad, and their professional ideology. The suggestion that discretion may mean little more than the application of 'gut instinct' or a 'hunch' about a particular case is worrying. It may well mean that prosecutors rely on their own sense of right and wrong in deciding the meaning of gross negligence and in interpreting the opinion of medical experts.[85] Given the subconscious but powerful influence of prejudice discussed in Chapter 2, this thought is indeed cause for concern.

While it is not surprising that most of the prosecutions reviewed by Quick involved professionals operating in 'high risk settings' such as surgery and anaesthesia, a disturbing feature was the disproportionate number of non-white practitioners featuring in these prosecutions.[86] We have alluded to the role of racial prejudice earlier, in Chapter 3 and in our discussion on attribution of character. Quick speculates that this may be attributable to the fact that in the UK a higher number of foreign-trained doctors work in poorly performing hospitals, where in turn the ongoing opportunities for training are inferior to those provided in more sought-after institutions. These difficulties may be confounded by inade-quate language skills and the expectation that these doctors will exercise responsibilities beyond their levels of skill in the absence of adequate supervision,[87] which arguably creates a 'perfect storm' for medical mis-adventure to occur. This has led Quick to conclude that these doctors face an increased likelihood of making errors and committing violations that lead to harm, and of greater vulnerability to subsequent prosecution

[83] Quick, 'Prosecuting "gross" medical negligence', 421, 422.
[84] Quick, 'Prosecuting "gross" medical negligence', 429.
[85] Quick, 'Prosecuting "gross" medical negligence', 435–36.
[86] Quick, 'Prosecuting "gross" medical negligence', 436.
[87] Quick, 'Prosecuting "gross" medical negligence', 437.

because of prejudice (presumably often subconscious prejudice), and suggests that these factors add to other arguments pointing powerfully towards a case for abolishing gross negligence manslaughter.[88]

Another important factor in the prosecutorial discretion bears consideration. In reviewing the range of factors that might explain the increase in criminal prosecution, Quick notes that the crime of 'medical manslaughter' is beginning to achieve 'cultural recognition and acceptance'. This is a feature of society's changing social perceptions of professions and a decline in trust. Furthermore, the emerging phenomenon of lay knowledge of risks and errors may have led 'to an awareness of the limits of expertise, and represents a public relations problem for those seeking to maintain trust in expert systems'.[89] This rising suspicion of medical professionals and the corresponding diminution of trust is a feature of the postmodern malaise and the dominance of individualism. It has its parallel in the rise of 'popular punitiveness' in the realm of criminal justice, with the associated rise of the 'public voice' and the declining influence of social and legal expertise.[90] As part of a general 'anti-elites' attack, popular punitiveness portrays criminal justice agents, including judges, lawyers, legal academics and policy-makers, as being 'out of touch' with popular sentiment on matters of criminal justice.[91] The ascendancy of popular punitiveness has also been accompanied by a powerful movement favouring the interests of victims in criminal justice, whereby the risk of victimisation becomes, in a negative way, the catalyst for the construction of a sense of community.[92] As Madeleine Bunting has noted, the grand narratives of communism, socialism, neoliberalism, fascism and religion have foundered and shattered into 'a mosaic of millions of personal stories', in relation to which we have lost the capacity to create common narratives of idealism, morality and hope.[93]

According to Quick, in the context of patients being harmed, 'dangerous docs' have been demonised within a climate of rising complaints against healthcare professionals and media portrayals of the costs of errors and violations. This climate of increased suspicion of medical

---

[88] Quick, 'Prosecuting "gross" medical negligence', 437.
[89] Quick, 'Prosecuting "gross" medical negligence', 428, and see A. Giddens, *The Consequences of Modernity (Redwood City, Stanford University Press,* 1990) 130.
[90] See D. Brown, 'Recurring themes in contemporary criminal justice developments and debates' in J. Tolmie and W. Brookbanks (eds.), *Criminal Justice in New Zealand* (Wellington, LexisNexis, 2007) 7, at 28.
[91] Brown, 'Recurring themes', 28.   [92] Brown, 'Recurring themes', 31.
[93] M. Bunting, 'Where is the new vision to unite us?' *The Guardian Weekly,* 3 July 2009, 19.

professionals has probably had an impact on the way in which prosecutors have framed the factors relevant to the exercise of their prosecutorial discretion. Influences of this type do not appear to have threatened the long-established restraint in resort to the criminal law in medical contexts in Canada, nor indeed in Scotland. In New Zealand, new forms of accountability, the emergence of a strong patient safety movement and radical changes to systems of self-regulation by the medical profession have changed the way citizens regard and respond to errors made by the medical profession. This seems to have been associated with widespread acceptance of the virtual abandonment of prosecutions for medical manslaughter.[94] As noted earlier, in England and Wales, in recent years, there is some evidence that there may have been a fall in the numbers of health professionals facing charges of manslaughter arising from inadvertent harm to patients.[95] This is unlikely to be due to any decrease in deaths linked to errors and violations, so it is possible that there has been some alteration in prosecutorial policy. McDowell and Ferner suggest that this change, if real, may reflect the difficulties in obtaining a conviction under current English law on criminal negligence manslaughter. They refer particularly to the apparent circularity of the test of gross negligence, noting that 'it is a crime if the jury think it ought to be a crime'. They also refer to the increasing prominence of clinical teams in hospital medicine, commenting that the opportunity for error has been increased at the same time as responsibility has become more diffuse.[96] We have discussed the importance of teamwork earlier in this book, and have noted the problems inherent in communication and coordination that this brings. We would certainly agree that scapegoating an individual through criminal prosecution is profoundly unjust in the context of clinical teamwork, particularly when the individual is a junior doctor and those responsible for his or her training and supervision are allowed to go unscathed.[97]

We do not believe that the solution lies in the construct of 'corporate manslaughter'.[98] Instead, we think that this source of injustice is simply one more argument that the criminal law is poorly constructed to deal

[94] See Paterson, 'From prosecution to rehabilitation', 229.
[95] McDowell and Ferner, 'Medical manslaughter'.
[96] McDowell and Ferner, 'Medical manslaughter'.
[97] This has occurred on several well-known occasions in Britain.
[98] A. Samanta and J. Samanta, 'Charges of corporate manslaughter in the NHS' (2006) 332 British Medical Journal 1404–5.

with the majority of things that go wrong in healthcare. In this, we agree with the comments of Paterson, cited earlier in this chapter. It is interesting that, in the first corporate manslaughter case to be brought against an NHS trust (Maidstone and Tunbridge Wells NHS Trust in Kent),[99] the judge directed the jury to return not guilty verdicts on the basis of inadequate evidence on which to convict. He commented that it was understandable that the family of the patient who died from a postoperative cardiac arrest wanted to know why she had died, and wanted someone to be held accountable. He then said, 'But this is not a public inquiry into her death. It is a criminal trial with two defendants facing serious charges. The test for gross negligence manslaughter is very high and cases are rare. A misjudgement has to be so grave that it is a crime.'[100] This is exactly the point. In this case, questions of training and supervision of doctors below the rank of consultant were raised, and there is no question that these are important. However, criminal courts are not well suited to elucidate failures in the wider aspects of provision of patient care that really matter and need to be addressed, but are often somewhat poorly defined, may or may not constitute gross negligence, may be multiple and may be rather indirectly related to the patient's death. In Chapter 10 we will speculate on potential approaches to the regulation of healthcare that might be more effective for promoting safety and more just than either the civil or the criminal legal systems that pertain in many countries today.

A New Test – Recklessness

Paterson suggests that there is a place for the criminal law in clinical settings, but only a very limited place. He suggests that a health practitioner who kills a patient by *reckless* acts or omissions may warrant prosecution for manslaughter, but also suggests that in the 'vast majority' of unexpected patient death cases, more harm than good is likely to result from a manslaughter prosecution.[101] Similarly, Quick has argued that the bar should be raised to recklessness. This would represent a more onerous threshold for prosecutors, so it is likely that fewer prosecutions would result, and therefore fewer opportunities for assessments based on

---

[99] The charges included a locum consultant anaesthetist.
[100] C. Dyer, 'First case of corporate manslaughter against NHS trust collapses' (2016) 352 *British Medical Journal* i585
[101] Paterson, 'From prosecution to rehabilitation', 247.

character to creep in.[102] Subjective recklessness as the culpability threshold for medical manslaughter would provide better protection than the (allegedly objective) gross negligence standard against the risk of prosecution in weak cases.[103] Quick notes that one recent English appellate decision has favoured the view that a defendant's (subjective) state of mind is a relevant consideration in relation to the issue of gross negligence and will often be 'the critical factor in the decision'.[104]

Importantly, in England, the few cases that do lead to conviction tend to involve 'classic subjective recklessness'.[105] For example, in one case a defendant proceeded with a risky procedure despite warnings that it was too dangerous, and in another the defendant administered a fatal dose of adrenaline contrary to the advice of three colleagues. At the least, these were not unintentional errors made in the heat of the moment – they appear to have been examples of violations.[106]

Lessons from the New Zealand Medical Law Reform Group

In New Zealand, as we have noted, the Crimes Amendment Act 1997 was passed as the result of sustained advocacy by a small group of doctors and lawyers (the New Zealand Medical Law Reform Group), supported by substantial research, consultation and debate.[107] In its submission to the Justice and Law Reform Select Committee in 1996, this group made several key points, drawing on the deliberations of Sir Duncan McMullin, a former judge of the New Zealand Court of Appeal, appointed to review the issues. We suggest that some of these points pertain today, in all comparable countries, as much as they did then in New Zealand. These points are as follows:

1) No special case should be made for doctors: there are aspects of medical practice that place some doctors at greater than average risk for manslaughter prosecutions, but the principles at stake apply to all who have a duty to undertake dangerous things, notably including

---

[102] Quick, 'Medical manslaughter and expert evidence', 114.

[103] Quick, 'Medicine, mistakes and manslaughter', 199.

[104] See *R* v. *Misra and Srivastava* [2005] 1 Cr App R 21 and see O. Quick, 'Medicine, mistakes and manslaughter', 199.

[105] Quick, 'Medicine, mistakes and manslaughter' 201.

[106] See C. Dyer, 'Doctor who injected adrenaline against advice found guilty of manslaughter' (2009) 338 *British Medical Journal* 545; and see O. Quick, 'Medicine, mistakes and manslaughter' 201.

[107] P. D. G. Skegg, 'Criminal prosecutions of negligent health professionals: the New Zealand experience' (1998) 6 *Medical Law Review* 220–46.

(but not restricted to) nurses, police officers, rescue workers, fire fighters and airline pilots.

2) The fact that human error may have tragic consequences does not (of itself) mean that the errors were therefore a crime, but it does justify every effort to reduce recurrence of those errors. This depends, amongst other things, on a culture of open reporting and active engagement in the continuous improvement of patient safety.

3) As outlined in Chapters 2 and 3 of this book, error (being unintentional) cannot be prevented simply by trying harder, and draconian threats (such as that of criminal prosecution) are no more likely to succeed in deterring error than the possibility of dying in an aeroplane crash (such as that involving the Air France flight discussed in Chapter 1, for example). Instead, systematic initiatives, including those aimed at culture and communication, are the key to managing errors and reducing the harm that can follow errors and violations. It follows that the criminal law is ineffective in improving the safety of healthcare, and moreover that inappropriate criminal investigation actually impedes this objective by inhibiting openness in reporting errors, and by delaying or even preventing more sophisticated and comprehensive analysis of the underlying causes of the event in question.

4) Severe punishment is unjust in the absence of *mens rea*, and it is also unjust (not to mention illogical) to punish only the individual who actually makes a fatal error when various other people, multiple factors and a large element of chance have also contributed to the situation.

5) The situation in New Zealand in the 1990s and that in England and Wales in the first part of the current century were out of line with mainstream modern philosophy in relation to the law, ethics and patient safety.

6) Inappropriate resort to the criminal law often reflects a lack of public confidence in alternative means to ensure the accountability and safety of the activities in question: instead of investing in criminal prosecutions (which are typically very expensive) the focus should be on improving other aspects of the regulation of healthcare and the assurance of patient safety.

In this chapter we have reviewed the place of the criminal law in healthcare from a perspective informed by the events in New Zealand in the 1990s, and by a further twenty years of international experience and debate. Avoidable harm in healthcare is without doubt a very serious problem. On the other hand, contrary to some rhetoric, healthcare is becoming progressively safer as innovative improvements continue to occur in various aspects of the system.[108] Nevertheless, more progress is needed, urgently. This must include improved ways of facilitating and ensuring the engagement and accountability of all who work in healthcare, from hospital managers to those specialist doctors whose task it is to save lives through the exercise of their highly developed expertise at any hour of day or night, to the large army of supporting professionals each of whose contribution may safeguard or sabotage the outcome for any individual patient. As we have repeatedly emphasised, modern healthcare depends on teams, not on individuals. The criminal law is particularly inappropriate for regulating and enhancing team performance. New ways of thinking about the regulation of healthcare are required. In Chapter 10 we will go beyond the possibilities discussed in Chapter 8 into the realms of speculation. To extend the boundaries of the discussion we will discount the very real barriers inherent in any serious attempt to change long-established ways of thinking and doing things, and explore novel ideas to enhance the pursuit of excellent healthcare that the public can rely upon to be safe.

---

[108] For example, evidence for this can be found in the ongoing reduction of rates of mortality after surgery: see M. E. Semel, S. R. Lipsitz, L. M. Funk, A. M. Bader, T. G. Weiser and A. A. Gawande, 'Rates and patterns of death after surgery in the United States, 1996 and 2006' (2012) 151 *Surgery* 171–82.

10

Rethinking Accountability in Healthcare

Ideas about accountability in healthcare have not been static. The causes of unintended and avoidable harm to patients are varied and complex, and perceptions of how best to regulate healthcare have changed alongside changes in social values. For most of the last century there was a strong focus on blame for things that went wrong in healthcare. As we have seen, this often manifested through lawsuits or criminal prosecutions. Following the publication of the US Institute of Medicine's report, *To Err Is Human* (the IOM Report), the official patient-safety movement was born.[1] The IOM Report embraced a 'no blame' culture to underpin a comprehensive strategy by which government, healthcare providers, industry organisations and health consumers could reduce errors. However, it has become increasingly apparent that accountability of individuals within the system is also important, if only in respect of the expectation that everyone should engage fully in efforts to improve safety. Thus, the concept of a 'just culture' has emerged.[2] Repeated failures in the delivery of safe and appropriate healthcare (in many different countries) have been followed by initiatives and reforms intended to improve accountability and promote higher quality and safer healthcare. Numerous organisations and agencies have been established, either by governments or within the private sector, to promote these ends in different ways. Healthcare expenditure has increased dramatically over the same period throughout the OECD. Overall, the outcomes of healthcare are

---

[1] L. T. Kohn, J. M. Corrigan and M. S. Donaldson (eds.), *To Err Is Human: Building a Safer Health System* (Washington, D.C., National Academy Press, 1999).

[2] S. Dekker, *Just Culture: Balancing Safety and Accountability*, 2nd edn (Aldershot, Ashgate Publishing Limited, 2012); J. Braithwaite, R. L. Wears and E. Hollnagel, 'Resilient health care: turning patient safety on its head' (2015) 27 *International Journal for Quality in Health Care* 418–20; J. Reason, *Managing the Risks of Organizational Accidents* (Aldershot, Ashgate, 1997). The need for this type of just culture was the key message of the first edition of *Errors, Medicine and the Law*.

improving steadily, at least in high-income regions of the world. Yet far too many patients continue to be harmed, inadvertently, by the healthcare intended to help them and many of those who work in healthcare seem to feel demoralised and over-burdened by increased expectations for compliance with regulations and procedures whose value is often seen as unproven.

In Chapter 8 we discussed both the advantages and the limitations of the civil law in responding to the problem of iatrogenic harm in healthcare. We discussed different approaches to achieving the objectives of compensation and accountability, and to some extent (often secondarily) punishment. Punishment, of course, is a central objective of the criminal law. In Chapter 9, we noted that the criminal prosecution of practitioners whose patients die because of failures in care has increased in England and Wales in the new millennium and discussed reasons for this. There is no doubt that the public do sometimes see a need for strong measures when things go badly wrong. With this in mind, we considered suggestions for increasing the scope of the criminal law along French lines, to encompass harm that falls short of death and wilful neglect of the type seen in the Stafford Hospital scandal. However, the criminal law is poorly designed to regulate healthcare, or to deal with essentially well-motivated people who have simply made mistakes. In particular, we have advanced strong reasons to believe that it is not an effective deterrent to human error, which is by far the biggest single cause of harm from healthcare. Resort to the criminal law seems often to result in little more than a costly aggravation of the harm that provoked the prosecution, for patients and those close to them, and also for those who deliver healthcare. There is certainly little reason to believe that criminal prosecutions advance the cause of patient safety. In fact, the reactive nature of both the criminal law and the law of torts is a major limitation in that regard. Both also consume precious financial and human resources that could be better directed towards proactive efforts to make the healthcare safer and better in the first place. In Chapter 8 we made the fundamental point that the best way to respond to avoidable harm in healthcare is to avoid it – by ensuring that safe and appropriate care is provided to all patients who need it in the first place. None of the approaches discussed so far start from a stance of a proactive focus on improving the system.

In the conclusion to Chapter 8, we listed six objectives for a good system for regulating healthcare. In this chapter, we will consider ways to achieve these objectives, given a will to embrace the need for improvement. There are many barriers to progress and the challenges differ with different jurisdictions and different healthcare systems. One size does not fit all, and flexibility will always be required in the implementation of the various principles that seem to be important in the pursuit of well-regulated, affordable, safe, high-quality patient-centred healthcare. In Chapter 8 we acknowledged the importance of the underlying social culture in which healthcare and legal systems operate, and suggested that it will probably be easier to refine the existing system in any particular country than to implement radical change. Thus, the ideas that follow are given in the spirit of rethinking accountability in healthcare rather than as prescriptions to be applied mechanistically.

Bad Apples or Good but Fallible Doctors, Nurses and Hospital Managers?

The IOM Report took the view that most errors in healthcare were not the result of individual recklessness or carelessness. They were not usually a problem of 'bad apples', but instead reflected faulty systems, processes and conditions, which led people to make mistakes, or failed to avoid harm.[3] Furthermore, as we have seen in previous chapters, outcomes for patients seldom depend on individuals. Instead, outcomes usually depend on the collective functioning of groups of practitioners working with paramedical, administrative and other staff, supported by information systems and other forms of technology within organisations, whose resources and processes are strongly influenced by the policies and decisions of senior management and those responsible for governance. Blaming an individual practitioner who makes what is perceived to be a single error in a complex chain of events, and is thus seen to be in the position of holding the 'smoking gun', is often just an easy alternative to the more important imperative of identifying and addressing the underlying influences that made the errors and its consequences more likely. These influences may include the decisions and actions of the funders and administrators of healthcare, and of those responsible for the supervision of junior doctors. These are the influences that might well lead to future recurrences of the same events, even if an individual perceived as having 'done wrong' is sanctioned or replaced. They are also the influences that determine the overall culture of an organisation, and set the road to excellence on the one hand, or generalised failure of the

---

[3] See p. 2 of Kohn, Corrigan and Donaldson (eds.), *To Err Is Human.*

type seen in the Mid Staffordshire NHS Trust on the other.[4] Thus, the authors of the IOM Report took the view that the best way to avoid errors was to design health systems to make them more resilient. Wachter and Pronovost have recently restated this view:

> Most errors are committed by good, hard-working people trying to do the right thing. Therefore, the traditional focus on identifying who was at fault is a distraction. It is far more productive to identify error prone situations and settings and to implement systems that prevent caregivers from committing errors, catch errors before they cause harm, or mitigate harm from errors that do reach patients.[5]

The phrase 'trying to do the right thing' aligns with our definition of error in Chapter 3. We believe that the basic assumption that people are usually well motivated and also reasonably competent is an appropriate *starting point* for any response to harm in modern healthcare. Indeed, it is this basic assumption that has underpinned calls for a 'blame free' culture. The focus in such a culture would be entirely on the system and the importance of reporting to facilitate identifying opportunities for improvement. There is much to be said for this philosophy. It has facilitated risk management based on so-called 'improvement science', which usually implies some variation on the concept of 'rapid cycle improvement' along lines that have been articulated in an international standard:[6]

1) establish the context;
2) identify the risks (hence the need for appropriate monitoring of outcomes);
3) analyse the risks;
4) evaluate the risks;
5) treat the risks;
6) monitor the results and review the approach; and then
7) repeat the cycle.

---

[4] See the discussion of teamwork in Chapter 2, and L. A. Curry, E. Spatz, E. Cherlin, J. W. Thompson, D. Berg, H. H. Ting, … E. H. Bradley, 'What distinguishes top-performing hospitals in acute myocardial infarction mortality rates? A qualitative study' (2011) 154 *Annals of Internal Medicine* 384–90.

[5] R. M. Wachter and P. J. Pronovost, 'Balancing "No Blame" with Accountability in Patient Safety' (2009) 361 (14) *New England Journal of Medicine* 1401–6.

[6] Standards New Zealand, *Risk Management (AS/NZS 4360:1999)* (Wellington, 1999). This is a slightly more comprehensive statement of the idea of cycles based on Plan, Do, Check, Act (PDCA): see chapter 11 in B. Runciman, A. Merry and M. Walton, *Safety and Ethics in Healthcare: A Guide to Getting It Right* (Aldershot, Ashgate, 2007).

This is an iterative process, and consultation and communication are expected to occur at each step, to engage people in making the initiative really work, as well as to learn from each initiative. In this context many of the people who need to learn are experts who are actually responsible for patients and for carrying out the practices in question, so communication may be as much about clarifying expectations and understandings as about education, and should always be explicitly understood to be a two-way process.

A critically important group in all of this is, of course, the patients, or, more generally, the consumers of healthcare.[7] It has become increasingly apparent that the outcomes of initiatives to improve care are better when patients or their representatives are involved at every stage of the process. In the present context this begins with a duty to disclose when things go wrong. For patients who have been harmed, an acknowledgement that things have gone wrong and a sincere apology will often go some distance towards healing. In a more proactive context, patients know what matters to them, and may have unique insights into the best ways to ensure that things are done. Including patients (or consumers) in the planning and perhaps even in the implementation of the processes for improvement can substantially increase the likelihood of success.

For many instances of unintended harm in healthcare, notably those that involve the sorts of error made even by very well-intentioned people, a blame-free approach of this type is absolutely appropriate, and separating the response to the problem from any suggestion of discipline or reprisal facilitates the advance of safety.

However, it has become increasingly apparent that binary solutions – to blame or not to blame, to call to account or not to call to account, to punish or not to punish – are inadequate. A total prohibition on blame

---

[7] The term 'consumer' has gained popularity in this context and may sometimes be more appropriate, for example in relation to services for people with long-term disabilities who are not otherwise unwell. This term also includes those such as families, who may not be sick themselves but are intrinsically involved in the care of those who are. On the other hand, some of the people in need of healthcare are very ill indeed, and it is very difficult to consult such people at the time they are admitted, acutely, in extreme ill health. The word 'patient' does serve to underline the considerable vulnerability that is often characteristic of those who most need acute healthcare services. It is also relevant that most of the people who work in healthcare are themselves consumers of healthcare from time to time, so there is also an element of engaging with people from outside the system (sometimes called lay people) that matters in this context.

fails to recognise the distinction between errors and violations.[8] Blame is not appropriate for errors, but if violations of safe practice are allowed to persist without sanction, it is understandable that patients, hospital administrators and the public in general might feel aggrieved. After all, the improvement of patient safety is one of the major arguments for a blame-free culture, and tolerance of unsafe practice is not an obvious way to achieve that goal.

An important point about any systemic response to inadvertent harm in healthcare is that people are an integral part of the system. Some initiatives do not depend on people for their effectiveness – for example, pin indexing is an engineering solution to the problem of potentially fitting an incorrect cylinder to an anaesthetic machine, such as nitrous oxide instead of oxygen. It is a solution that effectively prevents this type of error without the need for any further human input. Other initiatives will only succeed in improving safety if people conscientiously engage with specified processes on an ongoing basis. Hand hygiene and The World Health Organization Safe Surgical Checklist (the Checklist)[9] are initiatives of the second type. Imperfect hand-hygiene practices on the part of hospital staff are likely to result in the transmission of infection from one patient to another, and thus in increased rates of hospital-acquired infections. The reduction of these rates will not be brought about by policies or posters that articulate good practices: it requires the people who care for patients to change long-established habits and become much more meticulous in their daily compliance with those practices. The Checklist goes beyond the checklists used by pilots and aims to promote teamwork and communication at the same time as preventing the omission of certain key steps during three phases of every surgical operation. There is a considerable body of evidence to show that its proper use can improve patient outcomes substantially.[10] However, its use will only avoid errors and improve safety in surgery in the hands of people whose brains are engaged and who participate positively in achieving all of its objectives. Mindlessly ticking boxes on a form will

---

[8] See Chapters 3, 4 and 5.

[9] A. B. Haynes, T. G. Weiser, W. R. Berry, S. R. Lipsitz, A. H. S. Breizat, E. P. Dellinger, . . . A. A. Gawande, 'A surgical safety checklist to reduce morbidity and mortality in a global population' (2009) 360 *New England Journal of Medicine* 491–9.

[10] For views on this, see for example J. D. Birkmeyer, 'Strategies for improving surgical quality – checklists and beyond' (2010) 363 *New England Journal of Medicine* 1963–5; L. L. Leape, 'The checklist conundrum' (2014) 370 *New England Journal of Medicine* 1063–4.

not achieve much, and hostile or reluctant compliance with the process may actually be counter-productive.

We do not, therefore, accept the idea that people have no responsibility for the safety of patients, and that only systems change will catch errors and mitigate harm. We are not alone. Since the IOM Report was published, academic thinking around the management of safety issues has moved substantially towards a model that balances the 'no-blame' approach with a renewed requirement for 'accountability'. Incompetent practice or egregious behaviour must be identified and dealt with. More than that, it is reasonable to expect those who work in healthcare to support, facilitate and participate in sensible initiatives to promote patient safety (such as those related to hand hygiene and the Checklist). Professor James Reason has long argued that 'a no-blame' culture is 'neither feasible nor desirable'.[11] In 1997, he wrote:

> A small proportion of human and unsafe acts are egregious ... and warrant sanctions, severe ones in some cases. A blanket amnesty on all unsafe acts lacks credibility in the eyes of the workforce. More importantly, it would be seen to oppose natural justice. What is needed is a just culture, an atmosphere of trust in which people are encouraged, even rewarded, for providing essential safety related information – but in which they are also clear about where the line must be drawn between acceptable and unacceptable behaviour.

Wachter and Pronovost recently provided an insightful analysis of how an appropriate balance between accountability and blame should be achieved.[12] The story of the *Keystone Project* provides helpful insights into this analysis.

Pronovost and the Story of the Keystone Project

Dr Peter Pronovost is an intensive care specialist[13] at Johns Hopkins Hospital in Baltimore. A central venous line (CVL) is a catheter introduced into major veins in the body, often running all the way into the chambers of the heart. These lines are sometimes used in very sick patients to measure pressures in the heart, and to administer drugs intravenously that cannot readily be given into more superficial veins, in the arm, for example. (We have discussed aspects of their use in

---

[11] See p. 301 of J. Reason, *Managing the Risks of Organizational Accidents* (Aldershot, Ashgate, 1997).

[12] Wachter and Pronovost, 'Balancing "No Blame" with Accountability in Patient Safety'.

[13] Also known as 'Intensivist'.

Chapters 1 and 7.) It was widely believed that a certain rate of infection (called central line-associated bacteraemia, or CLAB[14]) was an inevitable concomitant of the use of CVLs. Pronovost's team questioned this received wisdom. They did five things to reduce the risk of infection that were relatively generic and could apply in principle to many other interventions to improve patient safety. These were:

1) education – about the problem and the solution;
2) facilitation of compliance – they created a catheter insertion cart to make it easy for the doctor inserting the line to find everything he or she needed;
3) a checklist that outlined the essential steps for sterile insertion of the lines;
4) enforcement of compliance; and
5) checking daily whether the inserted CVL was still needed, and removing it as soon as possible.

The practice points on the checklist (hand hygiene, chlorhexidine skin antisepsis, maximal barrier precautions and optimal catheter site selection) were all supported by strong evidence and already well understood, but compliance with them was often poor. As discussed in Chapter 7, poor practice is frequent in healthcare, even when evidence-based guidelines have been developed and widely promulgated.[15] One might well ask why. Pronovost and his team sought answers in the literature on human factors, notably work by Cabana et al.[16] on barriers to the uptake of guidelines. Several important things emerged for improving compliance. First, the evidence supporting the requested practices should be convincing. Second, the relevant practitioners should agree that the problem mattered, and therefore that the response was warranted. Third, the things asked should be possible, and preferably easy, to do. Finally (the novel step), compliance should not be negotiable: thus, at

---

[14] In the United States, the acronym CLABSI is commonly used (for Central Line-Associated Bloodstream Infection).

[15] See, for example, E. McGlynn, S. Asch, J. Adams, J. Keesey, J. Hicks, A. DeCristofaro and E. Kerr, 'The quality of health care delivered to adults in the United States' (2003) 348 *New England Journal of Medicine* 2635–45; W. B. Runciman, T. D. Hunt, N. A. Hannaford, P. D. Hibbert, J. I. Westbrook, E. W. Coiera, . . . J. Braithwaite, 'CareTrack: assessing the appropriateness of health care delivery in Australia' (2012) 197 *Medical Journal of Australia* 100–5.

[16] M. D. Cabana, C. S. Rand, N. R. Powe, A. W. Wu, M. H. Wilson, P. A. Abboud and H. R. Rubin, 'Why don't physicians follow clinical practice guidelines? A framework for improvement' (1999) 282 *Journal of the American Medical Association* 1458–65.

Hopkins, nurses were empowered to stop the procedure if the doctor did not follow the items on the checklist.

The result was a dramatic decrease in the rate of CLAB, with an estimated saving of forty-three CLABs, eight deaths and nearly 2 million US dollars over five years. In the now famous Keystone Project, this initiative was then rolled out across Michigan, with similar success, across the whole state.[17] Similar improvements have subsequently been achieved elsewhere – in New Zealand, for example, where CLAB has not been completely eliminated, but its incidence has been reduced to a tenth of the levels formerly considered acceptable.[18]

The example of CLAB is somewhat unusual in that an important problem was amenable to a relatively simple 'bundle' of practices. Also, the outcome (infection) was relatively straightforward to measure. Many problems that beset healthcare are more difficult to deal with. Evidence is often absent or unclear. Context is important, and a rule that might apply in one situation might be unhelpful in another. Nevertheless, two key messages from the Keystone Project are instructive.

The first message is that received wisdom about the inevitability of current complication rates should be questioned. If the rate of CLAB could be reduced dramatically, why not the rates of other hospital-acquired infections – for example, those occurring after hip and knee replacements? Why not the rates of other types of complication too – for example, the rate of stroke after cardiac surgery?

The second message relates to normalised deviance. Practices for inserting CVLs were often poor, despite the fact that evidence to support better ways of doing things was already to hand and reasonably well known. It is true that the strength of evidence is more compelling now and that a return to previous practices would probably not be tolerated today. Nevertheless, practices related to the use of CVLs were not to an acceptable standard in the past. A key (and controversial) part of the

---

[17] P. Pronovost, D. Needham, S. Berenholtz, D. Sinopoli, H. Chu, S. Cosgrove, ... C. Goeschel, 'An intervention to decrease catheter-related bloodstream infections in the ICU' (2006) 355 *New England Journal of Medicine* 2725–32.

[18] J. Gray, S. Proudfoot, M. Power, B. Bennett, S. Wells and M. Seddon, 'Target CLAB Zero: A national improvement collaborative to reduce central line-associated bacter-aemia in New Zealand intensive care units' (2015) 128 *New Zealand Medical Journal* 13–21.

initiative was the non-negotiable expectation for compliance with the items on the checklist. This point supports the idea that practitioners should be held accountable for at least some aspects of their practices. Accountability lies at the heart of the concept of a just culture.

Unfortunately, good news does not necessarily travel fast. It might be expected that every practitioner in the world who inserts CVLs would have read the publication reporting the results from Michigan, and that most (at least) would have adopted the bundle of best practices immediately. Not so. In New Zealand, for example, the work of Pronovost's team to achieve change had to be repeated though a national initiative. Inertia is a powerful bedfellow of poor practice.

Wachter and Pronovost have identified several other practices that could contribute substantially to reducing patient deaths and injury if they were applied more consistently. These include:

- marking the surgical site to prevent wrong site procedures;
- compliance with hand hygiene protocols;
- following guidelines for handover at the end of shifts; and
- performance of 'time out' during surgery, before the incision is made.[19]

In the domain of spinal surgery, Casey[20] has listed events that are strongly influenced by inadequate practices:

- infection;
- caudal equina injuries (compression of the spinal nerve roots in the tail bone);
- damage to the spinal cord; and
- missed fractures.

We have already alluded to the problem of poor hand hygiene amongst hospital staff in the transmission of infection from patient to patient. The first global challenge of the World Health Organization, 'Clean care is safer care,' was a major international effort to improve hand hygiene in hospitals.[21] Again, enough evidence has long been available to

---

[19] Wachter and Pronovost, 'Balancing "No Blame" with Accountability in Patient Safety'. Note that 'time out' is a component of the WHO Safe Surgical Checklist.

[20] A. T. H. Casey, 'The ugly face of medical negligence: where has justice gone?' (2014) 23 (Suppl 1) *European Spine Journal* S1–S3.

[21] D. Pittet and L. Donaldson, 'Clean care is safer care: the first global challenge of the WHO World Alliance for Patient Safety' (2005) 26 *Infection Control & Hospital Epidemiology* 891–4.

demonstrate the importance of hand hygiene in reducing infections. Unfortunately, hand hygiene amongst those who care for patients in hospitals has tended to fall far short of the standards that are required: absolute perfection is probably unnecessary, but consistently good hand hygiene[22] has been shown to reduce hospital associated infections considerably. In part, poor practice in the past reflected inadequate facilities for hand hygiene. In at least some countries today, this barrier to good practice has been removed. Dispensers of alcohol-containing solutions or gels (and soap and water) are readily to hand when needed. This goes to the point that making the right thing easier to do is a key element of improving compliance. Thus, action was required, not only from clinicians but also from hospital managers supported by hospital leadership. The whole 'team' matters, and, as we have indicated several times in this book, the team can be very large: in this example, the WHO led the way with its international 'Global Challenge'. National agencies responsible for the quality of healthcare ran campaigns to promote hand hygiene and established national processes to audit hand hygiene practices and associated rates of relevant infections.[23] Improved outcomes have been achieved, although slowly and often only to a limited degree.

It is easy to find many examples where outcomes could be improved for patients through better compliance with particular aspects of good practice. Part of the difficulty lies in determining which practices really matter. Another part lies in ensuring that everything necessary for any particular practice is readily accessible and well maintained. However, the greatest part lies in achieving compliance once agreement on particular aspects of appropriate practice has been achieved, even after compliance has been made easier. Punishment was not a prominent feature in any of the above examples, but there was an insistence on compliance, backed up by substantial efforts to make expectations clear and to explain the reasons for them.

---

[22] The term 'hand hygiene' is used because the quick application of an alcohol-containing gel or liquid is often adequate, and actual *washing* is only necessary from time to time, notably when hands actually become soiled.

[23] See for example: S. P. Stone, C. Fuller, J. Savage, B. Cookson, A. Hayward, B. Cooper, . . . A. Charlett, 'Evaluation of the national Cleanyourhands campaign to reduce *Staphylococcus aureus* bacteraemia and *Clostridium difficile* infection in hospitals in England and Wales by improved hand hygiene: four year, prospective, ecological, interrupted time series study' (2012) 344 *British Medical Journal* e3005.

The Concept of a Just Culture

The term 'just culture'[24] has been coined to express a balanced approach to accountability in healthcare in which the inevitable failures that occur in complex systems that include humans are distinguished from the much less frequent actions or decisions that may justifiably be considered blameworthy. The former should be dealt with without blame, but a proportionate element of sanction may well be appropriate for the latter. Today, there seems to be a broad consensus in many industries, notably including healthcare and aviation, that diligent professionals seeking to the do the *right* thing should not usually be punished when things go wrong. On the contrary, they should be encouraged to report errors and mistakes openly, without fear, as part of their contribution to ongoing efforts to improve safety. Punishment should be reserved for those whose acts, in Reason's terms, are egregious, suggesting a high level of culpability. Algorithms have been developed to assist with making this distinction.[25] These algorithms may be more difficult to apply in practice than one might at first imagine. The value of an open culture in which everyone feels part of a concerted effort to ensure the safety of patients without undue fear for their own safety is considerable. Therefore, care is needed in deciding where the line should be drawn between the appropriateness or otherwise of sanctions: there should be little room for doubt in cases deemed culpable. Of course, decisions and actions do not fall neatly into two categories. Rather, they are spread along a scale. We have expressed this idea in Chapter 5 by describing five levels of blame. At the extreme ends of the scale, the appropriate response will be easy to identify and understand. At the boundaries between levels it may be harder to know whether a particular event should be placed above or below the line. Algorithms alone are not enough: expertise, experience and judgement is required. It is therefore critically important that an organisation aiming for a just culture invests adequately in developing the required capacity to handle the processes of deciding how any particular event should be managed. All (or at least the vast majority of) members of staff

---

[24] D. Marx, *Patient safety and the 'just culture': a primer for health care executives* (New York, Columbia University, 2001); S. Dekker, *Just Culture: Balancing Safety and Accountability*, 2nd edn (Aldershot, Hampshire, Ashgate Publishing Limited, 2012); J. Reason, 'Achieving a safe culture: theory and practice' (1998) 293 *Stress* 302–6.

[25] See, for example, J. Reason, *Managing the Risks of Organizational Accidents* (Aldershot, Ashgate, 1997).

should be confident in the process and in the people responsible for the process.

Most of the essentials for safe practice are well established in health-care. In particular, systems for training health professionals of all kinds and ensuring that they are properly qualified to enter practice are well developed. Most problems that arise (at least in well-resourced countries) seem to relate less to ensuring adequate expertise in the first place than to the maintenance of competence in the longer term, and to failures in compliance with certain procedures and standards that are widely held to be important for patient safety – participation in the Checklist and proper compliance with hand hygiene, for example. Abusive or bullying behaviour has recently received considerable attention as a problem in healthcare in Australia and New Zealand.[26] This could be seen as a slightly different matter, but it may be a manifestation of a common underlying attitudinal problem, and at any rate should not be tolerated. The question, then, is how best to deal with those practitioners who fail to maintain expected standards of practice and behaviour?

In the example of CLAB, it is interesting that substantial improvement in practice was achieved without needing to punish anyone for his or her previously poor practices. In part this suggests that properly explaining and articulating expectations, and gaining the agreement of relevant practi-tioners about their importance, can achieve much. However, given that this was done, it is at least arguable that an essential element to the success of the Keystone Project was that compliance with required processes was not negotiable. It is necessary to win the hearts and minds of highly trained experts if one expects compliance, but having done so it seems reasonable to set clear expectations and insist that they are met and facilitate the actions so that they can be met. The establishment of a just culture must mean that no one will be punished unfairly for (unintentional) errors, but it must also mean that deliberately poor practice will not be tolerated. Therefore, we need to consider the question of sanctions.

Sanctions in the Context of Healthcare

A key element of a just culture is the concept of *proportionality in sanctions*. The legal and regulatory consequences of an act or decision

---

[26] See, for example, Expert Advisory Group on discrimination, bullying and sexual harass-ment, Report to the Royal Australasian College of Surgeons (2015) http://www.surgeons.org/media/22086656/EAG-Report-to-RACS-FINAL-28-September-2015-.pdf, accessed 11 January 2017.

should be proportionate to the level of culpability involved. Indeed, when blameworthiness is low, the response may be better framed as remedial than punitive.

As we pointed out in Chapter 4, a low risk of serious consequences is usually less effective in changing behaviour than a much higher risk of minor consequences. Thus, spot checks and fines are more effective in improving compliance with various aspects of road safety than the terrible (but improbable) prospect of death in a car or motorcycle crash. This raises the idea of regular proactive audits in healthcare to monitor compliance with safety rules or of regular tests of important aspects of expertise or technical competence. This idea may seem novel to many health professionals. Many practitioners, particularly doctors, hold dear their perceived right to autonomy in practice. They might acknowledge the appropriateness of punishment for major transgressions, but many might be less convinced about the justification for minor punishments of minor transgressions. This idea might well be construed as undermining their professionalism. One answer to this, of course, is that it is the transgressions themselves that undermine their professionalism, not the consequent sanctions (so long as the sanctions are appropriate in nature and severity). However, this answer may not be well received by all practitioners. To make matters more difficult, in many parts of the world, there has long been a shortage of doctors.[27] This shortage may have increased the sense of invulnerability of some individual doctors – in the past many organisations would have found it very difficult to replace a dismissed doctor, and even the thought that a doctor might became disaffected and leave of his or her own volition may have acted as a restraint on justifiable criticism. This situation may well be changing in some countries, with far more doctors produced today than in the past, but at any rate, considerations of this sort are not adequate reasons to tolerate poor practices. Rather, they may add to other reasons for careful thought on how best to achieve an agreed way of managing the need for compliance with certain specified standards and behaviours.

It is worth turning to other industries for inspiration. For example, commercial pilots are expected to undergo regular training and tests in flight simulators; if they fail one of these tests, they are taken off flying.

---

[27] It is interesting that shortages of nurses have also been quite common but these shortages do not seem to have produced quite the same cultural response.

This may sound harsh, but further training is promptly instituted, followed by further testing, with a view to returning the pilot to a state of competence and to work. Dismissing the pilot without a reasonable attempt at remediation would be unduly harsh. As with doctors, it would also be an unattractive option for the airline: pilots, like doctors, take years to train. Thus, this approach of regular training, testing and retraining is in the interests of all concerned: the airline, the public and the pilots. Importantly, even the prospect of a short period off work seems to be sufficient to provide substantial motivation to maintain expertise and competence. This prospect functions as a sanction, but a sanction whose aim is not so much to punish the pilot as to protect the public (and, arguably, the pilot and the airline as well). It is a sanction based on a reasonable proposition grounded in the professional activity in question – in this case, that pilots should not fly unless able to demonstrate their competence to do so safely. In fact, this principle is strongly embedded into airline culture and extends far beyond the requirement for regular training and testing. For example, a refusal to participate in prescribed safety practices (such as the use of checklists) while flying would certainly not be tolerated, even by fellow pilots.

There are some somewhat similar examples in healthcare. The Australian and New Zealand College of Anaesthetists has a well-established programme for the maintenance of professional competence within a framework of continuing professional development. Certain skills are expected of specialist anaesthetists. Four particularly important examples of these skills have been identified. For example, one of these skills is the ability to manage a patient with a 'difficult airway'. Anaesthesia often involves administering drugs that paralyse the muscles by blocking the junction between muscles and nerves. The paralysis makes it impossible for the patient to breathe, so the anaesthetist must ventilate the patient's lungs using specialised equipment. Usually a tube will be placed through the mouth or nose and into or just above the trachea to facilitate this. Placing the tube is a little difficult to do in any patient, but occasionally it is very difficult and, rarely, the anaesthetist may not be able to maintain oxygenation of the patient at all. Failure in oxygenation results in rapid brain damage and death, and is a rare, but feared, complication. It is now expected that training in the advanced skills required to deal with this sort of problem will be undertaken regularly, typically through simulation (as in the airline example). Unless evidence is provided that appropriate training has been taken for two of the four skills at least once within every three years, it is no longer possible to obtain certification for completion of CPD. Most hospitals in Australia and New Zealand require this certification before providing privileges to practise. In contrast with the airline industry, however, the training typically provides formative feedback, but there is still no requirement to pass a summative assessment. Furthermore, it may be questioned why evidence of the maintenance of all four skills is not required in every three year cycle.[28] Nevertheless, this approach includes proactive identification of important risks, the development of a process to address them, and insistence on compliance in participating in that process. It is a major step in the right direction, and (interestingly) seems to have been welcomed by most anaesthetists in this college. It is interesting to speculate that the obvious relevance of the four skills to patient safety is more compelling than the theoretical benefits allegedly associated with regular critical reflection on one's own practice – a feature of the previous iteration of this programme that has now been reduced in prominence. It seems likely that participants in this programme to maintain professional standards might well accept an equivalent approach to that of the airline industry. There is a strong argument to support the idea that a failure to demonstrate adequate proficiency in an essential skill should result in suspension of practice until remediation has been achieved.

Wachter and Pronovost have taken these ideas in a slightly different direction and suggested some putative penalties for more general failures to comply with expected best practices. For example, in the context of hand hygiene, they suggest 'education and the loss of patient-care privileges for 1 week'.[29] This approach shifts the emphasis from one of proactive training and testing of core skills to one on monitoring practice and behaviour and responding to problems as they arise. We will expand on the topic of monitoring the performance of practitioners later in this chapter. For the present, our interest is in the question of enforcing compliance with good practices. Wachter and Pronovost explain that their proposed scheme of punishments is only intended to be indicative and illustrative. Locally relevant approaches would obviously be needed, but the central idea that

---

[28] The programme is regularly reviewed – the current version reflects a particular stage along an evolutionary process.
[29] Wachter and Pronovost, 'Balancing "No Blame" with Accountability in Patient Safety', at 1405.

unsafe practice should not be tolerated is closely aligned to the approach taken by the airlines.[30]

There is a difference between regular tests of competence in a classroom or simulator and audits of unsafe practices of people while actually at work. In the former case, with the pilots, return to work depends on the successful completion of remedial training in a simulator and then passing an appropriate test. The whole process is grounded in a sequence of steps that includes identifying a deficiency in competence, stopping flying, taking steps to address the deficiency, demonstrating a return to competence, and then returning to flying. The duration of the period of the suspended right to fly depends not on any assessment of culpability but on the practical considerations of retraining and retesting, and could vary substantially. In the medical context, with the suggestions of Pronovost and Wachter, the duration of the sanction seems to be a more arbitrary matter, motivated by notions of declarative punishment rather than the time taken to complete remedial training. This difference may reflect a difference in the nature of the failing in question: a repeated failure to comply with hand-hygiene requirements (for example) is not typically a matter of competence or knowledge: it is one of attitude. Thus, the purpose of the proposed sanctions appears to be primarily one of deterrence and enforcement. It is unclear how an airline would handle a similar situation, in part because the culture in commercial aviation makes it very unlikely that a pilot would simply flaunt a prescribed procedure: as we have observed above, such behaviour simply would not be tolerated. Once again, this point brings into focus the importance of grappling with the widespread view of compliance as optional for many aspects of safety-oriented procedures in healthcare.

In Chapter 4 we outlined an initiative in Colombia, where a department of anaesthesia has introduced a system of fines for common minor offences, such as arriving late for the start of a list. Absolute liability applies (i.e. no excuses are accepted), but the fines are reasonable in magnitude and are put into a jointly held account to support discretionary activities for the department, including research. These minor sanctions have apparently been very successful in improving compliance

---

[30] Wachter and Pronovost, 'Balancing "No Blame" with Accountability in Patient Safety'. In some institutions a week without operating privileges might be viewed as a vacation rather than a sanction, although this may be offset by the impact of the punishment on the practitioner's reputation.

with certain expected behaviours.[31] It does not seem likely that this precise approach would be readily embraced in many other parts of the world. On the other hand, it does show that behaviour can be shifted with the aid of a very low level system of sanctions, particularly in an already well-motivated group of professionals. Perhaps all that is needed is a firm head of department willing to take minor offenders aside and have an appropriately framed conversation with them. In a professional context, we think that such conversations would be taken seriously by most people, particularly if it was understood that further steps would follow if the offending continued. Departments with strong heads willing to insist on proper practices are far from unknown, but there seems to be considerable room for this aspect of clinical leadership to be strengthened. Ideally, it should permeate the culture of the entire organisation.[32]

Wachter and Pronovost underpin the idea of proportionate sanctions with a series of principles that increase the reasonableness and obvious validity of the sanctions. These would apply irrespective of the exact details of any particular sanction, and may contribute to informing the choice of sanction. First, there has to be an important clinical reason for the required practice (e.g. in the case of hand hygiene, infections, which are indisputably a serious problem). The practice must be supported by good evidence (e.g. hand hygiene has been shown to influence the rate of infection). Clinicians must have been educated about both the importance of the problem and the justification for the practice. The practice must be possible and should be facilitated (in this example, by providing hand gel containers widely). Consultation and the development of consensus are critical if change is not only to be achieved, but also to be sustained. This consultation should cover the practice, the steps needed to make it easy, the methods of audit and the sanctions for non-compliance. There should be no question of imposing unfounded and arbitrary rules, and no one should be taken by surprise. A distinction should be made between occasional inadvertent failure to comply and recidivist or deliberate behaviour. The first step for failed compliance should be a warning, perhaps with counselling. At some point, however, repeated transgression should trigger at least the possibility of an explicit sanction and further transgressions should result in an escalation of the level of sanction, leading ultimately to the possibility of dismissal, or, more generally, loss of licence to practise. Each situation should be

---

[31] Ibarra, P., 2015: personal communication.   [32] See footnote 4.

assessed on its merits, and serious punishment should very rarely be needed, but once reasonable expectations have been agreed and made clear, compliance should not be optional.

This discussion has included two related but different issues. One relates to unsafe behaviours in clinical practice, such as non-compliance with prescribed processes to improve safety or enhance outcomes. The other relates to competence and expertise. An overarching idea lies in the notion of a commitment to achieving acceptable outcomes for patients. Actually, the aspiration should be for excellent outcomes, not just acceptable ones. If excellent outcomes can be demonstrated, important failures in competence or behaviour will be unlikely. This raises the important question of monitoring and reporting the outcomes achieved by practitioners, institutions and nations.

The Public Reporting of Data on Surgical Outcomes

One of the consequences of the Bristol enquiry in the UK was the publication of outcome data for individual cardiac surgeons.[33] Today, it is possible to access results for index procedures by individual cardiac surgeons in the UK and some states of the United States. There are three potential reasons to report data of this type: to ensure that each surgeon is practising safely, to promote transparency in healthcare and to inform choice for individual patients. The open publication of individual practitioners' results may also provide a form of reward or sanction for performance: reputation and, possibly, success in private practice are at stake. However, this practice is controversial, and it is worth considering its merits in more detail.

Our principal concern is to promote safer and better outcomes for patients. Risk-adjusted mortality for coronary artery surgery has decreased in Britain since public reporting of outcome data was adopted.[34] However, the extent to which this improvement can be attributed to public reporting is not clear. The process has included the

---

[33] The events involving paediatric cardiac surgery in Bristol are outlined in Chapter 1. In respect of reporting data on surgical outcomes, see B. Keogh, 'The legacy of Bristol: public disclosure of individual surgeons' results' (2004) 329 *British Medical Journal* 450–4.

[34] B. Bridgewater, A. D. Grayson, N. Brooks, G. Grotte, B. M. Fabri, J. Au, . . . B. Keogh, 'Has the publication of cardiac surgery outcome data been associated with changes in practice in northwest England: an analysis of 25 730 patients undergoing CABG surgery under thirty surgeons over eight years' (2007) 93 *Heart* 744–8.

establishment of a cardiac surgical database to provide the reported results and the benefit of this information may not depend on public disclosure: it may be that simply knowing one's own results and those of others is enough to drive improvement. Also, there have been many incremental improvements in the surgical, anaesthetic and perioperative management of patients undergoing cardiac surgery over the period in question that have nothing to do with public disclosure. The truth is that the results of all forms of surgery are gradually improving, whether publically disclosed or not.[35]

Appropriate statistical interpretation is important if data of this type are to be used to monitor the performance of individual practitioners. The key point is that valid statistical conclusions in this context require surgeons to perform a certain minimum number of essentially similar cases with a high enough rate of a measurable and relevant outcome or complication (such as death). Small numbers may lead both to false positive and false negative conclusions. Obviously, the case mix of one surgeon may differ from that of another. Often more experienced and skilled surgeons will take on a greater proportion of high-risk cases. Thus, standardisation and risk adjustment are both important. Cardiac surgery lends itself to this sort of analysis because it includes several relatively standardised operations with relatively high mortality rates – notably coronary artery bypass grafting, which has a mortality rate of 1–2 per cent in many units. Even in this speciality it seems that, in the UK, surgeons would have to perform three times their typical number of coronary procedures to generate enough power to detect a poor performer eight times out of ten. In most other surgical specialities the numbers of standardised procedures with adequately high rates of mortality are totally inadequate for this purpose.[36] Furthermore, in some specialities, mortality may be less important than morbidity. In Chapters 7 and 9 we made the point that in neurosurgery, for example, various manifestations of brain damage are more common, and probably more feared, than death. Complications of one sort or another can be monitored, but

---

[35] M. E. Semel, S. R. Lipsitz, L. M. Funk, A. M. Bader, T. G. Weiser and A. A. Gawande, 'Rates and patterns of death after surgery in the United States, 1996 and 2006' (2012) 151 *Surgery* 171–82.

[36] K. Walker, J. Neuburger, O. Groene, D. A. Cromwell and J. van der Meulen, 'Public reporting of surgeon outcomes: low numbers of procedures lead to false complacency' (2013) 382 *The Lancet* 1674–7.

this is much harder than monitoring death. The costs associated with the development and maintenance of the requisite databases (with adequate levels of detail and reliability) should also be considered.

There is, however, an even more compelling reason to believe that this approach is ill conceived. In Chapter 2, we discussed teamwork in healthcare in some detail. We cited evidence that most outcomes in healthcare today depend to a great degree on teamwork. Take cardiac surgery. Outcomes do not depend on individual surgeons alone, but on the contributions of many people including anaesthetists, intensive care specialists, intensive care and ward nursing and junior medical staff and so on. In many units today, surgeons hand over the care of patients to an intensive care team at the very time that their condition is most critical. The degree of surgeons' involvement in that phase of care does vary. In some units the intensive care is under the control of the cardiac surgeons, in others it is under the control of intensive care specialists. To put this in context, though, even those surgeons who would claim intimate involvement in the intensive care of their patients will often complete one long and difficult operation, hand over care of that patient to the nursing and junior medical staff in the intensive care unit and then return to the operating room to attend to the task of undertaking a similar operation on another patient. Whatever the precise arrangements, patients undergoing cardiac surgery (or indeed any form of substantive surgery) always depend on a number of clinicians for their final outcome. Failures in teamwork and communication are a prominent cause of adverse events in healthcare, generally. Even simple things, such as inadequate hand hygiene by ward staff several days later, may alter outcomes. The importance of the wider team can be seen in studies that show that if a surgeon works in two units, or moves units, his or her results are likely to differ between units.[37] Furthermore, for many patients accessing public health services, choice of surgeon is not possible. For these patients, it is the results of every surgeon in the institution that matters, and of the institution as a whole (i.e. the 'team'). The events at Stafford Hospital (see Chapter 1) make this very clear. Even for those who access private services and perhaps can choose their surgeon, understanding the available data may not be straightforward. Questions of equity arise in this regard, in relation to variations in health literacy amongst other things. As with so many things, the idea of putting

---

[37] R. S. Huckman and G. P. Pisano, 'The firm specificity of individual performance: evidence from cardiac surgery' (2006) 52 *Management Science* 473–88.

individual surgeons' results into the public domain seems sensible at first blush, but turns out to be beset with difficulties, and indeed serious flaws, when considered in detail.

We believe the driver should be for collective excellence rather than for individual excellence. Thus, we advocate the public reporting of outcome data aggregated to the level of the unit or institution.[38] This is likely to provide very different incentives from publically reporting the results of individual surgeons. In the former case there will be a vested interest by all concerned to make sure that every surgeon, and indeed every person and part of the system, is performing well. Improving the outcome of the whole unit should, surely, be the aim, and reporting should be designed to promote that aim. Through aggregation, reporting at the unit level also goes a long way towards addressing the question of the required number of cases. There is an argument that the most important metrics relate to countries as a whole – the aim should be excellent outcomes for all patients in any given country.[39] Access comes into the equation when consideration is extended to this level. There is little point in having one or two outstanding surgeons if most patients are unable to access their services because of geographical or financial barriers. It makes much more sense to try to ensure that all patients have ready access to services of a uniformly high standard.

In New Zealand, the Health Quality and Safety Commission recently reviewed these questions in some depth. Amongst other things, the Commission recommended:

1) the public reporting of judiciously chosen, adequately risk-adjusted measures at the team, unit or organisational level rather than the individual level;
2) development of agreed national standards of data collection, relevant definitions and measures across New Zealand, and agreed risk adjustment models to account for case complexity and risk; and
3) that publication should include clear explanations of context, and of the limitations and interpretation of the data, in different formats and media to ensure that the information is accessible to people of all levels of health literacy.

---

[38] See, for example, S. Goodacre, M. Campbell and A. Carter, 'What do hospital mortality rates tell us about quality of care?' (2015) 32 *Emergency Medicine Journal* 244–7.

[39] See for example R. Hamblin, G. Bohm, C. Gerard, C. Shuker, J. Wilson and A. F. Merry, 'The measurement of New Zealand health care' (2015) 128 *New Zealand Medical Journal* 50–64.

The above considerations do not mean that institutions should not monitor the performance of individual practitioners internally. On the contrary, there are many different ways to evaluate such performance, and a holistic approach using a selection of metrics and assessments can go a long way towards ensuring that each individual is performing at an acceptable level. To be meaningful, this sort of assessment is of necessity more complex than simply reporting mortality data, and does not lend itself to public disclosure in detail. On the other hand, we think the public are entitled to know whether or not this is being done in any particular hospital or practice. Similarly, the Commission made a further recommendation: it supported work 'to strengthen and align the processes within organisations to demonstrate doctors' on-going competence' and suggested that these processes should be made more transparent. The Commission went further and recommended that 'boards of health care organisations should be asked to attest to their presence, and to their confidence that all practitioners are participating and achieving acceptable standards'. This is clearly aligned with our view that those who fund, manage and govern healthcare services should share the responsibility for the safety of these services with those who actually care for patients. Finally, the Commission recommended 'increased education and training focused on enhancing teamwork within organisations'.[40]

The general principle, then, is that appropriate metrics should be reported publically at unit level, and appropriate internal practices of review, audit and assessment should be used to ensure that all practitioners are performing adequately within each unit. This principle could be applied to any speciality, including general practice: it is a matter of identifying the metrics and methods that are most appropriate for each context. The process could include patient reported outcomes (such as measures of quality of life), measures of patient experience and measures of cost as well.[41] Even in the context of primary healthcare, it should be

---

[40] R. Hamblin, C. Shuker, I. Stolarek, J. Wilson and A. F. Merry, 'Public reporting of health care performance data: what we know and what we should do' (2016) 129 *New Zealand Medical Journal* 7–17. Readers should be aware that, at the time of writing, one of the authors of this book is chair of the board of the New Zealand Health Quality and Safety Commission, and will note that he is also an author of the paper cited here, but many other people were involved in developing (and indeed leading the development of) the Commission's recommendations and much consultation of experts, authorities and organisations went into them.

[41] M. A. Shulman, P. S. Myles, M. T. Chan, D. R. McIlroy, S. Wallace and J. Ponsford, 'Measurement of disability-free survival after surgery' (2015) 122 *Anesthesiology* 524–36;

possible to find measures that will at least elevate a red flag if a rogue practitioner like Harold Shipman is deliberately harming large numbers of patients, but such practitioners are rare outliers, and this should not be seen as the primary motivation for publically reporting selected data on the performance of healthcare teams. Instead, the motivation should be the promotion of excellent standards throughout the healthcare system. With this in mind, a balance should be struck between the burden and costs of measurement and reporting and the need for the public to be assured that services are of a safe and satisfactory standard.

Therapeutic Jurisprudence

We come now to the question of the role of regulation and the law when a practitioner or institution fails to obtain acceptable results over time (as in Bristol or the Stafford Hospital), or when things go wrong in a particular case. Earlier, we discussed the essentially reactive nature of lawsuits, criminal prosecutions and disciplinary actions against health practitioners. We also reflected on the fact that these processes are poorly designed or adapted to the specific context of healthcare and how in consequence they often tend to add to harm that has already occurred, even from the perspective of patients. In particular, the moment a lawsuit is initiated or criminal proceedings commenced, the commitment to open disclosure to the patient is inhibited (to say the least) and so are the opportunities for early internal identification of what really went wrong with a view to prevention of recurrences. The legal imperative to remain silent becomes very strong. Furthermore, any hope of ongoing trust between the injured patient and the relevant practitioners and institution tends to be completely destroyed. It is by no means given that the outcome will satisfy either party. The route to resolution will be long, hostile and emotionally challenging for everyone. Even in the unlikely event that a particular practitioner has crossed all normal boundaries and demonstrated a flagrant lack of care for a patient, it is surely a reasonable assumption that the rest of the healthcare team, including senior management and clinical leadership, will be motivated by concern for the injured patient. At the very least, they ought to be.

B. F. Gornall, P. S. Myles, C. L. Smith, J. A. Burke, K. Leslie, M. J. Pereira, . . . A. Forbes, 'Measurement of quality of recovery using the QoR-40: a quantitative systematic review' (2013) 111 *British Journal of Anaesthesia* 161–9; R. Hamblin, G. Bohm, C. Gerard, C. Shuker, J. Wilson and A. F. Merry, 'The measurement of New Zealand health care' (2015) 128 *New Zealand Medical Journal* 50–64.

Seen in this light, one of the worst aspects of adversarial legal processes is that they remove important sources of support for the injured patient. For this reason alone there is a high likelihood that the intervention of the law will simply make a bad situation worse.

Could a better way be found? Could there be ways to integrate the legal and regulatory elements essential for dealing with things that go wrong in healthcare with healthcare's own processes of measurement and improvement? Earlier in this book we discussed the concept that accidents are ultimately inevitable in a complex system even when all possible things are done to ensure safety. Surely, then, the common objective of assuring that services are adequately safe and of a satisfactory quality for everyone should include provision for responding effectively on those occasions when things do, inevitably, go wrong? Could such integration enhance rather than impede active processes of continuous improvement in pursuit of uniform excellence of care? What if one started with the idea that the regulation of healthcare and those who provide it ought to be proactive rather than reactive? What if the explicit aim in responding to harmful events in healthcare was to contribute to the rapid healing of all concerned – most notably the affected patient, but also the relevant clinicians and the system itself?

Therapeutic jurisprudence is a movement in the law that studies the ways in which the operation of the law affects people's emotions, behaviours and mental well-being. It had its origins in the area of mental health law in the late 1980s. Psychiatric patients may sometimes be committed, with a view to preventing harm to themselves or others. Committal is a process of the law, so the process of committal is dictated by specific legislation. The founders of therapeutic jurisprudence, Professors Bruce Winick and David Wexler, discovered that such legislation, while specifically designed to help the people being committed (as well as to safeguard the public), often had a detrimental psychological effect on them in practice. Many people who are committed have not knowingly done anything morally wrong, yet the process involves an appearance before a judge. The details vary between legislatures, and have changed over time, but the nature of the relationship and of the interaction may be quite traumatic for the patient. Judges are imbued with the authority of the State to interpret and apply the law, and indeed to punish. There is, therefore, a daunting imbalance of power, and for many patients this alone may create a perception that the purpose of the process is punishment, even if the judge is motivated (amongst other things) by a genuine wish to help people suffering from mental illness. The way in which judges address these patients can make a big difference: courtesy and respect for their value as a person can enhance their sense of self-worth and well-being, whereas a lack of either can aggravate their sense of blameworthiness and alienation, which may have the effect of exacerbating their condition rather than assisting them along the journey towards recovery. This led Wexler to develop the idea of law *as* therapy, and from that emerged the idea of explicitly examining the therapeutic and anti-therapeutic consequences of the law to achieve a more humanistic healing perspective. In its attempts to achieve this goal, therapeutic jurisprudence has embraced insights from other fields such as psychiatry, psychology, social science and criminology. These have helped exponents of the therapeutic jurisprudence approach to better understand the effects of the complex ways in which the law operates, and to envision a therapeutic approach to the law in general.

Thus, the forging together of the two elements in the movement's name – 'therapeutic' and 'jurisprudence' – suggests a deliberate linking of the study of the law with the power to effect beneficial change – in effect, to heal. In this regard, therapeutic jurisprudence moves the legal discourse from a focus on rules and prescriptive procedures to consideration of alternative legal arrangements designed to increase the possibility of therapeutic outcomes. It recognises that law is a social force that has consequences in the domain of psychology. With its focus on the law in action, therapeutic jurisprudence is more closely aligned with legal realism than the austere positivism of modernist legal theory. Its primary concern is with how legal systems actually operate and affect people psychologically.

Therapeutic jurisprudence is relevant to this discussion because of its designation as the 'study of the role of law as a therapeutic agent'.[42] If the law is to operate as a therapeutic agent it ought to have something to say about the management of patient safety and the blaming culture in medicine. Helen Kiel has noted that therapeutic jurisprudence provides a theoretical framework for an interdisciplinary approach to issues around impaired doctors, by drawing from social science and medical research to develop evidence-based strategies for their treatment.[43]

---

[42] See D. Wexler and B. Winick, *Law in a Therapeutic Key: Developments in Therapeutic Jurisprudence* (Durham, Carolina Academic Press, 1996).

[43] H. Kiel, 'Regulating impaired doctors: a snapshot from New South Wales' (2013) 21 *Journal of Law and Medicine* 429–40.

This framework has been successfully applied in both drug courts and mental health tribunals[44] and has the potential to enliven debate around the effects of vicarious trauma in the regulation of both medical and legal professionals.[45] Professor Ian Freckelton has observed that therapeutic jurisprudence has potential for the boards that regulate health practitioners by giving 'specific recognition to the health repercussions of each aspect of the operation of the law in practice ... and offer[ing] the possibility for the law to draw creatively for both its processes and its outcomes from the insights of the mental health professions'.[46]

Therapeutic jurisprudence offers a perspective from mental health on the law in general through its strategy of identifying psycho/legal 'softspots' and bringing processes of law reform to bear on those dysfunctional areas to produce better outcomes. Kiel notes that therapeutic jurisprudence is 'clearly implicit' in provisions of the law that incorporate strategies to achieve compliance in the management of impairment on the basis of 'persuasion rather than punishment'. She further observes: 'These strategies are said to be more effective than deterrence-based approaches in terms of preventing recidivism. By allowing impaired doctors to continue in practice while receiving treatment, the law acts as a therapeutic agent. By placing conditions on a doctor's practice, the law demonstrates the concept of 'creative compliance'.[47] Thus, the ideas that underlie therapeutic jurisprudence would seem to have much to contribute to the debate on the role of the law and other forms of regulation in healthcare. Therapeutic jurisprudence seeks to replace the harmful effects of traditional legal processes with a process that seeks healing for all concerned – both the victim of and the perpetrator of an offence. If the latter goal is seen as worthwhile even when intentional wrongdoing has led to the legal

---

[44] See note 6 at p. 432 of H. Kiel, 'Regulating impaired doctors: a snapshot from New South Wales' (2013) 21 *Journal of Law and Medicine* 429–40.

[45] See, for example, A. Levin and S. Griesberg, 'Vicarious trauma in attorneys' (2003) 24 (1) *Pace Law Review* 245–52; P. Jaffe, C. Crooks, B. Dunford-Jackson and Judge Michael Town, 'Vicarious trauma in judges: The personal challenge of dispensing justice' (2003) 54 *Juvenile and Family Court Journal* 1–10; J. Tanay, 'Psychic trauma and the law' (1969) 15 *Wayne Law Review* 1033–59; J. Osofsky, F. Putnam and Judge Cindy S Lederman, 'How to maintain emotional health when working with trauma' (2008) 59 *Juvenile and Family Court Journal* 91–102.

[46] I. Freckelton, 'Disciplinary Investigations and Hearings: A Therapeutic Jurisprudence Perspective, http://www.aija.org.au/TherapJurisp06/Monograph%20Papers/10% 20Freckelton.pdf, cited in Kiel (above, note 27) at 432.

[47] H. Kiel, 'Regulating impaired doctors: a snapshot from New South Wales' (2013) 21 *Journal of Law and Medicine* 429–40. See p. 432.

response, how much more so must this goal be when dealing with healthcare professionals who are 'good, hard working and trying to do the right thing?'[48]

At this point it is worth revisiting this assumption. What about the small minority for whom the assumptions of conscientiousness and good intentions do not apply, or only partially apply? What about practitioners who are impaired, or less than acceptably competent? What about those who do in fact behave recklessly, or with intent to harm?

The example of Harold Shipman, found guilty of multiple murders, is easily dealt with. People of this type need to be removed from the system and punished, but we believe they are exceptionally rare. The example of Dr Channagiri Manjanatha, the anaesthetist from Saskatchewan who left his patient unattended, and then falsified his account of the events, seems at first to be relatively straightforward as well (but we will return to it below). Again, few would dispute that this behaviour was totally unacceptable, or that punishment was in order. The difficulty arises with practices that are less obviously distinguishable from normative standards of practice, but that arguably reflect less commitment to doing the right thing. As we have seen, these are the failures that account for a substantial proportion of poor outcomes from healthcare. Failure to observe expected hand-hygiene practices is just one example of a failure of this type. It is an example of failure that has been so widespread that almost everyone who works in a hospital has probably transgressed at some point. Yet, as we have seen, a practitioner is less likely to be punished for a failure in hand hygiene than for a fatal drug error, even though the former may well constitute a conscious violation (at least to some degree) while the latter would typically be a completely unintended error, as seen in the case of Dr Yogasakaran, who was clearly trying to do his best in difficult circumstances but was convicted of manslaughter.

In part, this distinction is a reflection of moral luck. Many anaesthetists have given the wrong drug in error, without being sanctioned, primarily because, by good fortune, no harm ensued, or if it did, the link to the error was not clear. For example, a failure to administer prophylactic antibiotics before surgery may contribute to a postoperative wound infection that develops several weeks later, but the connection between the two events may never be established. In a similar way, the link

---

[48] Wachter and Pronovost, 'Balancing "No Blame" with Accountability in Patient Safety', at 1401.

between an episode of poor hand hygiene and a subsequent infection will seldom be obvious. In both cases, the failures usually appear to be without consequence. As a general point, this goes a long way to explaining why compliance with best practice is often imperfect: people simply don't see the results of their actions, so they don't believe they matter. Earlier in this chapter we discussed possible approaches to shifting this perception and establishing that compliance with practices known to be important is not negotiable. This would be one element of an approach based on therapeutic jurisprudence. We explained earlier in the book that it can often be difficult to distinguish between errors and violations. An approach that sought to deal constructively with failures in practice while respecting the legitimate interests of all parties might sometimes finesse the need to distinguish precisely between errors and minor violations. After all, in either case the objective would be to address the needs of the patient and improve safety and prevent recurrence without adding to the harm that has already occurred, either through expensive and adversarial legal processes or even through unduly harsh discipline.

Therapeutic Recalibration

What is really needed is a recalibration of the perceived acceptability of certain practices: a sort of 'therapeutic recalibration', as it were. The boundaries for this approach could be quite wide. Some things are simply beyond any attempt at therapeutic restoration (the case of Shipman, for example), but the number that are is probably small. For example, Dr Manjanatha returned to practice after a period in prison. If an outcome of this type is contemplated as a reasonable long-term aim under conventional legal processes, then perhaps an approach based on therapeutic jurisprudence might offer a more effective and efficient way to achieve it. Some serious behaviours, such as working while under the influence of drugs or alcohol, falling asleep while administering an anaesthetic or aggressive, bad tempered or bullying behaviour in the workplace, often reflect underlying physical or mental illness rather than irredeemable defects of character or lack of good intentions. Of course, rehabilitation is not always possible, and return to practice may not always be the best aim. Drug addiction amongst anaesthetists, for example, has a very high rate of recidivism (although not 100 per cent), so in this context it might be sensible to explore alternative careers that provide less ready access to drugs. This may still be consistent with the idea of addressing the needs of patients and society while causing no more harm to practitioners than intended (in the sense that deliberate punishment may sometimes be appropriate). Indeed, the idea of therapeutic jurisprudence, in the context of the present discussion, emerged from the very issue of how best to deal with impaired doctors.

Therapeutic jurisprudence, then, offers a fresh means of envisioning the issue of patient safety and responding in a consistent and effective manner to a substantial proportion of the behaviours that lead to patient harm, whether inadvertent, arising from impairment, or reflecting normalised deviance. It does this by adopting insights from social science to examine the extent to which a particular legal rule of practice[49] may, or may not, promote psychological or physical well-being in the people affected by the law. An approach based on the ideas of therapeutic jurisprudence might shift our understanding of accountability from one in which those actions that lead to harm are typically punished (if the harm comes to attention), while, at the same time, widespread normalised deviance from appropriate practice is tolerated to one in which the prevention of harm is proactive and not optional. The detail of what constitutes appropriate practice should be negotiable, but not compliance with safety practices for which substantial consensus has been reached. We need to recalibrate the thermometer of acceptability in relation to practice to inform an integrated approach in which the law (and other regulatory authorities) works collaboratively and proactively with health professionals to drive improvement and increase patient safety: in short, 'therapeutic recalibration'.

One major aim of this therapeutic approach would be to reduce the incidence of and need for medical malpractice litigation, both civil and criminal, by taking collective responsibility for patient safety. Even when things go badly wrong, the approach would recognise that the vast majority of practitioners are committed to helping, not harming people, and also that errors are an inevitable and unavoidable element of human performance within complex systems. However, the most fundamental point about 'therapeutic accountability' is that practitioners should not be at liberty simply to 'walk away' from circumstances in which patients are harmed without taking part in the response to that harm. The responsibility for the event should be seen as collective – involving

---

[49] This is a legal rule, usually statutory, which requires that a particular person undertake a particular duty in defined circumstances. For example, such a rule might place a requirement on a judge to give a corroboration warning in defined circumstances.

the wider team, rather than just one individual. The first priority should be the immediate medical and emotional needs of the patient and those close to him or her. Also, there should be early acknowledgement that things have gone wrong, with full disclosure of the relevant facts as they become clear. Patients should never have to resort to litigation to find out what went wrong. An apology should accompany this disclosure even if no obvious wrongdoing has occurred: healthcare should not cause avoidable harm to patients, and the mere fact of such harm warrants a straightforward and compassionate expression of regret that it has occurred. Thus, the response to any episode of potentially avoidable harm might include the following elements:

1) proactive commitment to providing safe, appropriate and effective treatment with the least possible risk of harm;
2) managing and treating harm when it does occur as a priority, with no additional financial cost to the harmed patients;
3) excellent communication with patients at all times, including open disclosure when things go wrong;
4) ready access to reasonable compensation through a system that does not require proof that negligence has occurred, and is separate from any process of discipline or sanction; and
5) a process to identify why things went wrong that will lead to an appropriate response, including some or all of apology, systems change, retraining and proportionate sanctions when appropriate.

There is increasing agreement that the first three of these elements are worthwhile, and they are already promoted in many countries around the world, in various forms and stages of evolution. The fourth, the provision of compensation without the necessity to establish fault, is a real barrier to progress in most parts of the world except the Nordic countries and New Zealand, which, as we have seen, have well-established and highly functional national systems for doing this. In Chapter 8 we discussed the merits and the disadvantages of the tort system as a means for providing compensation to patients injured by healthcare, and we will not revisit these arguments here. Suffice to say that it is enormously helpful to separate the process of compensating patients who have suffered avoidable harm from the process of holding practitioners and institutions accountable for their practices. Doing this opens the door for new and effective ways of pursuing the fifth of our objectives.

It is in the fifth of these domains that the ideas of therapeutic jurisprudence and recalibration have much to offer. The starting point would be the establishment of a 'just culture', in the terms envisaged by James Reason and others.[50] Within such a culture it would be possible to lay down processes for the proactive identification and effective management of safety issues in ways that included rather than marginalised practitioners. The aim would be to achieve (as far as possible) universal compliance with agreed safety practices, thereby rendering the need to punish failures in compliance redundant. Infrequent errors made in the context of otherwise safe practices should be understood as inevitable and should not be the subject of sanction, but it should be an expectation that every reasonable effort is made collectively and collaboratively by all concerned (practitioners, administrators, senior management and funders) to minimise their occurrence. Wilfully culpable behaviours, including persistent refusal to participate fully in the pursuit of excellent practices and repeated lack of compliance with expected standards, should be sanctioned in a proportionate manner that aims to correct the behaviour rather than further marginalise the individual. For those that simply will not or cannot engage constructively, these sanctions should include measures to end their involvement with healthcare – for example, removal of licence to practice. On one hand this final sanction should be a last resort, but on the other, it should not be unreasonably withheld for too long. The idea, in therapeutic jurisprudence, is not to allow recidivist egregious behaviour to be tolerated for prolonged periods. This would simply fail to serve patients' legitimate expectation of a safe system. Rather, it is to ensure that everyone concerned has a reasonable opportunity to understand clearly what is expected, and the opportunity to meet the expectation before more draconian steps are taken. There are two reasons why this matters: first, because it is fair and just; and second, because it is efficient – few countries can afford to discard the expensive resource of highly trained practitioners, administrators and other expert staff too lightly. Rehabilitation, including further training to address particular deficiencies if necessary, is worthwhile where possible.

A therapeutic jurisprudence approach would change the nature of the discourse from one of adversarial debate to a more inquisitorial dialogue with a greater sense of a collaborative effort between regulators, health professionals and patients to find good solutions together. Therapeutic recalibration would have both remedial and preventative elements, since the aim of any recalibration should be to avoid harm but also to fix

---

[50] J. Reason, *Managing the Risks of Organizational Accidents* (Aldershot, Ashgate, 1997).

defective practices that have caused harm when they do occur, and to work with involved professionals to prevent the recurrence of similar events in the future. While some patients will continue to be harmed in the normal course of their care, the incidence of this harm should be reduced through appropriate continuing education and training to maintain and improve standards of performance accompanied by iterative review and improvement to systemic factors that influence safety.

The Law, Therapeutic Jurisprudence and an Integrated National Framework

We have said that the boundaries of an approach based on therapeutic jurisprudence could be wide. As discussed in Chapter 9, there was a substantial increase in the prosecution of health professionals for manslaughter during the 1990s in New Zealand. When a patient died unexpectedly in the operating room police officers would frequently descend on the operating theatres and begin investigations that drew more from training and experience in the investigation of burglaries, assaults, rapes, murders and other crimes than from any expertise in hospitals or healthcare, or in the ways in which things go wrong in complex systems. Furthermore, since they were drawn from the general police force and returned to normal police activities once their involvement in the case was over, there was little opportunity to develop such expertise. This was not a process endowed with any therapeutic elements at all. It was manifestly anti-therapeutic.

The police involvement reflected a superficially reasonable idea, namely that death is a serious matter and warrants investigation in the interests of protecting the public. The Shipman cases would support this view, but unfortunately it misses the point that a great number of patients die in hospital, one way or another. Distinguishing those in which police involvement might be appropriate from the vast majority in which it is not appropriate is not readily done by a general police response triggered simply on the grounds that a particular death happens to have occurred in association with an operation in a hospital. Shipman's murdered patients died at home, after all. Also, as we discussed in Chapter 9, death is not the only unintended serious outcome associated with healthcare and there is no logic in singling it out from all the other ways in which patients can be injured.

A more sensible approach would be to expect an internal review of all forms of major unintended harm, at least to a basic extent, within a process capable of identifying any cause for concern and escalating the level of investigation as appropriate. The police and the courts should seldom be involved. However, the public may well ask how they are to know that such processes are in place and working adequately, and may understandably have reservations about leaving these matters entirely to those within healthcare. This raises the question of models by which legal or regulatory authorities could interact regularly and proactively with those responsible for the provision of healthcare more effectively, to become expert in this field while remaining independent of it. An approach of this sort could facilitate the continuous improvement of safety while at the same time providing independent assurance to the public that the safeguards they expect are in place. We envisage the implementation of the principles of therapeutic jurisprudence as very much a team-based activity. There would have to be alignment at all levels of both the health and the legal system, from national regulators and the leaders of healthcare organisations to those whose job is directly concerned with patient care, and everyone in between.

The Health and Disability Commissioner in New Zealand

One model that goes some distance towards achieving many of these goals is to be found in the Office of the Health and Disability Commissioner in New Zealand (the Commissioner). In Chapter 7 we recounted how, in the late 1980s, a Committee of Inquiry, headed by then District Court Judge Dame Sylvia Cartwright, was tasked with investigating allegations in relation to the treatment of cervical cancer at New Zealand's premier woman's hospital. The *Report of the Committee of Inquiry into Allegations Concerning the Treatment of Cervical Cancer at National Women's Hospital and into Other Related Matters* revealed that women had been unknowing participants in a clinical research trial, the purpose of which was to study the course of the disease, while treating the cervical cancer in situ. As we mentioned in Chapter 8, a result of the inquiry was a recommendation by Judge Cartwright that New Zealand law be amended to 'provide for a statement of patients' rights and the appointment of a Health Commissioner'.

The Health and Disability Commissioner has now been established as a statutory role under the Health and Disability Commissioner Act 1994. The Commissioner's role is to promote and protect the rights of health consumers and to facilitate the efficient resolution of complaints relating to a breach of those rights.[51]

Any consumer can complain to the Commissioner. No cost is involved. Advocates are available to assist in the process. The Commissioner's scope of influence is wide, and includes all registered health professionals and others within the system, such as senior managers. The approach taken is substantially inquisitorial. Usually it begins with a letter to the health professional about whom a complaint has been made, or to the person responsible for the organisation in question if the complaint is more broadly based. The response to this letter is important and may determine the next steps. The aim is to seek resolution at the lowest level possible, and to identify opportunities for improvement, whether these relate to the system in general or to particular practices or individuals. In some cases, if the response provides an adequate explanation for events, and perhaps some acknowledgement of the complainant's perspective and an apology for whatever harm has been suffered, no further steps will be necessary. Often, a more substantive investigation is carried out, with input from experts called by the Commissioner, and the opportunity for response by those complained of. This may result in finding that the code has been breached, and such findings may or may not involve disclosure of the names of the individuals or organisations involved. Usually, a careful and detailed report will emerge that, in addition to reaching a finding as to whether a breach of the code has occurred, outlines the relevant issues and provides advice for improvement in the future. If egregious behaviour is identified, the case is referred to 'the appropriate authorities', which might be a disciplinary tribunal or even the police. The Commissioner and the staff of the Commissioner's office interact regularly with practitioners and healthcare organisations. Two of the first three Commissioners have been legally qualified, and the Office employs lawyers with an interest in medico-legal matters. There is much about the functioning of the Commissioner's office that aligns well with the ideas of therapeutic jurisprudence. Similar models have been adopted in some states of Australia.

The biggest limitation of this system is that it is still primarily reactive to things that go wrong. A reactive arm would be needed in any overall regulatory approach, and in many ways the Commissioner's office addresses this need very well. The gap lies in the proactive components

---

[51] Health and Disability Consumer Act 1994, s6.

of therapeutic jurisprudence and recalibration – the idea that account-ability begins with a concerted collective effort to avoid harm in the first place, and, further, to promote excellence of care. One aspect of the challenge is to know how well practitioners and institutions are actually doing. In part the solution lies in the reporting of outcomes data, which we have discussed earlier in the chapter. The open publication of simple, but appropriately selected risk-adjusted metrics aggregated at unit level to monitor the overall performance of a team or institution should be the norm, and should be accompanied by more holistic internal processes of review that will provide early warning of the possibility that an individual practitioner is failing to perform at an acceptable level.

This brings us back to the question of how the public is to know that such processes are in place. We have already mentioned one approach to achieving this: the idea that those with the responsibility for the govern-ance of healthcare institutions (typically boards of directors) should be required to attest to their presence, presumably annually.

Monitors

A variation on this theme, which may well go hand-in-hand with attesta-tion, would involve the establishment of officers who specialise in the monitoring and regulation of those who work in healthcare, within a therapeutic jurisprudence framework. Ideally, these people would have legal training supplemented by training in the nature of human error and in the principles of improvement science (as it is sometimes called) in the context of healthcare. By virtue of the specialised nature of their responsibilities they would build expertise on these foundations through experience over time – after all, as we have discussed in Chapter 2, this is the way expertise is always built. They might be called by a variety of titles, but for now we suggest the term 'monitor' because their primary role would be to act, on behalf of the public, as independent monitors of the processes to assure and improve the quality of healthcare within institutions.

It would be important that these monitors were financially and organisationally independent of the institutions they were monitoring. At the same time they should be sufficiently integrated into the relevant activities of the institution to be able to develop a clear understanding of the context in which patient safety is being assured and advanced. In countries like New Zealand that already have appropriate national agencies, such as the office of the Health and Disability Commissioner, these agencies could employ such officers and then deploy them to hospitals, practices or other healthcare institutions to work alongside the health professionals and managers responsible for assuring and improving standards of practice. The role we envision would not be one of ticking boxes on a schedule of items for compliance. Instead, all processes and data related to performance would be completely open to these officers in a way that would allow them to gain a deep understanding of the risks, the solutions, and the challenges. They would treat information on individual practitioners as confidential, but represent the public in monitoring the processes by which practitioners' performance was (in turn) being monitored and in evaluating the results of that monitoring as well.

A key responsibility of these officers would be the oversight of processes for implementing a just culture. They would be responsible for the triage between human errors in which the focus should be on the system and avoidance of future occurrences, and actions that might warrant a different process, with a focus on discipline. The combination of a legal background and specific training and experience in healthcare would mean that they would be well placed to carry out or oversee the use of appropriate algorithms for determining when to invoke discipline, and how. A scaled approach could be implemented, drawing on internal processes at the lower levels of wrongdoing, and then on the processes of national registration and disciplinary bodies, and finally the courts.

In the event that a monitor was not satisfied that all the necessary processes were in order in a particular institution, the first response would be to work with the relevant staff to address the identified deficiencies. If, for some reason, there was resistance to improvement, and the shortcomings persisted, the monitor would have the power to escalate the matter to the central agency for further action, which at some point would become a publically disclosed matter.

These monitors need not necessarily have full time commitments to any given location – in the case of a small general practice, for example, the likelihood is that these duties would require only a modest commitment of time, particularly if things were going well. Indeed, having responsibility for more than one institution or practice might facilitate the sharing of good ideas, and assist a monitor in calibrating his or her views of what constitutes an appropriate framework and level of commitment for assuring patient safety. Conversely, a major hospital might need several such officers.

In some countries, these ideas may seem to be so far from current reality as to be purely idealistic and hypothetical. The principles are the important thing. The detail through which an approach based on the concepts of therapeutic jurisprudence could be introduced to any particular country will vary enormously. Countries such as New Zealand and the Nordic countries already have many of the required elements, so these principles could be implemented with little more than fine-tuning of systems that are already working relatively well. In many jurisdictions the starting point would have to be the more difficult challenge of shifting the compensation of treatment-related injury from the civil courts to a system that did not depend on demonstrating fault. Many large institutions in the United States (and elsewhere) already have policies to provide compensation directly to patients who have been harmed, alongside disclosure and other measures within wider frameworks of risk management that seek to resolve problems at the lowest level possible. It is not difficult to envision ways in which indemnity insurance companies could work with institutions to embrace the underlying concepts outlined in this chapter. The barriers to bringing a successful lawsuit are substantial, and it does not seem beyond the bounds of possibility that approaches could be set up in private systems of healthcare that would take away many of the reasons that presently drive injured patients to civil actions or complaints to the police. If patients who had been injured felt that they were being fairly treated, were confident that open disclosure was occurring and knew that all concerned were genuinely engaged in preventing future episodes of harm, many might be willing to work with their doctors and other hospital staff to achieve satisfactory outcomes for all. The prospect that it might be possible to maintain trust between patients and the professionals under whose care they were unintentionally harmed would be a very important advantage of any successful application of the principles of therapeutic jurisprudence.

Conclusion

One of the tenets that underpins this book is that the most effective (and inexpensive) way to deal with preventable harm from healthcare is to make healthcare safer: in other words to decrease the likelihood and severity of harm before it happens. The argument for this is more acute now than when this book was first published, because of the increasing realisation that the demands of healthcare are tending to outrun the available resources. Resources spent on inefficient and ineffective regulatory and legal processes are resources that cannot be spent on improving healthcare, and in the end, as we indicated in Chapter 8, the resources for responding to things that go wrong in healthcare come from the same limited pool as those for the provision of healthcare. Another tenet is that processes of accountability must be just, and therefore (amongst other things) must reflect the evolving empirical and theoretical body of knowledge that informs our understanding of the performance of humans within complex systems. Ideally, no one working in healthcare should need to be punished when things do go wrong because practices should always be excellent from the outset. This implies that normalised deviance should not be tolerated. The key to safe and excellent patient care would seem to lie in a culture based on efficient service provision within a framework of proactive risk management through repeating loops of causes and consequences as proposed here, with appropriate monitoring and functional links between the legal, regulatory and healthcare branches of the system. In such a culture, when something does go wrong, the processes for dealing with the aftermath will already be in place, ready to be brought into action quickly, easily and justly. The ultimate outcome should be improved safety and outcomes for everyone – patients and practitioners alike.

~

Conclusion

This study started with a chapter on accidents. How those accidents are viewed – and how we regard untoward occurrences in human affairs – has been the subject of our enquiry. It is our view that many of our current responses to such events are not only morally and scientifically unsophisticated, but may also be unhelpful in promoting better and safer practices. If we want to reduce the damage caused by accidents, then we should ensure that the legal response is fashioned with an awareness of the insights that psychology, accident theory and an understanding of complex systems can now afford. At present the law in many cases adopts a blunt approach, which fails to take these insights into account. This is in the interests of neither the patient nor the doctor.

We have not been concerned with intentionally produced harm, which may quite uncontroversially merit blame. It is worth noting, though, that even in situations where blame is entirely appropriate, a strongly punitive response may not necessarily be the most effective method of dealing with the problem. There will, of course, be situations where a good case can be advanced for a strongly deterrent approach. An example of this is where punitive measures are used to deter the deliberate flouting of safety or environmental regulations by corporate actors. It may often be appropriate for both the corporation and individuals within it to be held liable – healthcare today is a team endeavour, and the outcomes of healthcare depend much more on the integrated functioning of entire units or institutions than on the competence of any single individual. The errors made by individuals are important, but these fade into insignificance when set against the potential difference for patients' outcomes between excellent institutions and those that simply aren't functioning well at any level. This is made abundantly clear in the story of the failure of the Mid Staffordshire NHS Trust. There is current interest in corporate criminal liability, which recognises that responsibility for an offence may be institutional as well as individual.[1] In this respect it provides a model for our own critique of the allocation of blame. We have argued that singling out an individual actor – sometimes one who occupies a relatively junior position within a highly complex organisation – may obscure the real nature of responsibility for an event in which a patient is harmed. Contemporary legal theorists have stressed the need to escape an individual focus and to recognise the sociological facts and economic realities of corporate wrongdoing.[2] The aim of this approach is to identify what lies behind an individual act. The fact that an employee has breached the criminal law in the context of his or her employment does not necessarily mean that he or she has acted in the pursuit of some personal objective or gain. It may well be appropriate for the individual to bear liability in such a case, but to punish such a person as if he or she had been acting in isolation is to miss the point of offences committed in a corporate context. These offences are often committed in pursuit of corporate gains, sometimes in response to considerable corporate pressure. The real offender may be in the boardroom or may even be the corporation itself. There are, of course, difficulties in conceiving of the corporation as a moral actor, but there is a strong consensus in jurisprudence that the corporation is capable of being envisioned in this way. These are important principles, but, as we indicated in Chapter 9, in practice the criminal law is a blunt instrument and poorly designed for dealing with the context of well-intended people attempting to deliver healthcare with restrained resources and many other challenges. Perhaps the most important role for the criminal law in the regulation of healthcare lies in its declaratory function: it is important that social expectations are made crystal clear, but the very fact that resort to the criminal law has become necessary is in itself evidence of abject failure to meet those expectations.

---

[1] B. Fisse and J. Braithwaite, 'The allocation of responsibility for corporate crime: individualism, collectivism and accountability' (1988) 11 *Sydney Law Review* 468–513; A. Samanta and J. Samanta, 'Charges of corporate manslaughter in the NHS' (2006) 332 *British Medical Journal* 1404–5; C. Dyer, 'First case of corporate manslaughter against NHS trust collapses' (2016) 352 *British Medical Journal* i585.

[2] C. Wells, *Corporations and Criminal Responsibility* (New York, Oxford University Press, 1993). There is a substantial philosophical literature on the issue of the moral responsibility of the corporation; the classic exposition of the problem, from the point of view of moral philosophy, is that of P. French, *Collective and Corporate Responsibility* (New York, Columbia University Press, 1984).

The social efficacy of blame and related sanctions in particular cases of deliberate wrongdoing may be a matter of dispute, but we accept their necessity – in principle – from a moral point of view. Distasteful as punishment may be – and it is, after all, the infliction of pain – we cannot escape the social, and possibly moral, need to punish people for wrongdoing, occasionally in a severe fashion. The communicative nature of punishment is important. Punishment indicates to all concerned that an act is unacceptable to society, and it affirms the value of the person who has been wronged. These are needs that are deeply ingrained in human society and it is difficult to imagine a world in which the concept of punishment was absent; indeed, such a world would bear very little resemblance to our own. At the same time, we should bear in mind that punishment is in many respects a primitive device and that in some circumstances the forgiveness of wrongdoing is not only the morally correct response but also the most constructive one. Increased interest in forgiveness among contemporary moral philosophers and social theorists has drawn our attention to the role which forgiveness plays in the promotion of social healing, most notably in the wake of political and social turmoil.[3] But even at an individual level, the encouragement of forgiveness breaks the cycle of retribution and bitterness and, from a utilitarian point of view, may have the advantage of diminishing social conflict. A society in which blame is overemphasised may become paralysed. This is not only because such a society will inevitably be backward-looking, but also because fear of blame inhibits the uncluttered exercise of judgement in relations between persons.[4] If we are constantly concerned about whether our actions will be the subject of complaint, and that such complaint is likely to lead to legal action or disciplinary proceedings, a relationship of suspicious formality between persons is inevitable. Life in a blame-obsessed system will be very different from life in a supportive and appropriately forgiving system.

---

[3] There is a burgeoning literature on forgiveness. A work which looks at the topic from a variety of points of view (including the psychological and political) is R. D. Enright and J. North (eds.), *Exploring Forgiveness* (Madison, University of Wisconsin Press, 1998). In the philosophical literature, a useful treatment is the debate between Murphy and Hampton in J. G. Murphy and J. Hampton, *Forgiveness and Mercy* (New York, Cambridge University Press, 1988). See also R. C. Roberts, 'Forgivingness' (1995) 32 *American Philosophical Quarterly* 289–306.

[4] This theme is developed further in D. W. Shuman and A. McCall Smith, *Justice and the Prosecution of Old Crimes* (Washington, D.C., American Psychological Association, 2000). See also N. Lacey and H. Pickard, 'To blame or to forgive? Reconciling punishment and forgiveness in criminal justice' (2015) 35(4) *Oxford Journal of Legal Studies* 665–96.

Blaming behaviour in relation to deliberate wrongdoing may be morally acceptable, and indeed necessary, subject to a proper recognition of the function of forgiveness, apology and other social institutions of an emollient nature. Its role in the context of non-deliberate actions is another matter altogether, even when those actions have caused harm. It is at the heart of our argument that undue emphasis on blame in relation to such incidents is unjustified and counter-productive. What is required is a clear-eyed, properly informed examination of the grounds for blame, and a firm fixing of these grounds to criteria which are both morally defensible and pragmatically productive.

We have argued that many errors are not the product of failures or shortcomings of a culpable nature. Indeed, we suggested in Chapter 2 that certain types of error are inextricably linked to those human strengths (such as distractibility and creativity) which differentiate us from machines and which have contributed to our success as a species. Our analysis reveals that to attribute blame for an error is to misunderstand the very nature of what is happening when an error is made. Slips or lapses, for example, will be made by the most conscientious of people, and do not of themselves demonstrate any culpable failing sufficient to justify the attribution of blame. The same is true of mistakes – decisions taken entirely with the intention of doing the right thing and made carefully, but wrongly. Errors are not the product of choice.

Why should such errors not be culpable? If one believes that moral culpability depends on the making of a free choice, then any human action that is not the result of such a choice cannot involve blame. In Chapter 3 we argued that errors, under the tight definition that we have provided, are examples of precisely this. This is by no means a novel position in moral philosophy; indeed, the place occupied by freedom in theories of moral responsibility finds its roots in Aristotle and has been central to theories of responsibility since then. It is on the basis of the absence of a free choice of course of action that those who act under coercion are exculpated; similarly, those who act in ignorance are not usually held to be culpable, on the grounds that their actions do not represent an informed choice of the resulting harm.

Culpability may attach to the consequence of an error in circumstances where substandard antecedent conduct has been deliberate, and has contributed to the generation of the error or to its outcome. In these cases, the making of a prior choice by the actor may lead to responsibility for subsequent situations where choice is absent. These choices, which may involve breaking a rule or failing to take proper account of a general principle, are not errors – they are violations. In Chapter 4 we made the point that not all violations will be equally culpable; nevertheless, at least some responsibility will always attach to a violation, precisely because violations involve choice. In so far as negligence is constituted by a violation, it will be culpable. If, however, it is constituted by no more than an error, then moral culpability will be absent. In practice, the making of an error will often be construed as negligence. We have argued that, in the case of errors, the only failure is a failure defined in terms of the normative standard of what should have been done. There is a tendency to confuse the reasonable person with the error-free person. In other words, the test has shifted from what *could reasonably* have been expected to have been done to what *ought* to have been done. Even though the courts have repeatedly said that the reasonable person test is anchored in realistic expectations of people, the reasonable person test has progressively failed to take account of the inherent human limitations of actual reasonable people. We have illustrated, in Chapter 5, how the precise formulation of the test may change the focus from an action, such as a drug administration error, which may appear unreasonable in itself, to the person. The answer to the question 'Could other people in this position reasonably have made the same error?' will in many cases be in the affirmative, supported by data from incident reporting and other studies that show a widespread occurrence of the same problem.

To help clarify this, we introduced, in Chapter 5, a classification of blame in five levels. Level-two blame is appropriate for error, in which no moral culpability is involved. At this level, *blame* may be better thought of as *accountability*. Care has fallen below the expected standard, so if the error contributes to harming a patient, accountability includes minimising the consequences to that patient. It also includes making every effort to understand and (if possible) address the reasons for the failure. However, for the reasons advanced in Chapter 3, a punitive response is entirely inappropriate. In level three, there has been a prior awareness on the part of the actor that the substandard aspect of his or her behaviour fell short of what could be expected. In other words, choice was possible. While nobody can avoid errors on the basis of simply choosing not to make them, people can choose not to commit violations. The caveat, of course, is that many factors in the system may make violations more or less easy to avoid, and there are circumstances in which certain violations may be inevitable or even appropriate. In general, though, at level three the actions have genuinely failed the reasonable person test, even allowing for the human limitations of the reasonable people. At level three there is still no intent to cause harm or conscious disregard for the safety of others. In Chapter 4, we discussed at length the range of circumstances in which violations may occur.

There is an inescapable tension in the law of torts between the principle of compensation for loss caused by another and the principle that only those who deserve to pay compensation should be required to do so. This contradiction is not one that tort scholars or the courts have resolved satisfactorily. It remains the case that negligence liability in the common-law systems is founded on fault, and this notion of fault is not one which is entirely amoral in nature. The transfer of loss from the person who has suffered it to the person who has caused it depends on the latter having fallen below a standard that it is thought he or she reasonably ought to have met. This is unobjectionable, even if it means that those who were by no means *subjectively* negligent will be held liable. Thus, a person may be held liable even if he is doing his best if this best fell short of the reasonable person's expected performance. We would simply add that the reasonable person's expected level of performance must take account of the fact that the reasonable person is a human being, with the normal limitations of even the most conscientious human being. It is this point that has often been overlooked.

If the standard ceases to represent the level that can in reality be expected of the reasonable person, then it could be argued that the moral underpinning of negligence liability has been lost. This possibility is discussed in Chapters 6 and 7. The courts have never deliberately sought to produce such a result. They have frequently stressed that the reasonable person test means what it says. Unfortunately, there have been times when a divergence has developed between the standard that the courts clearly intend and that which has in practice been demanded. The reasons for this include the nature of expert evidence, an understandable desire to ensure compensation for loss and, above all, insufficient appreciation of the nature of human cognition and performance.

There are other reasons, apart from those of legal theory, why the standard of care should reflect a reasonably and realistically attainable level. If the standard becomes too high, those who are potentially liable – especially those engaged in high-risk activities such as medicine – will feel that they are the victims of unduly harsh assessment. It could be pointed out to them that civil liability entails no moral opprobrium, and that it is merely a matter of loss redistribution, which has the same moral implications as insurance. But this is naïve. The impact of civil liability on defendants *is* serious. A doctor, for example, who is sued for negligence is likely to feel that his professional capability is publicly questioned. Litigation is an intensely stressful experience, from the point of view both of the plaintiff and of the defendant, and to be the object of an action for damages which one feels is not justified is a highly disruptive and distressing experience. It might be argued that this is to place excessive weight on the sensitivities of professional persons, who must accept the consequences of the harm they have caused. Yet this objection ignores the point that there are two sets of interests at stake here: the interests of the plaintiff and the interests of the defendant. A correct balance of these two sets of interests should ensure that tort liability is restricted to those cases where there is a real failure to behave as a reasonably competent practitioner would have behaved. We have suggested that the inappropriate raising of the standard of care threatens this balance. Similar considerations apply to disciplinary measures.

How do we respond to the position of the victim of a personal injury that has been the result of an act that falls into our second level of blame – that is, below the level at which we feel the reasonable person test should apply? Clearly, at this level an injury has been caused by a level of performance that falls short of best practice. One cannot but sympathise with the victim who argues that the accident should not have happened. Such patients are entitled to a timely and satisfactory explanation of events, and usually an apology. Mediation has much to offer. If a way could be found for compensation to be paid without any finding of negligence with all that that entails in terms of blame and moral censure, this would be highly desirable. It is this desire that has fuelled a long-standing debate in tort law as to alternatives to the current system. This debate is by no means over. We have examined some possible solutions in Chapters 8 and 10.

A consequence of encouraging litigation for loss is to persuade the public that all loss encountered in a medical context is the result of the failure of somebody in the system to provide the level of care to which the patient is entitled. The effect of this on the relationship between a patient and his or her doctor (and other clinicians) is distorting and will not be to the benefit of the patient in the long run. It is also unjustified to impose on those engaged in medical treatment an undue degree of additional stress and anxiety in the conduct of their profession. Equally, it would be wrong to impose such stress and anxiety on any other person performing a demanding function in society. There are numerous examples outside medicine of this process: social workers, for instance, face stress in the discharge of their duties arising from possibilities of complaint and proceedings for wrong decisions in high-risk activities such as child custody and child safety matters. The same can be said of many other occupations. Throughout this book we have stressed that it is not primarily the occupation of the individual that is relevant, it is the general issue of culpability in particular circumstances. There is no reason why this pressure should be felt by any reasonably competent person who is conscientious in the discharge of his or her responsibilities. Expectations must be realistic. It is essential that standards are attainable. This implies recognition of the nature of ordinary human error and human limitations in the performance of complex tasks.

The criminal punishment of negligence is a matter of particular concern. In Chapter 9 we outlined the substantial moral overtones carried with criminal punishment, and indeed even with criminal charges. Conviction of any substantial criminal offence requires that the accused person should have acted with a morally blameworthy state of mind. Recklessness and deliberate wrongdoing, levels four and five of our classification of blame, *are* morally blameworthy, but any conduct falling short of that should not be the subject of criminal liability. Common-law systems have traditionally only made negligence the subject of criminal sanction when the level of negligence has been high – a standard traditionally described as *gross negligence*. In fact, negligence at that level is likely to be indistinguishable from recklessness, in that some degree of deliberate risk-taking or knowing disregard for the safety of others will usually be involved. Occasionally, however, a criminal prosecution may occur in cases in which this standard is not reached. This is objectionable because it involves the criminal punishment of persons whose moral culpability may be very low or non-existent.

Blame is a powerful weapon. When used appropriately, and according to morally defensible criteria, it has an indispensable role in human affairs. Its inappropriate use, however, distorts tolerant and constructive relations between people. Some of life's misfortunes are accidents for which nobody is morally responsible. Others are wrongs for which responsibility is diffuse. Yet others are instances of culpable conduct, and constitute grounds for compensation and, at times, for punishment. Distinguishing between these various categories requires careful, morally sensitive and scientifically informed analysis. The law sometimes undertakes this, and attributes liability – civil and criminal – appropriately. In many other cases, however, crude legal notions of negligence fail to achieve a distinction between unavoidable and inevitable mishaps (which are frequently true accidents) and culpable or faulty behaviour. Injustice is the result.

Too many patients are harmed, inadvertently, by healthcare. An important barrier to progress in reducing the incidence of harm in healthcare and in finding better ways of handling these injuries when they occur is an undue emphasis on blame. Blame is reactive, and promotes an adversarial response, which in turn feeds upon blame. A sophisticated and constructive approach to the attribution of blame is required and a proactive approach is needed if harm from healthcare is to be reduced. In Chapter 10 we suggested that current legal and regulatory responses to incidents of such harm frequently do little more than make bad situations worse. We have drawn from the concepts of therapeutic jurisprudence to advocate a rethinking of accountability and suggested approaches that should be proactive rather than reactive, and integrative rather than adversarial.

We have seen much progress in the understanding of safety in healthcare since the first edition of this book was published. In many countries, progress has also been made towards more enlightened and effective legal and regulatory approaches to managing the very difficult and substantial problem of inadvertent harm to the very patients that those who work in healthcare seek to help. If the importance of one theme has become clearer over the intervening years, it is that of teamwork. The real challenges in healthcare lie in the coordinated efforts of many individuals working at all levels in a system that ranges from politicians to those who we depend upon to keep our hospitals clean. In the second edition of this book we have attempted, again, to provide a reminder of just how important is the link between moral fault, blame and justice, and to emphasise that this matters not only in relation to individuals, but also in relation to the ways in which people work together and share collective accountability. Further, we have tried to show that the law is itself an integral part of the overall system by which we try to deliver safe and effective care to all who need it. Furthermore, the law has considerable potential to influence the way healthcare is delivered, for better or for worse. We would argue, therefore, that those who regulate healthcare and administer justice when things go wrong are not exempt from this collective accountability. In the end, our patients deserve a legal response to harm in healthcare that is proactive, well-informed, sophisticated and effective in enhancing the care they receive.

INDEX

absence of fault, 213
ACC. *See* Accident Compensation
   Corporation
acceptable standards, 368
Accident and Rehabilitation and
   Compensation Insurance Act, 290
Accident Compensation Act, 290
Accident Compensation Corporation
   (ACC), 288–90, 296
accidents, 41–2
   blame attributed in, 183, 206–7,
      392–3
   compensation for medical, 271–2
   damage reduction of, 385
   defining, 40–1
   foreseeability in, 38–9
   harm included in, 37–8
   human behaviours in, 36–7
   intentionality in, 38
   medical, 10, 13, 271–2
   mistakes causing, 160–2
   moral culpability and, 3–4
   non-accidental injury and, 43
   Perrow and consequences of, 68
   punishment and normal, 63–8
accountability, 12, 282–3
   blame and, 389–90
   compensation part of, 273
   just culture and, 357–8
   patient harm and practitioner, 304
   patient safety and improved, 292
   regulations and, 380–1
Action for Victims of Medical
   Accidents, 304
actions, 201, 204–5, 210–11
   appropriateness of, 151–4
   civil, 311
   complex sequence of, 201
   learned sequence of, 113

legal, 246–8
   moral culpability of, 206
   negligence and moral quality of, 202
   negligence and sequence of, 201
   reflex, 200–1
   with risk, 150, 204–6
   violations as antecedent, 160–2
activities, dangerous, 117
acute illness, 171–2
acute myocardial infarction, 100–1,
   179–80
addiction, 374–5
administrative overhead, 296
administrative support, 172
adversarial response, 393–4
adverse events, 58–60, 65
   healthcare avoidable, 2–3, 375–6
   preventable, 55–8
advertent wrongdoing, 329–30
affordances, 77–8
AIMS. *See* Australian Incident
   Monitoring Study
Air France flight 447, 33–6
air travel, 36
Airbus A330, 33–6
airline industry, 33–6, 67–8, 115
airspeed, 34
algorithms, 357
American Academy of Actuaries, 287–8
anaesthesia, 16–20, 27, 29–30, 39
   breathing circuit problem in, 160–2
   complexity involved in, 61–2, 64–5
   crisis situations faced by, 42–3
   CVC inserted by, 27–9, 239–41
   drug addiction in, 374–5
   drug administration of, 59–60, 66,
      197, 360–1
   hypoxic patient of, 136, 174–5
   keeping up with literature in, 250